TIM BURTON'S BODIES

This anthology was completed during the lockdown of 2020 and so we dedicate it to all those who lost their lives that year

TIM BURTON'S BODIES
Gothic, Animated,
Corporeal and Creaturely

Edited by Stella Hockenhull and
Frances Pheasant-Kelly

EDINBURGH
University Press

Edinburgh University Press is one of the leading university presses in the UK. We publish academic books and journals in our selected subject areas across the humanities and social sciences, combining cutting-edge scholarship with high editorial and production values to produce academic works of lasting importance. For more information visit our website: edinburghuniversitypress.com

Edinburgh University Press Ltd
The Tun – Holyrood Road
12 (2f) Jackson's Entry
Edinburgh EH8 8PJ

Typeset in 10/12.5 pt Sabon by
Servis Filmsetting Ltd, Stockport, Cheshire
and printed and bound by CPI Group (UK) Ltd,
Croydon, CR0 4YY

A CIP record for this book is available from the British Library

ISBN 978 1 4744 5690 6 (hardback)
ISBN 978 1 4744 5692 0 (webready PDF)
ISBN 978 1 4744 5693 7 (epub)

CONTENTS

List of Figures viii

Notes on Contributors ix

Acknowledgements xiv

Introduction 1
Stella Hockenhull and Fran Pheasant-Kelly

PART ONE ANIMATED BODIES

1. Transformation: Metamorphosis, Animation and Fairy Tale in
the Work of Tim Burton 15
Samantha Moore

2. Agreeing to be a 'Burton Body': Developing the *Corpse Bride*
Story 27
Emily Mantell

3. Tim Burton's Unruly Animation 42
Christopher Holliday

4. *Corpse Bride*: Animation, Animated Corpses and the Gothic 54
Elif Boyacıoğlu

PART TWO   CREATURELY BODIES

5. Burton, Apes and Race: The Creaturely Politics of Tim Burton's
    Planet of the Apes   69
    Christopher Parr

6. Dead Pets' Society: Gothic Animal Bodies in the Films of
    Tim Burton   81
    Rebecca Lloyd

7. Too Dark for Disney: Tim Burton, Children's Horror and
    Pet Death   94
    Claire Parkinson

8. Monstrous Masculinity: 'Becoming Centaur' in Tim Burton's
    Sleepy Hollow   105
    Stella Hockenhull

9. Anomalous Bodies in Tim Burton's Bestiary: Reimagining *Dumbo* 118
    Frances Pheasant-Kelly

PART THREE   CORPOREAL BODIES

10. All of Us Cannibals: Eating Bodies in *Charlie and the Chocolate
    Factory* and *Sweeney Todd: The Demon Barber of Fleet Street*   135
    Elsa Colombani

11. 'I Might Just Split a Seam': Fabric and Somatic Integrity in the
    Work of Tim Burton   148
    Cath Davies

12. The Semiotics of a Broken Body: Tim Burton's Use of Synecdoche 161
    Helena Bassil-Morozow

13. Art and the Organ Without a Body: 'The Jar' as Burton's Artistic
    Manifesto   174
    Fernando Gabriel Pagnoni Berns

14. 'Hell Here!': Tim Burton's Destruction of Michelle Pfeiffer in
    Batman Returns   185
    Peter Piatkowski

PART FOUR   GOTHIC, MONSTROUS AND PECULIAR BODIES

15. The Grotesque Social Outcast in the Films of Tim Burton   203
     Michael Lipiner and Thomas J. Cobb

16. 'A Giant Man Can't Have an Ordinary-Sized Life':
     On Tim Burton's *Big Fish*   219
     José Duarte and Ana Rita Martins

17. Tim Burton's Curious Bodies in *Miss Peregrine's Home for
     Peculiar Children*: A Contemporary Tale of the Grotesque   233
     Marie Liénard-Yeterian

18. Asexuality and Social Anxiety: The Perils of a Peculiar Body   245
     Alexandra Jayne Hackett

19. Burton's Benevolently Monstrous Frankensteins   260
     Robert Geal

Bibliography   273
Film and Television   294
Index   297

FIGURES

2.1   Topsy Turvey Heads designed for portrait gallery in Victor's
house, Emily Mantell for *Corpse Bride*   28

2.2   Topsy Turvey Heads designed for portrait gallery in Victor's
house, Emily Mantell for *Corpse Bride*   28

2.3   Concept for Second Hand Store scene, Emily Mantell for
Corpse Bride   31

2.4   Final appearance of Second Hand Store in *Corpse Bride*   31

2.5   Wedding dress for Victoria, Emily Mantell for *Corpse Bride*   32

2.6   Victorian sewing blanket, Emily Mantell for *Corpse Bride*   32

2.7–2.10   Possible Effects of Land of the Dead on Land of the Living,
Emily Mantell for *Corpse Bride*   35

2.11   Creating the Film Script   38

2.12–2.19 Corpse Bride transformation, *Corpse Bride*   39–40

8.1   Daredevil, *Sleepy Hollow*   112

10.1   Violet, *Charlie and the Chocolate Factory*   140

10.2   *Sweeney Todd: The Demon Barber of Fleet Street*   145

19.1   *Frankenweenie*   266

19.2   *Edward Scissorhands*   266

19.3   *Frankenweenie*   271

19.4   *Frankenweenie*   272

NOTES ON CONTRIBUTORS

Helena Bassil-Morozow is a cultural philosopher, media and film scholar and academic author whose many publications include *Tim Burton: The Monster and the Crowd* (2010), *The Trickster in Contemporary Film* (2011), *The Trickster and the System: Identity and Agency in Contemporary Society* (2014), *Jungian Film Studies: The Essential Guide* (co-authored with Luke Hockley 2016) and *Jungian Theory for Storytellers* (2018).

Fernando Gabriel Pagnoni Berns works as Professor at the Universidad de Buenos Aires (UBA) – Facultad de Filosofía y Letras (Argentina). He teaches courses on international horror film and has authored a book about Spanish horror TV series *Historias para no Dormir* (Universidad de Cádiz 2020). He has edited a book on the Frankenstein bicentennial and is currently editing books on director James Wan and the Italian *giallo* film.

Elif Boyacıoğlu received her BA in Communication and Design, and MA and PhD in History from Bilkent University, studying death in European medieval societies and related supernatural and folkloric beliefs. She completed a second BA in Animation at the Irish School of Animation, BCFE, Dublin; her animated short *The Teacup* was screened in over fifty international film festivals, winning seven awards. She is currently an Assistant Professor at the Faculty of Communication at Başkent University.

Thomas J. Cobb was awarded his doctorate at the University of Birmingham in April 2018. He is interested in film's relationship with the

American political context and Hollywood's role in allegorising US foreign policy. He works as an academic writing tutor at Coventry University and has worked as a visiting teaching associate at the University of Birmingham, where he taught Discovering North American Literature and Introduction to American and Canadian Studies. His forthcoming monograph is entitled *American Cinema and Cultural Diplomacy: The Fragmented Kaleidoscope* (2020).

Elsa Colombani is an independent scholar. She is the editor of *A Critical Companion to Stanley Kubrick* (2020). Her thesis focused on the influence of Gothic literature and cinema in Tim Burton's films. A frequent collaborator of the *Critical Companions to Contemporary Directors* series, she has recently published a chapter in *Tim Burton, a Cinema of Transformations* (2018), as well as a study of Netflix films in the French periodical *Commentaire* (2019).

Cath Davies is a Senior Lecturer in Constellation (Critical/Contextual Studies) at Cardiff School of Art and Design, Cardiff Metropolitan University. Her continuing PhD by publication research interrogates the relationship between fabric and corporeality. Articles addressing this include 'What Lies Beneath: Fabric and Embodiment in Almodóvar's *The Skin I Live In*' (2017) in *Fashion, Film, Consumption* and 'Strike a Pose: Fabricating Posthumous Presence in Mannequin Design', in *Journal of Material Culture* (2020).

José Duarte teaches Cinema at the School of Arts and Humanities (Universidade de Lisboa). He is a researcher at ULICES (University Lisbon Centre for English Studies) and the co-editor of *The Global Road Movie: Alternative Journeys around the World* (2018). His main research interests include Film History, North American Cinema and Portuguese Cinema.

Robert Geal is Lecturer in Film and Television Studies at the University of Wolverhampton. He is the author of *Anamorphic Authorship in Canonical Film Adaptation* (2019), as well as numerous articles and chapters in journals and edited collections such as *Literature/Film Quarterly*, *The Routledge Companion to Adaptation*, *New Review of Film and Television Studies*, *Film International* and *Adaptation*. His second monograph, *Ecological Film Theory and Psychoanalysis: Surviving the Environmental Apocalypse in Cinema*, will soon be published.

Alexandra Jayne Hackett is a filmmaker who has directed numerous short films (credits include *Knots Untie* and *Jay Bird*) and is currently working on her first feature-length project, *Red Velvet Time Machine*. Since gaining an MA in Filmmaking in 2019 at Sheffield Hallam University, she is now pursuing doctoral study in Film Studies. She has also curated the Black Bird Film festival, Wolverhampton (2018–19), showcasing local talent and raising money for a different charity each year.

Stella Hockenhull is an Honorary Research Fellow at the University of Wolverhampton, where she was previously a Reader in Film and Television Studies. Her research interests include landscape and painting in British cinema, women film directors, and animals in film. She has published a number of monographs including *Aesthetics and Neo-Romanticism in Film: Landscapes in Contemporary British Cinema* (2013) and *British Women Film Directors in the New Millennium* (2017), and numerous articles and chapters in edited collections such as 'Celebrity Creatures: The "Starification" of the Cinematic Animal' in *Revisiting Star Studies* (eds S. Yu and G. Smith 2017).

Christopher Holliday teaches Film Studies and Liberal Arts at King's College London, specialising in Hollywood cinema, animation and contemporary digital media. He is the author of *The Computer-Animated Film: Industry, Style and Genre* (Edinburgh University Press 2018) and co-editor of the edited collections *Fantasy/Animation: Connections Between Media, Mediums and Genres* (2018) and *Snow White and the Seven Dwarfs: New Perspectives on Production, Reception, Legacy* (2021). He is also the curator and creator of the website/blog/podcast *fantasy-animation.org*.

Marie Liénard-Yeterian is Professor of American Literature and Cinema at University Côte d'Azur. Her fields of research are Southern Literature, American Theatre and the American South in film. She has published numerous articles, monographs and edited collections, including *Faulkner et le cinéma* (2010), *A Streetcar Named Desire: From Pen to Prop, Play and Film* (2012), *Nouvelles du Sud: Hearing Voices, Reading Stories* (2012) and *Le Sud au cinéma* (2009), and is currently working on a book on the grotesque on screen.

Michael Lipiner is currently pursuing his doctorate degree in film studies at Bangor University in Wales. A native New Yorker, he resides in Israel where he is the programme adviser for the Diplomacy and International Communication in English program at Leo Baeck Education Center in Haifa. He also created the ongoing film studies programme at Bayside High School in conjunction with St John's University in New York City where seniors receive college credit. He is interested in American cinema and its cultural implications for which he teaches, writes about and gives lectures. He has published a play and articles in *Quarterly Review of Film and Video, The International Journal of Comic Art and E-Learning* and *Digital Media*.

Rebecca Lloyd is an independent researcher, with publications on Gothic environments and creatures including *Gothic Animals: Uncanny Otherness and the Animal With-Out* (eds Heholt and Edmundson 2020); *Haunted Landscapes: Super-Nature and the Environment* (eds Heholt and Downing 2016), and is co-author on 'Anne Rice' for *The Encyclopedia of the Gothic* (2013). She is also writing on historical crime fiction.

Emily Mantell is an RCA Animation graduate. Her films have travelled the world on the festival circuit. *Gifted* won the best student film in the British Animation Awards in 2004. After working on Tim Burton's *Corpse Bride*, she won a Creative Pioneer Award from NESTA for Prude, a business she ran for two years. Emily has also worked on BAFTA award-winning films and is currently Animation Course Leader at the University of Wolverhampton.

Ana Rita Martins is an English lecturer in the Department of English Studies at the School of Arts and Humanities (Universidade de Lisboa) and a researcher at the ULICES (University of Lisbon Centre for English Studies). Her main research interests include monsters and monstrosity, medieval romance, medievalism, fantasy and science fiction.

Samantha Moore is a UK-based, international award-winning animation director and is coordinator for the Masters' courses in Media at Manchester School of Art, and Associate Professor in Animation at University College Volda (Norway). She has made work on diverse subjects, from competitive sweet pea growing to cutting-edge microbiology, and her own experience of having twins. Her most recent film, *Bloomers* (2019), has won several international awards, including Best British Film at the London International Animation Festival (2019), and was nominated for a British Animation Award for Best Short Film (2020).

Claire Parkinson is Professor of Film, Television and Digital Media and Co-director of the Centre for Human Animal Studies at Edge Hill University. Her publications include the books *Animals, Anthropomorphism and Mediated Encounters* (2019), *Popular Media and Animals* (2011), *Memento* (2010), *Routledge Companion to Cinema and Politics* (2016), *American Independent Cinema* (2012) and *Beyond Human* (2012). She is currently Principal Investigator on two Arts and Humanities Research Council-funded projects that explore multi-species storytelling.

Christopher Parr is a PhD candidate at the University of Wolverhampton. He is currently researching antihuman attitudes in twenty-first-century science-fiction cinema and has presented papers at various national and international conferences on *Planet of the Apes*, prestige horror and the films of actor Doug Jones.

Frances Pheasant-Kelly is Reader in Screen Studies and Director of the Centre for Film, Media, Discourse and Culture at the University of Wolverhampton. She has written over sixty-five publications, including *Abject Spaces in American Cinema* (2013) and *Fantasy Film Post 9/11* (2013), and is the co-editor of *Spaces of the Cinematic Home: Beyond the Screen Door* (2015). She is currently working on several monographs, including *The Bodily Turn in Film and Television* and *A History of HIV/AIDS in Film, Television and the Media*.

Peter Piatkowski is a London-based writer specialising in film, pop culture, feminist and queer studies, music, literature and travel. He was raised in Chicago, where he attended school and ultimately earned his MA in English Literature from DePaul University and his MFA in Creative Writing, Nonfiction from Roosevelt University. He taught English writing and reading with the City Colleges of Chicago and has had work published in numerous journals, anthologies and magazines.

ACKNOWLEDGEMENTS

This collection arose from a conference on Tim Burton's Bodies, organised by the Centre for Film, Media, Discourse and Culture at the University of Wolverhampton in 2018, and held at Light House Media Centre, Wolverhampton. The editors would like to thank the University of Wolverhampton for their generous support of the event and the subsequent research time that has enabled this publication. We are more than grateful to Kelly Jeffs, Jas Kapur and all other staff at the Light House who worked so hard to make the conference successful. Thanks also to staff at the University, especially Amrit Chodda, Donna Hughes, Nicky Bhatti and Jill Morgan, Helen Page and Luke Bristow. Special thanks to postgraduate students Tim Gough, Chloe Homewood, Paul Jonze, Safire Jones and Dan Whorton, who all made the conference run so smoothly. Finally, and not least, many thanks to the staff at Edinburgh University Press, especially Gillian Leslie and Richard Strachan, for bearing with us during lockdown.

INTRODUCTION

Stella Hockenhull and Fran Pheasant-Kelly

The theme for *Tim Burton's Bodies* derives from Tim Burton's international reputation and critical acclaim for fantasy horror films that are inhabited by ghosts, animated corpses, grotesque and horrible bodies or otherwise 'different' beings. It also emerges from his acknowledged proclivity for character-over-narrative-driven films. The aim here is to reframe analyses of Burton's work and provide insights into his somatic sensibilities to filmmaking by employing the 'body' as a central organising theme. At the same time, the book employs rigorous theoretical underpinning and a range of methodologies from a variety of disciplines as relevant to each aspect of character/film or group of films, simultaneously examining Burton's mainstream works as well as some lesser-known productions. While the overall approach involves textual readings, this collection of international scholarship on the theme of bodies has the added insight and experience of a crew member involved with *Corpse Bride* (2005), as well as animal studies' perspectives on the representation of creaturely beings.

Bodies are central to Burton's films in ways that exceed their obvious necessity to narrative. In considering the array of anomalous, extraordinary and transgressive beings that pervade his canon, this study broadens the focus of living forms to include animated, creaturely, corporeal and Gothic bodies. Fundamentally, Burton celebrates the body, whether human, animal, animated or anthropomorphised, and more particularly if it is in some way unusual or off-kilter. Therefore, as well as often subordinating narrative to distinctive visual design, for which he is noted, he also prioritises the physicality of characters. His productions, either as director or producer, span short film and music video to theatrical releases, his earliest work including several short films, ranging from *The Island of Dr Agor* (1971), *Vincent* (1982) and *Frankenweenie* (1984) to the later *Stainboy* (2000). Burton has also been involved in television, directing *Alfred Hitchcock Presents: The Jar* (season 1, episode 19) (1986) and *Faerie Tale Theatre: Aladdin and his Wonderful Lamp* (season 5, episode 1) (1986), as well as several commercials, including a French chewing gum advert (1998) and two for Timex-1-Control watches (2000). Aside from music videos for The Killers (directed in 2006 and 2012), Burton is best known for his cinematic directorial output, with nineteen major productions to date (although, despite his role as producer for *The Nightmare Before Christmas* (Selick 1993), this film is usually attributed to him). The first of these was *Pee-wee's Big Adventure* (1985) and thereafter followed a series of commercially successful and critically acclaimed films, his most recent enterprises including *Miss Peregrine's Home for Peculiar Children* (2016) and *Dumbo* (2019). He has achieved Academy Award nominations for *Corpse Bride* and *Frankenweenie* (2012) and won numerous other awards as well as attaining worldwide box office figures totalling \$4.447 billion approximately to date. The most lucrative was *Alice in Wonderland* (2010), which earned over a billion dollars worldwide.[1]

The Body in Film

Scientific Bodies

In contextualising Burton's filmic affinity for physical form there follows an overview of key academic studies and trends as they relate to the body in cinema and visual culture, although it is beyond the scope of this volume to consider all previous discourse published in this field. Burton's fixation with bodily-ness, discernible in his earliest films, corresponds to a broader Western cultural obsession with the nuances of physicality that has emerged in the past fifty years, hereafter referred to as 'the bodily turn'. Although such a phenomenon is already noted by other scholars (Brophy 1986; Boss 1986; Cooter 2010), there is limited discussion of its extent or its possible causes. Nonetheless, Bryan Turner does identify a more long-standing 'somatic society' in social theory (1996: 6) and Mariam Fraser and Monica Greco suggest that the 1980s is a threshold for thinking about the body (2005: 3). Arguably, this bodily turn results from the intersection of various medical, socio-cultural and political factors that coincided in the early 1970s. Even before this revived focus on the corporeal being, however, the body has always been a source of fascination and scrutiny and, prior to the invention of cinema, audiences gathered for public displays of execution and anatomy (Stephens 2011). The development of cinema facilitated this affinity for the corporeal, with the socio-cultural, technological and political zeitgeist at any given moment dictating how the body is contemporaneously represented. Initially, it was at the centre of documentaries and a 'cinema of attractions', which was characterised by novelty and shock that usually involved the spectacle of human figures, and often afforded the same morbid pre-cinema aspects of gazing at the dead and the executed. In this vein, Marina Dahlquist, Doron Gaili, Jan Olsson and Valentine Robert's anthology *Corporeality in Early Cinema* (2018), which traces the 'Body Under the Scalpel' through to 'Death by a Thousand Cuts', documents early photographic and cinematic records of 'mental patients', nudity, indigenous cultures, dance and sports performers and strongmen, as well as images of death and dying. The late nineteenth century also witnessed the recording of human and animal motion in the sequential photography of Eadweard Muybridge and Jules Etienne Marey, their imagery effectively functioning as a precursor to early cinema, with the subject of the human form in motion captured by Jonathan Auerbach (2007) in *Body Shots: Early Cinema's Incarnations*. Lisa Cartwright (1995) too reports on early cinema's recording of animals, albeit from a scientific perspective that focuses on physiological experimentation rather than motion. In charting medicine's visual culture, she goes on to consider the human body as object of the medical gaze. In a related way, Tim Boon (2008) analyses public health and scientific documentaries, with examples including the microscopic body, natural history subjects, children's bodies in vaccination promotion campaigns and malnourished bodies in the post-Depression era. Other scientific approaches to physicality in film are wide-ranging and include Anneka Smelik's (2010) collection which centres on more contemporary interfaces between science and visual culture. For instance, an essay by Michel van Dartel examines 'haptic visuality' in its scientific form whereby vision is substituted with vibration on the skin (2010: 126). Also reflecting recent scientific development with regard to onscreen bodies, Jackie Stacey examines the 'cinematic life of the gene' (2010) whereby she considers the effect of genetic engineering and cloning on filmic imagery. Relatedly, while not focusing solely on film, Susan Squier (2004) explores the interactions, influences and overlaps between culture and science.

Circuses, Freakshows and Performing Bodies

Especially relevant to Burton's filmmaking and connected to the aforementioned cinema of attractions are those films that centre on bodily deformity and aberration, such as Tod Browning's *Freaks* (1932) and David Lynch's *The Elephant Man* (1980). Scholarship on the extraordinary and anomalous body, which has increased in recent decades partly owing to the bodily turn, includes work by Rosemarie Garland Thomson (1996; 1997), Rachel Adams (2001) and Angela Smith (2011), and associated analysis of circus bodies (Tait

2005; Tait and Lavers 2016). Correspondingly, Adrienne McLean's (2008) study of ballet, the body and narrative cinema traces the history of dance from the early studio days through to the post-studio era. It considers aspects such as the embodiment of the eponymous red shoes in Michael Powell and Emeric Pressburger's *The Red Shoes* (1948) as an aspect of compulsive behaviour (McLean 2008: 152) and their association with promotional material involving 'long legs' (McLean 2008: 166), as well as investigating aspects of gender and sexuality concomitant with ballet.

Animal bodies, particularly those belonging to circuses, are also a noticeable feature of Burton's films and have recently come to the fore in scholarship generally, with significant works including *Primate Visions* (Haraway 1990), *Simians, Cyborgs, and Women* (Haraway 1991), *The Selfish Gene* (Dawkins 2006), *Ethics and Animals* (Gruen 2011) and *Animal Liberation* (Singer 2015). Those works addressing a specific film and visual cultural context comprise *Popular Media and Animals* (2011), *Beyond Human* (2012) and *Animals, Anthropomorphism and Mediated Encounters* (2019) authored by Claire Parkinson (formerly Molloy), a contributor to this collection. Other recent studies of animals in visual culture include *Picturing the Beast* (Baker 2001), *The Animated Bestiary* (Wells 2009), *Creaturely Poetics* (Pick 2011), *Animal Life: The Moving Image* (Lawrence and McMahon 2015), *Screening the Nonhuman* (George and Schatz 2016) and *Deleuze and the Animal* (Gardner and MacCormack 2017).

Bodies of War

Of less importance to a consideration of bodies in Burton's outputs are those works countenancing the representation of the body at war. While Burton does include abject visuals, and a theme of death underpins many of his films, these invariably involve surreal or fantastic circumstance and are removed from real images of the wartime body. In the latter respect, Susan Sontag (2003) debates the response to images of horror arising from news footage of warfare and its aftermath, while there is extensive study of documentary imagery arising from the Holocaust, including works by Oren Stier (2015) and Sander Gilman (2003). Karl Schoonover (2012) examines the spatial relations involved in Italian Neorealism between the imperilled body of the sufferer and the spectator and 'is focused on internationalising pity's spatial order [whereby] for neorealism, corporealism is a graphic force capable of opening Italy to the global spectator' (2012: xiv–xv). Related to Italian film, Angela Dalle Vacche considers how Italian culture is translated to the screen body whereby she explores the connections between Italian Renaissance painting and cinema in terms of the 'human figure, the theatricality of space, and the allegorical dimension of the visual narrative' (2014: 4).

Bodies of Gender, Race and Stardom

In contrast to bodies of war, the star bodies of classic Hollywood are discussed by Richard Dyer in his book, *Heavenly Bodies* (2004), whereby he details how the screen image of major Hollywood stars was constructed. During the post-war period and following the demise of the Hollywood studio system, a relaxation of censorship led to increasingly sexualised representations of the human body and, subsequently, the emergence of the queer body, as discussed by Harry Benshoff (1997) and Michele Aaron (2004). At the same time, the civil rights movement and growth of feminism, which began to challenge the stereotyped and prescriptive roles of women and blacks in film, resulted in studies of the racial and/or gendered body by authors including Lola Young (1996), Chris Holmlund (2002), bell hooks (2008) and Frantz Fanon (2020). Likewise, Yvonne Tasker focuses on spectacular gendered bodies (1993) and Barbara Creed is known for her thesis of the monstrous feminine (1993). Concurrently, as a reflection of the post-Vietnam War era and the distinct militaristic position projected by Ronald Reagan, films such as *Rambo: First Blood* (Kotcheff 1982) and *Die Hard* (McTiernan 1988) articulated masculinity through an emphasis on the 'hard body' (Jeffords 1993). More recently, and foregrounding the films of independent women directors, Kate Ince (2017) considers female subjectivities through *The Body and the Screen*.

Affective Bodies and Subjectivity

While scholarship pertaining to the body usually pivots around textual representation, a number of academic works instead consider the body of the spectator in terms of affective modes. For instance, Luke Hockley utilises aspects of Jungian psychotherapy to consider how 'the body of the spectator and the cinema screen are interrelated sites of meaning' (2014: 1), Julian Hanich (2012) elaborates on abjection and disgust as aesthetic strategies for fear and audience affect, and Xavier Aldana Reyes analyses the affective-corporeal dimensions of horror (2016). In compiling various filmmakers' contributions to bodily representation, Steven Shaviro likewise examines the reactions of the spectator and 'foregrounds visceral, affective responses to film' (1993: viii), while Alanna Thain explores a similar relationship through examples such as the Hollywood films of David Lynch and Alfred Hitchcock's *Vertigo* (1958). In terms of other less tangible aspects of the body, Davina Quinlivan examines the place of breath in cinema (2014), Laura Marks (2000) proposes a 'haptic visuality' whereby certain images enable the spectator to experience cinema as a physical embodiment of culture, and Kaja Silverman (1988) surveys the voice in *The Acoustic Mirror: The Female Voice in Psychoanalysis and Cinema*.

Abject Bodies and the Posthuman

During the late twentieth century, genres became saturated with explicit body imagery, especially the abject interior body. More recently, the onscreen body has become even more graphic with, for example, the tortured form recorded on film by military police at Abu Ghraib (Danner 2004), terrorist executions accessible on the Internet and the first public autopsy for 170 years, performed by anatomist Gunther von Hagens (2002), available on television. Relevant to the filming of terrorist detainee abuse at Abu Ghraib and other detainee camps, Judith Butler (2009) discusses the tortured body while Steve Allen (2013) considers sadomasochism, body modification and torture in fictional productions such as *8mm* (Schumacher 1999) and *Boxing Helena* (Lynch 1993). While a sense of the violated physical body is increasingly incidental to many contemporary mainstream films and television dramas (for example, the post-millennial cycle of James Bond films) for reasons related to vulnerable post-9/11 masculinities, it has, since the 1970s, become a key aesthetic in numerous artworks as well as genres such as horror, science fiction, reality television, medical drama, medical documentary, fantasy and forensic crime drama. A consideration of the body therefore dominates associated texts, such as *Body Trauma TV* (Jacobs 2003), *Cultural Sutures: Medicine and Media* (Friedman 2004) and *Spectatorship, Embodiment and Physicality in the Contemporary Mutilation Film* (Wilson 2015). Aside from a relaxation in censorship, the trend towards displays of the interior body is arguably informed by medical developments since the 1970s, including MRI, CT and keyhole surgery, while an inclination towards what Mark Seltzer (1997) describes as a 'wound culture' – the public fascination with opened and torn bodies – has further engendered tropes of viscerality.

With the advent of motion-capture technology and CGI, so too is the posthuman-, post-anthropocentric- and cyborg-body increasingly foregrounded in films of the late twentieth and early twenty-first centuries, with productions ranging from *The Terminator* (Cameron 1984) to *Avatar* (Cameron 2009); accordingly, this turn to the posthuman body is reflected in a range of edited collections and monographs addressing the interfaces between the body and technology, and features work by Judith Halberstam and Ira Livingston (1995), N. Katherine Hailes (1999), David Bell and Barbara Kennedy (2000), Neil Badmington (2000), Elaine Graham (2002) and Rosi Braidotti (2013). Relatedly, Niall Richardson (2016) examines transgressive bodies in film and popular culture in a study that extends across hyper-muscular, fat, trans-sexed and disabled bodies, and Xavier Aldana Reyes (2014) similarly analyses corporeal transgression in Gothic horror film and literature. Robert Furze (2015) too explores the visceral screen through the films of David Cronenberg and John Cassavetes, while Michele Aaron (1999) engages with the 'dangerous pleasures' of the body through an examination of productions ranging from Cronenberg's *Dead Ringers* (1988) to William Friedkin's *The Exorcist* (1973).

THE FILMS OF TIM BURTON

It is at the confluence of this bodily turn with discourses of disability, the freakshow and circus, corporeality and transgression, as well as the abject, Gothic and posthuman, that Burton's work is located. These modes intersect with a broad diegetic chronology that extends back to 1799 in *Sleepy Hollow* (1999) and forward to the year 2029 in *Planet of the Apes* (2001). Indeed, Burton's films are often grounded in the abject, corporeal body, as exemplified by *Sweeney Todd: The Demon Barber of Fleet Street* (2007), *Corpse Bride* and *Sleepy Hollow*. More specifically, imagery directly involves death, dissection, decay and reanimation, as evidenced in *Sleepy Hollow*, *Frankenweenie* and *Corpse Bride*. If Burton particularly embraces chimeric, transitional, ambiguous and circus bodies as in *Big Fish* (2003), *Dumbo* and *Edward Scissorhands* (1990), spectral bodies are found in *Beetlejuice* (1988), transgressed bodies in *Mars Attacks!* (1996) and animal bodies across a range of films including *Planet of the Apes*, *Frankenweenie*, *Mars Attacks!* and *Sleepy Hollow*.

Certain of these somatic qualities are identified in other analyses of his work, but they tend to feature peripherally rather than centrally. Instead, scholarly studies either direct their attention to theoretical aesthetic framings, such as the uncanny, the grotesque and the abject, or otherwise take a thematic approach that pivots around subjects such as space, film soundtrack, German expressionist and Gothic influences or, at other times, the monstrous body. Such works include Johnson Cheu's edited collection, *Tim Burton: Essays on the Films* (2016), which comprises three sections, the first of which, 'Outsider Characters and Other Oddities', has some connection to the theme of bodies. Indeed, one chapter focuses on 'The Typical and Atypical body in *Charlie and the Chocolate Factory*' and another examines 'Corporeal Mediation and Visibility in *Sleepy Hollow*'. However, neither chapter overlaps with the theoretical approaches adopted in *Tim Burton's Bodies*. Subsequent sections of Cheu's anthology concentrate on the nature of adaptations, technology, artistry and stardom which are only indirectly related to bodies. Like Cheu's anthology, *The Works of Tim Burton: Margins to Mainstream* (2013), edited by Jeffrey Weinstock, is also divided into three sections. These examine aesthetics, influences and contexts and thematics, and comprise aspects such as the spaces of Burton's films, the director's trash cinema roots and a consideration of Danny Elfman's music and auteurist fandom. While none of the essays centre on bodies, Carol Siegel's chapter has some connection to Alex Hackett's examination of sexuality in *Edward Scissorhands* – while Hackett acknowledges Siegel's argument, her claim differs in that Hackett sees Scissorhands as an asexual being rather than one involved in sado-masochistic rituals.

More recently, *A Critical Companion to Tim Burton* (2017), edited by Adam Barkman and Antonio Sanna, comprises three sections based on the spaces in which Burton's films are set and entail: 'Constructing Worlds', 'Fairy Worlds and Nightmares' and 'Identity and the World'. In considering a broad range of aspects associated with these three areas, the essays extend from the fabrication of fantasy spaces of the films and the associated *mise-en-scène* and narrative construction through to how identity might be interpreted. While certain chapters explore characterisation, the subject of the body is not explicitly addressed, with the collection generally preoccupied with spaces and settings.

Conversely, Jennifer McMahon's edited collection (2014), *The Philosophy of Tim Burton*, debates the philosophical significance of Burton's productions and is organised around three key areas: identity, authority and art. The first part considers identity and the nature of the self; the second looks at the domain of the social and how Burton's films comment on authority; the final part focuses on aesthetics. Overall, the book differs fundamentally to the somatic focus of *Tim Burton's Bodies*.

Aside from these edited collections and a number of fan-based guides, there are several scholarly monographs devoted to Burton. These include Alison McMahan's *The Films of Tim Burton: Animating Live Action in Contemporary Hollywood*, which considers the industry aspects of Burton's films, spanning animation, CGI, marketing, adaptation and Elfman's music. Her primary argument is that Burton's films are what she terms 'pataphysical' and possess certain characteristics: they make fun of established systems of knowledge and rituals, display an alternative narrative logic, use special effects that are 'visible' as opposed to invisible, and have thin plots and characters that are not rounded because the narrative depends more on intertextual, nondiegetic aspects (McMahan 2005: 3). McMahan's monograph therefore is focused and narrow and does not discuss bodies in any direct form.

In a series of interviews with Burton, Mark Salisbury (2006) discusses all his films up to that point, devoting a chapter to each, with the discussions extending to most aspects of the filmmaking process. Since this edition, however, Burton has directed many more films, including *Sweeney Todd: The Demon Barber of Fleet Street*, *Alice in Wonderland* (2010), *Dark Shadows* (2012), *Frankenweenie* (2012), *Big Eyes* (2014), *Miss Peregrine's Home for Peculiar Children* (2016) and *Dumbo* (2019).

Helena Bassil-Morozow too has made a significant contribution to scholarship in her monograph on Burton, titled *Tim Burton: The Monster and the Crowd* (2010). Bassil-Morozow, one of the contributors to this collection, employs Jungian and post-Jungian psychology to explore the isolation of Burton's protagonists. The book's six chapters consider the various guises of Burton's protagonists, including the child, monster, superhero, genius and maniac as well as monstrous society, and while her study is character-based, it has a psychological rather than a somatic focus. In contrast, *Masters of the Grotesque: The Cinema of Tim Burton, Terry Gilliam, the Cohen Brothers and David Lynch* (2012), authored by Schuy Weishaar, provides limited coverage of Burton's outputs owing to its inclusion of several other directors in the book. In a chapter titled 'Tim Burton's Two Worlds', Weishaar discusses the various manifestations of the grotesque, and while alluding to the corporeal body, the chapter does not wholly engage with physicality.

TIM BURTON'S BODIES

Tim Burton's Bodies thus contributes to a gap in the literature in relation to a coherent consideration of bodies as a centripetal force in Burton's work. What this book does differently is to spotlight actual physical attributes and figure behaviour of characters and the meanings that these may impart in terms of race, class, gender, sexuality, humanimality and disability. Its distinctiveness not only derives from its concentration on the body, but also in its consideration of nonhuman animals. Uniquely, it features a chapter written by a crew member who worked on *Corpse Bride*. Moreover, while this anthology analyses films that have already been scrutinised many times over, it also entails a study of Burton's two most recent films, *Miss Peregrine's Home for Peculiar Children* (2016) and *Dumbo* (2019). The volume comprises nineteen chapters in all that are categorised according to themes corresponding to the various types of body that predominantly populate Burton's films, namely: 'animated bodies', 'creaturely bodies', 'corporeal bodies' and, finally, 'Gothic, monstrous and peculiar bodies'. Discussion chiefly spans his cinematic outputs, with Samantha Moore's chapter on metamorphosis and transformation introducing the theme of 'Animated Bodies' in Part One. Noting Burton's early affiliation with Disney studios, she discusses how Burton exploits the various properties of animation before explaining that he employs metamorphosis in several ways. First, she suggests that it may be instigated via the actions of characters, for example, in *Sweeney Todd: The Demon Barber of Fleet Street*; secondly, via unresolved metamorphic longing; and thirdly, in literal metamorphic change as in *Beetlejuice* and *Alice in Wonderland*, which Moore analyses as case studies. Also contributing to 'Animated Bodies' is Emily Mantell, who recounts her experiences of working on *Corpse Bride* as a 'Burton Body'. Mantell describes the development of the story and reveals how story teams and their ideas informed the final script. Further focusing on *Corpse Bride*, Elif Boyacioğlu considers the relationship between animation and the Gothic, paying particular attention to the uncanny, especially in its connection to stop-motion animation techniques. Analysing *Corpse Bride* as an example of Burton's creative hybridisation of genres, she centres on its Gothic and comic treatment of the animated corpse. Christopher Holliday's chapter on Tim Burton's 'unruly bodies' completes Part One, whereby he acknowledges qualities of unruliness in the director's artistic practices, expressive film style, his industrial position at the margins and even in his appearance. Referring to *Corpse Bride* and *Frankenweenie*, Holliday first considers the cultural and gendered values of unruliness when applied to Burton's animated bodies. He then analyses Burton's animated bodies in light of the fundamental unruliness of stop-motion aesthetics.

Part Two, 'Creaturely Bodies', details the role of the nonhuman animal in Burton's films, and opens with Christopher Parr's analysis of the creaturely politics of *Planet of the Apes*. Parr explores how the apes in Burton's reimagining are ambivalently signalled as racial others in a way that reflects similar coding in prior films of the franchise and several of Burton's previous outputs. The chapter considers Burton's version in relation to Franklin Schaffner's earlier adaptation (1968) and contributes to the discussion surrounding race in Burton's films. 'Creaturely Bodies' also takes into account the theme of dead pets, explored first by Rebecca Lloyd who debates how Burton's productions, predominantly Gothic in tone and seemingly celebrating excess and transgression, in fact reveal the meanings attached to the animal form that maintain human dominance over the animal body. Lloyd analyses *Vincent*, *The Nightmare Before Christmas*, *Mars Attacks!*, *Corpse Bride* and both versions of *Frankenweenie*, where animals are central to the narrative, to explain how representations of humans and animals castigate transgression of boundaries and the excessive body. Relatedly, Claire Parkinson considers dead dogs, albeit contextualised as autobiographical references to Burton's own pets. Framed by the concept of children's horror, Parkinson explores the repeated depictions of dead dogs and the cultural and social meanings attached to the bodies of animals, pet death and grief. In contrast, Stella Hockenhull's chapter centres on the lesser role of the horse and its appearance in the Gothic horror adaptation, *Sleepy Hollow*. Engaging with Monica Mattfield's (2017) concept of 'becoming centaur', whereby the body of a horse enables its rider a heightened masculinity, Hockenhull discusses the representation of the headless Horseman, in combination with his black stallion, Daredevil, but extends Mattfield's concept to suggest a sublime effect: a symbol of monstrous masculinity or, in this case, 'becoming monstrous centaur'. In the final chapter of 'Creaturely Bodies', and making connections between Burton's fixation with misfits, outsiders and unusual bodies, Frances Pheasant-Kelly analyses Burton's incarnation of Sharpsteen's 1941 classic, *Dumbo*. She contends that while Burton's adaptation follows the original, it concurrently addresses contemporary concerns for animal welfare by first highlighting the human/animal divide, and then diegetically operating to close this gap. The chapter also considers the position of Disney productions in the technologising of animals to situate anthropomorphised creatures on the side of a dialectic opposed to 'animal'.

Elsa Colombani's analysis of cannibalism in *Charlie and the Chocolate Factory* (2005) and *Sweeney Todd: The Demon Barber of Fleet Street* opens Part Three of the collection, titled 'Corporeal Bodies'. Colombani explores the similarities and evolutions from the metaphorical cannibalism of the former to the literal anthropophagy of the latter, charting the disappearance of the individual body into the mass of consumerist society to its reappearance through the body pieces of the cannibalised as well as that of the cannibal. Also investigating corporeality, Cath Davies examines the relationship between dissolving bodies and materials in Burton's work. Her essay centres on the interweaving of textures, surfaces and materiality of characters in *The Nightmare Before Christmas* and *Corpse Bride* to probe how they gain agency through clothing. Correspondingly, Helena Bassil-Morozow considers the physical or psychological brokenness of Burton's characters. Expressly, Bassil-Morozow interrogates the ways in which images of hands and eyes are utilised by Burton in a range of his films, with a focus on *Charlie and the Chocolate Factory*, *Sweeney Todd: The Demon Barber of Fleet Street* and *Big Eyes* (2014); she argues that the literal or narrative fragmentation of characters reflects the intrinsic conflict of modernity – that between individual identity and societal conformity. In the vein of fragmented bodies, Fernando Gabriel Pagnoni Berns scrutinises Burton's direction of 'Alfred Hitchcock Presents: The Jar' (season 1, episode 19) (1986), a television episode that pivots around a disembodied organ, and is therefore relevant to this collection. Berns suggests that Burton's preference for experimental narratives runs through the ways that he reimagines the human body and, even when working with actors rather than puppets, he reconfigures the body to dispense with realism. In this regard, Berns argues that 'The Jar' is a manifesto of things to come, with Burton's ideas on artifice and the antirealist body emerging in subsequent productions such as *Beetlejuice*, *Sleepy Hollow* and *Big Eyes*. Such reconfiguration of the body is likewise identified by Peter Piatkowski in his analysis of *Batman Returns* (1992). Engaging theoretically with the work of Richard Dyer (2004) on stars, Piatkowski first identifies a stable of performers with whom Burton typically works, including Johnny Depp, Helena Bonham Carter and Danny DeVito, and notes how these actors each have unconventional star images that conform to his characters and style. However, in *Batman Returns*, Piatkowski notes that he deviates from this method of casting by including Michelle Pfeiffer, whose screen persona is defined by her glamour and whose onscreen image is that of a traditional classic Hollywood star. Piatkowski's essay examines how Burton uses Pfeiffer's star image to advantage and then dismantles it through her corporeal and psychological deterioration.

The final part of this collection, 'Gothic, Monstrous and Peculiar Bodies', begins with Michael Lipiner and Thomas J. Cobb's analysis of the grotesque social outcast in Burton's oeuvre. Lipiner and Cobb focus on how his cinematic treatment of the grotesque, in all its incarnations, shapes this figure to mirror mainstream American culture in the guise of a Gothic or cultural body, often metaphorical of popular lore, and which appears in the various forms of a persecuted monster. Examining *Beetlejuice*, *Edward Scissorhands*, *Batman Returns* and *Miss Peregrine's Home for Peculiar Children*, the essay suggests that Burton's manifestation of the grotesque offers universal and multifaceted implications, thereby subverting the homogeneity of American suburbia. Marie Liénard-Yeterian also discusses the grotesque in *Miss Peregrine's Home for Peculiar Children* and explores the cultural work performed by the assorted curious and monstrous bodies in the film's imaginary world, while addressing Burton's ability to interweave different generic traditions. Specifically, Liénard-Yeterian debates the notion of 'monster' embedded in the motif of these curious bodies, which are poised at the intersection of the Gothic and the grotesque in their staging of an encounter with terror. José Duarte and Ana Rita Martins too consider Burton's representation of monstrosity in their study of *Big Fish* (2003). Their essay enquires into the importance of weird and monstrous bodies while also identifying the work of American photographer Diane Arbus as a potential visual inspiration for the film. It further analyses the unusual bodies presented in the diegetic stories told by protagonist Edward Bloom (Albert Finney) and suggests that they propose a chance to consider changes in how anomalous bodies are viewed in the 'real' world. Peculiar and unusual bodies are at the centre of Alex Hackett's analysis of *Edward Scissorhands* and *Charlie and the Chocolate Factory*. Adopting a psychoanalytic approach, Hackett contends that both protagonists are asexual beings, thereby differing from previous analyses of sexuality in Burton's films. The final contribution to the book examines 'Burton's Benevolently Monstrous Frankensteins'. Here, Robert Geal reappraises *Edward Scissorhands* and *Frankenweenie* to interrogate usual interpretations of Burton's films that celebrate outsider status. Rather, Geal challenges these to suggest that Burton's intertexual engagements with Mary Shelley's novel *Frankenstein* [1818] (1974), which inform the aforementioned films, include elements that are progressive, but compromise these aspects with arguably misogynistic revisions that invert some of the novel's proto-feminist potential.

In all, Tim Burton's cinematic world of human and nonhuman bodies in their various forms provides a unique point of departure to present a range of new ideas and theoretical frameworks that enable innovative insights into his work.

NOTE

1. https://www.imdb.com/title/tt1014759/ (accessed 30 June 2020).

PART ONE

ANIMATED BODIES

1. TRANSFORMATION: METAMORPHOSIS, ANIMATION AND FAIRY TALE IN THE WORK OF TIM BURTON

Samantha Moore

Animation has always been a haven for eccentrics and misfits, a place for film-makers who have a singular vision and where the laws of physics rarely apply. Everything in animation is fabricated, often from the feverish imagination of a single individual, so it is the natural habitat of the auteur. Animation is the form which Tim Burton gravitated towards as a child; he recalls the stop-motion animation of Ray Harryhausen in *Jason and the Argonauts* (Chaffey 1963) having a profound effect on him, stating, 'I've always loved monsters and monster movies' (in Salisbury 2006: 2). This mode of moving image also offers evidence that we cannot believe and, according to Paul Wells, the liminal space between real and unreal is where much of the deliciousness of animation lives (Wells 1998: 20). Moreover, animation allows for the possibility of impossible change, of metamorphosis either figurative or literal. Burton's early short animated film, *Vincent* (1982), is about a young boy longing to metamorphose into his hero, Vincent Price. As Burton suggests, '[i]t's like at Hallowe'en, people dress up and it allows them to get a little wilder, they become something else. That's one of the aspects of film making that I've constantly enjoyed, the transformation of people' (in Salisbury 2006: 56). Many of Burton's films have metamorphosis at their heart, but less often in the literal than the figura-tive sense. He gives us metamorphic process instigated by his characters, for example, in *Sweeney Todd: The Demon Barber of Fleet Street* (2007), where Benjamin Barker/Sweeney Todd (Johnny Depp) and Nellie Lovett (Helena Bonham Carter) turn their victims into pies. Most poignantly (and most often), he presents the spectator with unresolved metamorphic longing, for instance in *Edward Scissorhands* (1990), whose titular character longs to transform. Occasionally he gives us literal metamorphic change, as in *Beetlejuice* (1988) and *Alice in Wonderland* (2010), which will be explored in more detail in this chapter. Metamorphosis will also be examined as it relates to the subversive nature of animation, and the uncomfortable relationship that one of Burton's key influencers, Disney Studios, has had with it.

Metamorphosis in animation is the fluid transformation, frame by frame, of one thing (person, object, animal) into another. It can be done via any animated medium – clay, model, paint, drawing or computer-generated imagery (CGI) – and can be used in assorted ways for a variety of reasons. Metamorphosis can replace editing tasks such as scene cuts; as Barry Purves points out (2014: 184), to edit in-camera seamlessly and lyrically may be achieved by using under-the-camera techniques such as those employed in Caroline Leaf's oil paint on glass film, *The Street* (1976). Furthermore, it can be utilised to condense information, space or time, for example in *The Owl Who Married a Goose*, another Leaf film (1974), where a water splash turns into snow falling to signal seasons turning. Metamorphosis can be used to draw comparisons between apparently unrelated subjects, or to create an emotional reaction, for example in Bill Plympton's *Your Face* (1987) which, with its 'nearly continuous metamorphosis of body violations and self-ingestions', concentrates solely on 'a man's insipidly smiling face' (Crafton 2012: 279–80), provoking humour and the uncanny.

From attending the California Institute of the Arts' (CalArts) animation programme to getting his first job working on the animated feature *The Fox and the Hound* (1981), Burton was steeped in traditional Disney animation training. This was despite its clear disconnection, artistically and philosophically, from his signature style. His recollection of his time at CalArts and Disney is ambivalent at best, but it cannot be denied that by hiring him, 'Disney gave Burton a source of income and an identity – the identity of an animator, which he retains to this day' (McMahan 2005: 22). Burton acknowledges that the animation training he received has inflected his visual vocabulary ever since: '[h]aving a background in animation sort of broadens the scope of what you can do visually' (in Salisbury 2006: 51). Metamorphosis is a fundamental part of the vocabulary of animation, but it became forbidden at Disney as they pursued 'believability' of characters above all else (Pallant 2011: 35). Therefore, the neat animation trick of metamorphosis, that vital tool for instigating disturbance, was ignored by the company that trained him and, arguably, this influenced the ways that he used it in his films.

Whenever metamorphosis is used in film it creates a disorderly presence: disrupting character, undermining the film structure or upsetting internal logic. According to Norman Klein, the frame becomes an 'unreliable space [which reveals] the mechanisms of the medium' (in Wells, 1998: 134). Metamorphosis draws attention to the anarchic nature of the animated form. It does not bother to disguise its temperamental similarities to dream or delusion and makes no attempt to present a realistic perspective on a standard timescale. There is an inherent untrustworthiness about metamorphosis: it recalls dreams, night-mares and hallucinations, states we have experienced but in an unreal internal sense, and so to see it made manifest is profoundly unsettling. Vivian Sobchack comments about morphing, stating that 'its effortless shape shifting, its confu-sions of the animate and inanimate [. . .] its homogenizing consumption of others and otherness, are uncanny – uncanny not only in the sense of being strange and unfamiliar but also in the sense of being strangely familiar' (2000: xi). Morphing broadcasts animation's ability to represent the interior but, in the style of dreams, we have no idea where it is going. Donald Crafton sees the metamorphic process as partially malign: a cannibalistic, self-destructive exercise on the part of the animator. As he states,

> Metamorphosis is autophagic in two fundamental ways. Set in motion by the animators – or their primordial hand – the forms come into being swallowing up the ones before them and cease to exist when they are eaten up by their successors. And, to the extent that the on-screen bodies represent the animators' creative processes, their termination reflects the demise of the filmmaker. (2012: 278)

This destructive model is particularly true for stop-motion animation made in front of the camera, like Leaf's direct animation (paint, or sand, on glass) or Jan Svankmajer's clay models that must literally be destroyed before the next frame can be made.

Wells posits that metamorphosis may be the central defining quality of animation itself (1998: 69) because, for him, it is unique to the animated form. Metamorphosis can be used in a live- action frame by borrowing from stop-motion and utilising techniques like time-lapse (taking individual frames at set intervals and then playing them back continuously, to give the effect of time speeding up/caving in), as exemplified in Peter Greenaway's *A Zed and Two Noughts* (1985). Time-lapse, as in all forms of metamorphosis, can be profoundly unsettling and emotionally distancing to watch, since it is related to life, but is not lifelike at the speed we experience it. For example, in Greenaway's film, a dead swan writhes, zombie-like, as its body festers, while a dead crocodile appears to be breathing post-mortem as its stomach swells and sinks during the rotting process. However, metamorphosis in this sense (in camera, using real objects or people) can only be in one direction – that of time passing: the signs of growing, ageing, decaying. Animated metamorphosis, on the other hand, has what Sergei Eisenstein describes as 'freedom from ossification' and is not tied to 'the rungs of the evolutionary ladder' (1986: 5). Cause and effect are not necessary with animated metamorphosis – one can have effect, effect and effect *ad infinitum*, leaving the cause open to the opinion of the viewer. Blu's *Muto* (2007/8) is an animated, life-sized graffiti film shot in a city, with the normal urban population relegated to mayflies while the animation ploughs through the cityscape at several times the size and a fraction of the speed of everything else. As Crafton states, 'Blu pushes the bodies of his grotesque beings through never-ending metamorphoses based on cycles of parthenogenesis and reincarnation' (2012: 272). The characters circle through endless loops without discernible narrative structure, but with a compelling visual style that no other medium could achieve.

Metamorphosis, then, is grotesque, nightmarish, disorienting, destructive, unsettling and uncanny: qualities it shares with the fairy tale and that may be associated with Burton's work. However, as noted, unlike the fairy tale, metamorphosis was explicitly rejected by Disney. As a fledgling animator, Burton's early training came exclusively from Disney, which had a monocultural approach to the way that animation should be made. Concerning his time at Disney, Burton says:

> [i]t was like being in the army; I've never been in the army, but the Disney programme is probably about as close as I'll ever get. You're taught by Disney people, you're taught the Disney philosophy. It was kind of a funny atmosphere, but it was the first time I had been with a group with similar interests. (in Salisbury 2006: 7)

Burton did not explicitly choose Disney, but rather, as animation director and fellow CalArts alumnus Brad Bird said, 'it was literally the only game in town' (in Kashner 2014). Disney was the pre-eminent animation company in the world at that point and in many ways had defined what animation was seen to be capable of, prioritising 'artistic sophistication, "realism" in characters and contexts, and, above all, believability' (Pallant 2011: 35) in their films. Disney's work was famously admired by Eisenstein for their use of metamorphosis in its 'ability to dynamically assume any form' (1986: 5). Ironically, what he admired them most for they rejected after the success of *Snow White* (Hand et al. 1937) and the comparative failure of the more visually inventive *Fantasia* (Algar et al. 1940). Such striving for realism and believability meant that they rejected the very thing – metamorphosis – that gave animation its disruptive edge, and the disruptive edge was what made it a tempting medium for Burton. This was the start of an equivocal relationship between Burton and Disney. He needed their support but the basic tenets of Disney's beliefs (order, reality) were at odds with his own (disruption, outsider status). Burton's own sensibility was much more in tune with an early rival of

Disney studios, the Fleischer Brothers, whose privileging of visual spectacle over character development better suited his filmic concerns.

Unsurprisingly perhaps, metamorphosis is not represented in the 'twelve principles of animation'. These were a set of axioms famously recorded by Ollie Johnston and Frank Thomas, two of Disney's 'nine old men'.[1] The twelve principles are essentially a set of technical rules for animators, designed to create believable physicality in Disney's animated worlds, which was increasingly the aim of their work as it developed through the first half of the twentieth century. These principles include squash and stretch, anticipation, staging, straight ahead action and pose to pose, follow through and overlapping action, ease in and ease out, arc, secondary action, timing, exaggeration, solid drawing and appeal. Of the twelve principles, arguably only 'exaggeration' is not directly related to making the animated movement more realistic, and even that must take its cue from the internal believability of the work. Metamorphosis, however, is the opposite of the realistic/believable physicality of the twelve principles and bears no reference to reality. Klein points out that as 'the transformation begins [. . .] the laws of nature collapse' (2000: 21), and that collapse could not be allowed to happen in a Disney film.

Burton would have been aware of the twelve principles when he joined the Disney-funded CalArts' animation programme in 1976, and adherence to this methodology was the one which he was meant to be apprenticed to during his time at Disney when he entered the company proper in 1979. Disney at this time was very catholic in the individual styles of the animators it took on: 'rough or clean, intuitive or analytical, it did not matter. It was the combination of styles that made Disney films rich and nuanced' (Johnston and Thomas 1995: 95–6). However diverse or unusual the personal style of the animator was, the end result would always have to be ironed out to look like a Disney product. Burton says, 'what's odd about Disney is that they want you to be an artist, but at the same time they want you to be a zombie factory worker and have no personality. It takes a very special person to make those two sides of your brain co-exist. So I was very emotionally agitated at that time and couldn't function very well' (in Salisbury 2006: 10). Animation director Gary Trousdale is quoted by Sam Kashner as saying that Disney 'didn't know what the hell to do with Tim. They were scared of him. So they just stuck him into an office. That's when he came up with the original [1984] "Frankenweenie"' (2014). Burton would continue to wrestle with this coexistence of being an insider and simultaneously an outsider throughout his work.

In order to identify how Disney's lack of metamorphosis inflects its storytelling in comparison to other studios of the era, two treatments of the same scene are examined: the wicked queen's transformation in films of the *Snow White* fairy tale. As noted, metamorphosis has no place in the twelve fundamental principles of animation and, in fact, as a tool, is barely used by Disney. Disney's emphasis was on the 'believability' of the movement and characters, sometimes characterised as 'realism'. Chris Pallant notes that 'as a product of Disney's insistence on realism in *Snow White*, cartoonal metamorphosis is, with the exception of the Queen's transformation into the witch, largely absent' (2011: 43). Arguably, 'cartoonal metamorphosis' is thin even here: almost all this sequence could have been achieved with straight editing of a live-action scene. The 1937 Disney scene is entirely plot- and narrative-dependent; as Wells points out, the transformation scene brings 'clarity to an extended narrative' by using the narrative function of 'a disguise' (1998: 73), rather than emphasising the magical nature of a transformation. This scene is a key plot point in the film and shows the lengths to which the queen (Lucille La Verne) will go to get her way rather than highlighting her magical capability.

The spectator is given a breakdown of the ways in which the queen's 'disguise' will function (voice, hair and hands) in the future plot development of fooling Snow White (Adriana Caselotti). It is also couched in terms of character; there is a strong sense of her feelings of sacrificing her youth and beauty, her intense physical pain is clearly signalled, and finally her malicious glee is evident as she completes the protracted and difficult process. The transformation itself uses little actual metamorphosis in its animation; it depends on live-action techniques like an out-of-focus 'camera' shot as the queen drinks the potion. The only metamorphosis happens as the hair whitens (although her face remains the same) and a close-up reveals the hands ageing dramatically into those of a crone. The scene uses a theatrical rather than metamorphic flourish to provide the final reveal: a swirl of the queen's sleeve as she shows her hag face to 'camera', the sequence using the language of live action almost exclusively. This is entirely in tune with Disney's intentions for the animation. Klein cites Johnston and Thomas, suggesting that '[w]hen the animator distorts the figure, he [sic] must always come back to the original shape. Donald and Goofy can be made to bulge and implode but must never lose their "personality", never turn into other *things* in the way Warner's characters did [italics in original]' (2000: 25).

Comparing this to the Fleischer Brothers' version of *Snow White* (1933), the queen (Mae Questel) is shown simply stepping through her mirror, which serves as a metamorphic plane, as she steps from queen into hag with an insouciant bravado. There is no sense that this sequence is plot driven; it is a gag (the mirror tells her to hide her face so she changes into someone else). It is not even the first time she has metamorphosed in the film: during Betty's (Mae Questel) first meeting with her she briefly becomes a pan of two fried eggs for no other apparent reason than, with her unusually long nose and googly eyes, her three-quarter-view face looks like a frying pan of eggs. The metamorphic sequences in the Fleischer film do not rely on character and plot development to drive them (there's no good reason that the Fleischer queen should turn into a hag other than that it is an accepted plot point for this fairy tale). Jack Zipes asserts that '[t]he Fleischers rarely worked from a script, and even if they did, they would ad lib and change it beyond recognition' (2011: 120), and this feeling of spontaneous fun with no high emotional stakes pervades the film. In the Fleischer *Snow White*, the wicked queen uses her magic metamorphic mirror to turn Koko (Cab Calloway) the clown into a ghost, with weirdly long legs and a creepily familiar rotoscoped animation based on Calloway's movements. As Sobchack describes it, the metamorphosis in this case has 'transformed the structure of spectatorial pleasure', disrupting 'the spectator's traditional modes of identification with central human characters and displac[ing] them' (2000: xix–xx). He is no longer Koko but he continues to sing as if no change has been effected, perpetuating the dreamlike atmosphere.

Eventually the queen's final metamorphic sequence begins when the mischievous mirror rebels against her and turns her into a dragon, disappearing itself at this point. Finally, she turns inside out like a giant sock and the story ends. This kind of fundamental character transformation (size, shape, species) could not have happened at Disney, where character was far more revered. According to Disney, Klein says, 'once a character's body was shown – rubbery, watery, humanlike – its substance was irreducible. Walt was convinced that revealing the drawing behind the flesh could wreck the atmospheric effects that he prized so highly' (2000: 25). Significantly, Johnston and Thomas argue, rather wistfully, '[w]e still wonder what we would be working on today if *Fantasia* had been as successful as *Snow White*' (1995: 511). However, as Pallant points out, 'the financial and critical success of *Snow White*, coupled with the comparative failure of *Fantasia* (1940), led to the former becoming an aesthetic blueprint for much of the Disney-Formalist period. The artistic paradigm promoted by *Snow White* has since become known as "hyperrealism"' (2011: 35–6). Burton's perspective was indelibly shaped – both positively and negatively – by the Disney ideology. As he argues,

> Because I've never read, my fairy tales were . . . monster movies. To me they're fairly similar. I mean, fairy tales are extremely violent and extremely symbolic and disturbing, probably even more so than *Frankenstein* and stuff like that, which are kind of mythic and perceived as fairy-tale like. But fairy tales, like the Grimms' fairy tales, are probably closer to movies like *The Brain that Wouldn't Die*, much rougher, harsher, full of bizarre symbolism. (in Salisbury 2006: 3)

The fairy tale is such a familiar subject of animation as to be almost synonymous with it. Metamorphosis is a key ingredient of fairy tale; in fact, Marina Warner argues that the fairy-tale form is defined by metamorphosis. As she avers, 'More so than the presence of fairies, the moral function, the imagined antiquity and oral anonymity of the ultimate source, and the happy ending [. . .] metamorphosis defines the fairy tale' (1995: xv–xvi). Fairy tale is also a recurring concern of Burton's, although he says, 'I think I didn't like fairy tales *specifically*. I liked the *idea* of them more [italics in original]' (in Salisbury 2006: 3). Burton's fairy tales are filtered through his own lens of concerns and ideas, much like Disney's were, and emerge similarly askew as a result. If metamorphosis, as Sobchack says, 'reminds us of our true instability' (2000: xii), then so do fairy tales, with stability under constant threat from wolves and wicked witches, poverty and familial deaths.

Burton's affinity with the fairy tale is clear, and this unstable base gives him a good opportunity to explore his love/hate relationship with the status quo: the untransformed. Even when he is using original material, such as in *Beetlejuice* (1988), the characters are very clearly fairy-tale inflected and therefore disposed to metamorphosis. The Maitlands are the isolated but unspectacularly ordinary husband and wife who wish for a child, and the Deetz family are the inattentive king and needling stepmother who have a poor unfortunate (step) daughter. In typical Burton style, the sympathetic protagonists are the monsters (the ghosts of the Maitlands), and the antagonist usurpers (the Deetz family and entourage) are the legitimate house-owners. The 'good fairy' who effects transformation is Betelgeuse (Michael Keaton) himself, a grotesque character mixing an anarchic cartoon sensibility (definitely not Disney) with creepy sexual innuendo. Metamorphosis is used by the marginalised characters, often as defence. Barbara Maitland (Geena Davies) attempts to use metamorphosis as a way of scaring the Deetzes from 'her' house; she transforms into Hallowe'en mask cliché (faces ripped off, eyeballs popping out) but the pretentious Deetzes' horror is triggered only by the bland interior decorating and her metamorphosis remains unseen, so she changes back.

Betelgeuse, unlike the Maitlands, is unselfconsciously metamorphic throughout the film. He uses his metamorphic power as the ultimate childlike wish fulfilment ('if I had a magic wand . . .') to magically transform any given situation. Zipes states that animation applied to fairy tales involves 'first and foremost transformation' (2011: 82) because only there can we see instantaneous punishment applied, justice dispensed and desires granted. Betelgeuse is first seen as a drawn advert: part man, part beetle, holding a huge hammer. Next, he is part of a diorama, uncannily real but on the scale of the 'tiny' models he is among. He casually changes or distorts parts of himself at will; for example, when he is attempting to persuade the Maitlands to hire him, his outfit changes to mirror Adam's (Alec Baldwin) clothes. Sound and visual effects are used to make clear his similarity to a riotous cartoon character; smoke comes out of his hat, his head swivels uncontrollably, and 'cartoon' sound effects accompany some of his movements – like the lewd squeeze of his groin in salute to the departing Maitlands, emphasised by the sound of a car horn. In the scene where he first encounters the Deetz family, his metamorphosis into a monster is almost complete, except for his recognisable hair. He becomes a snake-like creature, reminiscent of Harryhausen's Medusa from *Clash of the Titans* (1981), emerging nightmarishly from the stair banister rail. When he is banished by Barbara Maitland and returns (in a car crash) to the model town and his normal form, he sprouts knives from his body to stop Barbara from picking him up to tell him off. Riffing off the phallic knives and his sexual frustration, Betelgeuse conjures up a brothel complete with demonic sex workers, horrifying the Maitlands.

Betelgeuse's position as subversive agitator is rooted in the fact of his metamorphic ability. He is couched as plot instigator and troublemaker: a classic fairy-tale trope like Rumpelstiltskin who creates as many problems as he solves. Barbara and Adam Maitland explicitly take on metamorphosis as a strategy to help them in their predicament, and yet their position as sympathetic protagonists remains intact and unthreatened. Later in the film they must scare on command to prove to their afterlife case worker, Juno (Sylvia Sidney), that they can be effective ghosts. They metamorphose their heads into grotesque masks which bear no resemblance to their normal faces, but – far from losing their 'personality' as Disney feared metamorphosis would inevitably effect – they remain familiar and recognisable. Adam sprouts eyeballs on all his fingers, but clearly they are each as short-sighted as his original eyes because he has to hold up his spectacles to them to look at Barbara. They need to change quickly to their normal selves in the next scene when they unexpectedly meet Lydia (Winona Ryder), and Adam has a problem changing back; but, as in the Fleischer brothers' film, *Snow White*, the metamorphic change is played purely as a throwaway visual gag, not a focus of the plot or reflection on the character, and is not commented on in the dialogue.

In *Beetlejuice* the transformations come very deliberately via analogue stop-motion and puppet-based effects rather than digital effects, which give a vitality to the sequence and fulfil Burton's visceral pleasure in stop-motion. As he states, 'Growing up watching the kinds of movies that I did, like Harryhausen . . . I always found the effects to be a little more human. There's a certain sort of handmade quality about them' (in Salisbury 2006: 62). When he interviewed Harryhausen in 2012, Burton talked about the special energy created through actually touching the puppet when stop-motion animation is created. All animation is made frame by frame, whether digital or analogue. Hand-drawn 2D animation or digital 3D animation can be reviewed and changed incrementally, as the frames can be individually revisited. However, in analogue stop-motion animation, mistakes or missteps cannot be smoothed out afterwards because each take is a record of the animator's performance in animating that model. If the sequence needs to be changed or slightly improved it must be re-shot. In all the stop-motion animated sequences in *Beetlejuice* there is an uncanny aura about their movement reminiscent of Harryhausen's work, which draws attention to their hand-constructed origins. The spectator is sub-liminally aware of the hands that have made and moved them because they are slightly imperfect and 'kind of cheesy' (Burton in Salisbury 2006: 61). Burton's love for and fascination with Harryhausen's work is well documented; *Jason and the Argonauts* is the first film that he remembers watching (in Salisbury 2006: 2), and in *Corpse Bride* (based on a Russian folk tale, 2005) there is a homage to Harryhausen's work in the skeleton song-and-dance scene. When interviewing Harryhausen to coincide with the Blu-ray release of *20 Million Miles To Earth* (Juran 1957), Burton says passionately, 'people don't really realise how beautiful and special animation itself is [. . .] three- dimensional [computer] animation [. . .] I still don't feel has the same quality' as handmade stop-motion animation (2012).

In *Alice in Wonderland* (2010), however, directed by Burton for Disney, the animation is entirely CGI. When Alice (Mia Wasikowska) first shrinks in size there is none of the cheesy, handmade effects of *Beetlejuice*; her flowing dress immaculately blossoms up around her as she disappears within it. When she steps into Wonderland, it is into a seamlessly integrated CGI environment, designed to be seen in 'Disney digital 3D'. Perhaps this is a logical extension of Disney's aspiration for the 'hyperreal' believability developed during *Snow White*, culminating in the apparently 'live action' partially animated remakes of *Dumbo* (Burton 2019) and *The Lion King* (Favreau 2019).

Alice is the most metamorphic being in this film but lacks agency; she changes in relation to her environment and in reaction to her treatment by others in Wonderland. She follows orders and instructions from people and things – whether she is attending a garden party or obeying the command 'drink me' on a bottle – reluctantly but reliably. Her body is a site of conflict and her body size is constantly commented on by others. At the same time, her passive metamorphosis is helpful in allowing her to continue in her escape from the real-world dilemma she finds herself in: ostensibly whether she should marry her aristocratic suitor, Hamish (Leo Bill), but actually, in deciding who she is and what she should do with her life. Warner points out that, in fairy tales, while male beasts are usually under the influence of a malign curse, female ones are frequently willing participants in their transformation, as they are often running away from the advances of an unwelcome lover. 'Their metamorpho-sis changes their problematic fleshy envelope, which has inspired such undesir-able desire, until a chosen, more suitable, more lovable lover can appear who will answer the riddle, undo the animal spell, disclose their identity and their beauty and release them to speak again' (Warner 1995: 353–4). Burton's Alice superficially has more power than the typical transformed fairy-tale heroine; at one point she says, 'from the moment I fell down that rabbit hole I've been told what I must do and who I must be. I've been shrunk, stretched, scratched, and stuffed into a teapot [. . .] this is *my* dream. I'll decide where it goes from here [emphasis in dialogue]'. Later, before the final battle is due to be fought, with Alice as the champion who must defend them, the White Queen (Anne Hathaway) tells her, 'you cannot live your life to please others, the choice must be yours'. However, the words seem hollow as Alice is as much a pawn of the plot at the end as she was in the beginning. Since the Caterpillar's 'Oraculum' foretold her slaying of the Jabberwocky at the start of the film, there does not seem much of a choice to be made.

The original Lewis Carroll (1865) version of *Alice in Wonderland* is essentially a metamorphic fairy story. Like animated metamorphosis, the story is full of effect, effect and effect with little sign of a cause (or a plot) as Alice travels from one strange character interaction and scenario to another. In Burton's Disney version, this metamorphic Wonderland is bracketed by a plot about a hypocritical society where nothing is as it is meant to seem: her brother-in-law is unfaithful, and her proposed fiancé does not like her very much. The falsehoods are not allowed to be acknowledged by Alice as everyone around her strives to keep the status quo intact. Wonderland here also seems to be a series of multiple effects, but the metamorphoses that Alice undergoes quickly become inextricably linked to the wider dilemma of how she literally fits in, and so the cause becomes glaringly obvious. Zipes claims that Burton 'queers the narrative of *Alice in Wonderland* by crossing genders, mixing sexual identity, and creating all sorts of bizarre animated characters who remind us that there is no such thing as normal, whether in reality or in our imaginations' (2011: 301). That is true to a point. For example, Alice changes from an archetypal princess into a warrior-prince who slays the Jabberwocky, but ultimately it always comes back to a patent binary conflict between good and evil with little room for ambiguity or unpredictability; everything happens in service of the plot. There is a duplicity in Burton's delivery of the fairy-tale ending. Angela Carter (1990), in the introduction to her *Virago Book of Fairy Tales*, suggests that the goal of fairy tales is not to maintain the status quo, but to fulfil wishes and create utopias, and this is something Burton struggles with. The real world is far less attractive, colourful or appealing than the metamorphic wonderland, and yet, in film plots, the real world must be returned to for the ending to make sense. Even in *Beetlejuice*, where at the end the dead and undead happily coexist, the culmination is essentially very real-world-normal. As Warner says of fairy tales, 'magic paradoxically defines normality' (1995: 133). Barbara and Adam Maitland become the suburban middle-class couple with a child that they always longed to have, and the outcome is much duller and less anarchic than the rest of the film despite the upbeat Harry Belafonte soundtrack in the final scene.

In these examples of Burton's work, the characters who inhabit or enter the alternative as opposed to the real world are most likely to exhibit metamorphic characteristics, and the metamorphic characters are by far the most empathetic. In the Fleischer brothers' *Snow White*, the wicked queen is the most vital, interesting and keenly drawn character visible. Similarly, the spectator has absolute sympathy with Burton's metamorphic characters. Disney's purported fear that metamorphosis would ruin the audience's connection with the believability of the character does not hold. Physical metamorphosis after all is a universal human experience, whether via adolescence (Burton's favourite), accident, menopause, pregnancy or simple ageing. Metamorphosis brings change and chaos, turning the world upside down, such as happens to Alice in the scene where she experiences her first metamorphic transformation and lands on the ceiling. As Klein states, during metamorphosis 'gravity itself seems to disappear' (2000: 21). Burton's empathy with the metamorphic characters is matched by an uncompromising attitude to those who aspire to metamorphic status but fail. The Deetz family and their interior decorator/ghost hunter, Otho (Glenn Shadix), are constantly attempting to harness metamorphosis by transforming the house themselves, via art materials, yet are thwarted in their attempts to do so. The sycophantic courtiers who pretend to be outsiders to ingratiate themselves with the Red Queen (Helena Bonham Carter) in *Alice in Wonderland* are more despised than the villains. Only the true outsiders, the undead Maitlands, the amoral Betelgeuse and the guileless Alice, are able to transform at will.

Metamorphosis is life, vitality, excess, subversion, perversion, deviance: all the fun stuff. Metamorphosis is specific to animation and being an animator is ingrained in Burton's identity as a filmmaker. Animation is a disruptive, marginalised medium that constantly reinvents itself, more qualities that we associate with the director's best work.

NOTE

1. Disney's 'nine old men' were the core animators from Disney's 'Golden Age' of drawn animation, from *Snow White* in the 1930s to *The Rescuers* in the 1970s.

2. AGREEING TO BE A 'BURTON BODY': DEVELOPING THE *CORPSE BRIDE* STORY

Emily Mantell

> At the end of the day it's not the technique that the audience cares about; it's a great story, a visual feast, and great characters. They want to be taken on an emotional journey they have never been on before. (Schneider in Lasseter 1995: 26)

A story team's journey on an animated feature such as *Corpse Bride* (2005) is similar to that of the audience. It is emotional, full of story and character, has astounding visuals – and it is unlikely you will have experienced anything like it before. When agreeing to work on *Corpse Bride*, you are agreeing to wholeheartedly embody Tim Burton's imagination. By signing the contracts, you accede to keep production secrets and leave your life at the door for the duration of your stay. In exchange, you enter the Burton world – you become a 'Burton Body', a crew member. You become dedicated to Burton's incomplete vision, you enter the 'dark, edgy, and quirky realm of the "Burtonesque"' (Salisbury 2006: xviii), and with this agreement there comes glory 'but also its own, unique set of difficulties, not least in the expectations that both studios and audiences now have of him and his output' (Salisbury 2006: xviii).

Sixteen years later I can reflect on my experience and the processes and write with hindsight. I hope to give a fair account of what it is like to be a 'Burton Body' and to explain what story development means on an animation feature. This essay provides an overview of how story teams and their ideas inform the final script, observing that the screenplay is not the beacon of light in stormy seas, but more like a large ship loosely anchored nearby.

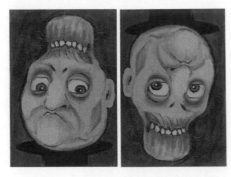

Figure 2.1 Topsy-turvy heads designed for portrait gallery in Victor's house, Emily Mantell, for *Corpse Bride*, 2005.

In 2004 I was one of the early crew members on Tim Burton's *Corpse Bride* at Three Mills Studios, London. My journey started in a large empty room designated to the story department, which would soon be bustling with story artists. Where there were once empty studios and offices, suddenly and intensely there is a surge of energy and urgency; something is created, and then as quickly as it arrives it disappears. Being part of that is special and difficult to explain.

Figure 2.2 Topsy-turvy heads designed for portrait gallery in Victor's house, Emily Mantell, for *Corpse Bride*, 2005.

Initially, there were early scripts, various pieces of concept art and production designs, Tim Burton's sketches, and a few storyboards. In the coming months, my job was to help set up the story department with the production crew and, later, to assist the storyboard artists with adapting their drawings digitally and preparing them for the editing team. Over time my role evolved to include more interesting creative tasks, including the *Corpse Bride* metamorphosis scene, topsy-turvy heads, script updates, concept art, concept art updates, gag concepts, suggesting story changes in team meetings and more.

Agreeing to be a 'Burton Body'

The term 'Burton Body' in this essay proposes the idea that the creative crew on feature animation development embodies the story and the characters both physically and mentally. It seems obvious to me now, but embodiment is a skill, an essential creative tool that varies in ability. Similar to writers, story artists are creating believable scenes, character arcs and emotional experiences that audiences should be able to connect with. To do so effectively, the creator needs to be able to emotionally and, at times, physically imagine themselves within the story or as the character. The world's leading TV showrunner/producer/writer, Shonda Rhimes, shares the ease with which this type of embodiment came to her from a young age: 'I've lived inside my head since I was a kid. My earliest memories are of sitting on the floor of the kitchen pantry. I stayed there for hours in the darkness and warmth, playing with the kingdom I created out of canned goods' (2015: 18).

The experience of being a crew member in the story team on *Corpse Bride* was an all-encompassing endeavour. Daily, we were absorbed by the story, the characters and the world. We rarely left 'The Land of the Dead' or the 'Land of the Living' and were immersed completely in the *Corpse Bride* world. If we weren't fabricating the events and emotions of the characters, then we were designing the experience of the audience. Imagining and embodying, this was our job. As Edwin Catmull notes, 'People who take on complicated creative projects become lost at some point in the process. It is the nature of things – in order to create, you must internalize and almost *become* the project for a while, and that near-fusing with the project is an essential part of its emergence [italics in original]' (2014: 91). To sustain long periods of work, the management team creates a family-led environment. The crew's embodiment was emphasised in the campus-like environment of production. In addition to this, your social life becomes crew-based, and regular after-work drinks and themed crew parties, with sometimes dressing-up as characters from the film, re-enforce the sense of an embodied experience.

A feature animated film can use anywhere between 300 and 500 cast and crew members. There are many roles, some creative and some operational. The operational crew, such as the production teams and accountants, argu-ably have less involvement with the story and characters, and therefore their embodiment is less intense. Their commitment and skills, however, enable the submersion of the creative crew into the Tim Burton realm. Hierarchical status on a feature animation doesn't differ much from the corporate world: with Tim Burton as founder and overseer of the film – executive producer (crea-tive and operational), followed by Mike Johnson the director (lead creative), Alison Abate the producer (lead operational) . . . and so it goes down through the production crew until you get to production assistants and junior creatives. On average, a feature animation can take anything between two and seven years in production, but a mere 120 minutes to watch. A huge crew dedicate themselves to a variety of tasks that go largely unnoticed, undocumented and unused; some processes may make it onto the 'special features – making of', and some ideas and assets may make it into the final film, but the majority don't. At the most basic level the entire crew embody the story by reading the script; they scrutinise each update and are witness to the development of the story as it moves forward. Meanwhile, they are surrounded by visuals created for the film – concept art, character puppets, animation tests, animatics, storyboards, sets and more. Eventually, and at varying different levels, the film and crew become strangely entangled as the 'tangible' and 'visible' make their way towards the final production.

As consumers of entertainment, art and culture we spend much of our time immersed in the story, characters and experiences, whether it is games, television, film, books or art. The more audiences/users are immersed, the more they live vicariously through the story and the characters, and the greater they embody the experience. As John Yorke notes, 'It's extraordinary to see the process by which their feelings are sublimated and they become inextricably linked with the fortunes of their fictional counterparts' (2013: 3). The more the audience embodies the character and story, the bigger the success the makers of the story feel their work has been (box office figures aside). Indeed, the creative crew are vital for this reason, and many talented individuals worked hard to complete the *Corpse Bride* vision. In the story team, our job was to get a good story out of the script, then run it through our brains, hearts and hands in the hope of making an authentic connection with the audience; we, of course, wanted to deliver the film that audiences expect from Burton. As Robert McKee maintains, 'Our appetite for story is a reflection of the profound human need to grasp the patterns of living, not merely as an intellectual exercise, but within a very personal, emotional experience' (1999: 12).

On *Corpse Bride*, the standard industry procedure of test screenings was held, in this instance, for child audiences; they watched rough cuts of the film, and their reactions were closely monitored by the crew. In general, facial expressions and responses are observed and, when it goes well, children look sad or happy in the right places, laugh when prompted, and leave with a sense of experience; if they don't react accordingly then it is back to the drawing board (literally in some cases) for the crew. The emotions are monitored because it is the clearest way of identifying whether the audience has connected with the story and characters, and whether they too are embodying the experience designed for them.

The story team have a huge influence over character and story, and it is a strange mix of working with micro details such as the emotional reactions of the character, and macro issues such as story structure.

The micro details process demands the story artists psychologically put themselves in the characters' shoes and embody their personality. For me, this practice necessitates deep concentration and working alone. The macro changes occur where big story fixes are needed. This requires team meetings, brainstorming, big-picture thinking, an ability to bounce ideas around and a good level of confidence in your ideas. A good understanding of story in general is important for the macro changes: knowing how character arcs work and how to break up the pace of the film/narrative. The story team's job is to be objective and subjective almost simultaneously; they must see the story objectively and be the characters subjectively. Often a scene would work for the plot, but the character's reaction wasn't authentic. Every gag, camera shot or story change has to be conceived, pitched, changed, pitched again and eventually accepted (if you're lucky).

Gags are the jokes that carry a scene through with visual humour; they have a large history in animation and are rarely included in the script. A story artist prides themself on getting a gag in the film and is usually congratulated by the other members of the team when they do. As the lowest- ranking story team member, I recall being celebrated by the rest of the story team when my concept of the 'secondhand store' was accepted as a gag. Below you can see the initial sketch (Figure 2.3) I nervously took to Mike Johnson. The amount of work added to the sketch to get to the final look (Figure 2.4) is evident in the images below.

Figure 2.3   Concept for Second Hand Store scene, Emily Mantell, for *Corpse Bride*, 2005.

Figure 2.4   Final appearance of Second Hand Store in *Corpse Bride*, 2005.

For each line of text in the script there could be between five and fifty drawings that demonstrate the mood of the scene, the attitude of the character and that visually incorporate key plot points (story beats). The story team can propose new ideas, or remove existing ones, and gradually they help to sculpt the final film.

There are elements of personification that are not seen by the outside world that add to the embodiment experience; an example of this was being asked to be the voice of Victoria on the rough cut of the film (many of the crew did the rough-cut voices). This meant acting the role, as well as trying to get the emotional tone of voice accurate. This was at roughly the same time that I was working on various visual expressions of Victoria's predicament – living a conformist life, forced into marrying someone she doesn't love and gradually losing her mind. I was asked to work on a wedding dress (Figure 2.5) that made Victoria look constrained, which further inspired me to push Victoria's need for escape, so I designed her sewing a blanket that would work as a ladder to aid her descent from the bedroom window (Figure 2.6).

Figure 2.5　Wedding dress for Victoria, Emily Mantell, for *Corpse Bride*, 2005.

Figure 2.6　Victorian sewing blanket, Emily Mantell, for *Corpse Bride*, 2005.

The story artists are given scenes from the script to visualise, then 'sell' the idea back to the director. This is a process which will often involve physically 'performing the boards' – using voices, high-energy storytelling and acting the board; artists put immense effort into the process, hoping that it will be approved. A performance sell may be done multiple times for each scene, and for a moment, the character, scene and story artist become one. All of this physical and cognitive embodiment is undertaken so that the audience truly identifies with the characters in the story. Yorke likens the reader's experience of story to that of an avatar: 'What an archetypal story does is introduce you to a central character – the protagonist – and invite you to identify with them; effectively they become your avatar in the drama. You live the experience of the story vicariously through them: when they're in jeopardy, you're in jeopardy; when they're ecstatic, you are too' (2013: 3). The concept of the crew embodying story and character starts with the lead creative – Burton himself. As Salisbury argues, 'Burton remains a filmmaker whose modus operandi is based entirely on his innermost feelings. For him to commit to a project it's necessary for him to connect emotionally to his characters' (2006: xviii). Even when describing the film after it has been made, Burton is deeply involved with the characters emotionally: 'You get everybody's feelings, you sort of feel for everybody involved in the triangle. You feel bad for Victoria, you feel equally bad for Victor, and there's manipulation on both sides, but you understand it' (in Salisbury 2006: 250). It was apparent in Tim Burton's sketches (which were pinned all around the story room) that he clearly empathised with and embodied the characters he created; each drawing was full of emotion, movement and energy and they remained a clear destination for the creative crew to head towards. Despite the many design and story changes, the drawings were the essence of the film.

STORY DEVELOPMENT

Animated features are mostly born in unconventional ways, with no set path. Indeed, the creative industries, in general, are not for those that enjoy order and protocol. Even within the in-house studios[1] that have a steady crew and accommodation, the journey towards the final film is not linear. Animation is fundamentally the combination of two industries that thrive on creative chaos (film and art), and both work because of exploration, trial and error. *Corpse Bride* was no different; it was a hotbed of ideas, creativity, errors and restarts. The first-time feature director, Mike Johnson, on collaborating on the project, remarked:

> One thing I learned from working with Tim is the importance of making space for creative experimentation. To stay loose and allow yourself time to play a bit. This isn't easy to do with the demands of a hectic schedule, but that creative spirit comes across on the screen, and I think it's a common thread of all films. It's obvious he loves what he does. The process is as important as the final product. (in Salisbury 2006: 25)

There is a common theme of a chaotic and confusing journey within animation feature development, even when an experienced leader with strong organisational skills and good leadership philosophies, such as Ed Catmull (Pixar), is at the helm of a production. The creative team still have to move slowly through the dark waters that inevitably make a film manifest. As Catmull notes, 'Where once a movie's writer/director had perspective, he or she loses it. Where once he or she could see a forest, now there are only trees. The details converge to obscure the whole, and that makes it difficult to move forward substantially in any one direction' (2014: 91).

In the film and animation industry the amount of work produced to 'sell' a project to investors before the 'green-light' varies considerably, but traditionally there would be a script involved. However, in the instance of *Corpse Bride* there was nothing but a few Tim Burton sketches and the seedling of an idea. As he stated, 'they green-lit it [*Corpse Bride*] without a script – without anything' (Burton in Salisbury 2006: 250). This isn't as uncommon as you might assume, and Burton suggests a history of starting animated movies this way: 'In getting started [on *Corpse Bride*] I sort of used *Nightmare* as the model.

And it's not a good model . . . *Nightmare* was developed almost like the old days at Disney' (in Salisbury 2006: 250).

In the early days, Disney Studios worked heavily with existing fairy tales, moving straight ahead into pre-production, and the visual concepts were as much a part of the development as the script. Pre-production work, such as concept art, character design and storyboards, was how the script developed, and was written and updated alongside these processes. As Paul Wells notes, 'Arguably, in many cases, the piles of sketches, storyboards, materials, artefacts and data files left at the end of the process in making an animated film, are the script' (2011: 89).

Despite the history of animation features developing story 'in house' through pre-production development, Burton acknowledges the lack of pre-production work and script at the 'green-light' stage, and also that *Corpse Bride* followed in *The Nightmare Before Christmas*'s (Selick 1993) footsteps, heading straight into pre-production without a script, perhaps causing more delays and story problems than necessary. As noted above, Burton suggests that having a script is preferable to not having one. McKee agrees; he believes that, despite the vast amount of scripts produced and rejected by the film industry, there aren't enough good ones. This forces underdeveloped scripts to be rushed through to production before they are ready, leading to big story fixes in the production phases. McKee is mostly referring to live-action scripts, where traditionally writers 'patiently rewrite until the script is as director-ready, as actor-ready as possible' (1999: 7). Burton is relatively unusual as he has experience in both live-action and animated feature films, giving him the perspective of working with finalised scripts, working scripts and no script at all.

By the time *Corpse Bride* was proposed by Burton to Warner Brothers' executives, the 'Burton Brand' had a track record of successful films, and a serious global cult following with the merchandising deals to prove it. Thus, it is not surprising that it was green-lit without a script. However, despite all of Burton's strengths, not having a script caused issues and the story team had a long journey ahead. Burton's script problems on *Corpse Bride* were frustrating, and he admits that the foundations and relationships were weak: 'I had scripts written, there were lots of people who worked on them. Carole Thompson wrote a version, but then we kind of had an argument . . . And then Pamela Pettler and John August came on board' (in Salisbury 2006: 250). Later in production, the script issues would become more pressing as we headed full speed into the production stages (animating) of the film. As a result, the development of the *Corpse Bride* story was altered and influenced by the scriptwriters and the story team equally: 'The script has changed all the way through, little bits of humour and business, kind of goes back to the old days of Disney where it was story people shaping as it goes. There has been a lot of that on this' (Burton in Salisbury 2005: 25).

Figures 2.7–2.10   Possible effects of Land of the Dead on Land of the Living, Emily Mantell, for *Corpse Bride*, 2005. Emily Mantell, for *Corpse Bride*, 2005.

An example of shaping things as we went along, and ideas that were played with, can be seen in the images above (Figures 2.7–2.10). I was asked to do some quick concepts of how the 'Living' might be positively affected by the 'Dead' and, from memory, the script we were working at the time had a similar ending, but there were so many script alterations and ideas coming from the story team that it was hard to keep track.

Many of the story concepts often come directly from the story department. The *Corpse Bride* script was an 'organic thing' (Burton in Salisbury 2005: 26), and the power and opportunities the story team had over the script were visible in the final film. Starting with the big fixes, we met regularly for story meetings where everyone was encouraged to throw ideas into the pot and battle out major plot or character issues. Eventually, micro changes evolved into macro changes: plot flaws turned out to be character issues. In the early stages of *Corpse Bride* there were two key elements for the story team to work with: the working scripts (which were already showing signs of being problematic), and the Burton sketches which showed strong character ideas and fixed visuals.

The exact origins of the tale of the *Corpse Bride* are not clear – and Burton doesn't seem to care much for these details; he had a simple yet great concept and proceeded. His inspiration came from a nineteenth-century Eastern European folk tale about a young man who accidentally marries a corpse who was murdered on the way to her wedding and is delivered to the Land of the Dead; he has to fix the situation and then return to his living fiancé. Burton made many character sketches, most of which didn't exist in the original tale, but gradually began to appear in the scripts, suggesting that the character sketches and ideas were leading the script but not necessarily helping the plot. Furthermore, identifying a clear central protagonist is arguably one of the largest plot/character issues a story can have, as it is this character that the audience must identify with. As Burton said, 'it was very difficult to find the balance for it [*Corpse Bride*], the right balance of the emotional and the humour, but also because it's a triangle, sometimes with that triangle thing, one character or another suffers. So, it became more the Corpse Bride's story' (in Salisbury 2006: 250). One of the ways in which Burton reached his decision was to focus more on female characters and emotion. When he was working on *The Nightmare Before Christmas*, the seed of *Corpse Bride* was already growing in his mind. As he suggests, 'One of the things I enjoyed on *Nightmare* was the emotional quality that the Sally character had: there was something there that I liked. It's nice to get the emotion in animation. And also, I was thinking about expanding my female characters. So, thinking about *Corpse Bride* was trying to do something with that emotional quality to it' (Burton in Salisbury 2006: 248).

Making the character of *Corpse Bride* the protagonist is a logical choice because, while Victor is struggling to work within the rules of the 'Land of the Living', he isn't as misunderstood as she is. In fact, 'Burton's characters are often outsiders, misunderstood and misperceived, misfits encumbered by some degree of duality, operating on the fringes of their own particular society, tolerated but pretty much left to their own devices' (Salisbury 2006: xviii). There were times in the story development where it was clear that *Corpse Bride* was being sidelined for Victor's story, and Burton's confusions over the protagonist and the story, in general, were duly experienced by the story team.

It gradually became apparent that despite Burton's ability to envisage fantastic film concepts, design beautiful characters and invent amazing worlds, he wouldn't be able to fix the escalating plot issues. Interestingly, this tallies with Jeff Gerke's (2010) well-argued point that if you are good at character development then it is unlikely that you will be good at plot development. He lists many examples of how successful creatives have overcome this issue by collaborating with people who have the opposite talents. Tim Burton's relationship with Danny Elfman is particularly significant in this context. Elfman is fundamentally known for the sound and music on Burton's film, but the collaboration is more profound than that. Watching Elfman in interviews and having felt his presence on *Corpse Bride*, it is clear that he has a strong control of the plot and is driven to move the story forward in an organised and assertive way. As Burton himself admits, 'He's always been a kind of guidepost, to try and help set the tone of the movie, capture the spirit of it' (in Burlingame 2016). Elfman and Burton's talents complement each other, and thirty years and sixteen films later they are still collaborating.

Despite the chaos of the working relationships and processes, and Elfman's input, the patchy story foundations and quick fixes began to show. The situation became pressured, with the story running over schedule and in danger of holding up the whole production. This is when I first heard the term 'creativity with a gun to your head', a phrase that perfectly encapsulates the intensity of this working situation and implies a compromise on quality. A story structure, or the skeleton of a story, is described by Brian McDonald (2017) as the 'armature', which is a sculpting term for the metal skeleton used inside a sculpture helping to hold it in place. Without this, the sculpture would flop. Puppets on a stop-motion film have an armature that is hard-wearing, functional and unseen but is an integral part of their make-up. Similarly, the same concept can be used within story contexts; without a decent story armature a film may flop. McDonald argues, 'The armature is your point. Your story is sculpted around this point' (2017: 20). For this purpose, midway through production, Jeff Lynch was hired as 'head of story' to resolve the story (armature) issues, as we needed to get back to the point of the film. It was clear that the armature needed some rethinking: Jeff worked closely with the story team, encouraging individuals to devise big plot fixes and move away from the current script. As he stated, 'There can be less emphasis on the script as a final source of story material . . . And sometimes you'll be starting from a concept' (Lynch in Salisbury 2005: 26). Lynch helped solidify story ideas that were being passed around, and a breakthrough came by simultaneously having Berkis, the antagonist, become the murderer of the Corpse Bride and the plotter of Victoria's murder. This facet gave the film an element of suspense and had the ricochet effect of enabling the development of the female characters. Eventually, both Victoria and the Corpse Bride were able to join forces and do the right thing: the Corpse Bride did so by handing back the groom to Victoria, realising what she thought she wanted (marriage) and receiving what she needed (justice and freedom), thus rounding off a perfect character arc. Victoria became empowered and freed, able to reinvent herself as a strong woman in charge of her own destiny. Ultimately, the film worked through 'Ideas, characters, jokes, and sight gags being added throughout the filmmaking process, contributed by everyone from Burton, Ranft, and Johnson to the storyboard artists themselves who worked with Lynch to break down the script, scene by scene, into thousands of drawings' (Salisbury 2005: 26).

Figure 2.11   Creating the film script.

STORY AND AUTHORSHIP

As a fledgling in the animated-feature industry I was surprised at how involved the storyboard staff were in moulding the story and script; like many outsiders, I had assumed the script would be our story bible, and that we were there to visualise story decisions that had already been made. Nonetheless, a steep learning curve quickly taught me how the story team were scriptwriters, using storyboards, concept art and verbal suggestions as a way of writing in new story ideas (Figure 2.11). As Wells argues, 'Storyboards are not an [illustration] of a script but another iteration of script, working as a model of editorial and creative construction in the same way as rewriting text' (2011: 94). Traditionally, story teams are rarely credited with major armature changes, which leads us into the complex realm of authorship. Wells describes the definition of 'script' as problematic, particularly for animated films: 'Animation arrives as an end product and as a result of many creative processes' (2011: 89). The issue of authorship is confusing because it is a result of many creative practices, and once you have seen inside the processes and experienced the struggle to establish where a specific idea comes from and how it was developed, you begin to understand why specific individuals are credited as story or script leads. In the instance of *Corpse Bride*, John August's name is on the final script, and Jeff Lynch credited as the head of story. The rest of the story team are credited for the most part, but this is not based on creative input, rather it is focused upon rank. Individuals working within the animation feature film world, especially the lead creatives, understand the story team's input. As John Lasseter remarks, 'the spirit of the storyboard artist's work is just as present and just as visible in the final film as the work of the animators and background artists' (2008: 9).

Higher-ranking creatives within the animated feature industry understand the value of a good story artist, and storyboarding as a career is known as an avenue into directing, mainly because of the multiple talents a story artist has. This includes the following skills: story, film language, drawing and, lastly, the ability to work fast and generate ideas. Rather than credited, the story team are rewarded by being noticed and promoted. Chris Butler is a useful example of this; on *Corpse Bride* he worked his way into the eyeline of Mike Johnson and Tim Burton, not because of his drawing skills, but because of his ideas and willingness to try things out in rough sketch form repeatedly. He has a logical mind, and an ability to see the bigger picture – to direct. Chris Butler went on to be storyboard supervisor on *Coraline* (Selick 2009), and writer/director of *ParaNorman* (2012) and *Missing Link* (2019).

CONCLUSION

Figures 2.12–2.13   Corpse Bride transformation, *Corpse Bride*, 2005.

I enjoyed my time as the story assistant (credited) on *Corpse Bride*, but mostly I enjoyed the variety of creative tasks I was given to do (some of which I have shown in this essay). Helping with the Corpse Bride transformation was perhaps the most rewarding task I was given. The transform work explored many options, from location, plot point and its meaning, right through to the way she would physically change. Finally, the decision for the dress to dissolve into butterflies at the end of the movie outside the church gives the theme of freedom, justice and empowerment to the film (Figures 2.12, 2.15–2.17, 2.19). The other images show different ideas being explored, such as crows transforming the bride (Figure 2.18) or a cocoon-style transformation (Figure 2.13). Figure 2.14 was part of a much larger series of images and storyboards I did that explored various transformations in the forest (early story idea), with Corpse Bride being mesmerised by the moonlight, or dancing into the light, or throwing her bouquet into the hole from where she was originally buried . . . and so the ideas went on.

While the crew are never visible to the spectator, their essence is always evident. Everything the audience sees and hears has been generated from the crew's minds, bodies and emotions. From the storyboard through to the final movement of the puppets onscreen, the technicians are visible. Their thoughts, feelings and ideas have transferred over into the film and new 'Burton Bodies' are created; the animated characters themselves are now the 'Burton Bodies' for the world to see and enjoy.

Figures 2.14–2.19   Corpse Bride
transformation, *Corpse Bride*, 2005.

Corpse Bride will always hold a very special place in my heart: the wonderfully unique cast of crew members, our collective successes and challenges, the day-to-day production practicalities and the creative struggles of bringing the project to life. Together we embodied the brilliant and visionary world of Tim Burton, united in the pursuit of storytelling. It was a truly unique experience. Working on *Corpse Bride* taught me, in Andrew Stanton's words, that 'Writing stories is hard. They are stubborn by nature. No matter how many times you master one, the next story is obligated to conceal its faults with an entirely new disguise' (in McDonald 2017: frontmatter).

NOTE

1. Pixar and Aardman are examples of in-house studios; they have permanent staff who have established in-house story procedures. They also have permanent buildings rather than 'pop-up' studios such as Three Mills, which was used for *Corpse Bride*.

3. TIM BURTON'S UNRULY ANIMATION

Christopher Holliday

Excessive, loose, disorderly, uncontrolled. As a cultural label rooted in the identification of transgression, 'unruliness' has come to define a range of irreverent, allegedly 'counter' behaviour that is in a persistent stand-off with the well-adjusted, and more compliant, obedient attitudes. The discourses of disruption and conflict that have underscored the shapes of unruly conduct largely within gender and cultural studies since the mid-1990s have, now, extended outwards to envelop alternative forms of power, leisure and labour. The transhistorical (or, perhaps, ahistorical) status of transgressive unruly body politics that confronts fixed heterosexual structures, and which emerged most forcefully in the writing of Kathleen Rowe (1995), has since been taken on by new media scholars as a way of explicating the specificity of current audiovisual media against more classical schemes of continuity and illusionism. Contemporary shifts towards 'intensified audiovisual aesthetics' (Vernallis 2013: 6) at the hands of digitally assisted technologies and practices have allowed for a discussion of unruliness as it plays out within scrambled, stuttering and swirling moving image culture. These degrees of stylistic transformation work to define the 'ever-present buzzing, switching, and staccato thinking' (Vernallis 2013: 3) demanded by hyper-mobile media, while providing new sites in which to examine unruliness as a form of rebellion that articulates its accelerated brand of dissent and disruption.

Beyond its cultural and political currency rooted in its satirising of social hierarchies – if not its links to the experience of unruly media objects – unruliness has also become part of a stable critical vocabulary used to explicate a certain kind of 'counter' cinema. However, although largely applied to traditions of cult media as an 'unruly pleasure' (see Mendik and Harper 2000), and also part of a wider commentary on film censorship that helps to regulate audience exposure to unruly entertainment, unruliness has also found a home in scholarship on California-born filmmaker, Tim Burton. Since his full-length film directing debut *Pee-wee's Big Adventure* (1985), and with a career spanning both live action and animation, Burton's qualities of unruliness have certainly come to be understood according to a wide range of principles. These relate to anything from his artistic practices and expressive film style to his industrial position at the margins, and even his unruly hairstyle. For Jason Horsley, Burton's entire authorship remains discursively grounded in his durable identity as an eccentric, unruly figure. He contends that 'Burton's movies for the most part seem made by a precocious, particularly perverse child, a prodigy; they are inspired, visionary, dreamlike, free-rolling, but often shapeless, unruly, indulgent' (Horsley 2009: 143).

This chapter considers the possibility of Burton's 'unruly animation' through an analysis of his two stop-motion animated films – *Corpse Bride* (2005) and *Frankenweenie* (2012) – in two interconnected ways. The first concerns the cultural and highly gendered values of unruliness when applied to Burton's animated bodies. In *Corpse Bride* and *Frankenweenie*, 'undead' characters occupy liminal spaces in their struggle to resist being confined and controlled; they are decimated and recharged, yet still create disorder through domination and by drawing attention to the very construction of identity through forms of spectacular reanimation. The chapter's second area of focus considers Burton's animated bodies in light of the fundamental unruliness of stop-motion aesthetics within the spectrum and multivalence of animated media. Through their self-conscious register, *Corpse Bride* and *Frankenweenie* narrativise the intermittent control, staccato and stuttering movement of visibly labouring three-dimensional stop-motion form. By mapping stop-motion animation's pervasive unruliness onto critical conceptions of unruly body politics, this chapter identifies how *Corpse Bride* and *Frankenweenie* might be considered as foremost examples of unruly animation.

The Unruly Animator

Burton's presumed unruliness can be largely squared to a causal understanding of three structuring principles that have consistently worked to frame his specific kind of authorial voice. The first of these emerges from a shared cultural understanding of Burton's transgressive behaviour, with a simmering strangeness to his character that persistently underwrites his star persona. Paul A. Woods argues that 'Burton is what some might call slightly eccentric, what with his wild, wild hair, a mass of unruly black curls that would terrify the strongest of combs' (2007: 147). The second element of Burton's unruliness perhaps emerges from – and is established by – this self-image of offbeat peculiarity. As a filmmaker he is often understood as something of a misfit auteur, whose 'star' eccentricity continues to support a critical and popular conception of his career as embracing multiple forms of transgression. A foundational moment qualifying the filmmaker's marginal status can be found in his well-documented adversarial relationship with the Disney studio, for whom he was hired as an animator in the early 1980s. Fuelled in part by the tumultuous conditions of the post-Walt period, Burton considered his role at the studio as equivalent to that of a 'zombie factory worker' (in Breskin 1997: 335), and he was unable to reconcile his artistic talents with the supposedly monotonous designs and character animation of Disney feature films. Yet Alison McMahan admits that 'Burton was not the only one who was chafing at Disney's schizophrenic atmosphere of dictatorialness and confusion. Others working at the company felt the same way, and they banded together with Burton on weekends and whenever they had spare time to make two live-action films, *Doctor of Doom* (1980) and *Luau* (1982)' (2005: 23). This framing of Burton's exceptionalism and lack of harmony with the industrial and ideological structures of the Disney studio has been further supported by his particular style of draughtsmanship.

A central component of his fractious working relationship with Disney was his resistance to the studio's hyperrealist style or 'Disney-Formalism', a hyphenated term recently coined by Chris Pallant (2011) that speaks to the stylistic uniformity of Disney's aesthetic honed during the 1940s and 1950s, though still in operation at the time of Burton's apprenticeship at the studio in the 1980s. Unable to fit in with Disney's visual tradition of anthropomorphic animals, including a self-proclaimed inability to draw 'cute foxes' (in Breskin 1997: 335), Burton's fertile imagination has instead been viewed as a proponent of a counter style rooted in the Victorian Gothic, with expressionist tendencies that fully support his dreamlike perversity and oneiric aesthetic register. Kristian Fraga argues that '[w]ith his keen pictorial instincts and his affection for all things fantastic, Tim Burton is a lightning rod for eccentric, stylized images – which may explain his distinctly unruly coiffure' (2005: 134). Matt Hills makes a similar connection between Burton's 'unruly, spiky, and squiggly sketches' that characterise his 'fluid, kinetic form' of drawing and his 'outsiderdom' that is symptomatic of the filmmaker's broader industrial occlusion (2013: 185–6). The unruliness of Burton is here understood artistically, implicated in a restless, disturbed and exaggerated style of drawing that emerges from a surrealist-influenced pictorial tradition and degrees of nightmarish creativity.

The pointed use of unruliness as a highly durable descriptor for Burton's work is reflective of, and reflected in, his erratic, disorderly authorship as much as his playfully unkempt visual appearance. Yet it is because of its widespread application to Burton that 'unruly' remains an umbrella term largely untested, or at best rarely qualified. Unruliness has, for example, obtained increasing critical purchase over the last two decades within the cultural politics of identity, promulgated largely in relation to second-wave feminist struggles for social transformation. In her 1995 book, *Unruly Women: Gender and the Genres of Laughter*, Rowe reflects on the availability of popular culture (specifically the narratives of mainstream film and TV) to 'figure' female unruliness and disorderly behaviour. Through 'fatness, pregnancy, age, loose behavior' (Rowe 1995: 33), alongside many other grotesque and unsettling violations of traditional neo-conservative gender ideologies, the unruly woman remakes femininity by inverting and diverting feminist cultural logic.

Written in the mid-1990s, Rowe's work builds on previous scholarly writing within film and cultural studies on stardom which largely conceived of star bodies as 'heavenly' (Dyer 1986), 'spectacular' (Tasker 1993) and 'impossible' (Holmlund 2002), rather than wayward, inappropriate and rebellious in their attacks upon presiding patriarchal power. Yet Rowe's identification of standards of female decorum also looks forward, anticipating postfeminist discourse by representing the very monstrous culmination of progressive femininity in need of monitoring and marshalling. Margaret Schwartz suggests that 'postfeminism cannot account for the opposite pole [of "trashy" female sexuality]' because 'Not every kind of exhibitionism or sexualized behaviour "counts" as acceptable' (2011: 229). The unruliness of the unruly woman therefore cannot be fully recuperated into the cultural logic of postfeminism because, as a 'topos of female outrageousness and transgression' (Rowe 1995: 75), its principles of excess mark it out as incongruous with postfeminist culture. Unruliness therefore transcends the final threat of postfeminism as it performs the ultimate (and unequivocal) reclamation of the self and the celebration of female liberation.

For Rowe, and the many scholars who have extended her initial formulations across the intersecting axes of female and heteronormative representation, unruliness is rooted in a framing discourse of nonconformity as it provides a challenge to normative female behaviour, decorum and beauty through efforts of power and deviancy (see Meeuf 2017; Mizejewski 2014; Pelle 2010; Petersen 2017; Richardson 2010; Rowe 2011). This certainly explains its anchoring to Burton as a particular kind of transgressive filmmaker. What connects Rowe's initial formulations with the terms of Burton's auteur status is that for both, twenty-first-century Hollywood entertainment media and its possible non-normative identities offer a space to think through unruliness as both an outcome of a pushback against abled-body politics, and as a new way of understanding performance/character/gender as 'more than' or 'too' in its self-management of identity. It is precisely under these broad terms of disruption that Carol Vernallis can be understood as further extending Rowe's polemic on unruly identity, by conceptualising the unruliness of intermedial relations within contemporary audiovisual media. Framed by the 'post-classical' moment, Vernallis understands 'unruly media' as emerging predominantly out of the 'malleable and volatile' boundaries between media forms, which results in a 'mixing-board' aesthetic that defines the contemporary era's convergent and still converging mediascape (2013: 4). Vernallis claims that in the instance of cross-pollinating media, 'influences ripple out maddeningly, creating interference, blendings, loosenings of boundaries in ways we've never seen' (2013: 3). Moving-image culture has become increasingly scrambled, stuttering and swirling, and it is these new audiovisual arrangements and resulting formal delirium that can be squared with a media ecology of unruliness.

The conceptualising of unruliness as a consequence of technological advance and seismic shifts in (post-)production practices usefully splinters notions of how the unruly might be further applied to – and allied with – the work of Tim Burton. As rhetorically both about content and form, unruliness speaks to the construction of particularly radical characters that spotlight power dynamics of social interaction as much as it does about the aesthetics of a spatio-temporal 'swirling vortex' and its visual speed of movement. Burton's stop-motion feature films, *Corpse Bride* and *Frankenweenie*, are supported by these complementary discourses of unruliness. They are first populated by characters who fall under Rowe's typology of unruly conduct, which are no less typical of Burton's body of work that interrogates a range of bodily differences, disfigurements and disassembly. However, it is the specificity of stop-motion aesthetics utilised in their execution that further strengthens the unruliness of these animated bodies. More than other forms of animated technology, the unique ontology of stop-motion embodies the features of 'reanimation and death' that Vernallis attaches to certain kinds of online 'unruly' media that are able to play with rebirth through the digital's creeping 'deathly taint' (2013: 138). It is therefore within this narrative/formal collision of unruly behaviour that Burton's precise image of unruliness might emphatically be found.

THE UNRULY BRIDE

From *Edward Scissorhands* (1990) to *Big Fish* (2003), many of Burton's films 'provide ample "meat" for satisfying discussions regarding [. . .] long-standing philosophical topics, including identity and authority' (McMahon 2014: 2). Indeed, for Ronald S. Magliozzi and Jenny He, Burton is a filmmaker entirely invested in 'the isolation of being disconnected from the world at large and the search for true identity' (2009: 17). *Corpse Bride* is a particularly striking exploration of identity politics through themes of the body, yet its engagement with unruliness allows the politicising of Burton's bodies and a greater consideration of their excessive agency that operates 'over the threshold'. A British/American co-production released in October 2005, *Corpse Bride* is a film concerned with the visibility of unruliness and unruly behaviour as a structuring principle of its bodily form(s). The qualities that Rowe attributes to unruly bodies offer a useful paradigm for thinking through the construction of femininity in the characters of Emily (Helena Bonham Carter) and, to a lesser extent, Victoria (Emily Watson). Within Rowe's taxonomy, four values stand out in particular as relevant to the former, the eponymous 'Corpse Bride':

1. The unruly woman creates disorder by dominating. [. . .] She is unable or unwilling to confine herself to her proper place.
2. Her body is excessive or fat, suggesting her unwillingness or inability to control her physical appetites. [. . .]
5. She may be androgynous or hermaphroditic, drawing attention to the social construction of gender. [. . .]
8. She is associated with dirt, liminality (thresholds, borders, or margins), and taboo, rendering her above all a figure of ambivalence. (Rowe 1995: 31)

Through her physical instability as a member of the film's 'undead' ensemble, Emily draws attention to the construction of gender by diagnosing the conditions of beauty through bodily exaggeration that reflect upon socially acceptable behaviours. For Rowe, the stable, even monumental, 'classical' body works to conceal by enforcing the structures of the self. Yet its unruly counterpart reveals 'gender' to be an altogether more incomplete and looser construct.

Emily's body is wrought with conflict and disruption, a 'leaking' corpse whose boundaries are always open to visual transgression. Among her many bodily disobediences, Emily's empty eye sockets are penetrated by maggots; during a piano-playing duet with Victor (Johnny Depp), her wrists break off and creep up her love interest's shoulder; and she transforms into hundreds of butterflies when sacrificing her own dreams of marriage during the film's climax. Jessica L. Williams argues that 'the grotesque image is often found in the process of exiting or entering the body' (2017: 147). In the case of *Corpse Bride*, Emily's excessiveness is anchored to the porosity of her bodily boundaries, which fuels her identity as a 'leaky' and unruly figuration through her lack of fixity. In the musical number *Tears to Shed*, Emily is told that being alive is 'overblown', 'overrated' and 'just a temporary state'. Her propensity for liminal states of being (passing between dead and living spaces; manipulation of bodily form; ability to metamorphose) further connects her to Rowe's schema for unruliness. Within the context of *Corpse Bride*'s narrative, Emily remains 'unwilling to confine herself to her proper place', and far from appearing well adjusted and invisible, she instead enacts her presence through forms of disruption. She fits the definition of the unruly woman who is typically 'associated with both beauty and monstrosity' and 'rooted in the social practices of the carnival' (Rowe 1995: 10–11). Her unruly qualities are, however, held as a source of potential power, and wielded against the misogyny of male characters who seek to control her (particularly antagonist 'Lord' Barkis Bittern [Richard E. Grant], whose initial deception resulted in her 'death'). Proclaimed as 'obviously delusional' by Barkis in a desperate act of diversion, Emily's subsequent refusal to marry Victor and climactic self-sacrifice mark the culmination of her unruly behaviour. Emily is a special kind of excess, a reflexive figure that acts out a resistance to coupledom and the social structures of marriage that wholly support the world of the living.

At the centre of *Corpse Bride*'s specific unruly register lies a discourse of the carnivalesque. Frances Pheasant-Kelly argues that in Burton's film, 'The emphasis on lower bodily strata and downwards movement described by Bakhtin coincides appropriately with Burton's signalling of a joyous and embodied afterlife existing deep below the surface of the living world' (2017: 26). The feelings of 'jubilation' germane to the carnivalesque (Pheasant-Kelly 2017: 23–4) and its roots in medieval folk culture are continually folded into *Corpse Bride*, which offers a Bakhtinian image of vigorous corporeality through the unruly actions of the undead rather than the funereal dreariness of arranged marriages and aristocrats. The clear division in *Corpse Bride* between the euphoria of the film's 'down below' space and the rigid economy of the Victorian world 'up top' (replete with modesty, propriety and custom) is arbitrated by the many unruly bodies that struggle to remain confined and resist control from beneath. The opening sequence of rhythmical clocks and ordered behaviour that cues the *According to Plan* musical number defines the austere rigidity of the living space and counterpoints the topsy-turvy joy of spatio-temporal fragmentation below that is marked on Victor's arrival by the colourful number *Remains of the Day*. With more than a passing reference to the cel-animated musical short *The Skeleton Dance* (Disney, 1929) and its medieval European *danse macabre* imagery, *Remains of the Day* fully showcases ambivalent bodies at the boundary. Their euphoria is expressed through improvisational song-and-dance (notably jazz), rhythm, appetite and gluttony, all rooted in laughter and liveliness in defiance of the status quo.

The oppositional power of the carnivalesque in *Corpse Bride* is in a reciprocal relationship with the troublemaking images and icons of unruliness, whose agents are the ill-disciplined undead that destabilise the world of order and coherence (paradoxically through vibrancy of colour and energy of life). Rowe herself suggests that 'The unruly woman often enjoys a reprieve from those fates that so often seem inevitable to women under patriarchy, because her home is comedy and the carnivalesque, the realm of inversion and fantasy where, for a time at least, the ordinary world can be stood on its head' (1995: 11). Among the disembodied folk that combine humour with the grotesque (including the comical 'head waiter' who suitably exists only as a skull and stands, figuratively, 'on his head'), Emily is decimated and recharged, inverted and recombined. Yet she still creates disorder through domination and inversion, and by drawing attention to the very construction of identity. It is additionally due to the animated medium's capabilities for queering identity through metamorphosis and transformation as part of its visual language that perhaps explains why it works so well in service of Burton's many unruly bodies. As a medium often mutable and sometimes illogical, 'the politics of identity arguably become more vibrant with the limitlessness of animation' (Batkin 2017: 6). But when Donna Mitchell argues that '[f]emale identity in Tim Burton's stop-motion films is often fragmented [. . .] [and] unstable' (2017: 231), the same charges of autonomy and dislocation can also be levelled at the specificities of stop-motion as a particular kind of animation that exists in an analogous state of unruliness.

The Unruly Medium

The narrative elements of unruliness as they are articulated through Burton's animated bodies in *Corpse Bride* are supported by the very identity of stop-motion as a uniquely 'unruly' form of animation. Stop-motion is currently enjoying a resurgence within contemporary Hollywood animation and beyond, thanks in part to eminent studios such as Aardman and Laika, and numerous directors who work predominantly in live-action cinema (Wes Anderson, Charlie Kaufman) increasingly experimenting with stop-motion techniques in a post-*Toy Story* (Lasseter 1995) animation era largely defined by computer-animated feature filmmaking. The epistemology and ontology of stop-motion within wider traditions of special effects, and indeed of animated media more broadly, is rooted in the pleasurable imprecisions and imperfections of the process. Neil Pettigrew suggests such unruliness is a striking function of its production, arguing 'this "jerkiness" – or strobing – is caused by the absence of a blur on the film, because the puppet is stationary during each exposure' (1999: 26). For Charlie Keil and Kristen Whissel too (and in ways that recall Vernallis's definition of unruly media), stop-motion holds a characteristic 'staccato or stuttered movement' (2016: 231) that often provides animators with a series of working challenges to overcome, but which equally defines the particular attraction of the frame-by-frame medium. As a consequence, the retention by stop-motion of its characteristic jerkiness is one of its strongest visual signifiers, and within its staccato movements lies a pleasurable unruly manifestation of its otherwise invisible labour.

Part of the critical anxiety around the smoothness of contemporary digital images is ultimately their obfuscation of the unruliness of stop-motion technique and aesthetics. Within the contemporary computer graphics industry, the simulation of motion blur effects as part of computer processing has permitted digital animation to accurately render the illusion of fluidly moving objects via the streaking or blurring of the image. This ability of digital imagery to '"perform" the conditions of the photographic image' (Holliday 2018: 209) has resulted in pristine animated images whose smoothness of action and motion are far removed from the kinds of stuttered movement attributed to stop-motion (see Moseley 2016). This is the argument made by Vivian Sobchack, who compares the phenomenology of crude stop-motion models in *King Kong* (Cooper and Schoedsack 1933) with the fluid digital bodies populating Peter Jackson's more recent 2005 remake. Sobchack demonstrates a preference for the former's 'jerky attempts, its laborious struggle, to achieve both "movement" and "liveness"' (2009: 390). Indeed, Sobchack's claim that the 'electronic (and invisible) labour' of computer processing has ultimately evaporated the intensive workmanship and 'effortful creation' (2009: 384) of animation production reflects, in turn, back onto the visibly labouring animation of Burton's stop-motion films. This is because the 'effortful' figures of *Corpse Bride* and *Frankenweenie* evidence human exertion from an external point of manipulation, just as Kong's constantly agitated furry texture discloses the pre-industrial work of stop-motion pioneer Willis O'Brien (whose manipulation during the film's production of the gorilla's material surface is visible in the finished film). Accordingly, whereas the agile body of the virtual Kong in Jackson's 2005 film is fully supported by its consistency in space and fluidity of action, the movements and mobility of the hand-manipulated puppet in the 1933 version inadvertently register the labour of its production one frame at a time.

The jerky agitations and imperfect continuity of Burton's stop-motion animated films offer a counter to the smooth pliancy and pristine visual illusionism increasingly available with digital imagery. Stop-motion provides spectators with unruly images that seem to stir and shake seemingly of their own volition, expressing something of the 'buzzing, switching, and staccato thinking' that Vernallis (2013) describes of more contemporary unruly media. In a discussion of *The Nightmare Before Christmas* (Selick, 1993) – a film based on Burton's 1982 poem, and produced by the filmmaker – Barry Purvis argues that the energy of the film's stop-motion is due to the very identity of the medium as 'rather unruly frenetic animation' (2008: 299). This freneticism and 'messiness' to stop-motion's quality of technique is directly folded into the opening sequence of *Frankenweenie*, in which the Frankenstein family settle down to watch Victor's (Charlie Tahan) stop-motion film 'Monsters from Beyond'. While *Frankenweenie* demonstrates a preoccupation with animation's illusion of life credentials in its narrative of Sparky (Frank Welker) the dog's electricity-induced resurrection, the specificity of unruly aesthetics is manifest in the film's doubly animated opening. As the film-within-a-film begins, the bespoke title cards (presumably drawn up by Victor-as-filmmaker) that announce the cast list give way to a short scene that depicts a monster attack on a city centre. Stop-motion is here used to (re)present itself, as Victor's mode of production creates the animated movement of traffic within a bustling urban setting, and then later the oncoming charge of an army tank designed to protect civilians from the monster attack ('send in the marines!'). As Susan Frankenstein (Catherine O'Hara), Victor's mother, proclaims upon first viewing, 'that looks great!'.

Frankenweenie's opening moments make a spectacle out of the 'struggle' (in Sobchack's terms) of stop-motion animation aesthetics, as Victor's attempts at animation for his short film are shown to express its fundamental jerkiness that emerges through his capturing of still images frame by frame. Unruliness therefore functions as a property of the distinction between the stop-motion aesthetics used by Burton and the more visibly 'labouring' stop-motion of Victor (as the film's surrogate animator). This distinction holds as a way of marking out the tentative nature of Victor's creative technique, if not playfully acknowledging the many challenges of working in a demanding medium and its inevitable staccato style. Yet the particularity of stop-motion becomes well served by the narrative of a film, which doubles Victor's labour as animator here with his subsequent reanimation of the family dog. The division in *Frankenweenie* (and indeed in *Corpse Bride*) between the living and the dead can be understood as representative of the 'before' and 'after' of stop-motion, whose objects lay dormant (yet, still, existent) but ready to come alive. For Annmarie Jonson, '[Stop-motion] bridges the threshold between, reveals the compossibility or undecidability of, both vivification and deanimation, life and death, the animate and inanimate' (2007: 425). The unique pro-filmic materiality of stop-motion is here sourced to open *Frankenweenie* as a particular kind of animated feature film. In the screen space of 'Monsters from Beyond', the inanimate objects that 'star' in Victor's short animation become endowed with noticeably jerky, staccato movements through the cinematic apparatus that qualifies their action. The outcome is a jarring representation of animated motion, and a startling counterpoint to the smoother movement of the Frankenstein family (who are no less animated) as they settle in for Victor's film screening.

The intermittent and stuttering images that open *Frankenweenie* draw attention to the materiality, liveness and agency of the objects under animated manipulation. 'Monsters from Beyond' therefore functions both as a citation of B-Movie monster cinema of the 1950s, and as a homage to the animated techniques used to achieve the fantasy of extraterrestrial or monstrous activity (in particular, the pioneering work of stop-motion animator Ray Harryhausen) (see Bassil-Morozow 2010). In this playful reanimation of older media, *Frankenweenie* delights in the pleasure of the animator's struggle. The incremental movement of three-dimensional objects in stop-motion – manipulated and handled by the animators between the frames – is shown to never be occluded or invisible. Rather, the trace of the animators' labour escapes into the pro-filmic event, made visible onscreen through the objects' characteristic jerkiness and recorded within its stuttering illusion of life. Discussing the imaginative possibilities enabled by CG technology, Aylish Wood has spoken of a similar 'leakage of technological inscription onto the screen interface' (2007: 24) that defines moments of action or a formal style that could only be achieved through digital animation. If animation therefore has the potential to 'leak out' onto screen to make its presence known, then in both *Corpse Bride* and *Frankenweenie* this 'leakage' is achieved via the unruliness of the visibly labouring stop-motion. Stop-motion is an unruly medium because it is excessive. Its images ooze and mark an upheaval, showcasing in its self-moving jerkiness the 'hidden' moves from 'animation to de-animation and back again' (Stacey and Suchman 2012: 2). Just as the unruly and ungoverned bodies that populate Burton's films are associated with 'thresholds, borders, or margins' (Rowe 1995: 31), stop-motion is a form of disobedient animation that always operates through the flexibility (or loss) of boundaries. It is a medium that creates disorder, refusing to be controlled but instead functioning as a liberation against the silence and invisibility of the processes used to create it. Unruly animation, therefore, gives agency to the animator's body that is conventionally left unseen or occluded.

Conclusion

Tim Burton is the ideal candidate to examine questions of unruliness that envelop both his construction of identity and manifest through the specificities of a medium that, in its laborious struggles, evokes the formal swirl and shifting experience of contemporary unruly media. As a filmmaker to which questions of 'counter' identity have often been levelled, unruliness allows a more nuanced consideration of how his characters challenge bodily orthodoxies through their own experiences of living with unruly bodies. In the case of Emily in *Corpse Bride*, the adjustment to her own unruly biology undergirds much of the film's drama and pathos, while in *Frankenweenie* it is Victor who must be receptive to Sparky's sudden unruly return. Yet the performance of nonconformity and dissenting attitudes in Burton's stop-motion films politically inscribes his animated bodies, and it is this interrogation of resistance and change through their ulterior behaviour that can be usefully understood through a framework of unruliness. Rowe's influential model of mid-1990s robust female disorder and, in turn, self-generated subjectivity, foregrounds the patriarchal misgivings towards such femininity at the same time as it presents the carnivalesque response to that suspicion. Burton's bodies therefore permit an examination of how marginality is negotiated and understood as precisely an experience by the marginal.

In *Corpse Bride*, Emily's unruliness enacts self-subjectivity as, through her appropriation of transgressive forms of rebellion (following her deathly removal from the social order by Lord Barkis), she is finally able to mobilise her oppositional power as an unruly body to force herself to be seen. However, the unruliness of *Corpse Bride* and *Frankenweenie* also qualifies the relationship between other kinds of bodies. Rowe suggests that in the case of unruly femininity, '[p]erhaps her greatest unruliness lies in the presentation of herself as author rather than actor or comedian, and indeed as author of a self over which she claims control' (1995: 65). This suggests that in service of authority and self-control, unruliness can occupy the space between the animator's body and the technologies, or instruments, used in their creative labour. Animation is able to make visible this potential unruliness because it involves the articulation of unruliness as a set of 'authored' qualities of performance. As part of its unruly register, then, *Corpse Bride* and *Frankenweenie* bring together the message of deviant bodies with the very unruliness of the medium.

4. *CORPSE BRIDE:* ANIMATION, ANIMATED CORPSES AND THE GOTHIC

Elif Boyacıoğlu

Tim Burton has, throughout his career, consistently utilised Gothic elements of storytelling in his works, be it narratively through subject matter or characters, visually through set, character or costume design, or the general atmosphere and mood: so much so that it has become one of his signature properties. However, he seldom creates films that can be classified into a single genre easily, which arguably makes his works more intriguing. *Corpse Bride* (2005) is a relevant example to read the nuances of Burton's creative hybridisation of genres. It provides insight into his relationship with the Gothic through an animation style and visual language that is inherently uncanny in nature: stop-motion. This study focuses on Burton's particular approach to the Gothic in *Corpse Bride* and considers those aspects of it that are retained and those that are subverted or changed through his perspective and narration. Attention is paid to how the stop-motion animation technique is employed in this process and what changes this brings to the story, visual design and genre of the film as well as the dark subjects it addresses. The concept of the uncanny will be applied throughout, primarily because it is implicitly connected to the Gothic and the emotions evoked by the content as well as the inherent nature of stop-motion animation itself. As such, the aim is to analyse how *Corpse Bride* approaches its subject matter and chosen genre through the medium of stop-motion animation. Here it should be noted that animation in itself is not a genre, but a medium that can be used to convey any category of film. The misperception is rooted in the fact that often the animation medium is related to children's content or the comedic genre. Accordingly, any genre hybridisation evident in *Corpse Bride* is not one between the Gothic and animation but between the Gothic and elements of comedy, though how Burton utilises animation in this process is of most significance here.

Researching Burton's filmography makes it clear that almost all academic work written about the director focuses, to varying degrees, on his particular style, at times labelled as grotesque, dark, twisted or ghastly; most scholars, in one way or another, point to his relation with the Gothic genre, and his manipulation of it. Though particular mention should be made of Helena Bassil-Morozow, who examines this relationship in *Tim Burton: The Monster and the Crowd: A Post-Jungian Perspective* (2010) and 'Individual and Society in the Films of Tim Burton' (2011), others similarly refer to this subject (McMahon 2014; Odell and Le Blanc 2005; Page 2007; Weinstock 2013). Here, the primary focus will be on Burton's specific presentation of the Gothic through the inherent properties of stop-motion animation and how these properties find common ground in the uncanny. A comparable approach can be found in Steven Allen's 'Bringing the Dead to Life: Animation and the Horrific' (2010), though there the emphasis is on how love, marriage and bereavement are represented, and how '*Corpse Bride* from 2005 and *Monster House* of 2006 reinterpret Gothic terror in relation to marriage and gender' (2010: 88). However, the attention to the types of animation utilised in both films concentrates primarily on the technical innovations in their respective fields rather than what the medium contributes from an aesthetic and narrative perspective. The contention here is that *Corpse Bride* extends beyond the superficial generalisation that animation is a children's medium and that any utilisation of an animation technique would automatically render a subject suitable to younger audiences. Rather, the essay examines how stop-motion animation is utilised to channel the Gothic, especially the uncanny, within the visual narration of the film, distinguishing and highlighting Burton's creative contribution to its comedic and Gothic duality.

THE GOTHIC

The Gothic genre first surfaced in literary form with Horace Walpole's novel *The Castle of Otranto* in 1764, and it was, in fact, Walpole himself with the subtitle of the novel, 'A Gothic Story', who named the genre (Just 1997: 9). There are several characteristics in Gothic literature that became staples of the genre: mysterious incidents, horrible and violent imagery, life-threatening situations, chilling despair, a villain seemingly greater than life with impossible power over either the heroine or hero, be it literal, physical or sexual, and most strikingly, the prominent presence of the supernatural (Botting 1996: 29). This presence could take the shape of ghosts, demons, decaying corpses, skeletons that walk and talk, a past that refuses to stay buried, mysterious and creepy noises and an eerie atmosphere. These elements turned out to be powerful and effective storytelling constituents. The word 'Gothic', itself changing from a 'term suggesting the barbaric and unenlightened; [. . .] to a literary term indicating the presence of the supernatural in a given work' (Clemens 1999: 15), became the embodiment of the novel, and from there the primary indicator of the genre that was emerging. The word Gothic was now synonymous with 'the grotesque, ghastly and violently supernatural' (Varma 1987: 13).

Many of its aspects, some transformed and others modified, were carried over into cinema. Gothic is unique in its narration as well as its effect on the spectator and the characters. As Mark Edmundson states, it 'is the art of haunting, the art of possession' (1997: xi), aspects that were amenable to the visual storytelling of cinema. The cinematic Gothic proliferated beyond the adaptations of Gothic novels, becoming essentially a hybrid genre; Gothic films could be found among the ranks of science fiction, drama, thrillers and horror. It could be said that Gothic 'resists territorialization by invading other genres' (Hendershot 1998: 1). In this sense, the Gothic genre is inherently open to hybridisation, which is a quality that Burton exploits creatively.

The Gothic is generally recognised by its aesthetic and narrative elements, with death and supernaturalism being pervasive themes (Morris 1985: 308). Accordingly, *Corpse Bride* presents a classical iteration of the Gothic, with its repressed characters and stark presence of ghosts and resurrected beings; in addition it contains thematic approaches, with betrayed brides killed on their wedding days, the dead, the past refusing to stay buried, and evil lurking behind unexpected corners. Here, the walking dead embody another inherent property of the Gothic, that is, the abject. As Julie Kristeva states: 'The corpse, the most sickening of wastes, is a border that has encroached upon everything' (1982: 3). In Gothic stories the dead returning become agents of transgression, while their defilement of borders and classifications, disruption of everyday life and instigation of unmitigated terror are features that Burton realises in the film.

Corpse Bride has its origins in folklore and is claimed to be either based on a nineteenth-century Russian folk tale (McMahan, 2005: 98), wherein a groom-to-be, while practising his wedding vows, accidentally gets married to a corpse-bride, or a tale first published in the seventeenth century detailing how the groom accidentally marries a demon (Ray 2010: 213), though there seems to be no consensus as to which one is the true source. As is generally the case, fairy tales in their unadulterated forms are visceral, violent and dark, and *Corpse Bride*, inherently, is no exception. It tells the story of Victor Van Dort (Johnny Depp), betrothed, through an arrangement between families, to Victoria Everglot (Emily Watson). Apprehensive about the wedding and having botched the rehearsal of the vows, he runs off into the forest and tries to repeat them, using a hand-shaped branch sticking up from the ground as a stand-in for Victoria's hand. Once he successfully says his vows and slides the ring onto the 'finger', Victor is unwittingly married to a dead woman, Emily (Helena Bonham Carter). Emily takes him to the Land of the Dead and asks him to drink poison to consummate their marriage. *Corpse Bride* therefore presents the audience with a story where characters are duty-bound in a repressed society, where the dead walk and the supernatural prevails; the latter is decidedly more fun than the living and mayhem inevitably ensues.

STOP-MOTION: AN UNCANNY TECHNIQUE

Stop-motion is an animation technique that is well suited to the Gothic genre, primarily due to its very nature wherein the inanimate object is animated, moving and acting as if alive. This is the perfect embodiment of the uncanny: that which does not act or is not as it should be. This particular definition of the uncanny owes more to Ernst Jentsch than Sigmund Freud, as it was he who initially identified, as one of the main sources of the uncanny, the 'doubt as to whether an apparently living being is animate, and, conversely, doubt as to whether a lifeless object may not in fact be animate' (Jentsch 1997: 11). While Freud acknowledges the validity of this effect, his main argument regarding the uncanny leans more towards the return of the familiar in a strange and hostile way: 'that species of frightening that goes back to what was once well known and had long been familiar' (Freud 2003: 124). However, the argument here is that both of these statements stem from the same human uncertainty: the inability to classify something as one thing or another. To do this, one needs to have familiarity with the context/object in question, as otherwise the urge to classify and failure to do so would not have the same disquieting effect. Similarly, boundaries and their encroachment are a strong element in the Gothic narrative tradition. The Gothic 'always blurs or even dissolves the boundary between life and death [. . .] The special contribution of the Gothic to this enterprise, as a stable genre of its own, is the creative domain of the undead, the should-be-dead-but-isn't, the never-was-alive-but-is, the looks-alive-but-isn't' (Wilt 2003: 41). Likewise, stop-motion is a technique that animates the inanimate whereby inert puppets imitate life. This ties into 'animism', which is intrinsically connected to the uncanny. As David Punter and Glennis Byron note, '[b]y "animism" is meant the way in which apparently inanimate objects come to seem to have a life of their own' (2004: 284).

In this sense, the uncanny is clearly present in the choice of animation technique in *Corpse Bride*, where lifeless puppets move, seemingly without outside help, and take on the properties of live beings with emotions and personalities. Centring on the innovative techniques utilised in *Corpse Bride*, especially where the facial expressions of the puppets are concerned, Allen states that they 'take on a more expressive, lifelike form' (2010: 88). Though the audience is still aware that the characters are inanimate puppets, they are invited to sympathise with their plight. That these puppets live, die, bleed, get hurt, harm one another and are frightened provides another level in the creation of feelings of uncanniness. Thus, an awareness of watching inanimate puppets clashes with the empathy that might be generated for the spectator and sustains a sense of uncanniness. Burton, aware of these factors, clearly preferred the medium of stop-motion for this project, making the conscious decision to wait for the opportunity to make the film as a stop-motion animation rather than hand-drawn or computer-generated. For Burton, 'there is a more visceral, deep-rooted emotional quality to the stop-motion, if the animation is right' (in Salisbury 2006: 316).

In *Corpse Bride* what is presented on the screen is a doubling of the uncanny. Further to the animation technique, those corpses and the dead featured in the film can be perceived as inanimate objects by definition. Any representation of them acting alive and moving thus evokes the uncanny, particularly its Freudian aspects such as the return of the once familiar in a strange form. This second layer also incorporates another connection to the uncanny, namely, anthropomorphism, which describes 'a subspecies of animism, whereby the inanimate is not merely invested with animate qualities but specifically "impersonates" the human. In Gothic terms, it is the figure of the dead coming back to life' (Punter and Byron 2004: 285). Emily, the Corpse Bride, corresponds with this category, and while not involving exactly impersonation, she does indeed try to look as alive as possible in her pursuit to win Victor's affections even while she is constantly tripped up by her own disintegrating body. The audience is repeatedly reminded that she is a corpse, regardless of how much she tries to pass as alive. While, due to Burton's style, the events are largely comedic in nature, there is no denying that the audience is watching and empathising with a partially decayed cadaver. This incarnation of the uncanny is also connected to the fear of the dead returning, which ties directly to one's fear of their own mortality. The inherent horror that a dead body 'cause[s] can also be explained to a great extent by the fact that thoughts of latent animatedness always lie close to these things' (Jentsch 1997: 15). Burton himself refers to this aspect when he comments, 'The great thing about stop-motion is that it's very tied to *Frankenstein*, which is to say, that you're sort of making something inanimate come to life' (in Salisbury 2006: 320). This source of horror is assimilated and manipulated by Burton through humour and comedy, though visually the cues remain clear, and the work retains its Gothic tendencies. As will become apparent, it is one of the main aspects of Burton's approach to Gothic properties that he employs in his films.

VISUAL STYLE

Corpse Bride opens on a gloomy, grey day, in a town with pointed Gothic Victorian-style architecture. While Burton was reluctant to state a specific locale and period for the film, he does indicate that the Victorianesque design was chosen deliberately to emphasise the repression in the world of the living (in Salisbury 2006: 325). This choice, as well as the costumes and technological indicators, place the narrative in the historical past. The visual tropes and mood in general are washed out, with Debbie Olson noting that 'the world of the living is a soft beige-white, a misty, milky drab color that is visually unappealing' (2014: 274). A related repression can also be seen in the costume design, whereby clothing appears rigid and uncomfortable, with form and presentation more important than comfort. Burton's style is equally evident in the character design and, echoing the world around them, the puppets sport harsher lines, sharp angles, spindly or stout bodies, long arms and legs, or squat ones with almost always angular features. These design choices are primarily possible due to the chosen medium of stop-motion animation that avoids the constraints of real-life locations or actors. In sum, the puppets, visually synchronised with their environment, further the complete immersion of the audience in an aesthetically Gothic world.

Corpse Bride employs tension-filled visual elements in its storytelling, involving camera movements and *mise-en-scène* that are consistent with the Gothic. Such elements facilitate the emotional impact of the various characters as they negotiate their journey through, and interact with, different environments. The stop-motion technique allows for realistic three-dimensional camerawork that can easily mimic live-action visual cues, which Burton utilises to the utmost. Cinematography is also used to inspire terror, horror, expectation and disquiet.

At the same time, Burton approaches this potential immersion of the audience in the feelings and emotional condition of the characters through another storytelling tool, that of humour. As Jeffrey Weinstock notes, 'In place of horror, Burton substitutes humor, sentimentality and hope' (2013: 27). A particular example arises in Victor's first meeting with Emily in the woods. The scene is set in the dark of night, the woods by no means inviting. Even while Victor is unaware of the imminent threat, the audience starts perceiving hints as to what is to come. Distant thunder, pronounced shadows, mist, deformed trees and assembling crows are among these indicators. The effects and music utilised here belong clearly to the Gothic, thus raising the tension. The camera on Victor, as he is in the process of practising his vows and putting the ring on the gnarled 'finger', adopts a canted angle, a further forewarning of things to come. When an unsettled Victor momentarily looks up from the 'branch', the gnarled hand moves. From this point on, the camera angles become more acute, and the following shot looks down on Victor and the hand sticking out of the ground. A reverse low camera angle reveals rows of crows amassing on the tall trees, as they too look down on Victor and the spectacle that is about to unfold. A high camera angle then resumes, framing Victor as he gazes upwards at the birds. At this instant, the audience is afforded a view of the hand moving and grabbing Victor's wrist, pulling him almost into the ground. The crows react by taking flight and swooping down towards the camera. Victor's struggle to pull his hand free is shown from a low angle, the crows circling behind him. Managing to release himself, he withdraws with the now-severed skeletal arm still attached to his wrist. Here, the first comedic hint is given as he shakes off the arm, although it is almost immediately counterpointed by the emergence of Emily from the earth, reaching out of the ground with her remaining arm. This shot uses a low camera angle to render her presence all-encompassing. It is at this point that Victor's terror, in response to the dead rising, is conveyed to the audience, the uneasy mood largely exacerbated by extremes of cinematography. In this scene, 'the barriers between the known and the unknown are teetering on the brink of collapse' (Punter 2007: 130). Emily subsequently rises from the grave, her form dominating that of Victor lying some distance away on the ground. As Misha Kavka states, in Gothic representation on the screen, 'the effect of fear is produced through the transformations, extensions, and misalignments of size and distance' (2002: 210).

After her atmospheric and terrifying ascent from the grave, Emily wails and intones 'I do', suggesting the 'marriage' as her design, though she does not appear malicious. Regardless, Victor's panic and his headlong escape are genuine, and the scene retains the makings of a terrifying flight. His fright is triggered by the dread of the dead encroaching on the realm of the living, and though we are invited to laugh at his fear, the terror is real. Through the set-up of the scene, camera angles and the visual cues, Burton intentionally manipulates the audience and Victor to make the initial and natural assumption that this, as yet unnamed, partially decomposed corpse is the monster/villain of the story. The audience, as well as Victor, witness in Emily's rising 'the tendency of the monster [. . .] to traverse space in an uncomfortably inhuman way' (Kavka 2002: 217), as she seemingly floats towards him. She is shown backlit on a hill in the woods while Victor scrambles back among headstones, though at this point the comedic elements start to properly surface. Here, Burton's voice and interpretation of the Gothic is clearly perceptible. Victor is not dignified in his escape, as he manages to hit a tree twice, and also treadmills transiently on a frozen stream. The way the chase sequence through the forest is created allows the audience to perceive a more light-hearted mood even as Victor is terrified. On the one hand the audience indeed witnesses something terrifying, while on the other, this spindly character is unable to make his escape.

This humour is accomplished primarily through a distancing from Victor, wherein the audience is invited not to share in his terror, but to enjoy his blundering attempt at escape. It is through the use of comedy that the character becomes someone to be observed rather than identified with; his reaction to the predicament is laughable, enabling situations to be created that would normally induce terror yet remain suitable for the target audience. In a sense, this distancing effect allows for the spectator to retain interest and connection to the narration but be immured from fear, which is then appeased completely when Victor awakens in the world of the dead, whose true nature is revealed as benign. The comedic elements fully surface in the macabre subsequent events. Burton, while retaining Gothic properties, thus manages to subvert and transform them into something else. This subversion is enhanced through the utilisation of animation and the exaggeration made possible by the technique, although the effectiveness of Emily's rising and the fact that the first part of the scene is essentially disquieting are indicative that, rather than the mere choice of medium, it is the vision of the director that calls forth such a unique subversion of the Gothic.

MONSTERS AND VILLAINS

In traditional Gothic literature, evil is represented quite obviously by characters that include monsters, demons, corpses, skeletons, evil aristocrats, scientists, husbands, madmen, criminals and the monstrous double (Botting 1996: 2). Emily's initial introduction and her movements, as well as actions within her first scene, establish her as a potential monster: dead but animate, doubling the effect of stop-motion and the coming alive of inanimate puppets. It is by disrupting classification systems that 'monsters problematize binary think-ing and demand a rethinking of the boundaries and concepts of normality' (Punter and Byron 2004: 264). Emily, acting alive, but visibly decayed and dead, provides a similarly problematic categorisation. She is firmly placed in-between and is initially visually and emotionally disturbing. Such liminality and in-betweenness 'is a key attribute of the grotesque-abject' (Hurley 2007: 139). The spectator is therefore left unsure as to her true nature and role within the story, whether villain or victim, hence her narrative uncanniness. Of significance is also the fact that, as was typically the case with classic Gothic villains, Emily as a monstrous body has power over Victor, the hero, afforded her through his unwitting marriage vow.

Through generic convention alone, Emily thus seems effectively cast as the monster/villain; however, she is simultaneously melancholic, the monstrosity embodied in her rotting flesh mitigated by her tragedy. Accordingly, in *Corpse Bride* there is no discernible evil, villainous character that is supernaturally inclined. Indeed, after the initial feint of Emily's introduction, all supernatural characters are rendered as quirky but essentially good, a counterweight to their dour living counterparts. Even though she has the makings of it, Emily does not come across as a monstrous villain, and she is actually perceived as more pitiful than scary, as well as whimsical and naïve. Producer Allison Abbate states that in the fairy tale 'the Corpse Bride is more of a monstrous, villainous character', though it seems that this darker version, too, shares in the love and self-sacrifice depicted in the animation (in Salisbury 2005: 21).

In a related vein, her comical attempts at hiding her decrepit condition, and the fact that she is 'physically disjointed, and internally broken' (Bassil-Morozow 2010: 42), contradict the usual perception of monstrosity. Emily's eye popping out at the most inopportune moments as well as the maggot that lives in her head, presumably eating her from the inside out, reminds the audience that she is indeed dead. Ironically, these properties are utilised to gloss over her monstrous nature through humour. This is another point where the abject is also subverted, since the physical encroachment of a moving corpse on the living is posited as acceptable for the audience through the rendering of her character. Whereas in a classical approach to the Gothic, this would normally be the very basis of the fear inspired by the monstrosity that threatens the hero, here it is the motivator that connects Emily to the spectator. At one point, the film becomes more about Emily being able to fulfil her wish of a 'happily ever after', rather than Victor's reunion with Victoria. Arguably, this endearment of Emily to the audience and the intermingling of humour and sympathy is only possible because the film is shot in stop-motion. Bodies falling apart, characters losing limbs, eyes and pieces of themselves, and particularly the decaying properties of Emily may well not have had the same endearing effect if the characters were played by live-action actors instead of puppets.

Even when Emily is angry, her face frightening and intimidating, the mood does not last, and her personality shines through. Because she often ends up crying during any argument, the audience is enabled greater sympathy with her than with Victor, and she becomes someone to support rather than to dread. This shift from being monstrous to engaging sympathy is another key to Burton's alternative treatment of the Gothic. Indeed, 'Despite her decay, Emily appears markedly more erotic than Victor's fiancée' (Ray 2010: 215). This seems to be intentional, because, although her dress is torn and tattered, its high slit allows glimpses of her legs; one is whole, and the other skeletal, making her design itself a dichotomy between life/sex and death/disgust. With her characterisation, 'Burton fleshes out a full-figured cadaver who embodies love and death, a dead woman who [. . .] teaches Victor about life and death' (McMahon 2014: 228). While there is a parallel trend in Gothic works in general wherein 'monstrous figures are now less often terrifying objects of animosity expelled in return to social and symbolic equilibrium' (Botting 2002: 286), the way that Emily's portrayal equivocates between monstrosity and inviting sympathy is a Burtonesque trope. It is also noteworthy that while Emily is ultimately not cast as the villain, she is indeed expelled, albeit through her own sacrifice, which allows things to return to 'normal'. Ironically, it is the completely mundane Lord Barkis Bittern (Richard E. Grant), Emily's murderous conman of a fiancé, who is the actual villain of the story.

UNCANNY CONTRADICTIONS

The deployment of the uncanny, a narrative force in most texts concerning the Gothic, is extensive in *Corpse Bride*. Apart from the nature of Emily's character, the uncanny is also present in the general concepts underpinning the film, such as the dichotomy that is created between life and death. As David Morris remarks, 'Death in the Gothic novel is not conceived in linear relation to life [. . .] It interrupts the hero on his wedding day; it intrudes upon timeless chapels of religion; it mixes corpses with marriage beds' (1985: 308). Victor and Victoria's marriage is literally interrupted by death and the dead. For Victor, the idea of a beautiful prospective wife is replaced by something that is dead and decomposed: Emily, the negative image of Victoria, still echoing her in the traces of beauty as well as her tragic background. In this sense, Emily, one could argue, is Victoria's grotesque double. After all, Victor himself originally substitutes, albeit unknowingly, Emily's hand for Victoria's while practising his vows in the forest. As Freud notes, 'The double has become an object of terror' (2003: 143), which is indeed initially the case but is later dissipated as Emily is introduced properly to the audience. Conversely, the idea of the double is once again visited when it is decided that Victoria should wed Lord Barkis Bittern, the very event that had led to Emily's original tragic demise: this time Victoria acts as Emily's double.

With his marriage to Emily, Victor gets locked into a parody of that prospective future-life played out in death. The consummation of this marriage, the ceremony wherein Victor is to drink the poison to join Emily in death, inevitably equates to the idea of consummation: that is, sex with death. Likewise, Emily's sacrifice, to allow Victor and Victoria to marry and build a life together, means that their future is bestowed upon them by the sacrifice of a dead bride, therefore creating an irony that in a way sums up the general approach that permeates *Corpse Bride*. In the scene, Emily, leaving the happy couple in the church, walks back towards the entrance holding her bride's bouquet: a reversal of the walk down the aisle. When she throws the posy it ends up in Victoria's arms, arguably signifying for Victor a 'happily ever after', the marriage Emily had so desired. When Emily reaches the door, an otherworldly breeze wafts her gown, while fragments of it break away as the camera zooms in to a close-up of her looking up at the moon. The camera continues to rise upwards, looking down on her as she takes a deep breath, smiles and closes her eyes; the small floating pieces then turn into blue butterflies. At this point her imperfections – the fact that she is a rotting corpse – are disguised by the light that seems to shine through and out of her and is obscured by the butterflies that she disintegrates into. Victor and Victoria approach the archway and watch the butterflies fly up towards the moon.

Emily is no longer monstrous in appearance, no longer a putrid corporeal body that can interact and touch, properties that would pose as threats in a zombie film. But ironically this is the moment at which she relinquishes her very existence. In this respect, the potential of a new life for Victor and Victoria is born from her 'death'. Equally, Victoria and Victor will fulfil that life in the world of the living that throughout the film was rendered as dreary and lifeless. Thus, Burton consistently plays with the concepts of life and death, substituting one for the other almost constantly.

Death, the Dead and Violence

Even though *Corpse Bride* is essentially 'a film devoted to death, murder, devious plans, sacrifice and love both in life and beyond the grave' (Page 2007: 433), the way that these elements are utilised and manipulated still makes it suitable for its chosen audience. Rated PG, and obviously a family film, it nonetheless retains traditional Gothic themes such as 'castles, ruins, vicious aristocrats, scary priests, undead maidens and evil mothers' (Bassil-Morozow 2010: 105). It also does not shy away from death as that is one of its principal concepts and Emily, a main character, personifies death (McMahon 2014: 227). The imagery of the dead disintegrating, losing parts and limbs, would normally be a source of horror. However, the revulsion of the violated body, the loss of body parts, dismemberment and decay is masterfully diverted by Burton, though the imagery in essence is comparable. Burton's vision 'combines gothic horror, black comedy, and a whimsical, oddball imagination' (Salisbury 2005: 13). His approach to death and the dead is light-hearted and is amplified though quirky designs and acting, and this is enabled by the animation technique deployed. The clear distinction in the rendering of the world of the living and the dead underlines this approach. 'Scenes depicting "the land of the living" are deliberately drained of colour, while "the underworld", far from being cold, is friendly and bright' (Bassil-Morozow 2010: 106), providing another instance where Burton adopts the blurring of boundaries inherent in the Gothic, and making sure the dead are more alive than the living.

Relatedly, subjects such as onscreen death in Mayhew's (Paul Whitehouse) unfortunate end are not flinched away from, though the general attitude of the film narration and characters does not allow for these to be read as tragedies. The next time Mayhew is onscreen he is more interesting and jolly. Burton uses the inherent properties of the Gothic to overturn the expectations of the audience; one such instance can be seen during the scene that depicts the rise of the dead to the world of the living (Page 2007: 433). The dead rising and corpses moving constitute effectively abject visuals, but Burton changes the nature of the scene entirely. When the dead creep out from the darkness, the set-up is initially reminiscent of the rising of the dead in horror films. However, with an abruptness that speaks of mockery, the perception is changed completely and everyone, relatives dead and alive, embrace joyfully. In this sense Burton capitalises on the well-established tropes of the genre and the expectations they create to further his own narrative and style, using them to create a unique animated Gothic hybrid.

In a similar vein, scenes where eyes pop out of skulls left and right are rendered in comedic fashion. Perhaps since Luis Buñuel and Salvador Dalí's first mutilation of the eye onscreen in *Un Chien Andalou* (1929), eyes are an especially strong motif to use in the creation of body horror and disturbance. This powerful effect is nonetheless disrupted by humour in Burton's case, and demonstrates his successful but diverse approach to the Gothic animation and its properties.

CONCLUSION

With its subtle manipulation of the Gothic perfectly deliberate in design, *Corpse Bride* is successful in making accessible a usually foreboding genre to its chosen target audience. As Colin Odell and Michelle Le Blanc suggest, 'The key to Burton's approach with his films lies in the way he takes an established genre and twists it' (2005: 14). The film maintains its Gothic identity even while Burton's narration and style, at times through the exploitation of certain properties of the animation technique chosen, subverts it. It is important to state that this hybridisation of genres cannot merely be laid at the feet of the utilisation of stop-motion animation. As noted, stop-motion animation has an inherent disposition for horror, uncanniness and resonance with the Gothic. It was indeed stop-motion that initially allowed some of the more imaginative monsters to come to life in early cinema, providing an ancestry of visual effects. In almost all aspects the properties of stop-motion animation that Burton emphasises are those that resonate with, and augment, the Gothic elements in his story. The hybridisation present in *Corpse Bride* is due primarily to the fact that Burton decided to create a story that was suitable for a wider and younger audience. He achieved this through his storytelling techniques, narrative choices, implementation of humour, and a visual as well as narrative style which he, at times, supported with the properties and narrative possibilities that stop-motion animation provided him. Perhaps more importantly, rather than glossing over or removing Gothic elements that could be perceived as terrifying or disquieting, Burton chooses to retain these features, changing how they might be perceived by playing on the expectations of the audience. These aspects are wholeheartedly embraced, emphasised and transformed to fit the vision of the director, thereby effectively changing the Gothic without losing its intrinsic properties. Burton's particular vision infuses the story with a light-heartedness even while it manages to maintain its distinctive style and darkness, touching on subjects that are by no means light, and which make the film identifiable as conspicuously Burton and especially Gothic.

PART TWO

CREATURELY BODIES

5. BURTON, APES AND RACE: THE CREATURELY POLITICS OF TIM BURTON'S *PLANET OF THE APES*

Christopher Parr

Tim Burton's 2001 'reimagining' (McMahan 2005: 160) of *Planet of the Apes* has an ambivalent relationship with both the novel on which it is based (Boulle 2011) and the original film which constitutes its clearest cultural counterpart (Schaffner 1968). While Burton's version shares many plot elements with Pierre Boulle's novel – a human lands on an explicitly alien planet, finds a civilisation of intelligent talking apes who oppress the planet's primitive humans, and eventually makes his way back to Earth where he finds the apes have taken over there as well – it mostly relinquishes its source's satirical elements for a straightforward adventure story. Meanwhile, though claiming no inspiration from Franklin J. Schaffner's film, Burton's borrows dialogue from the 1968 original: an ape paraphrases Charlton Heston's line from the original, growling, 'Get your stinking hand off me, you damn dirty human', while Heston himself appears in an uncredited cameo to repeat his famous closing cry of, 'Damn you! Damn you all to hell!'

The association of Burton's *Planet of the Apes* with its two source texts mirrors the film's equivocal relationship with both the race relations depicted in 1968's *Planet of the Apes* and Burton's complex affiliation with diversity throughout his career. This chapter explores how the apes in Burton's film are ambivalently signalled as racial others in a way that reflects similar coding in prior films of the franchise and certain of Burton's previous productions. The chapter first outlines a framework for studying race in cinema based on the work of Fatimah Tobing Rony (1996). It then summarises the racial dynamics of the first *Planet of the Apes* film, specifically the model developed by Eric Greene

(2006), before providing an overview of the sometimes debatable depictions of race and ethnicity in Burton's films. In textually analysing Burton's *Planet of the Apes*, the chapter considers how creaturely bodies are used to negotiate between these two positions and contributes to the discussion surrounding race in Burton's films: a subject on which there is, so far, limited scholarship.

RACIAL REPRESENTATION IN THE CINEMA: ETHNOGRAPHY AND HYBRIDITY

In her book *The Third Eye: Race, Cinema, and Ethnographic Spectacle*, Rony explores the representation of the 'native' in various cinematic modes. These include the ethnographic films of Félix-Louis Regnault, produced in the late nineteenth century, which were supposed to 'serve as an unimpeachable scientific index of race' (Rony 1996: 4), the early 'taxidermic' documentaries, such as *Nanook of the North* (Flaherty 1922), 'which hinge[d] upon a nostalgic reconstruction of a more authentic humanity' (Rony 1996: 14), and Hollywood-produced 'racial films', including *King Kong* (Cooper and Schoedsack 1933), which constituted 'a long line of films representing the person of African, Asian, or Pacific Islander descent as an ape-monster' (Rony 1996: 15).

While the first and second of Rony's modes are not relevant here, the third provides a useful lens through which to view the bodies of the apes in Burton's film. According to Rony, natives in Hollywood 'racial films' are usually '[l]andscaped as part of the jungle *mise-en-scène*, or viewed as the faithful Man Friday to a white Robinson Crusoe, or perhaps romanticized as the Noble Savage' (1996: 5), and all three of these representations can be found in the apes of Burton's film. Furthermore, though Burton's film is not ethnographic, and its only similarity with *King Kong* and other 'racial films' is the presence of apes, his version of *Planet of the Apes* continues the tradition of investing certain apes and ape-like characters with negative notions of animality and bestiality. However, several of the ape characters in Burton's film are sympathetic, even heroic. Just as Rony notes that the native in early films is a complicated figure, a 'site of a collision between past and present, Ethnographic and Historical, Primitive and Modern [capitals in original]' (1996: 15), the apes in Burton's film are a site of collision between the sometimes thoughtful racial representations of the original *Planet of the Apes* film and the arguably ambivalent portrayals present within Burton's body of work.

RACE IN *PLANET OF THE APES* (SCHAFFNER 1968)

In his book *Planet of the Apes as American Myth: Race and Politics in the Films and Television Series*, Eric Greene argues that the original cycle of *Planet of the Apes* films can be read as an analogy for race relations in the USA in the 1960s and 1970s. The series comprises the original *Planet of the Apes* and its sequels: *Beneath the Planet of the Apes* (Post 1970), *Escape from the Planet of the Apes* (Taylor 1971), *Conquest of the Planet of the Apes* (Thompson 1972) and *Battle for the Planet of the Apes* (Thompson 1973), and deals with such issues as animal rights, nuclear proliferation and the Vietnam war (Greene 2006: 72). However, Greene contends that the primary themes of these films are race, racial violence and the civil rights movement. Though Greene's argument extends across all five films in the franchise's original cycle, as well as the two television series and various novels and comic books, this chapter's elucidation of his claims will focus on the first film. This is because, of the five original films, the 1968 release has the clearest influence on Burton's production.

In Schaffner's version of *Planet of the Apes*, a group of human astronauts, travelling at light speed, crash-land on what they assume to be an alien planet. On this planet, talking apes are the dominant species, while mute and primitive humans are seen as vermin. The astronauts are captured by the apes; one of them, Taylor (Charlton Heston), suffers an injury to his throat and is unable to speak. Despite his handicap, Taylor manages to convince the chimpanzee scientist, Zira (Kim Hunter), of his intelligence, though the orangutan politician, Zaius (Maurice Evans), remains sceptical. When he regains his ability to talk, Taylor is still unable to convince Zaius that he is an intelligent being, so he enacts his escape from the ape city and flees to the wasteland known as the Forbidden Zone. Here, Taylor finds evidence that the planet's humans were once the dominant species. The film ends with Taylor venturing further into the Forbidden Zone and discovering the shattered remains of the Statue of Liberty, revealing that this is not an alien planet, but Earth in the far future. Humanity has wiped itself out, and apes have evolved to take their place.

As noted, the film deals with a number of issues, most notably nuclear war as exemplified by Taylor's furious cry of 'You blew it up' upon seeing the destroyed monument, which implies that there was a nuclear war in this Earth's past. While he acknowledges this, Greene presents an interpretation of the film in which the relationship between humans and the various species of apes is taken as a racial allegory. According to Greene, each film in the series 'is built around the conflict between a racially dominant group and a racially dominated group. The mediating figures are from a group previously discriminated against which is still marginalized and at odds with the dominant group' (2006: 24). In the case of the 1968 film, the dominant group are the orangutans who are presented as politicians and bureaucrats; the mediating figures are the chimpanzees who are intellectuals sympathetic to the film's humans but cowed by the orangutans; and the humans are the oppressed group, dominated by the apes (Greene 2006: 24). In terms of race, the orangutans represent the white establishment, the humans equate to African-Americans and the chimpanzees stand in for Jewish Americans, another minority who nevertheless often act as advocates for African-Americans (Greene 2006: 31–2).

Left out of this schematic are the film's gorillas, although Greene does note that they are located at the bottom of the ape society, 'limited to military service and low-skilled manual labor. Their opportunities have been constrained in much the same ways as those of African-Americans. And like African-Americans, they have been maneuvered into low-status service jobs' (2006: 31). The marginalisation of the gorillas creates a much more explicit racial analogy than does that of the film's humans. While the oppression of the humans at the hands of the apes raises the issue of animal rights and human exceptionalism, which can occlude the dynamic's racial element, the gorillas' lowly position in the apes' social hierarchy is a more immediate political statement. The gorillas' darker skin tones mark them as black (Greene 2006: 99), their relegation to menial jobs aligns them with many African-Americans of the time, and both of these factors cause the racially offensive uses of the words 'ape' and 'monkey' (Greene 2006: 5) to apply more readily to the film's gorillas than they do the chimpanzees or orangutans. In this way, both the humans and gorillas of Schaffner's film can be seen as symbols of blackness and race relations, a fact which will need to be considered when analysing Burton's film.

RACE IN THE FILMS OF TIM BURTON

Burton's work is recognised for often dealing with difference, from 'forbidden sexual identities', identifiable in *Batman Returns* (1992) (Siegel 2013: 199), and disability (Hall 2016) to, less noticeably, race. Paul Cantor (2014), for instance, argues that Burton's *Mars Attacks!* (1996) 'goes out of its way to suggest the multiethnic and multiracial character of the American people' (2014: 105). This is clearest in the band of characters who oppose the Martians in the film's Las Vegas scenes: the group comprises Byron Williams (Jim Brown), 'an African American Muslim', along with 'the very ethnic Danny DeVito character, and the Welshman Tom Jones' (Cantor 2014: 105). However, Cantor also notes that the Norris family, who become the *de facto* heroes of the narrative with their discovery of a method to defeat the Martians, are

> bigoted, close-minded, parochial, and devoted to saving their own family and their TV. And yet the movie seems to take the Norrises' side. For one thing, they are right about the Martians and willing to take action against them. The movie seems to suggest that there is something healthy about the ordinary human prejudice in favor of one's own. (Cantor 2014: 102)

Thus, Cantor suggests that, in *Mars Attacks!* at least, Burton displays an ambiguous attitude towards race, simultaneously celebrating multiculturalism and bigotry.

This ambiguous attitude is also visible in films which engage more obliquely with issues of race. While *Edward Scissorhands* (Burton 1990) can be read as dealing with disability (Hall 2016), Greene cites the film as an example of the kind of 'symbolic resolution or suppression of societal anxieties and tensions' (2006: 146) present in popular culture. Greene describes the plot of the film as an analogy for miscegenation, in which the outsider protagonist, Edward Scissorhands (Johnny Depp), is persecuted for falling in love with a white teenage girl and ultimately banished from the community. However, Edward's persecutors continue to benefit from his labour as they enjoy, even only in an aesthetic sense, the snow produced by his ice sculpting. Moreover, the suburban community goes largely unpunished for their harsh and unfair treatment of him (Greene 2006: 147). In this way, Greene argues, *Edward Scissorhands* advocates for segregation as a solution to racial tensions. Given the conservative connotations that accompany the film's stylised portrayal of American suburbia, this is a regressive position, more at home in a film from the 1950s than the arguably more progressive period of the 1990s. The film's stance is further problematic when it is considered that the only black character is the police officer who aids Edward in his return to his ancestral home, almost in an attempt to lend credence to the film's advocacy of segregation. What is more, the film's actual stand-in for black experience, Edward, is not only a white character played by a white actor but is made up to be as pale as possible, visually distancing the character from the very experience he is allegedly representing.

Wheeler Winston Dixon (1992) also notes the lack of diversity, whether in aesthetics or casting, in Burton's films. Discussing *Batman Returns*, Dixon points out that there 'is not a single African-American, Latin-American, lesbian, gay, or feminist character of any consequence in the entire film's narrative. "Difference" in any form thus guarantees narrative exclusion' (1992: 62). Anna Everett (1995) and Krin Gabbard (2000) go further, each suggesting that signifiers of racial diversity are not only utilised as signs of difference in Burton's films, but as signs of malevolence. With his use of 'blackspeak' and jazz music (Everett 1995: 30), Everett argues that the villainous Oogie Boogie (Ken Page) in the Burton-produced *The Nightmare Before Christmas* (Selick 1993) is a 'racially constructed arch-villain' who occupies a 'racially spatialized underground never-never land [. . .] wherein race, specifically blackness, functions as the perfect narrative interruptus' (1995: 29). According to Everett, *The Nightmare Before Christmas* engages in a 'subterfuge' by which

> the blackened arch-villain is not drawn with what could be thought of as black features or even coloration, but his speech, his environment, and his function as narrative obstacle clearly deploy socially recognizable codifications of racial blackness and thus racial undesirability: threatening and

racialized speech, 'jungle'music [sic] signifying a debased culture's jazziness (as jazz-like music is the preferred mode for soundtracks that want to convey a sense of the underworld, or savage and uncontrolled passions), and the villain's underground cave is the virtual heart of darkness for this script. (1995: 30)

Gabbard makes a similar argument with regard to Burton's *Batman* (1989), writing that the Joker (Jack Nicholson) 'arouses white anxieties about black youth by speaking in rappish rhymes and spray-painting graffiti on famous paintings in a museum while prancing to the funk of the artist then known and now once again known as Prince' (2000: 373). He goes on to claim that 'Tim Burton and his collaborators have avoided charges of overt racism by not showing black hooligans on the screen, but they have made the Joker more threatening by linking him to African American musical performances that are despised by many white Americans' (Gabbard 2000: 373). Meanwhile, Florent Christol perceives a colonial aspect to *Pee-wee's Big Adventure* (Burton 1985), in which 'Pee-wee inhabits a sort of pre-Civil War, racially-segregated universe', a universe which supports 'a conservative politics of historical disavowal [. . .] that partly challenges the popular image of Burton as a subversive, carnivalesque artist debunking traditional American myths' (2017: 162).

The examples given by Greene, Dixon, Everett, Gabbard and Christol demonstrate the uneasy relationship Burton's work has with issues of race and ethnicity. This difficulty was further highlighted in 2016 when Burton himself responded to criticisms of a lack of diversity in his films. After claiming that 'Things either call for things or they don't' (in Denham 2016), referring to whether his films should deal with issues of difference, Burton went on to say

I remember back when I was a child watching *The Brady Bunch* and they started to get all politically correct. Like, OK, let's have an Asian child and a black. I used to get more offended by that than just . . . I grew up watching Blaxploitation movies, right? I said, that's great. I didn't go like, OK, there should be more white people in these movies. (in Denham 2016)

Burton's comments suggest that while he is consistently acknowledged for embracing difference, paradoxically there appears to be issues with race in his films. In this respect, Burton's seeming equivocation will inform, along with Greene's racial interpretation of the 1968 film, the analysis of his version of *Planet of the Apes*.

TIM BURTON'S *PLANET OF THE APES*

Unlike Schaffner's film adaptation, Pierre Boulle's novel takes place on an alien planet, somewhere in the region of the star Betelgeuse. A group of space-farers from Earth land on the planet and are captured by talking apes who mistake the astronauts for the world's mute humans. One of the astronauts, Ulysse, convinces the apes of his intelligence, and begins working with them to uncover the origins of this planet's inverted species dynamic. He discovers that the planet used to be dominated by humans, who trained apes to imitate them. After the apes rose up in rebellion against their cruel masters, they continued to imitate them until they had created their own civilisation. Ulysse manages to escape the planet and return to Earth, where he finds that, in his absence, apes have overthrown humans here as well.

Though, as already noted, Burton's film is a 'reimagining' rather than an adaptation of the novel or a remake of the 1968 film, its plot owes more to Boulle's original book than it does to Schaffner's film. Set in 2029, Burton's production follows Leo Davidson (Mark Wahlberg), a United States Air Force officer who trains primates for space missions aboard the space station Oberon. When an electromagnetic storm approaches the station, Davidson's favourite chimpanzee, Pericles, is sent out to gather data. The station loses contact with Pericles and, against orders, Davidson flies out after him. After passing through the storm, he crashes on an unfamiliar planet. Here he is captured by a group of apes wearing intricate armour, along with a group of native humans. They are taken to a jungle city where Davidson learns that the apes are the planet's dominant species, and humans (who, unlike in the original novel or film, can talk) are used as slaves. Herein arises a racial allegory. Davidson is bought by Ari (Helena Bonham Carter), a chimpanzee and human rights activist. He manages to escape, free the other humans who were captured with him, and with the help of Ari and her gorilla servant, Krull (Cary-Hiroyuki Tagawa), flees the city. They decide to make their way to the forbidden temple of Calima, which also happens to be where Davidson believes his crew mates are waiting for him. They are pursued by General Thade (Tim Roth), a cruel chimpanzee who desires control of the ape society.

When Davidson and his group reach Calima, he discovers that it is actually the downed remains of the Oberon; the name Calima is derived from a par-tially obscured sign that reads 'Caution: Live Animals'. It transpires that the electrical storm sent Davidson forward in time, and that the apes and humans on this planet are descended from those who inhabited the crashed space station. Thade and the ape army catch up with the humans, and a large-scale battle is fought before the ruined station. The fighting is cut short when a pod descends from the sky and Pericles steps out. The apes revere Pericles as Semos, the founder of their society and religion, and a truce is negotiated between the humans and the apes. Davidson escapes the planet in Pericles's pod and manages to return to Earth. He lands at the Lincoln Memorial in Washington, DC; looking up, he sees that it is not Lincoln memorialised, but Thade, implying that the chimpanzee somehow also escaped his planet and arrived on Earth before Davidson. Police cars and onlookers gather, and Davidson looks on in horror as he sees that they are all apes.

Existing scholarship on Burton's production, such as that of Colin Odell and Michelle Le Blanc (2005) and Jim Smith and Clive Matthews (2002), is largely limited to brief overviews in chronological studies of the director's career. Alison McMahan provides a more comprehensive analysis of the film, claiming that, though 'much is made of the differences between apes and humans in this film, the emphasis seems to be more on class differences than on racial tensions' (2005: 178). Even then, McMahan argues that the film is unwilling to engage with any kind of social commentary, a reluctance most evident in the character of Davidson, who 'spends the entire movie trying to get back to his spaceship, ignoring, as much as possible, the huge social upheaval going on around him and refusing to participate except when he absolutely has to' (2005: 178). Oliver Lindner is critical of McMahan's reading of the film. Though he is primarily concerned with adaptation and the film's relationship to Boulle's novel and Schaffner's film, Lindner notes the

> broader implications of Leo's role as representative of contemporary American foreign policy [. . .] McMahan ignores the fact that Leo's conduct can be linked to America's rather informal military involvement in global affairs at the turn of the century, whereas Leo's alternative role as official leader of the humans on the ape planet would surely have been regarded as an undisguised reverberation of American arrogance and political hegemony that sits uneasily with a global audience. (2012: 124)

Nonetheless, Lindner's reading, like McMahan's, does not acknowledge any racial component to Burton's film. Kimiko Akita and Rick Kenney (2016) do discern a racial element, although theirs is a postmodern analysis concerned with audience engagement rather than Burton's racial politics. Page argues that Burton's production depicts 'how ignorance of the ways of other races and species can affect how they are treated' (2006: loc 2799). He goes on to claim that Burton's film is one 'which allows us to see how easy it is to misperceive, and therefore encourages us to be more thoughtful in matters relating to difference, not allowing ignorance to guide our actions' (Page 2006: loc 2802). This is, however, an uncritical reading of the film's engagement with issues of race, and one lacking in textual evidence. That existing scholarship does not address a racial component may largely be a result of the fact that the film is more of a fairy tale than an allegory, and one lacking in any real satirical content (McMahan 2005: 179). Arguably, however, Burton's *Planet of the Apes* presents a confused perception of racial issues in which the bodies of the apes become a focal point for both the racial allegory of Schaffner's film and the, sometimes ambiguous, race relations of Burton's other works.

This collision of racial perceptions first becomes evident early on, during the scene in which Davidson, along with a number of the planet's primitive humans, is captured by the apes. As Rony points out, 'the archetypal narrative of many forms of ethnographic cinema [. . .] mirrors that of the horror film' (1996: 163), and the introduction of the intelligent apes in many ways resembles the introduction of the monster in a horror film. The presence of the apes is initially alluded to when Davidson encounters the primitive humans in the jungle in which his pod crashes. They are shown in close-up, expressions of terror on their faces, and the only clue as to their pursuers is the diegetic sound of inhuman cries from behind them. After their brief encounter, the humans flee past Davidson and the film cuts together three shots of the jungle: movement in the underbrush, a shadow passing behind leaves, and a barely glimpsed figure running across a branch; these images are intercut with reaction shots of Davidson looking increasingly fearful. Davidson turns to flee with the other humans, before an overhead camera frames another shadowy figure leaping from tree to tree above its prey. The sequence subsequently features two shots of more shadowy figures dropping from the trees, before one drops directly in front of the camera and stands up; at this point it becomes the film's first close-up of an intelligent ape, a chimpanzee who lets out another cry before running out of frame. Burton's film therefore uses similar cinematic techniques as a horror film to position, at least initially, its apes as monsters. Given the pervasive racial allegory present in the *Planet of the Apes* franchise, as argued by Greene, these techniques also relate the apes to what Rony has noted as the ethnographic film's representation of the 'person of African, Asian, or Pacific Islander descent as an ape-monster' (1996: 15).

However, even before the apes are revealed to possess language and culture, their visual depiction complicates their representation as racial monsters. Their vocalisations and figure expression in this early scene may be animalistic, but the apes' costuming is at odds with this bestial nature. In contrast to the native humans who are dressed in primitive fur and leather clothing, the apes are wearing sophisticated metal armour, some of it adorned with intricate artistic flourishes, which implies that they possess an advanced culture, at least compared to their planet's humans. The juxtaposition of bestial figure expression and sophisticated costuming signifies, in this early scene, that the apes are a site of ambiguous racial representation.

After being captured, Davidson is brought to the ape city. Establishing shots reinforce the apes' advanced culture, with trade, music and fashion foregrounded; again, this aspect is contrasted with their animalistic appearance and behaviour. The film's equivocation towards issues of race continues into a dinner party scene later in the narrative. After being sold as slaves, Davidson and the humans with whom he was captured are forced to serve at a soirée being held by Senator Sandar (David Warner). It is here that Burton begins to engage with the original film's racial representations, as outlined by Greene, and the differences and similarities are telling. Though Ari, who is sympathetic towards the film's humans, occupies the same mediating position as the chimpanzees in the 1968 film, the other apes in this scene occupy positions that suggest that Burton is subverting the racial hierarchy of the original. Sandar, a chimpanzee, is a politician (a position held exclusively by orangutans in the original film), which is signified by his purple and gold robe. An identical robe is worn by Tival (Erick Avari), who is also a senator. That both a chimpanzee and an orangutan are senators suggests that Burton has abandoned the racial stratification which Greene (2006: 30) claims is featured in Schaffner's film. This is further reinforced by the appearance of a subsequent guest, Thade. He is a chimpanzee who is also a general, the kind of military position held only by gorillas in the original cycle of films: for example, General Ursus (James Gregory) in *Beneath the Planet of the Apes* and Aldo (Claude Akins) in *Battle for the Planet of the Apes*. This diverse distribution of species is evident elsewhere in Burton's adaptation. Unlike Schaffner's film, in which the apes who capture Taylor are all gorillas, in Burton's version the hunting party comprises both gorillas and chimpanzees. The latter also constitute the majority of the infantry sent against the humans in the battle before Calima, while the ape army in *Beneath the Planet of the Apes* is entirely made up of gorillas.

Even though, in many ways, the ape society of Burton's film dismisses the racial hierarchy of the 1968 original, there is one significant mode in which it adheres to that same social structure. Just as in Schaffner's film, the gorillas in Burton's version occupy the lowest positions among the apes. Without exception, they are servants, soldiers and underlings. In both films, gorillas are 'the lowest racial class [. . .] limited to military service and low-skilled manual labor' (Greene 2006: 31). There are two gorillas present at Sandar's dinner party, Attar (Michael Clarke Duncan) and Krull. Attar is Thade's *aide-de-camp* and is only seen in the background of shots; Krull is not a guest but a servant. In fact, Krull is barely positioned above the humans; he wears a simple jerkin whose muted colour is not dissimilar to that of the robes worn by the humans. Krull's lowly rank is reinforced throughout the scene as he is consistently depicted in two-shots with Davidson, thereby visually occupying the same position as the enslaved human. Although, as McMahan suggests, Burton's 'emphasis seems to be more on class differences than on racial tensions' (2005: 178), and his adaptation is ostensibly less interested in issues of race than the original cycle of films (instead focusing on animal welfare, largely through the character of Ari), it nonetheless includes the sort of problematic racial representations noted by Dixon (1992), Everett (1995), Gabbard (2000) and Greene (2006). That the gorillas in his film occupy the lowest racial position is emphasised by their obvious otherness. Their unambiguously dark skin tones mark them as racially black (Greene 2006: 99). Furthermore, their racial otherness is reinforced by the fact that the film's only prominent gorilla characters, Attar and Krull, are both played by non-white actors: Michael Clarke Duncan is black, while Cary-Hiroyuki Tagawa is Japanese. Non-white actors playing racially othered characters who occupy the lowest social position is potentially troublesome because of the negative connotations which, according to Greene and Roning, exist between apes, black people and natives. Greene notes that 'historically, discourses about apes and monkeys and discourses about race and "people of color" have been continually intertwined' (2006: 5), while Rony remarks that many ethnographic films in the early twentieth century 'depicted Africans and Asians as ape-men, lustful and savage' (1996: 179–80). Though Attar and Krull are neither lustful nor savage, both being rather stoic and noble characters, their lowly social positions and the fact that they are played by non-white actors embroils them in a concerning racial discourse. The gorillas appear to occupy a similar position in Burton's films to Oogie Boogie and the Joker; that is, though Burton attempts to avoid issues of race, he still utilises racially charged elements in his depiction of certain characters.

While Attar and Krull cannot be described as lustful or savage, Thade certainly can. As the film's antagonist, he is seen murdering his own subordinates after they discover Davidson's crashed pod. He violently lashes out when hearing that the humans have escaped his patrols, and brands Ari as a slave in a gesture that could be read as a symbolic rape. Thade is not a gorilla, rather a chimpanzee, and he is played by the white actor, Tim Roth. Despite these complicating factors, he remains an ape and is clearly signalled as savage and evil, and so is still implicated in the questionable racial coding of the film's apes. Other than the examples of violence listed above, Thade's savagery is signified largely through his bestial figure expression. Burton states that all the actors playing apes 'were schooled how to move and behave like apes for two to three days a week over two months at a special Ape School' (in Salisbury 2006: loc 2744). Despite this intensive training, most of the performers, or at least those walking on two legs, still move like human beings, with only the occasional slumped posture to indicate their simian nature. Thade, however, evinces a pronounced ape-like gait throughout the film. This is not visible in his first scene, as he is on horseback, but it can be clearly seen when he enters the slave auction to purchase a human for his daughter. Thade enters the auction in front of his daughter and Attar, and while the latter two walk upright, Thade affects a stooped, rolling gait which gives the character a menacing quality. Burton has said of Roth that he 'really captured part of the weird energy that chimps have, he really tapped into that scary quality' (in Salisbury 2006: loc 2759). It is this 'scary quality' that introduces a racial component to the depiction of Thade. The character's villainy is directly tied to his animalistic, overtly ape-like behaviour, and as noted, ape-like behaviour has historically established links in cinema to racial otherness, and especially blackness. This is similar to the 'subterfuge' Everett claims is at work in *The Nightmare Before Christmas* (1995: 30), whereby a character not overtly othered is still coded as different through the use of racial elements.

After the battle between apes and humans outside the downed space station, there is a reconciliation of sorts. The dead from both groups are buried together, with Attar eulogising, 'We'll leave the graves unmarked. No one who comes will be able to tell apes from humans. They'll be mourned together, as it should be, from now on.' However, the reconciliation is undercut both by the fact that Davidson, the human protagonist, is not present for Attar's eulogy, and that the human leaves the planet soon after. McMahan describes Davidson as 'a character firmly wedded to his own postadolescent state [who] spends the entire movie trying to get back to his spaceship, ignoring, as much as possible, the huge social upheaval going on around him and refusing to participate except when he absolutely has to' (2006: 178). This refusal to participate extends to the film as a whole in regard to its apes as a metaphor for racial otherness. As noted, McMahan argues that Burton's film appears to be more about class (2005: 178) or animal rights (2005: 181) than it does race. However, just as Davidson refuses to take part in the social upheaval of the film, Burton does not always resolve the ambiguous racial tensions embodied by his apes.

As the quotation above suggests, Burton is uninterested in dealing with issues of race in his films. Despite this, race and, particularly, negative depictions of racial otherness have appeared in several of his films. In *Planet of the Apes*, he attempts to displace the franchise's thematic concerns from race, as argued by Greene (2006), to class and animal rights. However, the director nonetheless, at times, codes his apes as inferior racial others. Burton's apes are much more bestial in their figure expression than those of the original cycle of films, alluding to established ideas of the savagery of non-white natives. Furthermore, though he attempts to disregard the racial stratification of the previous films' ape society, in his adaptation the obviously black gorillas remain the lowest class of ape, which again has connotations of non-white inferiority. While Burton's predilections therefore arguably lie more with the outsider and teenage angst, the apes in *Planet of the Apes* nevertheless provide an example of the director's uneasy relationship with racial issues.

6. DEAD PETS' SOCIETY: GOTHIC ANIMAL BODIES IN THE FILMS OF TIM BURTON

Rebecca Lloyd

A moment of epiphany for young Victor Frankenstein (Barret Oliver/Charlie Tahan) occurs in both the live-action short, *Frankenweenie* (1984), and the feature-length animation *Frankenweenie* (2012). His science teacher (Mr Walsh, played by Paul Bartel in the 1984 version, and Mr Rzykruski, by Martin Landeau in 2012) applies an electrical current to the spread-eagled corpse of a frog which is laid out before the class. Victor's face is observed from the frog's point of view as the boy is framed through the jerking legs of the creature: the animal body is clearly figured as the object of human knowledge. The frog has no control in the manipulation of its body, dismissed by Mr Walsh as merely 'an ex-frog', and the fact that the same perspective is used in both versions, almost shot-for-shot, reinforces how the animal body is rendered subservient to the human. What Victor learns results in the reanimation of his dead pet dog, Sparky (Frank Welker), while the subsequent actions of Victor and his classmates (in the 2012 version) signify aspects of the problematic use and representation of the animal body by the human across Burton's films. When the children in the later film revivify animals, creating uncanny life, their creatures become terrifying beings. Exceeding expected boundaries of scale, behaviour and even species, they threaten the town and its inhabitants, signifying the problem of the return of the supposedly disposable animal body in which human interest is short term and lacks understanding. The humans in both *Frankenweenie* films experience fear and disgust towards, and horror of, the animal that evades the limits established for it in the human-controlled world: even Victor helps to destroy the 'other' creatures in the 2012 version.

Ruth Heholt and Melissa Edmundson note that, in anthropocentric discourse, the insistence on a divide between the human and nonhuman 'has a long history' (2020: 2). Human identity in mind and body, from this perspective, must be distinctive and not-animal, and 'the suggestion of an unbreachable gap between human and animal imposes a binary hierarchy that emphasises the "nonhuman" essence of the animal' (Heholt and Edmundson 2020: 3). This act of separation, a socio-cultural construction that upholds and legitimates human power over the animal, determinedly situates the animal as 'other' in its embodied materiality (Heholt and Edmundson 2020: 9). Animals are not in themselves Gothic beings, but the social and cultural codes and conventions that render them as alien and 'Other and unknowable' ensures that 'in this schema the "animal" immediately becomes Gothic' (Heholt and Edmundson 2020: 3).

The Gothic text, as Fred Botting notes, is pre-eminently about transgression which, when acts portrayed in such texts exceed the boundaries of the social and cultural norms, 'serves to reinforce or underline their value and necessity, restoring or defining limits' (1996: 7). This chapter considers how Tim Burton's productions, predominantly Gothic in tone and seemingly celebrating excess and the transgressive, in fact reveal the meanings attached to the animal form that maintain human dominance over the animal body. These films, despite appearing to embrace the animal, particularly in the image of the pet, really show how transgression of the ideal human/animal relationship, which prioritises the human perspective, necessitates acts of containment as attempts to reinstate the status quo. Analyses of *Vincent* (1982), *The Nightmare Before Christmas* (1993), *Mars Attacks!* (1996), *Corpse Bride* (2005) and the two versions of *Frankenweenie*, where animals are central to the narrative, explain how representations of humans and animals in Burton's films castigate transgression of boundaries and the excessive body. All these cases insist on and perpetuate the anthropocentric discourse that situates the animal as always subordinate to the interests of the human, resisting alternative modes of existence. However, the analyses also show that, in being Gothic, and hence prey to ambiguity and ambivalence, attempts to stabilise the division between the animal and the human are undermined by the revelation that such a division is artificial. Further, there is evidence that Burton distinguishes between the 'good' and 'bad' human, represented as coterminous with the 'good' and 'bad' animal. This is most apparent in the films as instances where the human-as-animal and the excessive animal are treated as the threat that must be contained.

The field of Human Animal Studies highlights the political, philosophical and ethical issues in the anthropocentric worldview that insists on the subordination of, and complete control over, the animal. One strand of these debates considers how pets, as examples of the domesticated animal body, have been identified as being in the service of the human as status symbol, or for comfort and entertainment (Tuan 2007: 149). But, Yi-Fu Tuan stresses, '[t]he harsh story behind the making of a pet is forgotten. And the story must be harsh because the basis of all successful training is the display of an unchallengeable power' (2007: 148). Tuan argues that '[d]omestication means domination', since both terms 'have the same root sense of mastery over another being – of bringing it into one's house or domain' (2007: 143). This is, for him, most evident in what he terms 'the product – a docile and friendly pet' (Tuan 2007: 148). The making of the pet, equating to an act of creation, is achieved by the processes of breeding through artificial insemination and physical training, intrusive and disciplinary actions exposing the disturbing parameters of human desire for the ideal animal body in the pet (Tuan 2007: 149). In this respect, Victor reassures his parents in the 1984 *Frankenweenie* that a reanimated Sparky will save them from 'housebreaking another dog', a reminder that animals must conform to human space. Burton's works embrace pet owner-ship, but as Gothic texts they unintentionally reveal what has been repressed in the practices of pet-making identified by Tuan. Animals in Burton's produc-tions are situated to remind the viewer that humans are in control, but that such control must be continually reinforced because it is never final. Horror, in the films discussed here, appears to be contained, but the supernatural, reanimated and cross-contaminated pets in these productions have a more disturbing presence because Gothic texts can reveal what is repressed, which is how animals must be forced into fulfilling human needs and desires.

Relatedly, Donna Haraway, in her exploration of the notion of the 'compan-ion species', states that this is not the same as the 'companion animal' (2007: 363). The designation of 'companion species', she argues, should forefront the separateness between human and animal based on understanding and embrac-ing difference as equality (Haraway 2007: 363). The label 'companion animal' instead underpins a hierarchical relationship and, of relevance to the argu-ment in this chapter, Haraway notes the term 'has the pedigree of the mating between technoscientific expertise and late-industrial pet-keeping practices' (2007: 363). For example, the *Frankenweenie* films portray the regeneration of dead animals, nearly all of which are former pets, by children using science and technology, actions born of the children's desire to control the animal for their own purposes. The resultant beings are less than the 'ideal' animal because Burton presents the children as less than ideal themselves. Even Victor, the focus of sympathy in his loss, is a grave robber.

For Kelly Hurley, the Gothic body in *fin-de-siècle* texts serves as a key site on which anxieties and fears are played out, for the reason that the clas-sificatory drive produced alternative categories which challenged or exceeded human identity (1996: 9). Prior certainties about what it was to be human were destabilised, as scientific discoveries, both at the microscopic level and in the evolutionary theories after Darwin, 'required a radical rethinking of humanity's position relative to its environment' and, of particular relevance to the argument here, 'its intimate relation to lower species' (Hurley 1996: 56). Xavier Reyes argues that Gothic 'relies on the susceptibility to being under attack or scared that is instinctive to us' (2014: 2). The anxieties of the nineteenth century that linger on in questions concerning the identity of the human/animal body in the films under discussion here draw attention to the fears our animality generates.

Post-Darwin, the notion of 'the conception of the human-as-animal' raises the 'terrifying prospect of the animal "within" breaking out and uncontrollably expressing a wild, inhuman, monstrous side of the "human"' (Heholt and Edmundson 2020: 4). The awful revelation, Botting states, is that 'Nature, wild and untameable, was as much within as without [invoking] the bestial within the human [and] the pathological return of animalistic, instinctual habits' (1996: 12). In the act of othering, what is projected onto the other is all that must be refused in constructing the identity of the self. Hence the animal, in one strand of Gothic thinking, functions as 'a representation of otherness, fear, and the darker aspects of human psychology' (Höing 2020: 63). As Anja Höing points out, 'the monsters of traditional Gothic stories are relocated into other symbolisers' including the 'racial other', but for her this 'might just as well be a species other' (Höing 2020: 64). This is manifest in Burton's films.

Alongside the classificatory drives in the sciences, efforts to know, understand and care for the animal are evident. Harriet Ritvo (1987) notes how the rise of literature aimed at children often depicts animals in terms of education and instruction, as well as entertainment, a point underpinning Tuan's explanation of pet-making. She argues that such works promoted compassion as a preparation for adulthood, a rhetorical strategy indicating that 'the need to be kind to animals provided continual occasions to exercise self-control' (Ritvo 1987: 131). Further, Ritvo argues that, 'in adults as well as children, the treatment of animals could be an index of the extent to which an individual had managed to control his or her lower urges' (1987: 132). This can be linked to theories of degeneration and recapitulation, about criminal tendencies and racialised othering, which all raised the spectre of the regression of the human, a backsliding, to its evolutionary origins physically and mentally (Hurley 1996: 96–7). The threat inherent in the degenerate body is the exposure of 'the animal within' as 'the animal without', because this is where we originate and to where we are always in danger of returning: concerns that '[t]he human body, the human species, human cultures – all are balanced in such tenuous equilibrium that the slightest disturbance will send the whole human enterprise crashing down' (Hurley 1996: 77).

Throughout Burton's work there is remarkably little genuine compassion for the animal-as-animal. There is evidence, instead, that the correct relationship between the human and the animal, as a bargain that must be kept, depends on both categories being situated in their proper place through the symbolism attached to the animal from the human perspective. The films discussed here indicate that where the viewer is expected to understand some equivalence between the human and the animal, in *Mars Attacks!* for example, where attributes attached to the nonhuman are indicative of how humans explain the material world to themselves, any seeming parity is reliant on the boundary that distinguishes the human from the animal body remaining in plain sight, and that the human is always prioritised over the animal. Animals in Burton's work are freighted with meanings that articulate the anthropocentric world-view, and rarely offer the perspective of the nonhuman, which is constantly presented as the lesser being. As will be shown, the animal body in Burton's films is figured as the other, inevitably subject to the hierarchy of human over nonhuman in the discourses of domestication (particularly as pets) and science. But when this boundary is blurred, or breached, then the animal body must be returned to its rightful place in the hierarchy, whatever the cost. Therefore, when Sparky in *Frankenweenie* (both versions) is knocked down and killed in the road – an archetypical space of the human – the dog-as-body must be taken back under human control and, in an extreme demonstration of human power, reanimated. Victor, in the 2012 film, says 'I can fix that' about both his damaged home movie and his damaged dog, the animate body and the inanimate object thereby undifferentiated. The advertising for this film claims that it is 'a heartwarming tale about a boy and his dog', but there is more to the story of the human and the animal than this in Burton's work.

In the opening sequence of *Mars Attacks!*, for instance, the smell emanating from the herd of stampeding burning cattle is described by an onlooker as like 'barbecue', providing one of the most basic indications of how humans see animals: simply as food. But *Mars Attacks!* also presents other aspects of how humans deploy animals, revealing the workings of anthropocentrism. When the Martians, startled and alarmed by the dove freed by one of the crowd gathered to greet them, incinerate the bird, the President's daughter Taffy (Natalie Portman) suggests that the Martians might not understand the symbolism that links the dove with peace. This underlines how meaning is a matter of human attribution rather than a fact of animal being. But any questions this raises are quelled in the reassuring sequence when, as the Martian invasion collapses, the escapees from Las Vegas emerge from a cave. Heralded by the appearance of wild but essentially gentle creatures such as deer, order is clearly restored as a dove settles in Barbara's (Annette Bening) hands. Associations are made too between Tom Jones (himself), as a sexualised performer, and the animal: an eagle lands on his outstretched arm, signalling that he has something of the predator about him, and 'prey' creatures gather as he sings, his 'animal allure' evident. President Dale's (Jack Nicholson) dog is only shown in the domestic setting with him, in a photograph with Taffy displayed in the Oval Office, watching TV with the family, and sleeping on the floor in the presidential bedroom. The dog is a retriever, a family-friendly breed, signalling the 'family-friendly' view Dale has of himself as president. Muffy, Florence Norris's (Sylvia Sidney) cat, now resides, testament to the taxidermist's art, with her in a care home. Both the woman and the animal that represents her have been exiled, effectively 'dead' to the family. However, the animal body in Burton's work is an ambiguous body: Grandma clearly cherishes Muffy, but her stroking and kissing this lifeless creature are little acts of necrophilia, indicating the presence of the Gothic in the always-there potential of disturbance generated by the relationship between human and animal bodies.

As has been noted, Burton repeatedly links the human and the animal. An example of this in reverse arises in *Corpse Bride*, where Victoria's (Emily Watson) parents describe her face as 'like an otter in disgrace'. This claim by the Everglots rebounds on them, as 'bad' humans, in their failure to appreciate Victoria, because the bizarre association is so clearly incorrect. Conversely, the link between Emily (Helena Bonham Carter), the Corpse Bride, and her creaturely supporters, Maggot (Enn Reitel), the green maggot that resides inside her head, and Black Widow Spider (Jane Horrocks), is appropriate. As denizens of the underground world, they are all beings of death and decay.

It is in the figure of the pet as dead body that the boundaries, for Burton, must be fully reinforced. Briefly seen in a portrait during the opening sequence, Victor's (Johnny Depp) pet, Scraps, is now a skeleton dog in the Land of the Dead. Victor is thrilled when Emily returns the dog's bones as a wedding present, and Scraps enjoys himself in the Land of the Living, behaving as dogs do. But the animal must return to its proper place. Victor says of Scraps, 'You should have seen him with fur', because he is now a transgressive figure, ambiguously located in a nexus of past memory and present reality. As a dead dog whose living owner has moved beyond childhood to adult concerns of love and marriage, Scraps no longer belongs above ground.

Neither does Jack Skellington (Chris Sarandon/Danny Elfman) in *The Nightmare Before Christmas*. He exists beyond the boundary of the human, a spidery figure with a pumpkin head whose townsfolk are also interstitial bodies, part beasts and monsters. Jack's dog, Zero, is a ghost with empty eyes, his sheet-like ghost body billowing as he floats along and his glowing jack-o-lantern nose lighting the way for the ghastly parody sleigh journey to Christmas Town. The viewer is encouraged to consider Zero as a pet: although first seen arising from his tomb, he has a dog basket and candy cane chew in Jack's house (Jack calls out 'Zero, I'm home'), plays 'fetch' with one of Jack's ribs, and – the ever-faithful dog – warns Jack of danger.

An instance where attempts to link the human and animal body are shown as demonstrably wrong occurs when Jack, after his visit to Christmas Town, thinks of Santa Claus (Ed Ivory) as 'Santa Claws', describing him as a 'big red lobster man' to the inhabitants of Halloween Town. This is because they, and the things they make, exist beyond the borderlands of the properly unified and singular body of the ideal human. Jack is astonished to find there are no monsters in Christmas Town, since in Halloween Town monstrosity is the experience of everyday. A town musician plays a concertina made with the head and tail of a fish, the Wolfman sports a shirt over his beastly form, and the transformation of an 'old rat' into a hat demonstrates the commodification of the animal body. Dr Finklestein (William Hockey) states that constructing skeleton reindeer will be 'simple' because making animal (or animal-like) bodies is the norm. When bogeyman Oogie Boogie's (Ken Page) outer sacking body is unravelled by Jack, his innards are revealed as a mass of squirming bugs: an expression of the horror of the animal within, without. This echoes Jack disembowelling a teddy bear as he tries to understand Christmas presents: an obscene act of 'cruelty', no less repellent because the insides are soft stuffing.

Halloween Town is disturbing, and its beastly presences are terrifying. They can be juxtaposed with the 'correct' role of the animal and human in Christmas Town: the wooden polar creatures on the roundabout are 'proper' model animals and when Christmas is restored, the child, initially given a shrunken human head, gets a live puppy as replacement. The bodies are where they should be: in the restoration of comfort, pleasure and entertainment for all. As the film draws to a close, Jack's configuration of the human-animal 'Santa Claws' disappears as he recognises the true 'human' Santa Claus, now reinstated in his proper place.

Both Scraps and Zero as supernatural beings are safely in the realm of the dead. Conversely, Poppy the chihuahua and the retriever in *Mars Attacks!* are living animals, and these 'real' dogs suffer, invoking fear rather than containing it; as Scraps and Zero are already beyond the boundary, we can be assured of their proper place, and are comfortable with them. The destruction of Dale's retriever in the presidential bedroom, though, is doubly intrusive, exterminating both the animal and the human domestic space: only its skeleton is left, the inside out. Unlike Scraps, however, this dog will have no life after death.

The human skeleton is exposed in *Mars Attacks!* by incineration and evaporation, destroying skin, muscles and organs. More disturbing and horrific than bare bones, however, is Jason's (Michael J. Fox) hand, torn and ragged at the wrist, snatched up by Poppy, as well as the moment when a fish in Ross's (Martin Short) fish tank nibbles his severed finger. These body parts recall our physical vulnerability, as Reyes indicates (2014: 2). But Poppy is the most troubling image of all: she is the ultimate in human/animal horror as her head and body are divided and transposed so that her head is sutured to the body of her owner, Nathalie (Sarah Jessica Parker), whose own head tops Poppy's body. Vigilance, for Reyes, is essential to protect the always-threatened boundaries, since Gothic bodies 'are scary because they either refuse absolute human taxonomies or destabilise received notions of what constitutes a "normal" or intelligible body' (2014: 5). Here, the boundaries of body and human/animal are transgressed and so, as Gothic abominations, both Poppy and her human owner, hybrids both, must – and do – die.

But importantly Poppy, along with Jason's hand and Ross's finger, serves as a very visible example of the mortal threatened by the animal out-of-place, and, as such, her destruction signifies the attempt to contain that horror. Reyes argues that the Gothic body can 'undermine normative conceptions of what a body is forced to be and mean' (2014: 7). Poppy as a 'toy' breed represents the shallowness of her fashion-journalist owner, a doubling of human and animal. Both Nathalie and Poppy largely ignore Jason, who views the dog's yapping as akin to Nathalie's *Today in Fashion* show: nothing but empty noise. The way that Nathalie and Poppy are doubled in life is mirrored in the challenge to meaning by their reconstructed bodies: their very abnormality simultaneously confirms and refutes 'normal' because human and animal were always the same yapping lightweights. But revealing the boundary by transgression serves to expose the fiction of the coherence of humanoid identity as human.

There is evidence in *Vincent* and the two versions of *Frankenweenie*, where the bodies of nonhumans are central to the narrative, that the films conversely evoke strategies from anthropomorphic discourse to contain human and animal bodies. The terrors of the narrative of evolution are that species' boundaries may be porous, so control of any threat is pressing. Gothic texts are 'warning of dangers of social and moral transgression by presenting them in their darkest and most threatening form' (Botting 1996: 7). This necessitates acts of expulsion and containment as strategies of reassurance. Nonetheless, exposing what lies on the other side means that once revealed, it cannot be denied. This is notable in the ambiguous status of Victor and Sparky in the slippage of the distinction between human and animal, as interstitial figures. There might be strenuous efforts to eradicate the other, but once seen, never forgotten.

In *Vincent*, the boy protagonist conducts experiments on his dog, Abercrombie, 'in the hopes of creating a horrible zombie', as the narration explains, with which he can pursue his victims. The dog appears bound, mummy-like, capped with a multitude of wires and antennae, and 'smiles' and wags his tail before the electricity is sent through him. Abercrombie cuts a pathetic figure in his willingness to please his owner, considering that he is about to be tortured to death. He returns as Vincent's 'zombie slave', a terrifying and exaggerated animal shape, a haunting shadow. This short film references the mummy and zombie of Gothic works from the nineteenth century onwards: what is also significant, however, is that here these monstrous figures intersect with the animal body. The understanding (from the spectator's prior knowledge of texts across popular culture) is that both the mummy and the zombie are human in origin: reconfigured as animals, however, they are doubly disturbing. Taken in conjunction with the supernatural Zero and Scraps, the Poppy/Nathalie hybrid and the reanimated monster-pets of *Frankenweenie*, what is apparent are the ways in which Burton presents animals as monstrous beings. Even the 'best' of animals, embodied by Sparky, is a pet monster.

The degenerate human body, the beastliness of the human, and the repercussions of this are evident in *Frankenweenie* (2012), as the film delineates boundaries and the dangers inherent in their breaching. Victor's classmates are, in various ways, distorted and not 'normal' because, as Reyes notes, '[d]eformity is another staple of gothic bodies' (2014: 6). This is shown by their physical characteristics, and in their limited mental and moral capacities. Burton again references monstrous figures from popular culture; for example, Edgar E. Gore (Atticus Shaffer), inspired by 'Igor', and Nassor (Martin Short), the shadow of Karloff, are both characters of *Frankenstein* (Whale 1931). Others, however, are simply the physically and mentally unfit: Bob (Robert Capron) is a lumbering unthinking presence, and Weird Girl's (Catherine O'Hara) obsession with Mr Whiskers's faeces, which she claims demonstrate her pet cat's psychic powers, situate her with the abject (and animal) bodily functions of waste. Both girl and cat have staring eyes, equating human and animal, while her less-than-human status is evident in her 'name'. Toshiaki (James Hiroyuki Liao) is also represented as 'other' by his presence as a racial stereotype. None of them undertake scientific processes for the 'right' reason, which for Mr Rzykruski is the combination of head and heart in the love that should motivate the experiment. This can be compared with the experiments conducted by the Martians in *Mars Attacks!*, who do combine 'head' (science) and 'heart' (passion), but as nonhuman they can only produce the monster, Poppy/Nathalie.

In this case, both humans and Martians investigate each other's bodies, but the Martians' experiments are on living humans, rather than the alien corpse autopsy conducted by Kessler (Pierce Brosnan). A clear distinction is drawn between the calm 'scientific' Kessler and the excitable pleasure exhibited by the Martians, distinguishing between good science and bad. The 'good' human body is capable of genuine scientific understanding, and the appropriate relationship with the body of the other is demonstrated by Victor and Kessler, as intellectual beings with trim (that is, controlled) bodies. The children of *Frankenweenie* (2012), like the Martians, 'create' monstrous animal bodies from their 'bad' science, inevitable because these children are 'bad' bodies, less than human themselves. The anomalous and degenerate children and adults of the Frankenweenie world demonstrate their limitations in their lack of self-control, and in their treatment of animals before and after reanimation.

In the 1984 version of *Frankenweenie*, Mr Chambers throws his yowling cat out of the house, saying 'I hope you run into a ten-foot mouse'. This fits the narrative of the prejudiced neighbours who will drive Sparky to his second destruction and indicates how humans can find their own (apparently un-monstrous) pets inconvenient, to the point of wishing for their death. As a live-action film, visualising the act of physical dominance is a particularly vivid display of human power over the animal. Significantly, this cat returns in the 2012 version as Weird Girl's disturbing pet, Mr Whiskers, reinforcing the animal's unloved and perhaps unlovable nature from a human perspective. This will be notably figured in the horrific creature that Mr Whiskers becomes as the species-busting vampire bat-cat.

Victor's friends in the 1984 version ask if he will get another dog or a fish, as if animals are interchangeable, claiming that fish have no personality and 'you get used to them dying'. In the 2012 film, Edgar's fish, already dead in the pet shop, is the creature that Victor is blackmailed into electrifying. It subsequently becomes almost invisible, and eventually simply fails to exist at all, Edgar's comments of 'maybe they don't last' underlining the earlier film's view that fish lack a 'persona' and are hence insignificant. This recalls Tuan's argument that when humans take the animal into their homes, accommodation is only on human terms and, for the animal, this is not necessarily a permanent or happy state.

It is not only the domesticated animal that generates fear. In the earlier version of *Frankenweenie*, Rose (Roz Braverman), whose dog, Raymond, encounters the revivified Sparky, hysterically describes Victor's pet as 'six-foot tall, like a wolf', without evidence. Sparky is envisaged as a return to ancestral beginnings, and therefore pre-domestication and pre-acceptable, embodied as an excessive corporeality. Rose claims that 'it' tried to kill and eat 'my Raymond', and her response to a neighbour's allegation that the creature is a lion – 'I saw it. It's worse and it's bigger' – demonstrates the assumption that the wild (the natural) can overthrow the civilised, and that the boundary between them is uncertain and forever under threat. As Höing notes, 'human anxieties about animality and uncontainable wildness' posit wild animals as 'killing machines posing a constant threat to human culture' (2020: 65).

Burton references the bodies of popular culture human/animal monsters as Edgar finds a dead rat in a bin that, reanimated, becomes a wererat. Nassor's hamster, Colossus, crawls out of its crypt, a fanged miniature mummy (recalling Abercrombie). Shelley (Dee Bradley Baker), Toshiaki's turtle, becomes an enormous version of itself, akin to the creature in the kaiju genre film *Gamera, the Giant Monster* (1965), in which a flying, fire-breathing turtle, whose only friend is a boy named Toshio (referenced by Burton's 'Toshiaki'), is brought to life by nuclear weapons. Bob empties his packet of Sea Monkeys into a swimming pool, generating disturbing hybrid amphibious-like creatures suggesting the mutant mogwai of *Gremlins* (Dante 1984). The popcorn-fuelled rioting Sea-Monkeys are also synonymous with the basest, out-of-control kind of human, perhaps acknowledging that Sea-Monkeys were originally represented as humanoid in marketing campaigns of the 1960s and 1970s (Scott 2010). Weird Girl's Mr Whiskers brings her a bat which, fused by electricity with Mr Whiskers, becomes another hybrid being, the bat-cat as a vampiric figure. As with the Sea-Monkeys, this presents the erasure of boundaries. In all these cases, it is the collapse of the human/animal distinction that means these abominations must be destroyed because they are presented as dangers to human identity and therefore human life.

Botting notes that there is a shift during the nineteenth century towards texts that explore the uncanny and expressions of this in the double, mirroring and the *alter ego* (1996: 11). There are examples of doubling and mirroring in *Frankenweenie*. As already indicated, the repetition of the shot of Victor seen through the frog's legs is an act of doubling, and Poppy and Natalie are *alter egos*. Toshiaki (as Japanese) is mirrored, unflatteringly, by his Gamera-like creature as a reference to Japanese culture; Edgar's association with dirt and death generates the wererat; and the Sea-Monkeys that Bob creates explode into goo, their very viscosity an echo of Bob's own blubbery physique and what Hurley refers to as the 'propensity to become-slime' of the human body (1996: 34). Weird Girl and her cat-double are conflated into their mirror-being, the vampiric bat-cat.

Overall, the children create animals that are uncanny, whereby terror is produced in the recognition of something familiar, but different. The familiar becomes unfamiliar, so 'it violates a crucial binarism by which we organize the world' (Hurley 1996: 40). From this, 'the sensation of uncanniness is a symptomatic response to liminal phenomena, which confound and exceed the classificatory systems designed to contain matter' (Hurley 1996: 40). Even Sparky is frightened by his image in the mirror, recognising that he is not a 'right' body and, being *unheimlich*, returns to his grave to die again. Sparky's exaggerated shadow is the double of Vincent's zombie-dog, raising the question of whether he is an imperilled 'innocent' or the Gothic animal.

Sparky is monstrous because his body is neither a singular whole nor containable. He must be constantly repaired and, in both films, is patched with spotted material mirroring his 'monster' outfit in Victor's home movies. The necessity for repairs both signifies his state of perpetual deterioration and reveals the damage (never mentioned directly) that the car must have caused: a reminder of the dangers that animals face in the human world.

Sparky has the 'natural' instincts of the dog, just like Scraps and Zero, but pursuing these always leads to his downfall. His initial demise is not his fault but human failure to control him, ultimately leading to his death. In both films, before and after reanimation, Sparky is told to be a 'good boy' and stay in the backyard or house. Containment of the dog's body is the fact of his life and death, because only human permission allows a pet beyond the domestic.

For Avril Horner and Sue Zlosnik, 'serious Gothic' observes the boundaries that must be re-established, but 'the threat of their being breached again always remains' (1998: 3). 'Comic Gothic', however, enables 'a measure of detachment afforded by the comic mode' (Horner and Zlosnik 1998: 4) and provides 'the laughter of accommodation rather than the terror of disorientation' (Horner and Zlosnik 1998: 35). This may be observed in the staking of the vampire bat-cat, a scene that is comforting because there are known methods in dealing with vampires, while simultaneously managing anxieties about this disturbing boundary-breaking creature. The comic slumping of the creature's body distances the spectator from the experience of real pain, with laughter serving as cathartic release. The same can be said of Bob: splattered with Sea-Monkey slime, their 'blood and guts', his shocked expression is comical. He invites laughter, despite any revulsion, as it underlines his status already delineated as deficient in proper human qualities. When Toshiaki pulls out a camera to record Shelley's fiery death, the horror is deflected onto the racist 'joke' of the association of obsessive photography with being Japanese. Colossus, comically small, is squashed underfoot by Shelley, a gruesome end made ludicrous.

There is nothing comic in the demise of Sparky: the cut to the rolling ball rather than his broken body generates pathos, and his second death is a moment of pure horror. This is 'serious' Gothic purposefully managing our sympathy, and simultaneously reinstating the boundary between the 'good' animal and the 'bad'. We are not expected to trouble ourselves at the extermination of the monster-animals because they are a threat to the human. Sparky, the 'good boy', must be saved, but we should remember that he remains a monster, embodying the threat of the porous boundary.

To be a pet is not, necessarily, to be a Gothic animal. Pets are accepted into the domestic because we believe and expect them to be subject even to our children. But when pets exceed demarcated boundaries, they are out of place and dangerous, the external having been invited in but then revealing itself as a traitor. As Tuan notes, '[t]he dog must not be in doubt as to who is the master and as to the consequences of disobedience' (2007: 148). Disobedience by the animal, in being more than the proper animal, is, in Burton's films, rewarded with death. Beastly beings created by beastly children and other nonhumans cannot be permitted to live: the locus of anxiety in evading containment, they threaten the human and are cast into permanent death, including the supernatural Scraps and Zero. The pet out of place must be returned to beyond the borders.

Burton consistently draws parallels between humans and animals, as evidenced in the films discussed here, but moments of equivalence between human and animal serve to simply inscribe human attributes or human cultural conventions, rather than species' equality. The townsfolk seek Sparky's destruction for failing to have a 'proper' dog's body. They view him as the horror that exceeds boundaries in being undoglike, a perspective already established as 'correct' by the Gothic mode evident in the film. Burton must therefore find a way to accommodate this while still 'saving' Sparky from the pitiless expulsion experienced by the other 'inappropriate' pets. It is only when Sparky finally demonstrates the human attributes of selfless sacrifice for his owner that he is appropriately situated in the hierarchy of the human-animal binary by his preparedness to surrender his life for a human and, rehabilitated, is allowed to live again. The poodles and Sparky eventually find 'love': dogs thus refigured through the lens of the ideally gendered human relationship, a romance of tamed nature. As *Frankenweenie* concludes, the animal-as-human, more fitted to the hierarchy, is shown to be greater than the human-as-animal: Sparky is a proto-human because this is better than the nonhuman. Our hearts might be warmed by the tale but only because anxieties are assuaged.

Botting insists that 'Gothic is an inscription neither of darkness nor of light, a delineation neither of reason and morality nor of superstition and corruption, neither good nor evil, but both at the same time' (1996: 9). He also notes that Gothic texts can demonstrate our 'fascination with transgression and the anxiety over cultural limits and boundaries' (Botting 1996: 2). Burton attempts to insist on the proper relations between humans and nonhumans but, where the boundary between bodily forms is breached, Gothic ambiguity and ambivalence intrude.

Scraps and Zero are engaging and charming but are supernatural. Muffy the stuffed cat challenges the parameters of acceptable love. Victor (1984) has a Wolfman mug, the human/animal hybrid a reminder of the appeal of the unstable boundary. In the 2012 film, Victor, momentarily a dog-boy, howls to protect Sparky. Victor clings to the monster, but Burton allies the spectator with them both because the relationship is shown to be appropriate to the human-pet binary. The human 'good boy' accepts the undead 'good dog', but it is an undead dog nonetheless.

Thus, the containment of animal and human is never entirely successful, the excessive animal body threatening to return no matter how hard we try to kill it. A reanimated 'Sparky' is available as a plush toy, the cuddly Gothic for bedtime, because the Gothic animal, once seen, is forever at the edge of our vision. However, Burton always warns against the threat of the animal, of danger in disguise, because as Dr Finklestein comments, 'Nothing is more suspicious than frog's breath'.

7. TOO DARK FOR DISNEY: TIM BURTON, CHILDREN'S HORROR AND PET DEATH

Claire Parkinson

In the midst of marketing and promotion for the 2012 release of Tim Burton's stop-motion animated feature *Frankenweenie*, it seemed that the original 1984 short film with the same title was noteworthy in the story of Burton's career, primarily because it led to the then 25-year-old director being sacked by Disney. The studio had funded *Frankenweenie* (1984) – a live-action short – to the tune of $1 million and it was intended to accompany the 1984 theatrical re-release of *Pinocchio* (Ferguson 1940). However, when it was finished, *Frankenweenie* was deemed to be too scary for children, not in the Disney style, and the studio reportedly fired Burton for wasting company money (in Bovingdon 2012; in Itzkoff 2012). Burton's explanation of the circumstances surrounding his departure from Disney and the fate of the thirty-minute short beg the question, why did Disney back the film in the first place? After all, there was no doubt from the pitch and development stages that this film was a homage to the Universal monster horror movie *Frankenstein* (Whale 1931), reimagined as a story about a dead dog whose body is reanimated by a child. Added to this, Burton's own confusion about what happened, and his comments in interviews that it was 'kind of weird' and that he couldn't 'find logic in how things happen' (in Salisbury 2006: 39), magnify the strangeness of the situation that is subsequently explained by the director and others as a consequence of the change in Disney leadership from Ron W. Miller to Michael Eisner at the time of the film's expected release in 1984. The story of Disney subsequently 'shelving' the film and refusing to give it a theatrical release was, however, apocryphal, as *Frankenweenie* had a limited run in

Los Angeles in December 1984 to qualify for the Academy Awards and was released in the UK in 1985, where it preceded the Touchstone film *Baby: Secret of the Lost Legend* (Norton 1985). Moreover, there were changes occurring in the industry that demystify the circumstances surrounding *Frankenweenie* and provide some rationale for Disney's initial willingness to fund a children's horror film at that time.

In the context of Burton's career, the 1984 version of *Frankenweenie* is important for three reasons: it was Burton's first experience directing a star cast; it marks the point of his (first) departure from Disney; and, for the focus of this chapter, it establishes the loyal dead dog trope in Burton films, a theme that appears briefly in the stop-motion animation *Vincent* (1982), made two years prior to *Frankenweenie*. In *Vincent*, a child who wishes his life were that of Vincent Price, dreams that he experiments on Abercrombie, the family dog, in the hope that he might create a zombie dog and they can prowl the streets of London together looking for victims. This first Gothic interpretation of the boy and his (dead) dog narrative by Burton is fully imagined in *Frankenweenie* (1984) and the later 2012 feature-length stop-motion *Frankenweenie*, and also appears as the relationships between Scraps and Victor (Johnny Depp) in *The Corpse Bride* (2005), Zero and Jack Skellington (Danny Elfman/Chris Sarandon) in *The Nightmare Before Christmas* (Selick 1993) and Heraldo and Max Shreck (Christopher Walken) in *Batman Returns* (1992). Across these films, the bodies of loyal dogs are depicted in the form of reanimated corpses, a skeleton, a ghost and animal taxidermy, respectively. Burton (in Bovingdon 2012) refers to *Frankenweenie* as 'a memory piece', an autobiographical reference to the impact of the life and death of the family dog, Pepe, on Burton as a child. Given the importance of autobiographical references to Burton's work generally, the repeated depictions of dead dogs in his films therefore deserve consideration and, framed by the concept of children's horror, are explored here in relation to *Frankenweenie* (1984) and the cultural and social meanings attached to the bodies of animals, pet death and grief.

Frankenweenie received a PG rating in the US, a designation which Disney was reported to find at odds with the company's public image and its reliance on brand associations with childhood innocence and G-rated films. The consequences of a PG rating have to be set within the wider context of the time that saw the introduction of the PG-13 rating in 1984: in part, a response to parental concerns about the tone and content of *Gremlins* (Dante 1984) and *Indiana Jones and the Temple of Doom* (Spielberg 1984), both of which were considered to raise issues about the protection of children from unsuitable material (Zoglin 1984: 46). In addition, the home video boom of the 1980s, coupled with the slasher movie trend and, in the UK, the moral panic about 'video nasties',[1] all contributed to worries over children's access to horror film and unsuitable themes and content. Yet, children's horror can be understood as part of the ongoing development of a genre that underwent considerable reinvention throughout the 1980s, to the extent that, by the end of the decade, the home video and theatrical markets were oversaturated with horror movies (Muir 2004). Children's horror also responded to the changing tastes of younger audiences, who were reported to be turning their backs on G-rated films which were deemed by children as young as eleven to be 'old fashioned' (Harmetz 1984: 19). Jessica McCort points out that 'prior to the late 1980s and early 1990s, horror was not openly considered a distinct, significant vein within children's literature or culture [and] "horror stories for children"' were not a discrete category (2016: 7). Catherine Lester similarly argues that children's horror only emerges as a notable subgenre in the 1980s, but notes that there is an important distinction to be made between horror films that are 'merely "suitable" to be viewed by children and those that specifically target children as a core part of the audience' (2016: 24). Recognition that children and pre-teens constituted an audience for horror themes was reflected in the rise of child protagonists, for example, *Gremlins*, *The Goonies* (Donner 1985), *Teen Wolf* (Daniel 1985), *Little Monsters* (Greenberg 1989), *Stand By Me* (Reiner 1986), *Labyrinth* (Henson 1986), *The Lost Boys* (Schumacher 1987) and *The Monster Squad* (Dekker 1987), and tie-in merchandise that included toys and other child-oriented commodities (Lester 2016). With Hollywood driven by the economic imperatives of ancillary markets in the 1980s, nonhumans such as monsters, ghosts and aliens, as well as animated characters, represented lucrative merchandising opportunities due to their stylised appearances which 'lent themselves easily to reproduction as a myriad of product lines, more easily than do ordinary human beings' (Prince 2000: 139). A merchandising boom in *Gremlins*-related commodities confirmed the economic worth of creature characters in children's films, as did *Ghostbusters* (1984), the likenesses of the featured 'monsters' in both productions being widely licensed to appear on toys, clothes, games and other children's products.

If some studios managed to address the new core audience, the same cannot be said for Disney. The shift in young movie-goers' tastes was reflected in a series of box office failures for the studio in the early 1980s. An incompatibility between the Disney brand and young audiences prompted the then Disney president, Richard Berger, to claim, 'no matter what the movie, teenagers would spurn a Disney film', and he remarked somewhat wryly, 'If you put Disney's name on top of *Emmanuelle*, and had "X"-rated at the bottom, people would say, "We can bring our children"' (Harmetz 1984: 19). The strength of the brand and its associations with childhood innocence were equally perceived as Disney's weakness and, keen to exploit a teen and young adult audience, the company under Berger's lead established the Touchstone label in 1984. Although a PG rating conflicted with the Disney identity, the parent company adapted and responded to the new environment with

Touchstone, a label that provided a way to produce and distribute PG-rated films while maintaining a distance from Disney and its well-crafted brand associations. Burton had pitched the idea for *Frankenweenie* to Berger, who brought in the comedy writer Lenny Ripps to develop the script and Julie Hickson as producer. The industrial and cultural context of the time, and being at the forefront of Disney's move into films for the PG and PG-13 market, makes Berger's support for the *Frankenweenie* idea understandable. That it was distributed by Touchstone with another Touchstone film in the UK in 1985 also makes sense, although it is interesting to note that under the UK classificatory system, *Frankenweenie* received, without cuts, a U classification, which meant it was considered 'suitable for all' (BBFC), while the feature it accompanied, *Baby: Secret of the Lost Legend*, maintained a PG certification. Despite internal support for Burton at Disney, the change of leadership in 1984, coupled with new aggressive business policies and strategy that revived and modernised traditional Disney characters (Wasko 2005), was at odds with the sensibilities of both Burton and *Frankenweenie*. In terms of its timing, the film was made as Disney shifted its focus back to the family audience and sought to strengthen and exploit its brand associations with childhood. Disney Chief Executive, Michael Eisner, later explained the company's strategy in this way: 'We know our audience, and predominantly it is a family audience. We should not lament that others appeal more strongly to the disenfranchised teenage audience. They always come back when they become re-enfranchised adults with children' (Eisner 1995). Although having only a limited theatrical release in 1984, Disney did release *Frankenweenie* on VHS home video in 1992. This move was entirely in keeping with the Disney strategy to exploit its existing assets and, following Burton's box office successes with *Batman* (1989) and *Edward Scissorhands* (1990), the VHS release was timed to capitalise on the release of *Batman Returns* (1992) the same year.

Twenty-eight years later, *Frankenweenie* was remade by Burton for Disney as a feature-length animation; the story of Burton's previous precarious relationship with the studio added much to the director's well-marketed persona of the misunderstood artist with his own unique style. The autobiographical elements of both *Frankenweenie* movies served the marketing of the film and Burton's directorial identity very well. In terms of merchandising, among other products, Sparky the dog was reproduced as a plush toy, on clothes, as collectible stickers, a bobbing-head toy, a charm, keyring, mobile-phone cover, in various collectible figurine forms and as the '*Frankenweenie* Sparky the Dog' pet costume. With children's horror a well-established and generally uncontroversial subgenre by 2012, the animated version of *Frankenweenie* clearly targeted a younger audience and did so with the Disney branding. A ghoulish twist on the formulaic Disney 'boy and his dog' story, the narrative in both the

1984 and 2012 iterations paid respect to the memory of Burton's childhood pet and to the director's childhood love of monster movies.

In the 1984 live-action *Frankenweenie* film, a young boy, Victor Frankenstein, acted by child star Barrett Oliver, uses electricity to bring his beloved dog Sparky, played by a bull terrier (credited as Sparky), back to life. Victor's mother, Susan Frankenstein, is played by Shelley Duvall who, four years earlier, had portrayed the mother, Wendy Torrance, in Stanley Kubrick's *The Shining* (1980). Daniel Stern, who had come to public attention in the breakthrough role of 'Shrevie' in Barry Levinson's film *Diner* (1982), plays Victor's father, Ben Frankenstein. The film deals with the childhood trauma of losing a much-loved animal companion, the result of which is that Sparky's body is transformed through the process of reanimation from pet dog to monster. In an interview in 1985, Burton described his pitch for *Frankenweenie* to Richard Berger. The director explained that he had watched *Frankenstein* and begun to think about a dog he had lived with as a child: 'I started thinking just how incredible the whole idea of Frankenstein really is, of bringing the dead back to life. But all the versions of it so far have dealt with the horrible aspects of the idea. At some point, the idea of my dog and Frankenstein just connected and we started developing it' (in Mayo 1985: 4).

The film foregrounds the trauma of losing a companion animal and, in doing so, subverts the traditional child and dog narrative with the death of Sparky happening in a pre-title sequence. This opening scene establishes the bond between Victor and Sparky. A handmade title card appears on a screen to announce the film, *Monsters from Long Ago*, followed by a second handwritten card which says 'starring Sparky! As the Monster from Long Ago'. Dressed in a t-shirt adorned with stripy cardboard spikes and with a cardboard spike attached to his head in the manner of an elasticated party hat, the bull terrier walks into shot. Victor's 'direction' of Sparky is visible in the intra-diegetic film as a pair of hands pushing the dog back into shot. As Victor's home movie ends, the camera pulls out to reveal Victor, his mother, father and Sparky watching the projection screen in a suburban living room. At the end of the screening of his film, Victor throws open the living-room curtains and corrects his parents' comments about Sparky being cute: 'He's not cute, he's handsome', Victor insists as Sparky licks his face. Boy and dog go outside to play fetch, watched by Victor's parents and friends. Other than the unexplained use of black and white rather than colour, at this stage the film is loaded with all the signifiers of small-town moral sensibilities and boy-loves-his-dog sentimentality. The ball then rolls beyond the gate of the house and into the street. Sparky runs after it before the camera switches to Sparky's point of view which turns to the left to see the front of a car that fills the frame. There is the sound of a car horn, a cut to a long shot of the car undertaking an emergency stop, the sound of it hitting Sparky's body, and then a cut to Victor who stands up and screams 'No!' as the camera cuts to the ball rolling to a stop at the edge of the road, a possible reference to the Fritz Lang horror film *M* (1931). Although Sparky's death and his dead body are not seen, the combination of the dog's point-of-view shot, the series of rapid cuts and Victor's visceral scream creates a shock cut, a staple of the horror genre employed to give the viewer a physical and emotional jolt. David Diffrient defines the shock cut as 'a swift and jarring juxtaposition of two shots whose visual incongruity hinges on a profound contradiction: the intrusion of new narrative information as well as a temporal and/or spatial gap in a story's unfolding' (2004: 54). In *Frankenweenie*, Sparky's death is produced by, and constitutes, the shock cut without the need for the visual of his dead or dying body to underscore the affective jolt. The dog's subjective viewpoint is crucial in this regard; the novelty of its inclusion and sense of immediacy and movement contrast sharply with the shots that precede and follow it. Diffrient argues that horror films are distinguished by 'their frequent refusal to cut away from acts of violence [and instead] turn the site and sight of death into a spectacularly graphic touchstone' (2004: 55). *Frankenweenie*, a children's horror movie, offers up instead the shock cut and the site but not the sight of death. Although the visual language of the sequence borrows heavily from 1930s and 1950s horror and, in retrospect, can be read as unambiguous references to Burton's childhood love of old monster movies, such acknowledgement requires a level of film literacy that children in 1984 would be unlikely to possess. Add to this the live-action narrative and real dog, and it is perhaps unsurprising that Burton and others reported that in test screenings of *Frankenweenie* children became upset. The Motion Picture Association of America (MPAA) responded to Burton that the PG rating was due to 'the tone' of the film, and Disney became concerned about how it would be received by parents (Salisbury 2006: 39). As late as 2010, a reviewer noted that the animated version of the film 'could make the *Frankenweenie* tale much more accessible to those who may have had qualms about the death of a pet using a real dog, no matter how tastefully it was done' (Birch 2010).

Despite the obvious visual absence of Sparky's dead body, Burton's subversion of the boy- and-his-dog narrative in the opening sequence, the live action, intertextual sophistication and shock-cut cliché combine to produce a jarring affective moment. One interviewer remarked to Burton in 2012, 'There are emotions and experiences in *Frankenweenie* that audiences don't often associate with Disney features', to which Burton replied, with reference to the 1984 short: 'People get worried and they go, "Oh my God, the dog gets hit by a car". It's funny how people are afraid of their emotions' (in Itzkoff 2012). Burton's comments reflect an important intersection between the symbolic meanings and moral relevance that normalise the emotional response to a dog's death. On the one hand, the death of Sparky is a shocking event and the resulting display of grief by Victor is treated as an appropriate emotional response to the situation within the narrative; this is validated through wider cultural and societal norms that confirm dogs as family members with special moral relevance and status. On the other hand, grief for a companion animal remains socially complex and, despite the familial status of pet dogs, it is often regarded as a form of marginalised or unacceptable grief for adults. The death of a companion animal is frequently a child's first significant loss, a 'life changing event', the resulting grief of which is linked to the 'degree of attachment to the deceased pet [and] suddenness of death' (Kaufman and Kaufman 2006: 64). Some studies of grief have reported that children 'compared with adults, display more intense and longer duration pet bereavement' (Kaufman and Kaufman 2006: 64), while others argue that societal pressures maintain the marginalisation of pet grief such that there is a taboo against adults grieving openly for dead pets (Redmalm 2015: 19). Indeed, it is the case that children are socially enabled to experience and display grief in ways that would be considered inappropriate for adults, a dynamic that is normalised in *Frankenweenie*, where the intense emotional response to Sparky's death belongs to Victor and not his parents. However, Sparky is not the only dead animal in *Frankenweenie*, but he is the only one culturally normalised as legitimately deserving of human grief. Moreover, while pets exist as liminal beings, are humanised but not human, and are subjects who are legally defined as property objects and therefore ascribed an ambivalent moral status, in *Frankenweenie* dogs occupy a distinct category of pet that is distinguished from other species commonly kept as companions.

The background shots for the opening titles of *Frankenweenie* are of the pet cemetery where Sparky has been buried. A fire hydrant engraved 'R.I.P' leans to the left side of the frame, with the 'Walt Disney Pictures presents' title to the right. The comedic headstones – the fire hydrant, a stone fishbowl with 'Bubbles' and a sleeping fish engraved on it, a squirrel, a snake and a cat with crosses for eyes – attempt to lighten the mood and foreshadow the humorous tone of the rest of the film. These are the animals who are defined as pets, are worthy of burial and, by extension, deserving of human grief. This relationship between the burial of the body and the moral importance granted to a category of animals socially prescribed as 'pet' reflects the wider norms of animal classification and the arbitrary assignment of grievability for their deaths. In David Redmalm's study of pet grief, he notes that of the pet owners he interviewed, the snake, fish and large-scale bird owners did not grieve for their pets even though they stated that they would or had grieved for a dog or cat (2015: 30). In *Frankenweenie*, this hierarchy of morally considerable and grievable animals is reproduced, and the humour of the snake, the goldfish and the squirrel headstones is framed by the notion that they have been the subject of human grief and their bodies have gone through the human ritual of burial after death.

Dogs occupy a privileged position in a hierarchy of companion animals, where they are constructed as minded, conscious, purposive co-actors with subjecthood (Parkinson 2019). The difference between pet dogs and fish is made apparent in *Frankenweenie* when, during a conversation with his friends, Victor expresses his doubts that he will be ever be able to find another dog like Sparky. His friend responds: 'We got fish. They got no personality. You get used to them dying'. The darkly humorous tone to the conversation intentionally amplifies the distinctions between those pets who are individuated, given a name, ascribed with a unique subjecthood and therefore worthy of grief (Sparky the dog) and those who are non-individuated and unnamed, without the qualities of individual subjecthood and whose death has markedly less significance in moral or emotional terms (fish). The scene that follows this conversation introduces another dead animal, a frog, or, as the science teacher refers to him, 'an ex-frog', an intertextual nod towards the *Monty Python* 'dead parrot' sketch (1969). This sequence mobilises a further social classification of animal, the 'experimental object', an animal whose value resides in their observable body which is routinely treated as expendable and excluded from the moral community of animals who would be considered grief-worthy. When the teacher holds up the body of the dead frog laid outstretched on a piece of wood, the classroom of children voice disgust and turn away, averting their eyes and covering their mouths in a display of revulsion. Rebuking the children for their reaction, the teacher makes it clear that the dead body should be viewed from a scientific perspective. He then proceeds to apply electricity to the frog's lifeless body to illustrate its effects on the central nervous system. A shot of the frog's legs pointing straight up in the air, taut and twitching, pulls focus to Victor's face, wide-eyed and fascinated with the bodily spectacle before him. While the other children continue to express their revulsion, Victor rapidly sketches in his notebook. A smile on Victor's face is explained as the camera pans down to his notebook to reveal the plan to reanimate Sparky's dead body with electricity. The boy-and-his-dog narrative collides with the Frankenstein story as Victor and Sparky's relationship is about to become one of scientist and experimental subject/object. Even as the motivation for Victor's actions is grief at the loss of an irreplaceable individuated companion, it is this normative framing of their relationship that undercuts the monstrousness of Sparky's reanimated body. In terms of the film being a horror for children, the terror of a reanimated corpse is diminished by the sentimentality of a boy-and-his-loyal-dog story which rewrites the monstrous canine resurrection as a fantasy that love can overcome death.

Judith Butler examines at length 'the conditions under which a grievable life is established and maintained' (2004: 38) and suggests that grief can be conceptualised through aspects of irreplaceability, unpredictability and embodied loss (Butler 2004; Redmalm 2015). Those who are considered grievable are understood as unique identities by the griever; the unpredictability of loss has a transformative effect on the individual left behind because the relationality they experienced has gone and, finally, 'a grievable loss is always embodied', a reminder of the shared precarity of bodies (Redmalm 2015: 22–3). In interviews, Burton establishes the grievability of his childhood dog through the three framing concepts that Butler identifies. Individuated by name and his distinctive classification as a mixed breed, Burton marks out Pepe as irreplaceable: 'He was a mix, kind of a mutt, with a bit of terrier, and a bit of something else. I don't know what it was. It was kind of a mixture' (in Korkis 2012). In *Frankenweenie*, Victor expresses Sparky's irreplaceability. When asked by his friends 'Will you get another one?' Victor replies, 'I don't know if I can find another one like Sparky'. Burton also comments on the transformative effect of the loss of Pepe, saying, 'It's such an unconditional relationship [. . .] A lot of kids have that experience – I certainly had that experience with a first pet. You'll probably never have it again in your life in that way, it's so pure and memorable' (in Korkis 2012). But it is the vulnerability of Pepe's body that Burton recalls as being distinctive and suggestive to him of the Frankenstein reanimation story: 'Our dog had this thing called distemper and wasn't supposed to live more than a couple of years. He lived much longer than that, which kind of fed into this Frankenstein mythology as well' (in Korkis 2012). As Burton recalls, Pepe was a vulnerable and precarious body, as well as being a body that managed to elude death, noting that 'They said the dog was not going to live very long. He ended up living many years in spite of that, [. . .] but there was always the specter of that hanging over it' (in Alexander 2012). In *Frankenweenie*, Sparky's body undergoes transformation from living dog to reanimated 'monster' at Victor's hands, only to die again later in the film and be brought back to life for a second time by the adults. In Burton's recollections of Pepe and the narrative of *Frankenweenie*, both dogs satisfy the conditions by which Butler suggests a body becomes 'grievable'.

Certain companion animals are culturally normalised as 'grievable' and therefore remain morally considerable bodies after death. In *Frankenweenie* these bodies are then subject to the ritual of burial, a practice that has been common since classical antiquity when the 'burial of animals closely followed the pattern of human burials' (Bodson 2000: 28). However, the film also introduces a third category of animal body: that of food, which is used in the film to illustrate that Victor's parents do not know him as well as they think they do, but which also draws attention to the ambivalent and complex relationships humans have with (dead) animal bodies. Excited by his new-found knowledge that electricity can bring Sparky back from the dead, Victor runs home. His mother pauses her telephone conversation to tell Victor that she has the day off from work and is making his favourite meal for dinner. 'Roast beef?' Victor asks. 'I thought your favourite was chicken' his mother responds. 'Chicken's just great ma. Excuse me' Victor replies as he runs to his room to read a book entitled *Electricity and the Creation of Life*. The camera pans from a table loaded with books with titles that include *Life After Death*, *On Death and Dying*, *Science* and *Modern Chemistry* to Victor at his desk, reading intently. While the short exchange in the film is used to introduce the idea that Victor is in fact a misunderstood child, the use of meat to illustrate this familial disconnection can be read as a comment on the difference between the morally considerable and therefore grievable animal body and the morally unimportant dead body of a 'food animal'. Stepping outside of the normative classifications of animals as pets and food, the idea that parental concern for a child's grief over the death of one animal is expressed by feeding them the dead body of another animal has its own horrific symbolism. Indeed, the ambivalence of these cultural norms is made apparent if one considers the Western response to the idea of eating dogs, which Susan McHugh regards as 'perhaps the more controversial animal practice today, because of the tremendous range of feelings stirred' (2004: 31) and which I have argued elsewhere is 'a practice that is used to define the bounds of humanity and which simultaneously asserts the norms of human-canine relations' (Molloy 2011: 169). In this regard, *Frankenweenie* can be read as illustrative of the normative incongruity and cultural specificity of social categorisation of animal bodies.

The main conceit of *Frankenweenie* is its homage to Whale's *Frankenstein*, and through this narrative Sparky's body is reanimated. Victor's experimentation on Sparky's body is another subversion of the boy-and-his-dog narrative, although the exhumation of Sparky's body takes place off camera and throughout the experimental process his corpse is covered with a sheet. Sparky's body is transformed into a monstrous being, the signifiers of which reference Frankenstein's monster, with neck bolts and obvious stitches that hold the body together. At one point, Victor's mother helps him to re-stitch Sparky's neck, which has been shown in a previous scene to 'leak' water when he drinks. In being brought back to life, Sparky's grievable body is also the monstrous body which, in the context of children's horror, is made less horrific through his 'petification'. The process of petification is one in which an animal acquires meanings related to domestication and infantilisation. This can be understood as a strategy to address children as an audience for horror through ideological structures that co-constitute the categories of childhood and pethood (Feuerstein and Nolte-Odhianbo 2017). Child-pet relationships are constituted through a cultural politics that aligns pethood and childhood in ways that often blur the social realities of their difference. Within legal frameworks, for example, children have rights and subjecthood while pets remain property objects. Nonetheless, the power dynamics of the childhood/pethood alignment are culturally set in opposition to the figure of the adult, especially when addressed at children. *Frankenweenie* plays with this binary and presents the adults as emotionally detached, sinister, threatening or stupid. Victor has more in common with Sparky than with his human family, and the depiction of Victor and Sparky as playmates and co-creators (of films) reinforces the normative framing of the child-pet relationship. When the reanimated Sparky is introduced to the neighbours, they become fearful and then threatening – transformed into 'the villagers with pitchforks' – and chase Sparky to a miniature-golf course where, attempting to save Victor from a fire started by one of the adults, the dog is crushed to death. Once again, Sparky's dead body is unseen, hidden first under the burning miniature windmill blades which have fallen on him and then under a cloth as he is brought into the centre of a circle of cars. Only when the neighbours realise that Sparky saved Victor's life do they connect car battery charging leads to the bolts in Sparky's neck and use the electric charge generated by revving their cars to revive him once again.

Like many of Burton's films, *Frankenweenie* contains autobiographical references to some aspect of the director's life and interests. At the same time, the film opens up to a reading of the normative frameworks that constitute animal bodies socially and culturally. As a children's horror, *Frankenweenie* draws on the visual and narrative references of the genre but negotiates their use through the ideological structures and social conditions that inform our understanding of animal bodies as pets, experimental objects and food, and through the co-constitution of the categories of pethood and childhood. It also makes apparent the social norms that govern which bodies are grievable and through this cultural logic reconfigures the monstrous animal body as child-friendly.

NOTE

1. The term 'video nasty' referred to a film, usually horror, that was perceived to be excessively graphic or gory.

8. MONSTROUS MASCULINITY: 'BECOMING CENTAUR' IN TIM BURTON'S *SLEEPY HOLLOW*

Stella Hockenhull

Animals have played a major part in the films of Tim Burton, particularly those with a focus on the relationship between humans and dogs. Canines of various descriptions have featured as plot devices in his oeuvre, namely in films such as *Frankenweenie* (2012),[1] *Corpse Bride* (2005), *The Nightmare Before Christmas* (1993) and *Batman Returns* (1992). Conversely, horses have generally played a lesser role in his work except for their appearance in the Gothic horror adaptation, *Sleepy Hollow* (1999). Although Burton confesses to not being 'a big horse fan' (in Salisbury 2006: 164), he felt compelled to make this adaptation of Washington Irving's short story entitled *The Legend of Sleepy Hollow* (1820)[2] as a filmic example of an early American horror story. In keeping with Irving's tale, Burton uses the figure of a marauding Headless Horseman (Christopher Walken) and his black stallion, Daredevil, to create fear among the group of inhabitants in the settlement of Sleepy Hollow. Furthermore, he deploys this evil duo as a symbol of masculinity to contrast with, and to emasculate, the central protagonist, Ichabod Crane (Johnny Depp). Writing in 2017, Monica Mattfield introduces the concept that the body of a horse transforms its rider into a dominant and powerful entity through a process of what she terms 'becoming centaur'. In *Sleepy Hollow*, Burton too creates a figure that is dominant and masculine through the act of becoming centaur, but his imagining of the two-fold Headless Horseman, in line with a long-standing Gothic tradition in folklore and myth, is a monstrous invader that exploits the fears of the villagers. It is only towards the end of the film when Crane finally rides the stallion that he acquires similar power and dominance to that of the malevolent equine combination. This essay discusses the representation of horse and rider as becoming centaur in Tim Burton's *Sleepy Hollow* but extends Mattfield's concept to evoke what Sir Edmund Burke [1759] (1998) describes as sublime affect: a symbol of monstrous masculinity or, in this case, 'becoming monstrous centaur'.

BECOMING CENTAUR

Becoming centaur is a term used by Mattfield in her analysis of the role that horses played in eighteenth-century England. For her, through various means, the horse is transformed by its rider into a symbol of masculinity, a situation that has long existed in cinema. In the Western, for example, the horse glamorises the cowboy and shows his potency. Sometimes, 'The hero cowboy demonstrates his masculinity through breaking and taming his horse [which] is both free-spirited and courageous, traits that are transferrable to the rider' (Hockenhull 2017b: 104). In a similar vein, Mattfield suggests that men in the eighteenth century attained transformation through their mounts, converting the rider into a dominant, overpowering and fabulous figure. As she notes, 'They [the horses] were partners of choice for many men, and it was their presence that men sought to become, and to be observed as something other, something powerful, awe-inspiring, even mythical' (2017: 2). Mattfield argues that historically the horse had a pervasive effect on numerous aspects of culture, and widely influenced societal rankings while promoting an elevated model of masculinity to be admired. According to her, 'Horses influenced political discourse, social standing, scientific understanding of rationality, personal identity, and the performance of gender, while frequently transgressing the boundaries between what was considered human and what was understood as animal' (Mattfield 2017: 2). When horse and rider work together they operate as one; in other words, there is no human/nonhuman hierarchy. As Mattfield proposes, 'As human gender and subjectivity are formulated and negotiated through performance (performance being the "repeated stylization of the body, a set of repeated acts within a highly regulated frame that congeal over time" and that literally embody our existence of the world), so too are animal gender, subjectivity and being in the world [original brackets]' (2017: 9). Meaning emanates from the creation of the shared non-verbal language produced by the equine combination as a '*doing* or *becoming*, produced and reproduced in specific contexts of human/nonhuman interaction [italics in original]' (Birke, Bryld and Lykke 2004: 169). Mattfield adopts these idioms to produce the term 'becoming centaur [. . .] inhabiting the body of his horse, [. . .] embracing his mind to create a hybrid, dual-natured creature: a centaur' (2017: 10). The centaur display of eighteenth-century horsemanship that she refers to encompasses 'refinement, honor, strength, and spectacular personal display' (2017: 11), all traits associated with masculinity. As she explains, 'For a horseman to be a masculine man who could fulfill his civic duty to the nation, he was also required to "speak" the "languages" of horsemanship with perfection and grace. Men needed to be brave and ready to serve their nation, but they had also to be gentle, sensitive, and expert at interspecies communication' (Mattfield 2017: 12).

Mattfield's work discusses this interaction as a means of idealising masculinity to create political influence and power. In *Sleepy Hollow* and other films that fall within the horror genre, however, this collapse of distinction between nonhuman and human introduces the monstrous (Gregersdotter and Hållén 2015). To contextualise, commentators have argued that animals in visual culture have largely disappeared as nonhuman because they are either Disneyfied or treated anthropomorphically, such attribution of human qualities making them more suitable for film and television narratives (Berger 2009). Katarina Gregersdotter and Nicklas Hållén (2015) take this concept further to suggest that its reintroduction in cinema has taken place through the horror film. Animals in this genre usually perform a transgression against humans or society which consists of violent acts and typically human slaughter before the perpetrators are overcome. These massacres are habitually caused by humans who have either encroached on animal territory or have exploited them in some way. Typically the animal is anthropomorphised, producing human qualities to achieve results; those human characteristics attributed to the monstrous animal create otherness but are also simultaneously constructed through similarities between the species. As Gregersdotter and Hållén propose, 'in order to structure the narrative around the opposition between animal and human, otherness is constructed through sameness, since animals are ascribed human qualities – and, occasionally, humans are ascribed animal qualities' (2015: 207).

In *Sleepy Hollow* it is these human qualities that the horse acquires and those animal qualities that the human displays that create otherness, as well as the becoming monstrous centaur features of the Headless Horseman. Burton's film version of *Sleepy Hollow* is loosely based on Irving's short story and, in a similar manner to the writer, he retains the use of the animal mergence with the rider to create terror. This factor is acknowledged by Kirstin A. Mills, who analyses horses and horsemanship in Irving's story. She contends that, in general, the Headless Horseman accounts for much of the fear in Gothic fiction: indeed, for her 'The Headless Horseman stands alongside Dracula and Frankenstein's creature as one of the Gothic's most iconic "monsters"' (Mills 2020: 223). Mills explores what she terms the Demonic Horse in Irving's story and maintains that, for this figure to horrify, it is made up of two parts which merge: the horse and its mount. For her, 'the headless rider and the fearsome, Demonic Horse that he rides [. . .] accounts for much of the spectre's awesome terror' (Mills 2020: 223). As the name implies, he is a wild horse, only controlled by a heroic rider and, as Elsie B. Michie argues, 'Because it is ridden, the horse has a particularly intimate relation to the human body' (2007: 146).

Burton exploits Irving's description of the fearsome beast extensively to present this combination. Irving writes of the character Abraham Bones (Brom) that he arrives at a party 'on his favourite steed Daredevil, a creature, like himself, full of mettle and mischief, and which no one but himself could manage' (2014: 329). Akin to Irving's Brom, Burton's Headless Horseman is an excellent rider and, combined with the horse, the pair are threatening and hostile. However, whereas Irving's description of the headless rider is that of 'a figure on horseback, without a head [. . .] who is ever and anon seen by the country folk hurrying along in the gloom of the night' (Irving [1820] 2014: 313), it is a myth, and is used by Brom to play a trick on Crane in order to frighten him away.[3] Crane in the tale is a schoolteacher in the Dutch settlement of Tarry Town, New York, an area renowned for the appearance of the spectre of a Headless Horseman. A former Hessian trooper, the Horseman was, purportedly, decapitated by a stray cannonball and revisits each night the area where the event took place in search of his head. Crane competes with the local town thug, Brom, for the affections of wealthy heiress Katrina Van Tassel. At the end of Irving's tale, Brom plays a trick on Crane, pretending to be the Headless Horseman, and Crane disappears, leaving his adversary free to marry Katrina. Burton's story differs and the director makes a number of alterations to his narrative. He reimagines Crane as a bumbling and awkward police detective in place of a teacher and, instead of being a local inhabitant, he is a temporary visitor from New York City who is brought in to solve a series of murders. Irving's Headless Horseman is a yarn whereas Burton's creature exists as an apparition. Indeed, initially, Burton's protagonist does not believe in the existence of the Headless Horseman. As he explains, 'Murder needs no ghosts come from the grave. We have murders in New York without the benefit of ghouls and goblins'. Van Tassel, nevertheless, reminds him that he is 'a long way from New York, constable'. Crane later encounters the spectre and is finally convinced. Subsequently, he sets about ridding the village of the menace and, in the process, falls in love with the local landowner's daughter, Katrina Van Tassel (Christina Ricci).

BECOMING MONSTROUS CENTAUR

While the horse is not such a common feature in horror cinema, equine demons have long existed in traditional folklore and mythology, and these legends and stories have been found in various forms in most countries. The Wild Huntsman is one such tale and tells of a mythological figure leading a supernatural group of hunters. Alluding to medieval England, Mary Oldfield Howey makes specific reference to the terrifying characteristics of their animals: 'The horses which carried the hunters were coal-black with flowing manes and tails, and eyes that glowed like carbuncles. They appeared to breathe fire and smoke as they rushed with furious speed through the forest in chase [. . .] On some occasions, [they] are said to have vanished in smoke and flame from before the eyes of startled spectators' (2002: 57). Drawing on traditional folklore such as Oldfield Howey describes, which associates horses with the demonic unnatural, Burton depicts the Headless Horseman as a fiendish beast evoking what eighteenth-century philosopher Sir Edmund Burke would describe as sublime affect. Writing in 1757 (reprinted 1759), Burke's work on the sublime describes how terror is caused by various phenomena. As he suggests, 'Whatever is fitted in any sort to excite the ideas of pain, and danger, that is to say, whatever is in any sort terrible, or is conversant about terrible objects, or operates in a manner analogous to terror, is a source of the *sublime*; that is, it is productive of the strongest emotion which the mind is capable of feeling [italics in original]' (Burke 1998: 131). Burke lists aspects of the sublime as terror, obscurity and power. For him, terror 'robs the mind of all its powers of acting and reasoning as fear [. . .] it is impossible to look on any thing as trifling, or contemptible, that may be dangerous' (1998: 133). In this category he includes animals which 'though far from being large, are yet capable of raising ideas of the sublime, because they are considered as objects of terror. As serpents and poisonous animals of all kinds. And to things of great dimensions, if we annex an adventitious idea of terror, they become without comparison greater' (Burke 1998: 133). For Burke, the equine is one such creature. According to him, it has two functions. It is not only serviceable and practical, but can mobilise terror: 'The horse in the light of an useful beast, fit for the plough, the road, the draft, in every social useful light the horse has nothing of the sublime; but it is thus that we are affected with him, *whose neck is clothed with thunder, the glory of whose nostrils is terrible, who swalloweth the ground with fierceness and rage, neither believeth that it is the sound of the trumpet?* [italics in original]' (Burke 1998: 138). This combination of strength and danger he also links to other animals and the landscape, in particular the wilderness. Indeed, the sublime 'comes upon us in the gloomy forest, and in the howling wilderness, in the form of the lion, the tiger, the panther, or rhinoceros' (Burke 1998: 138).[4]

Obscurity is another feature of Burton's film inducing Burke's idea of fear of the dark and, in turn, night. This includes creatures of the night: 'the notions of ghosts and goblins, of which none can form clear ideas, affect minds, which give credit to the popular tales concerning such sorts of beings' (Burke 1998: 133). Not only are spirits and imaginary evil beings a cause for concern, the 'darkest woods, and the shade of the oldest and most spreading oaks' (Burke 1998: 134) are places to be wary of. Burke believes that power is enhanced through an animal's capacity to inflict pain and terror creating a hierarchy. As he argues,

> Look at a man, or any other animal of prodigious strength, and what is your idea before reflection [. . .] the emotion you feel is, lest this enormous strength should be employed to the purposes of rapine and destruction [. . .] An ox is a creature of vast strength; but he is an innocent creature, extremely serviceable, and not at all dangerous; for which reason the idea of an ox is by no means grand. A bull is strong too; but his strength is of another kind; often very destructive, seldom [. . .] of any use in our business; the idea of a bull is therefore great, and it has frequently a place in sublime descriptions, and elevating comparisons. (Burke 1998: 137)

By combining Mattfield's theory of becoming centaur with that of Burke's sublime, the headless rider in Burton's film is thus transformed via the body of his horse into a potent, dominant and awe-inspiring entity, producing a masculine otherness which results in becoming monstrous centaur. This spectre is first introduced audibly in the opening sequences but remains unseen at this point. Peter Van Garrett (Martin Landau), a local dignitary of the village of Sleepy Hollow, is travelling through the countryside by carriage when his driver is attacked and beheaded. Fleeing this massacre, Van Garrett encounters what the spectator believes to be the Headless Horseman. It is dark, but moonlight illuminates the man's face, creating an ominous and eerie glow. As he hides, the realisation hits Van Garrett that the Horseman has found him and, observed in close-up, he slowly raises his eyes upwards, indicating the size of the monstrosity set before him. Simultaneously, the snorting sound of the beast reaches his ears and he spins around haltingly, a terrified expression on his face. Presumably he has recognised the creature from the widespread legends that thrive in Sleepy Hollow. Accompanied by the swish of a sword being withdrawn from its scabbard, the camera cuts to an image of a scarecrow, its carved pumpkin head spattered with blood; from this it becomes clear that the man has been slaughtered.

As noted, in the aforementioned sequence the Headless Horseman remains unseen by the viewer but when the pair first appear visually in the film it is from the point of view of a local resident, Jonathan Masbath (Mark Spalding). Masbath has elected to protect the village and be on watch for the appearance of the Headless Horseman; he awaits its arrival in a wooden lookout at the edge of the forest, or as Burke might suggest, in the 'darkest woods, and the shade of the oldest and most spreading oaks' (1998: 134). Peering through a small slit in the wall, Masbath appears afraid. Subsequently, the pounding sound of horse's hooves informs of the spectre's approach and Masbath attempts to escape by running away through the dense trees. In a series of rapid edits, the camera cuts from the fleeing figure to images of a horse and rider which materialise at great speed from the mist. Masbath is diminished in the frame as he runs towards a clearing. Bathed in a blue light, the Headless Horseman emerges from the fog and the bodies of he and his mount fill the frame, overpowering the man. In this image, snorting steed and rider merge into one as an indeterminate whole; seen alternately from a front then rear perspective, they gallop furiously towards the unfortunate victim. An edit shows the Horseman from the rear, cape billowing from his shoulders, and brandishing a sword as he swipes at his victim. Subsequently he beheads the man then disappears into the fog; the ensuing shot reveals the severed head of the unfortunate victim. Masbath's death leaves Young Masbath (Marc Pickering), his son, alone and therefore a willing aid to Crane later in the narrative.

Throughout this sequence, the Headless Horseman has dominated the frame both visually and aurally, and Burton emphasises the animal's legs through a low-angle close-up shot to demonstrate his furious pace as he penetrates the mist and fog. The director uses sepia tones to visually fuse equine, rider and landscape, and the animal's speed of movement invokes Burke's notions of the sublime – its 'neck is clothed with thunder, the glory of whose nostrils are terrible, who swalloweth the ground with fierceness and rage [italics in original]' (Burke 1998: 138) – to suggest supremacy. Burton's unison of horse, rider and landscape enables the pair to blend in with their surroundings, and this coalescence facilitates a sense of menace which the director required for the completed look of the film. As he states, 'The saturated look I'm going for is [. . .] a binding together of the sets and the locations' (in Salisbury 2006: 176).

The Headless Horseman in *Sleepy Hollow* exemplifies monstrous inhumanity which reigns supreme in the settlement. This is evident when the tale is first told in flashback to Crane by the local landowner, Baltus Van Tassel (Michael Gambon). While the voice-over explains the story, the camera cuts to an image of the apparition. Van Tassel suggests that the Horseman's love of carnage brought him to America's shores, and an edit reveals a flashback of the flames of an open fire before a dissolve cuts to a close-up of the Horseman's face, now illuminated by the blaze of battle. A cut to a distant shot shows the mounted figure in silhouette, the raised swords of his adversaries filling the foreground. Horse and rider merge into one to create an outline and, using rapid editing, Burton cuts from close-ups of the Horseman's face showing glaring eyes and pointed teeth to wider shots of both horse and rider, the pair forming a black profile against a fire-lit sky. Here, the animal's body becomes an extension of the rider, creating what Mills terms the possibility for the disappearance of the human in this coupling. As she explains, in relation to Irving, he '[sees] a Gothic potential for terror and loss of the human within this close pairing of man and animal' (2020: 225). Indeed, the horse is as dedicated to destruction as his owner; the stallion too exists outside ethical boundaries and doles

Figure 8.1   Daredevil, *Sleepy Hollow*, 1999.

out retribution for his master's ill treatment. As Mattfield suggests, when horse and rider become centaur the former is 'shown to be as enraged, as violent, and as committed to the fight as the humans' (2017: 36). Van Tassel's description portrays the Hessian Horseman as a butcher and his horse is killed in battle along with his rider, who is buried with his severed head. As the voice-over continues, Daredevil is shown standing over the grave (Figure 8.1). He is a beautiful, proud animal: with neck arched, he is revealed from a low-angle shot in a monochrome composition which both enhances his size and sleek, black coat. Set against the gnarled and twisted trees and snowy setting, this is again the landscape to which Burke refers, and Burton uses cinematographic techniques to augment the beast's authority.

It is some way into the film that Crane first encounters the Headless Horseman. He has been conversing with the town official, Magistrate Philipse (Richard Griffiths), and the latter is leaving the settlement to escape danger. He attempts to convince Crane of the existence of the legendary creature, but the policeman refuses to believe him. Nevertheless, he is proven wrong. In fact, he stares in disbelief as, during their conversation which takes place in a severe thunderstorm, a galloping headless figure emerges from the woods. The Headless Horseman brushes past a scarecrow which is constructed from a pumpkin and ragged clothing, and hurtles towards Crane through the landscape. Set against a dark sky, this eerie sight constitutes what Edwin Page describes as a '"kind of natural expressionism" [which] can be seen as expressionist in that it is a twisted, exaggerated form of the natural world, one in which angst and torment can easily be imagined' (2007: 167). Decapitating Philipse, this headless apparition sits astride Daredevil who rears up in the air, overpowering Crane. Crane lies prostrate and powerless on the ground, indicated by a point-of-view shot as the camera looks upwards; the horse, with its headless rider atop, towers above him. Standing erect, Daredevil appears poised and at the command of his master, who is adept and capable. The animal's long flowing mane blows in the wind and his teeth are bared, making him appear a commanding and frightening beast.

While the Headless Horseman is not a hero figure, he is imposing and powerful, and masculinity is also bound up with performance. As Donna Peberdy suggests, '"to be a man" is a performance – something to be proved and acted out – it also points to the varying ways male identity is defined and performed' (2013: 3).[5] Thus, the headless rider, along with his demonic horse, perform manliness through domination and power. This is demonstrated as Daredevil rears up in the air a few more times, seeming to enhance his size. Subsequently, the camera cuts from a close-up of Crane's face illuminated by the lightning. Philipse's now severed head rolls towards him and the Headless Horseman spears it and gallops into the distance, at which point Crane faints: the difference between the equine pair and the constable is made palpable in this sequence. Indeed, the spectral creature has controlled the situation, commanding wonder and awe, its performance a display of masculinity. Here, the horse becomes an extension of its rider and, as Mills argues, horsemanship

> involved the rider's appropriation of the horse's body as an extension of his own, where the horse became a visible embodiment of the rider's animal power and virility, while his mastery of the animal signified his masculine dominance over these 'animal passions' (the animal within) and the natural world, metonymically figured by the horse as the animal without. (2020: 224)

The duo are controlling in that they hold the village of Sleepy Hollow hostage and, similar to the monster, Dracula, transgress boundaries between life and death and Christianity and Pagan ritual. They feed on the weaknesses of the village and are a parasitic other, blending as a single spectre, ruling and holding sway over the land. This form of control has been likened by philosopher Jacques Derrida to political hierarchy, suggesting male superiority over beings such as women, children, animals and those with less social authority. Derrida has described the sovereign state as '*animality*, or even as bestiality [. . .], either a normal bestiality or a monstrous bestiality itself mythological or fabulous [italics in original]' (in Cole et al. 2011: 1), and the Headless Horseman, a mercenary soldier, along with his horse is above the law, killing men, women and children alike.

If Daredevil is a symbol of masculinity, albeit a dreadful representation of such, he is positioned in distinct contrast to the animal that Crane rides. As noted, in terms of appearance, the black apparition is sleek, well proportioned and striking by equine standards. With reference to temperament, Daredevil is able and brave. Furthermore, his rider speaks the language of his horse; as Mattfield suggests, 'when taken together [. . .] political man as animal or animality form a three-sided sovereign that can dominate, domesticate, or kill as a being above the law, and as a being that does so as a social creature interested in personal gain' (2017: 29). Crane's horse is exactly the opposite. Named inappropriately Gunpowder, the animal is far from lively. His appearance is akin to his namesake in Irving's story, which describes the beast as 'a broken-down plow-horse [. . .] He was gaunt and shagged, with a ewe neck, and a head like a hammer; his rusty mane and tail were tangled and knotted with burs; one eye had lost its pupil, and was glaring and spectral, but the other had the gleam of a genuine devil in it' (Irving [1820] 2014: 326). Gunpowder is a functional animal and, in Burke's vocabulary, 'fit for the plough'. First sight of him occurs when he emerges from the stable; led by one of the local farmers, he appears short and stocky with a woolly, brown coat, thus differing physically from his elegant adversary. Furthermore, his inferiority is additionally emphasised because he is not a stallion, but a gelding,[6] and therefore lacks the feisty and energetic attitude of the Headless Horseman's mount. When Gunpowder first appears, he raises his head and stalls in a pose which suggests a reluctance to move at a pace, or in fact at all. He lacks the force and vigour of Daredevil, and hence emasculates his rider. Furthermore, in contrast to the black stallion who sports an elaborate and polished saddle and harness, he wears a small homespun blanket under his saddle.

Initially, this animal fits the persona of Crane, who is a timid and squeamish character. Described by Andrew O'Hehir as 'a Clouseau-like incompetent, his face a mask of involuntary tics and twitches. His scientific aspirations are portrayed as foolish and grotesque' (2000: 55), he appears uneasy and afraid when he first encounters his mount. Gingerly patting him on the rump, he states disingenuously that 'he should do just fine'. At this gesture, a cloud of dust emanates from the animal's fur, causing Crane to withdraw slightly in fear and disgust. When he initially attempts to climb aboard the animal he is unable to do so, ending up facing backwards in the saddle, further emphasising his urban ways as well as his placid, dull and unsophisticated horse.

Such weaknesses are first demonstrated when the spectator is introduced to Crane in his native city of New York before he departs for Sleepy Hollow. He is represented as a nervous yet caring individual, those characteristics not conventionally associated with masculine traits. In this scene, a corpse is retrieved from the river under his watch and Crane wishes to do justice to the body by undertaking a post-mortem, although this is against his heartless supervisor's wishes. A little later a burglar is brought into the police station and, without concern from the rest of the constabulary, is thrown into a deep underground dungeon, causing the detainee to cry out in pain. At this juncture, the camera cuts to a close-up of Crane's face; his eyebrows are raised, and his expression seems troubled at such treatment. Depp is an appropriate actor to play Crane. He has what Alison McMahan terms a 'natural clumsiness and overall lack of social grace' (2005: 71) and was deliberately chosen by Burton for his deficiency of superhero qualities, as is evident in many of his Hollywood contemporaries. As Burton points out, '*Depp plays Ichabod as a cross between Angela Lansbury and Roddy MacDowell* [sic] *with a pinch of Basil Rathbone.*

Typically of the actor, he's not your standard action-movie hero [italics in original]' (in Salisbury 2006: 177).

Crane's thoughtful attitude is further demonstrated when he prepares to leave New York for Sleepy Hollow. He carefully removes his pet bird from its cage and, opening the window of his apartment, releases it, thus permitting the creature to fly to freedom. Later, when he is informed of the ghastly deeds of the Headless Horseman, including his method of decapitating the victims, he stutters slightly as he reiterates the disturbing information that he has been told: that the heads disappear from the corpses subsequent to the slaughters. To emphasise his revulsion, an edit shows Crane's face; his eyes are half closed in a mock faint and his hands are shaking violently, evident through the rattling teacup and saucer that he holds. To contribute to his character flaws, he also has a fear of spiders and blood – the latter an odd anxiety given his profession.

By the end of the film, however, and through equine mastery, Crane is able to prove his manliness and overcome his fears. This occurs in the final chase sequence and chimes with Irving's tale when 'the goblin was hard on his haunches; and (unskilful rider that he was!) he had much ado to maintain his seat; sometimes slipping on one side, sometimes on another, and sometimes jolted on the high ridge of his horse's backbone, with a violence that he verily feared would cleave him asunder' (Irving [1820] 2014: 337). Here, Irving presents a pursuit but not with the same violence accorded the film. In Burton's version, the Headless Horseman appears behind the carriage that Crane, Young Masbath and Katrina are using to escape from Sleepy Hollow. In this instance, the spectre is less effective because the rider has vacated his horse and clambered up to the rear of Crane's vehicle to attack. The camera frames Crane as he stands to confront the Horseman but finds that only Daredevil is visible. A branch knocks Crane off the carriage and he inadvertently lands on the galloping horse but facing the wrong way. The horse does not slow his speed and Burton frames the animal's head in extreme close-up to demonstrate his force. Crane manages to turn around on the horse's back to face forwards and then gallop after the carriage; it is now the timid constable who masters the fierce animal instead of the Headless Horseman and, by doing so, appears in charge and powerful. The animal represents authority because it must be managed and it takes a strong male to do this. Eventually, in this action-packed sequence, Crane remounts the coach and reclaims control to the relief of Katrina and Young Masbath, thus saving both their lives. Crane now becomes centaur, although not a monstrous entity. Instead he demonstrates mastery over the horse that hitherto only the Headless Horseman could control. Furthermore, he succeeds in exposing Katrina's stepmother, Lady Van Tassel (Miranda Richardson), as the subversive force behind the spectre, and restores harmony to the village. As McMahan suggests, Crane acquires such masculine qualities when he eventually [. . .] proves himself as a man, which in his case means incorporating the reality of magic and the spirit world into his forensic, deductive methods [. . .] By confronting his personal deficiency, the hero is able to reconcile the masculine (the rational method) and the feminine (here represented by witchcraft), and therefore not only is able to solve the mystery and bring peace to the village, but can marry Katrina and look forward to a new, enriched life. (2005: 72)

Ultimately, this display of horsemanship enables him to prove his manhood through courage and physical strength, save Katrina and thwart the Headless Horseman. The couple return to New York City, but this time with Crane in control. At the end of the film he has acquired status and proven his masculinity by solving the crime and marrying Katrina.

Conclusion

Horses do not generally play a crucial role in Tim Burton's films, yet Daredevil and the horse that Crane rides in *Sleepy Hollow* are significant to the plot in a number of ways. The Headless Horseman adds terror and operates as 'a foreigner, an invader of sacred soil' (Newman 2001: 156). Furthermore, the pair introduce a monstrous masculinity through the interrelationship between man and horse. This negates the manliness of the key protagonist, Ichabod Crane, who is a timid rider and initially not at one with his steed. Eventually, however, he too masters the art of riding and becomes the dominant figure and centaur. As Mattfield contends, 'It was through the mediating presence of horses that the very humanity (or monstrous inhumanity), masculinity (or its lack), and honourable (or dishonourable) status of horsemen were created and secured' (2017: 13). However, ultimately whereas the Headless Horseman's success depends entirely on his horse which he takes with him to the grave, Crane's triumph is contingent on his knowledge of science as well as his positive attributes such as honesty, integrity, perseverance and a caring attitude. In true fairy-story mode, and unlike the tale from which Burton worked, evil is eliminated, and the couple unite to presumably live happily ever after. Meanwhile, the Headless Horseman, having reclaimed his head, along with Daredevil his trusty steed, retreats to the Tree of the Dead whence they came.

Notes

1. Claire Parkinson has analysed this relationship in 'Too Dark for Disney: Tim Burton, Children's Horror and Pet Death' elsewhere in this book.
2. Originally published in *The Sketch-Book of Geoffrey Crayon* (Irving 1819–20).
3. Burton was also influenced by an earlier Technicolor Disney adaptation by James Algar who amalgamated Irving's story with Kenneth Grahame's 1908 children's

tale, *The Wind in the Willows*, in a film entitled *The Adventures of Ichabod and Mr Toad* (1949). He followed this story accurately, even down to the comparison between the horses (McMahan 2005: 71).

4. Burke's theory of the Sublime is reflected in Gothic writing of the nineteenth century, particularly fiction. It exists in Western folklore such as Mayne Reid's serialised book *The Headless Horseman*, published between 1865 and 1866, and British and American First and Second World War literature frequently alluded to the subject. See Adam Piette and Mark Rawlinson (2012) (eds), *The Edinburgh Companion to Twentieth-Century British and American War Literature*, Edinburgh: Edinburgh University Press.

5. Peberdy is specifically referring to the film *Glengarry Glen Ross* (Foley 1992), although this broad definition can be applied to other film examples.

6. A horse that has been castrated. This process ensures that they are more docile to manage and ride.

9. ANOMALOUS BODIES IN TIM BURTON'S BESTIARY: REIMAGINING *DUMBO*

Frances Pheasant-Kelly

Introduction

While Tim Burton's live-action remake of the Disney animated classic, *Dumbo* (Sharpsteen 1941),[1] closely follows the original in its themes of motherhood and physical anomaly, it concurrently reframes certain aspects. Specifically, it comments on the corporate exploitation and confinement of nonhuman animals (hereafter referred to as animals) in zoos, circuses and theme parks, and explicitly foregrounds animal ethics. Burton also dispenses with the contentious gendered, racial and social stereotypes of Sharpsteen's version. In addition, while the primary element of Dumbo's outsize ears remains central to the story, Burton elaborates a relationship between humans and animals and interweaves their respective narratives. Like the source film, the remake follows the 'birth' of Dumbo, his separation from his mother, Mrs Jumbo, and his subsequent exploitation by unethical circus owners. Both versions reunite parent and 'child' in their resolution, providing typically Disneyfied happy endings. In this respect, Paul Wells explains that Sharpsteen's *Dumbo* follows the classical paradigm of the cinematic animal story which is usually characterised by a birth, the orphaning of a lead character and a quest. Resolution in this case occurs in the overcoming of obstacles and restoration of community, with 'Dumbo becom[ing] naturalized to the human world in succeeding as a circus performer' (Wells 2009: 125). In marked contrast, the end of Burton's film sees Dumbo reject the circus world in preference for his mother and a return to the wild.

Dumbo's physical aberration correlates well with Burton's past catalogue, which tends to focus on oddities, misfits and unusual bodies. However, the director is not only preoccupied with anomaly in the human form, as evident in films such as *Mars Attacks!* (1996), *Big Fish* (2003), *Edward Scissorhands* (1990) and *Corpse Bride* (2005), but is also renowned for regularly incorporating animals and humans that have animal qualities, illustrated, for example, by *Planet of the Apes* (2002) and *Frankenweenie* (2012). Indeed, he states that 'I like people who act like animals or vice-versa. Pee-Wee acts like an animal, Beetlejuice, Penguin, the Catwoman . . . Batman is an animal. I like animal people somehow. I don't know if it's an emotional response to things versus an intellectual response, but there is something about it I feel is important or is something I relate to somehow. It's just that primal, internal, animal instinct of people' (in Salisbury 2006: 193). This is most evident in *Planet of the Apes*, where Burton also gestures towards concerns with animal welfare. Moreover, if he celebrates human anomaly through performance, as in *Big Fish*, so too does he centre on performing animals. Presented as a flying elephant in a circus act, Dumbo therefore encompasses both performing animal and anomalous body, while, as noted, the film simultaneously addresses animal cruelty and confinement. Burton further overlies this revised focus with a theme of technology versus the natural world, the overall message being that the artifice of technology is always prone to failure whereas the natural order prevails. This nuance of Burton's remake resonates with a number of equivalent binaries that exist in current animal scholarship, including, for instance, culture/nature, human/wildness and human/animal. In terms of both *Dumbo* films as Disney productions, such dualisms also reflect on the artifice of anthropomorphism of animals and the broader Disney context, as considered by Umberto Eco (1986: 44) and Steve Baker (2001: 226), and which Burton arguably reiterates.

While there is extensive study of animals in visual culture (Baker 2001; Gardner and MacCormack 2017; Lawrence and McMahon 2015; Hockenhull 2015, 2016, 2017a; Parkinson 2019; Pick 2011; Wells 2009) and scholarship on the cinematic circus and zoo (Bouissac 1976; Cutler-Broyles 2020; Lawrence and Lury 2016; Stoddart 2000; Tait 2005), to date there is only limited analysis of animals in Burton's films generally (Akita and Kenney 2016; Sammond 2011; Wells 2009) or his version of *Dumbo* specifically. Currently, the latter is restricted to work by Brian McIlroy (2019) and Michael Charlton (2020). Both examine the two versions of *Dumbo* in the context of circus-themed films but do not discuss the crossover between cinema and animal discourse. McIlroy, for example, notes in Burton's film the connection between one of the protagonists whose mother has died of the 1919 Spanish influenza such that 'the young girl's empathy for Dumbo's classic separation from his mother elephant is therefore narratively twinned' (2019). He also observes that 'you sense that Burton can't stop himself from biting the hands that feed him: his

"Dreamland" run by an evil corporate entertainer played by Michael Keaton is a crude stand-in for "damn the workers" Walt Disney' (McIlroy 2019). Finally, McIlroy remarks that 'the Medici Circus run by Danny de Vito [sic] becomes a family circus with humans playing animals. Correct for our times' (2019). Michael Charlton's analysis focuses on the early version of *Dumbo*, which he interprets in terms of the Bakhtinian carnivalesque, with only passing mention of Burton's remake. However, he does note of Sharpsteen's *Dumbo* that 'here is one of the interesting peculiarities of the film, which from the very beginning contrasts the childhood joys of the circus [. . .] with anxieties about being outcast, neglected, or abandoned' (Charlton 2020: 106–7). Burton's remake retains this 'outsider' aspect, the concept being readily congruent with his previous works. The chapter therefore considers the intersection of bodily aberration and animal welfare, and refers to scholarship on circuses, zoos, freak shows and animal ethics. Engaging primarily with the work of John Berger (2009) and Peter Singer (1994), it textually analyses *Dumbo* to argue that, while Burton's adaptation follows the original and reflects the filmmaker's predilections for outsider status, it concurrently addresses contemporary concerns of animal welfare by first highlighting the human/animal divide, and then working to diegetically close this gap through specific aspects of characterisation, cinematography and *mise-en-scène*. This divide is evident in real-world zoos, circuses and sideshows and may be expressed in visual culture by the representation of otherness via stereotypes. It is less obviously apparent in Disney productions whereby, although animals talk and are given human qualities to a greater or lesser degree, the processes of industry and technology that enable this anthropomorphism position Disney creatures on the side of a dialectic opposed to 'animal'. The chapter therefore examines the film's introduction of a noticeable technological/natural binary and connects this to the collapsing of human/animal difference, as well as commenting on what Steve Baker (2001) terms the Disneyfication of animals.

The Human/Animal Divide

Burton's reimagining of *Dumbo* resonates with revised approaches to animal welfare that have evolved since the release of Sharpsteen's film and, it is argued here, signal a widely acknowledged diminution of the division between humans and animals. As Peter Singer notes, this awareness has been triggered by four key developments since the 1960s: a recognition of ecological crisis; the animal rights movement demanding an end to speciesism; a growing knowledge of animals and their capacity to make tools and communicate in sign language; and discovery of human genetic proximity to chimpanzees (1994: 173–7). As Singer further explains, 'the difference between us and chimpanzees is less than the 2.3 per cent that separates the DNA of chimpanzees from that of gorillas.

In other words, we – not the gorillas – are the chimpanzees' nearest relatives' (1994: 177). In a related vein, Donald Griffin reveals how this has been complemented by studies in cognition: 'the first step was a "cognitive revolution" [. . .] [which favoured] a cognitive psychology in which internal processes such as memory and decision-making are analyzed as principal factors necessary to understand behavior' (2006: 481). A second development involved the 'renaissance of scientific investigations of consciousness' and, by the 1970s, Griffin reports that these methods began to involve animals (2006: 480–1).

Zoos, Circuses and Sideshows

Historically, however, the relationship between humans and animals is hierarchical and is defined, at least in the past two centuries, by colonial impulses and the human control exercised over animals. In the essay 'Why Look at Animals?' (2009), John Berger notes that 'animals are born, are sentient and are mortal. In these things they resemble man. In their superficial anatomy – less in their deep anatomy – in their habits, in their time, in their physical capacities, they differ from man. They are both alike and unlike' (2009: 4). Berger considers such relationships as being inherent in zoo culture. Specifically, he suggests that 'the capturing of the animals was a symbolic representation of the conquest of all distant and exotic lands. "Explorers" proved their patriotism by sending home a tiger or an elephant' (2009: 21). As he further explains, zoos not only served the 'ideology of imperialism' but also functioned as a site of education and knowledge (2009: 21). Effectively, the zoo is a locus for studying and gazing at animals and, while Lori Gruen acknowledges that some contemporary zoos are important in terms of research and conservation, she notes that 'few animals have been saved from extinction by zoos and "some of them more by providence than prudence"' (2011: 139). Berger likens the zoo experience to that of visiting an art gallery whereby

> in principle, each cage is a frame round the animal inside. Visitors visit the zoo to look at animals. They proceed from cage to cage, not unlike visitors in an art gallery who stop in front of one painting, or then move on to the next [. . .] However you look at these animals, even if the animal is up against the bars, less than a foot away from you, looking out in the public direction, *you are looking at something that has been rendered absolutely marginal*; and all the concentration you can muster will never be enough to centralise it [italics in original]. (2009: 23–4)

The scenario that Berger describes unfolds in each version of *Dumbo* whereby the animal, in this case primarily the elephant, is the object of a marginalising gaze, both in terms of the zoo and the circus.

Adopting a similar critical stance, Anat Pick suggests that 'Zoos will never be able to offer the solution to the problem of disappearance of animals because their very inception and in their very being they are part of the problem' (2011: 104). She goes on to consider how this disappearance is covered up by an increasing appearance of animals in other forms. As she states, 'Fussed over, tagged, screened, projected, and surveyed, exhibited, simulated, incarcerated, conserved, even manufactured and invented, nature and animals are gaining an exclusive kind of cultural visibility' (2011: 105). The technological/artificial mode that Pick alludes to correlates with the technological/natural binary evident in Burton's film. At the same time, she comments that Jonathan Burt 'argues for a more nuanced theorization of the visual animal' (2011: 108) whereby he proposes that 'the theory that the animal is becoming increasingly virtual, that its fate is to disappear into technological reproduction to become nothing more than imagery, would make sense were it not for the fact that this imagery is not uniform but unavoidably fragmented' (in Pick 2011: 108). Likewise, Clare Palmer identifies a number of issues concerned with a strict human/nature dualism, the key point relevant to this chapter being that 'wildness forms part of a spectrum of relations, not one side of a dualism; animals can be more or less wild and more or less wild in different ways. In this sense there is no sharp, dualistic dichotomy between what is wild and what is not' (2010: 116).

Nonetheless, the positioning of Dumbo as a 'freak', and the exploitation of his extraordinary physical capacity by the circus and amusement park, initially accentuates a human/animal gap. Peta Tait describes how the freak sideshow, normally associated with abnormality and physical distinction, converged with the extraordinary and athletically superior bodies of the circus to produce a 'chimeric circus body' (2005: 138), a term appropriate to the diverse forms of Burton's film. As she explains,

> Perhaps it is not surprising that an idea of freakish appearance and strangeness contained within the late nineteenth-century freakshow became absorbed into imagined representation as one amorphous circus that collapsed together very different acts and bodies. Furthermore, as twentieth-century ideals of superior physical prowess became the prerogative of competitive sports, abnormality was allocated to the circus. (Tait 2005: 138)

Like the circus and the zoo, the freak show entails a fascinated and marginalising gaze, but rather than observing a performing or caged animal, the freak show usually involves human bodily anomaly. Traditionally, it is associated with humans having 'congenital abnormalities and progressive or hereditary conditions [that] yielded imaginative hybrids of the human and animal

[. . .]: the Turtle Boy, the Mule-Faced Woman, Serpentina, the Camel Girl [. . .] whose forms appeared to transgress rigid social boundaries' (Garland Thomson 1996: 5). Therefore, if Berger suggests that zoos and circuses enforce the human/animal divide and engender the animal subservient to the human, then the 'freak' human, in blurring the boundary between human and animal, complicates this division such that the human 'freak' too falls into a category of being gazed upon. *Dumbo*, on one level, articulates a reflexive position in that, as spectators of anomalous bodies at the cinema, we too participate in the power relationship extant in the zoo, circus and sideshow. Arguably, however, on another level, the spectator is not only invited to empathise and identify with Dumbo, and all other anomalous and disempowered bodies in the film, but is also encouraged to critically assess the corporate structures (zoos/circuses/Disney) that mediate such spectacles.

DISNEY AND THE HUMAN/ANIMAL DIVIDE

In assessing human/animal difference, Paul Wells proposes a conceptual tool that he terms 'bestial ambivalence' to address such oscillations in representation. This tool encompasses the various aforementioned binaries in that it accommodates

> a raft of polar extremes: the irreconcilable difference of animals and its opposite, the sociocultural assimilation of animals; D. H. Lawrence's view of the distance between humankind and its animal ancestors – 'the other dimension' – and its antithesis, Eisenstein's 'totemic' relationships; the 'wild systems' of the natural world and their appropriation with anthropomorphized human structures; and ultimately Nature itself and its supposed opposite, Culture [capitals in original]. (Wells 2009: 51)

Wells's framework entails three descriptors for animals: the pure animal, the aspirational human and the hybrid humanimal. The term 'pure animal' applies when the animal character 'is represented only through known animal traits and behaviors' (Wells 2009: 51); in the aspirational human context, the character 'demonstrate[s] favorable human qualities and heroic motifs' (Wells 2009: 52); and the hybrid humanimal 'operates at the metaphoric and symbolic level, and seeks to show when a conceptual idea is shared by the parallel terms that have evolved to define and explain both the human and animal world' (Wells 2009: 52). This framework, which is primarily concerned with discerning the degree to which an animal on screen is anthropomorphised, is therefore of relevance here.

DUMBO (1941) AND THE HUMAN/ANIMAL DIVIDE

If Sharpsteen's film freeze-frames an ideological moment in its verbal reference to freaks (the freak show being at its height between 1840 and 1940), so too do its stereotypical depictions position the animal as other. The first of such scenes arises early on after Dumbo has been united (albeit somewhat tardily) with his mother, Mrs Jumbo. Dumbo is 'delivered' by a stork, who gets lost *en route* and habitually rests on clouds to map-read, the heavyweight infant Dumbo constantly sinking through the clouds. Herein lies the first negative connotation attached to the elephant. Shortly after delivery, and upon revelation of his outsize ears, one of four haughty female elephants remarks loudly 'aren't they funny'. Aside from a troupe of clowns who are positioned lower down the circus hierarchy (in both films), here indicated by their broad New Jersey accents, social class is stereotyped via the four elephants. They are differentiated from Mrs Jumbo regarding accent and costume in their high-pitched American voices but also in their headdress, each wearing exotic caparisons while Mrs Jumbo sports a mob cap, imbuing her with a homely quality. Thereafter, the elephants are recruited to erect the circus big top. In pouring rain, they heave huge poles and tug on ropes with their trunks, alongside black workers. The cadenced extra-diegetic music and the lack of facial detail in the black roustabouts, together with the way in which they rhythmically work, is highly suggestive of the chain gang and its association with slavery. As Tessa Gorman notes, 'Historically, American chain gangs were instruments with which to terrorize, control and humiliate African Americans [. . .] Its beginnings can be traced to the roots of slavery in this country, as it was adopted in the colonies as a way to control and transport slaves' (1997: 441–3). There is, therefore, some equation between elephants and African American slavery, a notion that is repeatedly enforced throughout the film in the way that Mrs Jumbo and other animals are encased in leg irons and are caged as a means of control. Later in the film, racial difference is again implied in the sequence 'If I Saw an Elephant Fly', during which a murder of crows is clearly signalled as black, having African American accents and using vernacular such as 'brother'. As David Gillotta notes,

> The crows speak an exaggerated African American dialect and spend most of their time hanging around on tree branches (i.e. they are unemployed). Furthermore, the crows' role in the narrative, to help the unracialized and presumably white Dumbo – conforms to a long history of fictional African Americans helping white characters with their problems. (2013: 108)

While this sequence is considered contentious by some, other scholars argue that the crows actually turn out to be sympathetic to Dumbo. For Nicholas

Sammond, they 'are important for understanding why Dumbo's seeming disability, his difference, doesn't lead him into disaffection, depression or rebellion. Besides providing the physical object of the magic feather – a material token of their blackness – the crows also find Dumbo credible' (2011: 159).

RE-ENVISIONING ANIMALS IN *DUMBO* (2019)

Burton undoes these forms of stereotyping, and concurrently addresses the growing adversity to animal cruelty in recognition of increased awareness of animal cognition and consciousness. He achieves this by various techniques: the use of live action; close interaction and parallels between humans and animals, even though the latter here do not speak; adopting the cinematographic point of view of animals; punishing those who are cruel to animals; replacing animals with humans in the circus; and finally, returning Dumbo and his mother to their 'natural habitat' in India (albeit the scene appears to be computer-generated). At the same time, he retains identical motifs to the earlier version, such as a map of Florida viewed from overhead (this is framed from the storks' perspectives in the 1941 version), and similarly opens the film with a circus travelling by train, although the setting for Burton's adaptation is in the immediate post-First World War period. Fundamentally, the use of three-dimensional live action with CGI over two-dimensional animation makes the animals more credible for contemporary audiences. Unlike Sharpsteen's version, the film centres initially on two children, Milly (Nico Parker) and Joe (Finley Hobbins), who await their father's return from the war. The spectator is enabled their point of view as they wait anxiously at the railway station, the train's arrival generating clouds of steam. Through the steam they spot their father, Holt Farrier (Colin Farrell), their point of view shifting to an eyeline match, with close-ups of their faces registering alarm as they notice their father's amputated arm. Bodily difference is therefore foregrounded in the human figure. In fact, the trials of maternal loss experienced by Dumbo are replicated in those of the family, especially the two children whose mother, as previously mentioned, has died. It is this twinning of experience and bodily anomaly between humans and animals that first invites notions of equivalence.

As the children and their father return to their tent at the Medici circus, where Farrier has formerly worked as an equestrian performer, the camera traverses across other different and unusual bodies, including a snake charmer, strongman, juggler and mermaid, resting finally on circus owner Max Medici (Danny DeVito), himself of short stature. The film therefore continues to highlight human aberration. Like the original production, which itself was affected by financial issues,[2] there is mention of 'hard times' and animals are initially viewed by Medici in corporate terms of 'budgets, accounting and inventories'. Indeed, the opening panning sequences reveal a circus that looks rundown, and

Medici informs Farrier that he has sold his horses, thereby preventing Farrier from doing his 'stallion stars' act. Instead, Farrier is given the task of tending the elephants, which he reluctantly accepts, describing the beasts as 'scrawny and mangy'. There is therefore some antipathy regarding animals, who are viewed purely in commercial and monetary terms. Medici also emphasises to the circus folk that they must 'keep the cages locked!', highlighting a culture of creaturely confinement. However, following the spectator's first encounter with Mrs Jumbo, reportedly about to give birth (and the reason that Medici has invested in her), Farrier begins to change his attitude; when cruel trainer Rufus Sorghum (Phil Zimmerman) whips the elephant, Farrier swiftly punches him to the ground.

Unlike Sharpsteen's animated creatures, Mrs Jumbo does not speak but rather, like Dumbo, communicates with her eyes. Whereas Berger suggests that 'always its lack of common language, its silence, guarantees its distance, its exclusion, from and of man' (2009: 6), in this case, this is counteracted by close-ups that regularly focus on her eyes to signal intent and express emotion. In fact, the elephants' eyes are central indicators of their interactive ability and emotional state: a clue to this is given when Medici states that 'I saw something special in her eyes'. Concerned for Mrs Jumbo, Milly rushes towards her, saying 'something's wrong, she doesn't want to go', indicating an empathic understanding of the animal which persists throughout. Significantly, a key aspect of the film is the way that Burton mediates animal/human interaction to illustrate the diminishing of their respective differences. Another character important in this respect is the Indian snake charmer, Pramesh Singh (Roshan Seth), who treats the elephants with care and respect. The reason behind Mrs Jumbo's reluctance to move is soon revealed to be the newly born Dumbo, disguised in a bundle of hay. Like the original, the reveal of his gigantic ears is delayed, with the first sight of the creature being an extreme close-up of his one eye through the straw. When he fully emerges, Medici's reactions are similar to those of the four female elephants of the early film in that he echoes their exclamations of 'freak' with the words 'aberration and travestation'.

Just as Farrier is made to wear a false arm because, as Medici tells him, 'lots of children come to the show' and 'we don't want to scare them', so are Dumbo's ears, in his first public circus appearance, disguised with a baby's bonnet as he is wheeled into the ring in a huge pram. This posing of animals in human costumes amplifies anthropomorphism and, as Baker points out, is unacceptable for some animal rights philosophers. Baker also notes, however, that the 'reverse image, in which humans dress in animal costumes, may seem more problematic [although identifies] this kind of anomalous imagery as sometimes offering valuable opportunities to destabilise anthropocentric readings' (2001: xxxi). As he further comments,

> Disney material offers a potentially fascinating example [of unsettling the cute image] because it exploits both the anthropomorphic (in the animal characters themselves) and the therianthropic (in filling theme parks with people dressed up as those characters). Additionally, it seems to care very little about the distinction between these two classes of representation. (Baker 2001: 226)

The scenario of humans acting as animals becomes significant at two later junctures: when humans dress in animal costumes in the zoo at Nightmare Island, provoking an equivalent fear to the creatures normally housed there; and the replacement of animals with humans in Medici's circus in the film's resolution. Both situations do not occur in the original film and are thus relevant to a claim that Burton's reimagining attempts to resolve the human/animal binary.

It is at this point that Milly and Joe learn that Dumbo can fly, a feat that occurs some seventeen minutes into the film, compared to the original where Dumbo only takes flight in the closing sequence. His ability to fly is only realised when the two children encourage Dumbo to blow a feather (narratively, to blow his ears out of the way) and, through mimicking the children, he takes flight. There is, therefore, clear understanding between the children and Dumbo, who displays cognition and mimicry. In having Dumbo fly early on in the film, Burton thus focuses more on the positive aspects of the extraordinary body, while Rufus's ongoing cruelty is punished when Mrs Jumbo rears up, pulls down the big top and kills him. Notably, the scene includes an extreme close-up of her eye to show her anger and fear. This follows a scene where the crowd laughs at Dumbo when his ears are accidentally revealed. As a result of Rufus's death, Mrs Jumbo is locked away, close-ups focusing on the leg irons that prevent her movement. Here, Burton draws on the earlier film, which has identical close-ups of leg irons and also reflects usual practice in circuses. As Gruen reports, 'elephants used in circuses (and some zoos) are almost constantly chained by both a front and a back leg to prevent escape. These heavy chains often damage the elephants' legs, preventing the elephants from getting the daily exercise they need' (2011: 131). Like the original, the close-ups invite spectator sympathy and once more highlight the distinction between humans and animals as well as drawing attention to animal ethics.

Emotive scenes of Dumbo entwining trunks with his caged mother (who is now labelled as a mad elephant), through a series of shot-reverse-shots and close-ups, also mirror the original film, and when Mrs Jumbo is driven away, the spectator assumes the distressed animal's perspective. In an illustrative act of compassion for animals, Pramesh says to Jumbo, 'Beautiful creature, we'll take care of your son'. While being a key affective moment in the film, and typical of Disney's anthropomorphic strategies, the scene concurrently reflects the fact that 'elephants are highly intelligent, social animals who form close family ties. In the wild, their social structure is matriarchal [and] female elephants maintain lifelong bonds with their family group, and they remember each other, even when separated for years' (Gruen 2011: 130–1).

Providing a further twinning of human and creaturely lives, Milly is subsequently unable to sleep, Dumbo's loss seemingly triggering memories of her own mother, and she goes to find Dumbo, who also appears dejected. A close-up of Dumbo's eye, followed by an eyeline match as he reacts to Milly, reveals humanlike responses to her caring remarks, his responsiveness being signalled through direct eye contact. As Singer notes, 'Although human beings have a more developed cerebral cortex than other animals, this part of the brain is concerned with thinking functions rather than with basic impulses, emotions and feelings. These impulses, emotions and feelings are located in the diencephalon, which is well developed in many other species of animals, especially mammals and birds' (2015: 11).

Because of the chaos caused by the 'bonnet' scene, Dumbo is relegated to the clowns' section. According to Tait, there is a hierarchy of roles in the circus whereby '[i]dentity from the top of the social hierarchy was transferred to bodies physically performing at height in a literal deployment of the symbolic ordering of society' (2005: 34). Likewise, Farrier becomes a clown and, in a further equation between animal and human, both their faces, which are framed in close-up, are identically painted with 'sad' features. Dumbo's performance as a clown now involves him being raised on a platform high into the big top to extinguish a series of fires by expelling water through his trunk. The spectator assumes his point of view as he is elevated and looks downward, and is therefore encouraged to identify with him. However, the act goes awry because an excited monkey accidentally activates the levers that trigger the flames, providing the first example of the binary between technology and nature. Hereafter, close-ups of levers, dials and switches feature prominently. As a result, Dumbo is stranded above the flames without any means to extinguish them. Milly runs up a ladder and passes a feather to him and, as they had rehearsed previously, Dumbo sucks up the feather into his trunk and takes flight. Framed in long shot, he circles the big top before the camera cuts to his point of view just as he sprays some abusive boys with water, this again privileging spectatorial engagement with the elephant.

Medici subsequently promotes the animal's skills to sell-out audiences, which leads businessman V. A. Vandevere (Michael Keaton) to offer him a partnership. The latter's assistant, Neils Skellig (Joseph Gatt), like Rufus, is portrayed as cruel towards animals, this first suggested by the camera's downward tilt from Farrier's point of view to Skellig's grey shoes, which are, it is implied, made of elephant skin. As a result of the partnership with Vandevere, the Medici circus transfers to an expansive, glittering, Las Vegas-type amusement park, 'Dreamland', a reference to the Dreamland amusement park and sideshow of Coney Island (Adams 2001: 212) but also potentially to Disneyland. Ostensibly, Dreamland, presented as a corporate utopia, is dominated by the technological rather than the natural, and is a site where signs of power and control are ubiquitous. It soon becomes apparent that Vandevere is obsessed with money rather than human and animal welfare because, during Dumbo's first public appearance with Colette Marchant (Eva Green), a trapeze artist (and reluctant partner of Vandevere), he removes the safety net (to make the act seem even more daring). Indeed, during a rehearsal prior to the performance, Colette and Dumbo both fall into the safety net and end up sitting adjacent to each other in identical positions; framed in long shot, the parallels between animal and human again are accentuated. The lead-up to Dumbo's flying act involves performers using hoops to create enormous bubbles that spontaneously morph into elephants, reflecting the transformative potential of Sharpsteen's animation, and translating the surreal 'Pink Elephants on Parade' sequence from the original film as integral to the circus act. Dumbo watches entranced, nodding his head in time to the music, signalling his appreciation and falling between Wells's description of the aspirational human and 'humanimal' (Wells 2009: 52). As the pink elephants' act ends and cuts to audience applause, a single spotlight directed onto the ringmaster is reflected in Dumbo's eye, which is framed in extreme close-up, suggesting his mounting trepidation. Moreover, the full-frame reflection of the ringmaster addressing the audience means that the spectator literally views him through Dumbo's eyes. As the platform elevates, we again look down from Dumbo's perspective and are thus made to experience the same anxiety that he does. Although the act does not go as planned, causing Dumbo to cry out loud, he does indeed fly but, upon hearing the anguished response of his mother, he escapes the circus ring in search of her, and locates her in a zoo on 'Nightmare Island' within the Dreamland complex. Here, various 'props' are set up, and typically, as Berger notes,

> visibility, space, air have been reduced to tokens. The décor, accepting these elements as tokens, sometimes reproduces them to create pure illusion – as in the case of painted prairies or painted rock pools at the back of the boxes for small animals [. . .]. These added tokens serve two purposes: for the spectator they are like theatre props: for the animal they constitute the bare minimum of an environment in which they can physically exist. (2009: 25)

A menacing pre-recorded voice-over tells the diegetic audience that 'Nightmare Island is home to the most dangerous beasts in the world'. Technology is prominent, with locks and levers everywhere. (It is also evident in the 'Wonders of Science' attraction where Milly watches an animatronix family at work in the kitchen.) In this case, props and lighting are staged to project a sense of horror in line with the 'world's most dangerous beasts', these including low-key, red-toned lighting, artificial swirling mist and dark shadows. Such imagery also reflects the real horror of the chained-up animals, witnessed through close-ups of leg irons and blank staring eyes which summon up Berger's description of the zoo: 'Yet nowhere in a zoo can a stranger encounter the look of an animal. At the most, the animal's gaze flickers and passes on. They look sideways. They look blindly beyond. They scan mechanically. They have been immunized to encounter, because nothing can any more occupy a central place in their attention' (2009: 28). Indeed, the scene epitomises the marginalisation of zoo creatures, with Vandevere and Skellig planning to kill Mrs Jumbo (narratively, to prevent Dumbo being distracted by her cries), information that is relayed back to Farrier and the Medici troupe by Vandevere's chauffeur.

Once more, Pramesh, the Indian snake charmer, comforts Dumbo, who appears to fully comprehend what is being said. In response, Farrier comments, 'Dreamland doesn't deserve him', to which Colette adds 'No circus does', and in a bid to free Dumbo and his mother, Medici's troupe, who have now been fired by Vandevere, formulate a plan. Miss Atlantis, the Mermaid (Sharon Rooney), lures the guards into the zoo compound and then knocks them into the water. The troupe activate all the various levers to shut down lights, trigger fake mist and open cages. It transpires here that some of the 'world's most dangerous beasts' are actually humans dressed up as animals, a fabrication by Burton which not only 'destabilizes anthropocentric readings' (Baker 2001: xxxi) but also arguably critically comments on the Disney ethos and human responses to it. As Eco remarks,

> When there is a fake [. . .] it is not so much because it wouldn't be possible to have the real equivalent but because the public is meant to admire the perfection of the fake and its obedience to the program. In this sense Disneyland [and Disney] not only produces illusion, but – in confessing it – stimulates the desire for it: A real crocodile can be found in the zoo, and as a rule, is dozing or hiding, but Disneyland tells us that faked nature corresponds much more to our daydream demands. (1986: 44)

For a second time, Dumbo and Colette escape during their performance but this time alight on the Dreamland control tower, where Dumbo knowledgeably operates levers and switches to deactivate the theme park. The film now differs significantly from the original, as technological failure triggers chaos, leading Vandevere to rampage through the control tower. Various attractions ignite, and the robotic family that Milly had watched earlier now jerks randomly. As the control centre burns down, Vandevere shouts 'What's happened to my power?', suggesting a loss of control as well as a lack of mains energy, while Dumbo contrastingly gains subjectivity and agency. In order to rescue Milly and Joe, who are trapped in the burning complex, Dumbo glides in but then loses his feather, which he believes he must have in order to fly. Milly, in another example of their parallel lives, throws away the key that belonged to her mother (which gives her confidence) and tells Dumbo, 'Have faith in yourself' (rather than believing it is the feather that enables him to fly), which is one of the key messages of the film. In an analogous action, Farrier discards the fake arm, which proved useless anyway, and releases all the horses in a further example of animal welfare. A final mirroring of human/animal narratives unfolds as Dumbo and his mother return to India, along with Pramesh, who says to the two elephants, 'Let's go home' (suggesting they are a family). A point-of-view shot from Dumbo's perspective as he looks back at the children, Farrier and Colette likewise frames a newly formed family unit. The film closes with a sequence that pans across Medici's newly envisioned circus to feature a human flying elephant as he announces, in direct address to camera, 'No wild animals shall be held in captivity'. In contrast to its initial rundown appearance at the start of the film, the circus is now freshly painted and appears more prosperous. The closing sequence entails a rising crane shot that then tilts up and pans from the circus across the blue sky before descending to a natural setting, presumably India, to frame Dumbo and his mother looking out over a herd of elephants who respond to Dumbo as he flies past them.

CONCLUSION

If Sharpsteen's animated film suggests to the spectator that elephants have feelings, then Burton's live-action version, following Singer's four-stage evolution in its awareness of animal cognition and consciousness, progresses this notion for contemporary audiences. It achieves this by first highlighting human/animal difference and then closing the divide, persistently presenting Dumbo in Wells's categories of aspirational human and humanimal through point-of-view shots, close-ups of his eyes with direct eye contact, and expressions of understanding and tacit communication between humans and animals. In addition, it punishes animal cruelty, substitutes humans for animals in certain scenes and, finally, returns Dumbo and his mother to their natural habitat. In a related vein, Burton critiques Disney as a corporate institution and prescriptive force. One might perceive this in gendered terms, given that the characters associated with technology are power-obsessed men and those concerned with the preservation of nature and the natural world are coded as either 'other' or are female. One exception is Milly, who traverses these two poles as a scientist with a conscience. In a sense, therefore, gendered and racial elements persist, although in entirely different ways to the original film: Milly, Colette and Dumbo have a three-way mutual understanding, while Pramesh empathises closely with the elephants' plight. Even though Baker contends that 'Neither Disneyland nor the zoo will satisfy the demand for a morally or politically correct image of animals, an image of *animals as they should be seen*, of animals running free in our imaginary mythical wild [italics in original]' (2001: 194), one might suggest that Burton's version of *Dumbo* presents a more positive representation of animals, albeit he achieves this through the capacity of CGI and via the financial support of Disney.

NOTES

1. *Dumbo* was the most successful Disney production of the 1940s, grossing $1.3 million worldwide.
2. *Dumbo* premiered on 23 October 1941 and was released following the financial losses of *Fantasia* (1940) and *Pinocchio* (1940) due to the Second World War. It was made on a tight budget but, as Michael Barrier notes, 'The Disney people turned the shortage of both time and money to their advantage, so that *Dumbo* moves with a lightness and a quickness' (2003: 311).

PART THREE

CORPOREAL BODIES

10. ALL OF US CANNIBALS: EATING BODIES IN *CHARLIE AND THE CHOCOLATE FACTORY* AND *SWEENEY TODD: THE DEMON BARBER OF FLEET STREET*

Elsa Colombani

Why are you here?
So you can eat me.
The town decided to send a human sacrifice and I volunteered.
My arms are a little stringy but there's some good eatin' in my legs.
I mean I'd be tempted to eat them myself!
Big Fish

'Man devouring man' – such is the starting point of the devilish story of *Sweeney Todd* (2007), Tim Burton's adaptation of Stephen Sondheim's 1979 musical. While the demon barber of Fleet Street slashes the throats of his customers, Mrs Lovett (Helena Bonham Carter) uses their flesh to fill her pies, once known as the 'worst' in London, and which have now turned her bake-shop into one of the city's most coveted eateries. After Sweeney Todd (Johnny Depp) impulsively murders the barber, Adolfo Pirelli (Sacha Baron Cohen), Mrs Lovett comes up with the cannibalistic solution which conveniently provides the duo with a discreet way to dispose of the corpse's 'nice, plump frame' while uplifting her business in the process. As Jennifer Brown remarks, 'the conjunction of cannibalism with consumerism runs deep in the story of *Sweeney Todd*' (2013: 165), but if cannibalism allows Mrs Lovett to increase her capital, it provides Todd with an organised revenge from the injustice he suffered decades before when, then known as Benjamin Barker, he was sent to prison by the corrupt Judge Turpin (Alan Rickman), who wanted Barker's marital bliss for his own. Upon returning to London, Barker discovers that his family has been taken from him: he believes his wife to be dead and learns that his tormentor has been raising his daughter. Barker's life thus annihilated, he prepares his vengeance under the name of Sweeney Todd. The city he returns to looks as perverted as Turpin's morals. It is a dark and dirty place, in his words, 'a great black pit' filled with 'the vermin of the world'. London seen through his eyes is a rotten city, riddled with injustice (the child sentenced to death), poverty (the beggar woman) and abuse (the young Toby). Burton inherits this conception of society embodied by societal clusters – cities, suburbs, towns – from Urban Gothic, in which 'images of devouring, swallowing, drowning, and engulfing result in a sense of a cannibalistic city inhabited either by cannibals or the cannibalized' (Brown 2013: 154–5). His vampire-like cities, which draw his characters in before spitting them out, recall Karl Marx's frequent use of vampire imagery to personify the capitalist as 'a parasitic creature with cannibalistic appetites' (Piatti-Farnell 2010: 11).

Two years before *Sweeney Todd*, Burton had already taken a jab at capitalism and mass consumerism in his adaptation of *Charlie and the Chocolate Factory* (2005). In fact, as Lorna Piatti-Farnell remarks, the author Roald Dahl himself frequently used in his body of work 'metaphors of cannibalism to draw attention to consumerist tendencies and greedy commodity consumption' (2010: 2). Burton expands on these metaphors drastically in his version of *Charlie*, where the mechanisation and dehumanisation of society are directly to blame for the Bucket family's poverty. Charlie's father (Noah Taylor), for example, dismissed from the toothpaste factory he worked for, is replaced by a more productive machine. Beforehand, Grandpa Joe (David Kelly) had lost his position at Willy Wonka's factory when envious chocolatiers bribed some employees into selling Wonka's secrets, causing the latter to fire his entire workforce. Both interpreted by Johnny Depp, the characters of Willy Wonka and Sweeney Todd have much in common. Mainly, they each put into practice the Hobbesian notion that man is a wolf to man.[1] For his part, Wonka lures five children into his chocolate factory, promising them a special prize but only one winner, while setting traps along the way to punish the naughty ones. 'The plot of *Charlie*', summarises Greg Littmann, 'is one of the most familiar set-ups in horror films' (2014: 178). Meanwhile, horror is truly unleashed in *Sweeney Todd* when the barber uses his razor skills to assassinate his clients, as he embarks on a mission to exterminate Londoners. 'In all of the whole human race [. . .] there are two kinds of men and only two. There's the one staying put in his proper place and one with his foot in the other one's face. [. . .] We all to deserve die', he unmercifully sings.

This chapter aims to explore the similarities and evolutions from the metaphorical cannibalism of *Charlie and the Chocolate Factory* to the literal anthropophagy of *Sweeney Todd*. It examines how Burton stages the cannibalisation of bodies in both films through a similar movement from the macro to the micro: from the disappearance of the individual body into the mass of consumerist society, to its reappearance through the body pieces of the cannibalised as well as that of the cannibal.

Consumerism and Cannibalism: The Body of the Masses

When Sweeney Todd returns to London on a foggy night, the scene bears strong echoes of F. W. Murnau's *Nosferatu* (1922) and its vampire disembarking at Wisborg with hordes of rats to spread the plague. Todd refers to the city as a 'hole', sarcastically singing how there is indeed 'no place like London'. As the boat approaches the waterfront, torches can be seen on land, as if set ablaze, and they give the impression that Todd is, in fact, entering hell. The monochromic palette chosen by Burton and cinematographer Dariusz Wolski amplifies the ghoulish, almost lethal, atmosphere. This cut-throat feeling exudes from the dark, empty streets, summoning the terror of Jack the Ripper. Anthony's (Jamie Campbell Bower) woes testify as well to the perils looming on every corner when he is invited into Turpin's house only to be beaten up. A gloomy desert at night, London by day appears equally bleak and almost sunless. Its density, however, is much greater as passers-by crowd the streets. Throughout the film, the locations which Burton shows as crowded are systematically linked to food and consumption. One telling example is the scene at St Dunstan's market: starting with a panoramic viewpoint that moves from a low-angle to a high angle-shot, the director emphasises the density of London life, with shoppers rushing to the market. As Mrs Lovett and Todd make their way through the crowd, food-stands displaying potatoes, apples and cabbage (a testament to the poverty of the majority of the city's population[2]) are plainly noticeable. During the exchange between Beadle Bamford (Timothy Spall) and Todd that occurs after the contest with Pirelli, the backdrop changes to more 'meaty' colours which invoke the paintings of Francis Bacon,[3] as the characters stand in front of a butcher stall displaying a great range of pig carcasses. The scenery both foreshadows Todd's plans for the Beadle as well as underlines the carnivorous appetites that stir the population. If the serial killer prowls at night, the meat-eaters satiate their hunger during the day. But night and day reunite in Burton's film when Mrs Lovett's pie shop begins to thrive, crowding Fleet Street from dawn to dusk. If the fact that they are feasting on human meat remains unbeknown to the Londoners who flock to the shop, the viewer is a witness to Todd and Lovett's enterprise. Darkness has fallen both literally and metaphorically, as Burton operates a backward tracking shot for the spectator to better contemplate the masses sitting at their table and eating pies voraciously, their gregarious behaviour and gathering giving them the shape of one single body.

In *Charlie and the Chocolate Factory*, the crowd looks similarly indivisible.

During the sequence that follows the announcement of Willy Wonka's golden tickets, Burton takes us around the world and reveals the unvarying reactions, no matter how different the cultures. In Tokyo, teens and children amass in front of a candy store, anxiously waiting for it to open. Burton's *mise-en-scène* creates a feeling of anxiety with a tracking shot on the gathered shoppers followed by a tracking counter-shot on the saleswoman, standing alone like prey dreading the inevitability of the attack. The behaviour of the mob is repeated from Japan to Morocco and New York. Despite the change of colours and scenery, the crowds all rush to obtain the coveted Wonka bars, yet as plentiful as Andy Warhol's Campbell soup cans.[4] In *The Consumer Society: Myths and Structures*, Jean Baudrillard analyses consumerist behaviour in urban environments:

> The quantitative intake of food is limited, the digestive system is limited, but the cultural system of food is, for its part, indefinite. [. . .] in a society of industrial and urban concentration such as our own, where people are crowded together at much greater levels of density, the demand for differentiation grows even more quickly than material productivity. When the whole social world becomes urbanized, when communication becomes total, 'needs' grow exponentially – not from the growth of *appetite*, but from *competition* [italics in original]. (1998: 64–5)

Competition is precisely what Burton is targeting with these images of shoppers grabbing Wonka bars by the dozen. The consumers' frenzy is not the result of a sudden craving for chocolate, but the outcome of a contest: whoever finds the precious golden ticket will be distinguished from others, separated from the masses and identified as a winner. The St Dunstan's market sequence in *Sweeney Todd* is also where Todd and Pirelli compete for the title of the most dexterous barber. As for the busy Mrs Lovett, she boasts about the 'family secret' that makes her pies so much tastier than the others while serving her clientele. In a related way, Baudrillard writes:

> The strategic value of advertising – and also its trick – is precisely this: that it targets everyone *in their relation to others*, in their hankerings after reified social prestige. It is never addressed to a lone individual, but is aimed at human beings in their differential relations and, even when it seems to tap into their 'deep' motivations, it always does so in *spectacular* fashion. That is to say, it always calls in their friends and relations, the group, and society, all hierarchically ordered within the process of reading and interpretation, the process of 'setting-off' or 'showing-off' [*faire-valoir*] which it sets in train [italics in original]. (1998: 64)

Wonka's announcement consists more of an advertisement, an effective one at that, which triggers a massive shopping craze. Its emphatic address to the 'Dear people of the world' is not random and achieves precisely what Baudrillard formulates as 'everyone *in their relation to others* [italics in original]' (1998: 64). Burton makes it clear that Wonka's purpose is to tap into the general thriving of rivalry: to achieve more than the rest, to gain what the other has lost. Out of the five children that find a golden ticket, only one does not advertise his success. While the other four children are guilty of the same behaviour, Charlie Bucket (Freddie Highmore) is singled out because he moves against the flow. His individuality and status as the hero of the story are defined by his lack of distinctiveness. When the other children each hold a press conference (though it remains unknown if the media were sought after by the hungry-for-attention families or if they came on their own initiative) and smile at the cameras, 'showing-off' as Baudrillard writes, Charlie remains anonymous, 'happy to just be here' as Wonka will say upon meeting him. For Charlie, chocolate is not a prize to be won nor should candy be consumed thoughtlessly. Food is to the Bucket family a necessity.

'Charlie is an allegory: he is the only pure one', says Burton, while the other children are 'perverted'[5] (De Baecque 2005: 175). Indeed, in *Charlie*, the director associates the four corrupted children with images of devouring and destruction. In his first appearance, Augustus Gloop (Philip Wiegratz), chocolate all over his mouth, reveals his gluttony by biting and chewing on his golden ticket. Veruca Salt (Julia Winter) immediately appears as a spoiled brat whose extravagant demands are invariably fulfilled. Violet Beauregard (AnnaSophia Robb) is a karate kid who wants nothing more but to crush her competitors and finds her glory in chewing gum indefinitely. As for Mike Teevee (Jordan Fry), the chocolate-hater, he plays violent video games all day long, screaming at the virtual characters on his screen to 'die'. On arrival in Wonka's Eden-like garden, Charlie marvels at his surroundings while Mike immediately kicks a jello-filled pumpkin, bursting it open. The Eve-like image of Violet snatching an apple from a tree and biting it ferociously eloquently speaks to the perversion that has already taken hold (Figure 10.1). And yet, Wonka – and Burton – provide the visitors with a thinly veiled warning before unleashing them into the factory. 'Everything in this room is eatable, even I am eatable. But that is called cannibalism, my dear children, and is in fact frowned upon in most societies', says a weirdly smiling Wonka, who does not clarify where the practice stands under his rule. The line directly echoes Burton's short-film adaptation of the fairy tale *Hansel and Gretel* (1983), where the cannibal witch tempts the children into eating in order to fatten them up: 'Haven't you noticed yet? Almost everything in this house is edible'. If Wonka's factory is a trap akin to the witch's, the four children it aims to swallow up turn out to be cannibals themselves, ready to crush their adversaries in order to win.

Figure 10.1   Violet, *Charlie and the Chocolate Factory*, 2005.

As Francis B. Nyamnjoh remarks: 'As individuals and collectivities, many of us have somehow fallen prey to the idea that we succeed best (or delude ourselves that we are successful) when we literally, symbolically, metaphorically or indirectly eat up rivals and enemies' (2018: 5). The 'fat, fat, fat' Augustus flaunts his chocolate bar at a starving Charlie while Violet and Veruca strike a pledge of eternal friendship, their eyes burning with a heinous ambition. In the miniature society they represent, they abide by the 'eat or be eaten' playbook[6] that Sweeney Todd brutally unmasks when he declares, 'we all deserve to die' or, as Claude Lévi-Strauss would famously put it: 'We are all cannibals' (2016).

CANNIBALISING THE BODY: MECHANICS OF THE FOOD CHAIN

In the song 'Epiphany', Todd asserts his new identity as an 'eater' thirsty for blood – 'I want you bleeders' – and carnage – 'Not one man, no, nor ten men. Nor a hundred can assuage me'. In fact, blood seems to be Todd's only nutrient. His aversion to the food and drink Mrs Lovett serves him upon their first meeting testifies to his distaste for life itself. Moreover, his deathly pale face and the shadow under his eyes confer him an un-dead complexion. In characterising Todd, Burton multiplies references to vampirism: from the allusion to Murnau's *Nosferatu* at the beginning of the film to the fact that Todd chooses to slit throats, a favourite spot for the vampire's bite. When Todd impatiently waits for the Beadle's visit, Burton lingers on the barber's reflection in a broken mirror. If mirrors, by failing to reflect their image, reveal the vampire's true nature, the reflection of Todd's face lays bare his broken self. Burton also inserts a reference to Francis Ford Coppola's *Dracula* (1992) in the scene where Todd contemplates an old photograph of his bride and infant daughter. Caressing the image with his freshly bloodied hand, he leaves a trace of blood on the glass. The shot foreshadows the fact that Todd will in fact murder his own wife. Similarly, Count Dracula (Gary Oldman) seals Mina Murray's (Winona Ryder) destiny when he discovers her portrait among Jonathan Harker's (Keanu Reeves) belongings and spills ink on the photograph, Coppola filming in close-up the ink circling Mina's face like a pool of blood.

Like the vampire, Todd wishes to sow death: 'the lives of the wicked should be made brief', he sings. During the 'Epiphany' sequence, Burton illustrates the barber's extermination plan and immerses the viewer into Todd's mental projection. Amid the medium and close shots that predominantly frame the character, a reverse tracking shot with a high-angle set-up particularly stands out: visualising his devilish plan, Todd is shown moving backwards, then standing still in the middle of a crowded London street, his hands raised in the air and holding razors. Whereas his body is facing the camera, the multiple dwellers around him keep walking, in profile, failing to see the threat. Thus singled out, Todd's thin body appears like a razor slicing the crowd open. Johnny Depp's movements stress this fusion between body and blade throughout the song as the actor makes his gestures sharp and erect. In *Sweeney Todd*, the cannibal's body must be mechanised to be efficient. The 'A Little Priest' sequence – in which Todd and Lovett conceive their cannibalistic plan – is eloquent in this respect as it seals 'the marriage of violence and domesticity' (Jenkins 2014). As they converse on the taste of the flesh of Londoners, dividing them into social categories (such as priests, vicars, poets and lawyers), Todd and Lovett take hold of instruments – respectively a meat cleaver and a rolling pin – which will become their weapons. As Jennifer L. Jenkins remarks, 'Consumption defines the city in the Sweeney narrative, represented by a series of machines: the commodity producing factories [. . .]; the corpse-producing barber chair; and the meat grinder. All are machines of ingestion and degustation' (2014).

From the pie shop to the barbershop, the entire house materialises the devilish food chain the duo sets in motion and mimics the digestive system, something that Burton had already done in *Charlie and the Chocolate Factory*, as will be examined later. The attic becomes the devouring mouth, the butchery where Todd slaughters fresh meat. Then, sending the bodies through a trapdoor down to the cellar located in the city's sewers, the food journeys from the mouth to the intestines, where Mrs Lovett collects, chops and grinds it. Thus processed, the meat and its brown colour resemble excrement more than edible food, embodying Todd's statement of a world 'filled with shit'. Hence, as Jérôme Lauté remarks, 'Sweeney voluntarily transforms himself into an exterminating mechanism'[7] (2010: 139). His body akin to an efficient weapon, his barber chair converted into a deathly machine, and the house's well-oiled system in place, Todd proceeds to serialise his murders. During the reprise of the song 'Johanna', Todd engages in a bloodbath while reminiscing about his lost daughter, mercilessly cutting throats, at times with relish, at others thoughtlessly, almost mechanically, as if he were performing chain work. This image of Todd as a prolific and efficient vampire brings to mind the cannibalistic analogies used by Karl Marx to denounce capitalism, as Elspeth Probyn explains:

> Marx was fond of rather ghoulish turns of phrase, presumably in order to force his readers to feel the presence of capitalism and the possibility of revolution. [. . .] the associations with cannibalism and ingestion serve to render the analysis as well as the experience of consumption 'more intense, more satisfying'. (2000: 92)

Todd and Lovett relish their success as their 'machine[s] literally become[s] productive'[8] (Lauté 2010: 136). Lauté goes on to analyse how the spectre of Nazi death camps[9] comes to haunt the film when the young Toby discovers the meat grinder filled with the chopped body parts of Todd and Lovett's victims: 'at first fascinated by the freshly baked pies, he bites into one, comes upon a human finger, before noticing in the dark a stacking of teeth, a sinister echo to photographs exposing the golden teeth that were extracted from gas chamber victims [author's translation]' (2010: 137). Like Todd's fractured reflection in the broken mirror, the bodies of his victims are cut into pieces. Cannibalism, Lévi-Strauss comments, is 'a political act' of which the 'most brutal form [. . .] consists of killing enemies in order to eat them' (2016: 87).

The black smoke that emanates from Mrs Lovett's bakeshop which, the beggar woman alerts, 'comes from the mouth of hell', is foreshadowed in *Charlie*, in which Wonka's factory, though producing delicious candy, releases similarly ominous fumes. The icy and imposing architecture of the entirely grey building stands in stark contrast with its internal joyful display of colours. The outward aspect of the factory reflects its primary goal: that of an industry meant to produce and sell on a massive scale: 'here is an industrial, automatized, inhuman chain [author's translation]' (Masson 2008: 75).[10] The chocolatier's human workforce represents an additional grey area. 'Imported direct from Loompaland', says Wonka of the Oompa Loompas, whom he remorselessly uses as guinea pigs for his inventions. The fact that they are all interpreted by the same actor, Deep Roy, deepens the cold mechanics of the factory, where the labour force has no individuality but one single face replicated *ad infinitum*. Similarly, the Loompas are deprived of their own voice, conversing with Wonka through gestures and mimicry even though their sermonising songs attest to their speaking ability. The profitability of Wonka's machine, like Todd's, runs on the cannibalisation of bodies. Just like he baited the Oompa Loompas into working for him by promising them cocoa beans instead of wages, Wonka seduces the children into coming into his factory with candy. Wonka sets in motion his plan to punish the voracious children by metaphorically eating them up. In his analysis of the film, Alain Masson describes how the factory becomes a 'gastric representation' (2008: 76). Tubes indeed multiply in the building, functioning as digestive tubes. Augustus is thus trapped in an oesophagus-like pipe, stuck like a problematic nutrient the body refuses to assimilate. Veruca is subjected to the opposite journey and is expelled from the factory through the garbage chute like faeces. Furthermore, the cannibalistic nature of the children's physical punishment is all the more evident when they are identified and/or transformed into food. Augustus leaves the factory covered with chocolate and indulges in self-cannibalism – in a rewriting of the Prometheus myth[11] – condemned as he is to eternally lick his fingers: 'Augustus, please don't eat your fingers' scolds his mother, who remains confounded by her son's retort – 'But I taste so good!' Violet morphs into a blueberry and, after having the juice squeezed out of her, becomes as flexible as the chewing gum she was constantly masticating. Veruca, deemed a bad nut by the factory's squirrels, is consigned to burn in the incinerator with other leftovers but finally emerges covered in food waste. The sequence depicting Mike's chastisement illustrates Wonka's enterprise particularly well. Swallowed by the television set, the boy finds himself trans-ported into various programmes as Wonka flips through the channels. At one point, the shrunken Mike lands in a frying pan, quite aggressively handled by an Oompa Loompa disguised as a chef. After all, has Willy Wonka himself not admitted to having tasted human flesh, when Mike asks him if teleporta-tion works for people? 'Well, why would I want to send a person? They don't taste very good at all'.

Once more, machines enable the cannibal. Behind all the mechanisms that capture the children – 'slowly wheels go round and round, and cogs begin to grind and pound', sing the Oompa Loompas, like a Greek chorus – hide Wonka and his workers, who feign innocence and powerlessness. But Burton leaves no room for doubt as to the chocolatier's real part in the children's misadventures. The Oompa Loompas's songs and choreographies correctly seem 'rather rehearsed' to Veruca's father (James Fox), while Mike adds 'like they knew what was going to happen'. The Loompas are just another cog in the machine, whose musical numbers perfectly fit each child's sin. Burton's first clear indication of Wonka's masterful manipulation happens when Augustus has fallen into the chocolate river. As Mrs Gloop (Franziska Troegner) begs him to save her son's life, Burton shows Wonka in close shot as his eyes look upwards towards the glass pipe normally used to transport the liquid chocolate. The pipe moves forward, and the machine's obedience to its master's gaze is indicated when Wonka, once again in close shot, lowers his eyes towards Augustus. The next shot confirms the intention of the chocolatier as the machine descends towards the drowning boy to suck him up. Later, when the squirrels attack Veruca, he pretends not to find the right key and deliberately opens the gate once the rodents have completed their mission in deeming the girl a bad nut. Johnny Depp intensifies the cruelty of the character through his gaze and knowing smiles as each pun-ishment goes according to plan. As Stéphane Delorme underlines, Wonka himself seems to be mechanised: 'as a good automaton, he gives his organs autonomy: he starts to talk then suddenly stops, as his jaw drops; he smiles constantly, saddled with huge white dentures, while his wide open eyes freeze into the blue marbles of a mechanical doll [author's translation]' (2005: 32). In depicting Wonka's dehumanised machine-like body, Burton focuses on his character's face through numerous close-ups, which display his weird smile and strange teeth, quite logically giving the mouth a key role in the personality of the cannibal chocolatier.

CANNIBALISED BODIES: RE-HUMANISATION AND CLOSE-UPS

In *Charlie*, the main characters are all defined by the use they make of their mouths. Augustus gobbles his food and proves his palate's insensibility when he chews on his golden ticket, unable to differentiate paper from chocolate and caramel. Violet overworks her jaws by relentlessly masticating her chewing gum, while Mike misuses his mouth by his constant screaming and mumbling, as Wonka remarks. As for Veruca, Burton insists on her smile, which is too wide and calculated to be sincere. The mouth is the locus of identity in the film, as Wilbur Wonka will confirm upon recognising his son by examining his bicuspids. If Willy Wonka's dentures highlight his cannibalistic tendencies, they also hold the key to his identity. From dehumanising his characters through the depiction of their machine-like bodies, Burton undertakes a re-humanisation process by focusing on micro elements of their anatomy. This process transpires through a series of flashbacks that reveal Wonka's traumatising childhood. Raised by a dentist-father, little Willy is forbidden to eat candy (even on Halloween) and must wear a monstrous dental brace that encircles his entire head, as if to maintain the child's imagination imprisoned. The image was born out of Burton's own traumatic dental memories: 'It was such a painful, isolating experience, because I had one of the big braces that wrapped around your head. I remember getting them tightened was like somebody turning screws in your head' (in Salisbury 2006: 228). To the torture-like instrument appends the trauma of separation after Wilbur Wonka follows through with his threat of abandoning his son when Willy asserts his dream to become a chocolatier. Burton visually represents the violence of abandonment when Willy returns home to find a giant hole where his house used to stand. The tear in the midst of the block of buildings embodies Willy's psychological maiming, the indelible scar that will continue to haunt him. As an adult, he even proves physically unable to utter the word 'parent'. However, his teeth turn out to be identical to his father's; he has stopped eating candy and wears dentist's gloves to protect his hands. The son has become the punishing father; the cannibalised has become the cannibal. Helena Bassil-Morozow remarks how 'To demonstrate the fragmentation of the self, Burton uses visual metonymy in almost all of his films' (2010: 42). Teeth here define the chocolatier as much as scissor-hands characterise Edward (Johnny Depp), and as razors will later Todd. By exposing Wonka's past wounds, by giving him an empathetic background, Burton provides the ogre with a relatable identity that re-humanises him.

In *Sweeney Todd*, Burton moves from the teeth to the eyes. Before using his razors, Todd kills with his stare, on which Burton and Depp regularly insist in the key scenes that set the rhythm to his transformation into a serial killer. After hypocritically thanking the Beadle for acting as a judge in the barber contest, Todd's gaze follows Bamford's departure, Johnny Depp transforming his stare into a languid caress, which mixes an existential sadness with a pitiless death sentence. The actor's red make-up under his lower eyelids reinforces his enraged glare. In the Pirelli murder sequence, Burton concentrates on Todd's eyes with an extreme close-up shot in the seconds that precede the slaughter: panicked by Pirelli's blackmail, Sweeney acts impulsively and his eyes, which stare into the void before lowering towards the boiling kettle heard whistling offscreen, indicate his thought process. The following shots show him grabbing the kettle and striking Pirelli repeatedly. The horror of the act reflects in Todd's face, his eyes raving mad and his teeth showing: a testament to his murder frenzy. Gilles Deleuze writes that 'the close-up transforms the face into a ghost, and delivers it to ghosts. The face is the vampire'[12] (1983: 141). Todd's face in close-up is both the vampire sucking its victims dry as well as a ghost, the remembrance of the man he once was. Filmed in extreme close-up shots, his eyes come to represent both his inhumanity – the barbaric Sweeney Todd – and his humanness – the wronged and bereaved Benjamin Barker. This is perfectly exemplified at the end of the film when the barber burns Mrs Lovett alive. As he shuts the door of the baking oven, Todd's eyes appear in the rectangular opening to watch her incinerated body: the burning flames reverberate in his black pupils (Figure 10.2). The shot is all the more striking since it both reverses and mirrors the shot in *Sleepy Hollow* (1999) that shows in extreme close-up the lifeless eyes of Ichabod's mother, murdered by her husband in an iron maiden. The frontier is thin between each side of the looking glass as the mirror images expose the similarities between the victim and the executioner. In Todd's eyes, hatred rivals with tragic suffering. By using (extreme) close-up shots, Burton cannibalises

Figure 10.2   *Sweeney Todd: The Demon Barber of Fleet Street*, 2007.

his character's body, chops it apart with his camera, thus mimicking Todd's own actions while also revealing his insufferable torment in order to give him back his intrinsic humanity. 'Pity the meat!' writes Deleuze in his analysis of Francis Bacon's paintings, 'every man who suffers is a piece of meat' (2003: 23).

The similar paths of Willy Wonka and Sweeney Todd, however, do not come to a close in an identical fashion. While Sweeney's nihilistic vision concludes with his death at the hand of Mrs Lovett's adoptive child, Toby, Willy Wonka's purpose was, in the end, constructive.[13] Despite its ominous industrial architecture and its endless production of identical candy bars, the chocolate factory turns out to supply countless new inventions. Each room looks different and has its own purpose, from the 'Hair Cream' to the 'Invention Room' and the 'Nut Room'. Efficiency is humorously twisted: pink-skinned sheep are shorn to make candy floss; Oompa Loompas become mountaineers climbing the 'Fudge Mountain'; and the war room creates fireworks. Furthermore, while Todd refuses the possibility of a familial reconstruction, Wonka, after some hesitation, comes to grips with the idea of having a family. Reconciling with his father, the chocolatier then imports the Bucket house into his factory and the film concludes on their gathering around a plentiful dinner table.[14] Quite fittingly, Burton uses food to represent what ultimately differentiates Wonka from Todd. As Masson analyses, 'the family meal [. . .] offers the most legitimate fulfilment of unity. [. . .] The family appears as indispensable to the democratic ideal'[15] (2008: 77). In the end, the individual reintegrates the group, without losing sight of his values. Food is shared at the Buckets's table as it is in Wonka's factory. While swallowing the capitalist children through the pipes, Wonka offers nourishment to the one child who needs it most and yet does not eat, unless invited to. 'You look like you're starved to death', says Wonka while handing Charlie a chocolate-filled ladle, which the boy hastens to share with his grandfather. Food and family merge in Burton's imagination, which he nourishes with his own childhood memories: 'As a child I always had Italian friends. I didn't consciously do this, but I'd befriended these sweet, wonderful Italian families who'd give me food and take me in' (in McKenna 2005: 167). Inside the family home, food regains its meaning, and candy, no longer the cannibal's bait, regains its nonsensical primary function as Charlie Bucket concludes: 'Candy doesn't have to have a point. That's why it's candy'.

NOTES

1. According to the philosopher Thomas Hobbes, the primitive man is engaged in a perpetual war against others, driven by his animal instinct of self-preservation. From the statement that 'man is a wolf to man', Hobbes builds his theory of *Leviathan* (1651): the establishment of a third party which will ensure mutual respect between men as well as the protection and well-being of individuals, in exchange for man's renunciation of his natural liberty.

2. Early on, meat is established as a luxury product. In the song 'The Worst Pies in London', Mrs Lovett comments on 'the price of meat', which leads some bakers to take drastic measures, such as chasing down and killing the neighbouring cats, and then 'poppin' pussies into pies'. Furthermore, in *Charlie and the Chocolate Factory*, cabbage is synonymous with poverty as it is the only food that the Bucket family can afford at the beginning of the film.

3. Burton previously referenced Francis Bacon in the museum sequence of *Batman* (1989), when the Joker comes across the painter's 1954 *Figure with Meat*. See my analysis, 'Tim Burton's Artists of Death' (2017), in A. Barkman and A. Sanna (eds), *A Critical Companion to Tim Burton*, Lanham, MD: Lexington Books, pp. 47–55.

4. The unending rows of colourful Wonka bars shown in *Charlie* inevitably bring to mind Andy Warhol's 1962 work – a thirty-two-canvas display of Campbell's famous soups placed in rows like in a supermarket – a symbol of American mass consumerism. Burton would later explicitly quote Warhol in *Big Eyes* (2014), in which the director reflects on the value of art and the consumerism that results from its reproduction.

5. My translation.

6. Burton provides a literal example of cannibalism among children in the episode 'The Origin of Stainboy' of his animated series *The World of Stainboy* (2000–1). Abandoned by his parents, Stainboy is placed in an orphanage that welcomes strange children. There he witnesses Brie Boy breaking a little piece of Cracker Girl's head to eat it.

7. My translation.

8. My translation.

9. Burton frequently makes references to the Second World War throughout his oeuvre. The Joker threatening to kill the population of Gotham with toxic gas in *Batman*; the fascist-looking architecture of the city in *Batman Returns* (1992); the annihilation of humankind by Martians in *Mars Attacks!* (1996); the legend of the witch who 'makes soap out of people' in *Big Fish* (2003); Walter Keane's cynical invention of his tragic past in a post-war Europe in *Big Eyes*; the setting of *Miss Peregrine's Home for Peculiar Children* (2016) where monsters threaten to exterminate the peculiars – these are a few examples.

10. The image of the industrial machine is evidently displayed in the beginning credits of both *Charlie and the Chocolate Factory* and *Sweeney Todd*, which depict the machines' intricate but fluid workings of Wonka's factory and Todd's cannibalistic routine. In *Charlie*'s credits, only Wonka's gloved hand makes an appearance at the end of the productive work chain, while in *Sweeney Todd*'s the blood overflow is the only deadly trace of human presence.

11. In Greek mythology, Prometheus is punished for stealing fire from the gods. As he is attached to a rock, an eagle devours his liver. But each night the liver self-regenerates, prompting the predatory bird to renew his feast the next day.

12. My translation.

13. And reproductive as well, since Wonka's secret goal in organising the children's visit was to find an heir, someone who would be able to continue and reproduce his work as a chocolatier after his passing.

14. The importation of the Bucket house into the factory makes the ending of *Charlie* somewhat ambiguous. As revealed in the film's last shot, the snowflakes covering the house's roof are in fact icing sugar and thus artificial. Willy Wonka remains the misanthropic genius that he was, isolated from the outside world, though he now has a new family living on his land and under his control.

15. My translation.

11. 'I MIGHT JUST SPLIT A SEAM': FABRIC AND SOMATIC INTEGRITY IN THE WORK OF TIM BURTON

Cath Davies

Andrew Smith and William Hughes (2014) begin the introduction of their companion to Gothic literature with a quote from *A Christmas Carol* (Dickens 1843). Dickens describes the ghost of Christmas past as a figure without a clearly defined ontological form, a vision of 'dissolving parts [that] fluctuated in its distinctness' (in Smith and Hughes 2014: 1). This is an effective introduction, according to Smith and Hughes, to the Gothic preoccupation with fragmented bodies and psyches. Dickens's account thus provides a useful starting point for this chapter, which investigates Tim Burton's reconfigurations of Gothic discourses on 'dissolving' embodiment. While not addressed by Smith and Hughes, this representation of the ghost is a relevant framework to contemplate the formlessness of corporeality because Dickens frames somatic materiality through its juxtaposition with material decoration, describing how a 'belt sparkled and glittered' (in Smith and Hughes 2014: 1) and remained visible and intact in contrast to the spectral body. Arguably, the material integrity of the belt and its essential textures that attract light heighten the representation of corporeal dissolution while paradoxically assuming a structured form that 'figures' the ghost. It is the relationship between dissolving bodies and materials in Burton's work that forms the focus of this analysis. Smith suggests that Gothic literature 'explores how death shapes the subject's sense of what it means to be a person' (2014: 168). Accordingly, this chapter considers how Burton's characters in *The Nightmare Before Christmas* (1993) and *Corpse Bride* (2005) respond to their unruly embodiment. 'I might just split a seam' centres on the interweaving of surfaces, textures and materiality evident in the aesthetic design of Burton's characters, probing how his figures gain agency through clothing. It interrogates the role that fabric plays in suturing various manifestations of corporeal disintegration, highlighting what garments reveal about subjectivity and somatic integrity as the characters that inhabit Burton's world contemplate their own abject formlessness.

Burton's narratives foreground outsiders and feature characters who experience fractured identities and fragmented psyches (Carver 2013; Salisbury 2006). His work is equally populated with disfigured, often monstrous, bodies as his protagonists seek to orientate their abject forms within the confines of 'civilised' social norms (Carver 2013; Lackner 2013; Pomerance 2013; Salisbury 2006; Spooner 2013; Woods 2002). While Burton's figures navigate their unruliness in the fictional worlds they inhabit, they are also firmly ensconced within a generic tradition, inheriting the destabilised bodies and minds of their literary and cinematic predecessors. Thus emerges the premise that a Gothic sensibility pervades Burton's creative outputs. The inspirational context of Victorian literature and the horror film on the director is already well documented, with many studies outlining meta-textual themes and motifs that locate Burton's work within this tradition (Carver 2013; Salisbury 2006; Weinstock 2013; Woods 2002). This study draws upon discourses of somatic fragmentation typical of Gothic literature and examines how tropes of corporeal disintegration are intertwined with characters' interaction with fabric. Catherine Spooner's (2015) suggestion that Gothic is a 'genre through which bodies and their boundaries and surfaces are foregrounded and explored' (2015: 141) underpins the following investigation, and Gothic discourses thereby provide a conceptual framework to interrogate boundaries and surfaces of the body when interwoven with fabric.

In a literary and cinematic domain characterised by 'ghosts, vampires, rotting corpses' (Steele and Park 2008: 11), Gothic bodies are liminal entities that transcend ontological forms as life and death binaries are eroded. Physical boundaries of the body are diffused in a genre that foregrounds monstrous shape-shifting, hybridity and fluidity. Kelly Hurley's suggestion of Gothic literature's penchant for the 'morphic variability' (1996: 4) of 'abhuman' bodies evokes the visibility of somatic materiality. Her study probes the significance of the 'thingness of matter' (Hurley 1996: 31) that is polarised when bodies lose a recognisably human form. This heightened awareness of corporeal matter is pertinent in an investigation of unruly bodies in Burton's work when probing the role that fabric plays in rematerialising ontological disintegration. Arguably, characters in Burton's fiction negotiate their abject bodies in their relationship with fabric and adornment practices.

Costume in the Gothic often encapsulates themes of repression stereotypically associated with Victorian social restriction. Multiple textile surfaces and excessively adorned decoration and designs symbolically regulate bodies, repeatedly mirroring scenes of spatial confinement (Smith 2015). Frequently, Gothic costumes' embellished layers reveal characters' duplicitous intentions that are gradually exposed as the narrative progresses (Halberstam 1995; Sedgwick 1980; Spooner 2004; Talairach-Vielmas 2014). While Burton draws upon these traditions when fabricating his characters, this study focuses primarily on those whose debt to Gothic discourses lies in matters of dereliction. To sum up, through textual analysis this essay demonstrates the ways that fabric shapes somatic deterioration while signposting unruly bodies. Such a premise is located in Spooner's account of a Gothic sensibility in fashion designer Alexander McQueen's work, highlighting how clothing can depict a 'liminal state of the undead' that 'challenges a coherent and stable self' (2015: 151).

To ascertain the symbiotic connections between fabric and embodiment, between inorganic and organic materiality, 'I might just split a seam' first outlines *The Nightmare Before Christmas* and *Corpse Bride* characters' sartorial negotiations in the face of decomposing flesh. How these figures prioritise adornment practices to shape their deteriorating form will be explored. An alternative relationship with fabric underpins the analysis of Sally (Catherine O'Hara) (*The Nightmare Before Christmas*) and Selina Kyle (Michelle Pfeiffer) (*Batman Returns* 1992), with specific attention to the visibility of seams and stitching as the two characters use tailoring as an empowering act. Finally, the assumed binary between organic decomposing flesh and inorganic fabric will be eroded in a study of the wedding dress in *Corpse Bride*. An analysis of Emily's (Helena Bonham Carter) nuptial attire will consolidate the overarching premise that Burton's work interrogates discourses of containment and dissolution in the relationship between bodies and clothing.

Invisible Seams: Rematerialising Bodies

Within the Gothic novel, Glennis Byron suggests that there is a need to defuse 'agents of dissolution and decline' (2001: 133). Strategies to 'contain' posthumous bodies are evident in Burton's *The Nightmare Before Christmas* and *Corpse Bride* as the characters respond to their fragmented embodiment when death disrupts ontological certainties. In keeping with narratives that explore 'the desire to redefine and fix a "norm"' (Byron 2001: 133), this section considers how the character of Jack Skellington (Chris Sarandon) in *The Nightmare Before Christmas* uses fabric to disavow decomposition, seeking refuge in motifs of sartorial seamlessness to prevent further somatic disruption. Subsequently, the inhabitants of the afterlife in *Corpse Bride,* while suffering the same predicament as Jack, offer a comparison as they utilise adornment practices in more transgressive ways to fashion their skeletal frames.

The protagonist of *The Nightmare Before Christmas*, Jack Skellington, 'the pumpkin king', is a dapper gentleman who undergoes a series of costume changes throughout the film. When first encountered, he is dressed in a two-piece monochrome pinstripe suit comprised of a long-tailed jacket that finishes above the knee with narrow-legged trousers. The ensemble is completed with a matching cravat and black cat figurine brooch. His bespoke-tailored attire (handmade by Halloweentown resident seamstress Sally) draws upon a black-and-white colour palette that directly matches his skin tone and facial features – a white skull-like head with black eye sockets and stitched mouth. The look is befitting the Gothic milieu of Halloweentown, and his excessively long distorted 'uncanny coat-hanger legs' (Lennard 2013: 219) and flailing arms framed by this tightly fitted suit offer a complementary silhouette against the barren trees and twisted branches of the *mise-en-scène*.

Jack's pinstripe suit has been designed with a consistent colour palette and clearly illustrates his desire to appear well dressed at all times. The aesthetic dominates for the spectator, made evident in embellishments like the cravat and brooch that position his sartorial style in the domain of the Victorian dandy, marked by his preoccupation with 'the detail [. . .] the knot on a cravat, the material of a shirt, the buttons on a waistcoat, the buckle on a shoe' (Barthes 2006: 66–7). Jack's look could easily be transposed to the streets of Victorian London, recalling the eponymous hero of Bram Stoker's novel parading his sophisticated threads. The attention to detail in Jack's attire illustrates the importance of exterior appearance, whereby his character is clearly engaged in a process of self-fashioning. His later costume changes perpetuate this notion. When he is in bed, he is clad in beige pyjamas with matching bedcap as worn in bygone eras. On his decision to branch into the domain of Christmas, he instructs Sally to design his new Santa Claus outfit by presenting her with sketches of himself dressed in a refined version of Santa's suit, modified to flatter his elongated body. Indeed, he is aware that he cannot simply borrow the real costume as the original is designed for a portly rotund figure and Jack cannot tolerate ill-fitting clothes. After his bespoke version is constructed, he remains dissatisfied with the ensemble until he completes the outfit with the matching hat. Skellington can only aesthetically inhabit this new incarnation 'inside' if he is coherently matching on the outside. It is not enough for him to behave like Santa, he must look the part. Similarly, well-dressed attire is adopted by Danny DeVito in his role as the Penguin in *Batman Returns*. The Penguin, also known as Oswald Cobblepot, uses dandified ensembles to advertise his integration into civilised society, as sartorial embellishments signal an acceptable standing for him to penetrate the upper echelons of Gotham City. The role that clothing plays in fashioning an identity as a reflection of the inner self recalls schoolboy Vincent Molloy's performance of Gothic protagonists in Burton's first animated project, *Vincent* (1982). His desire to emulate the roles that Vincent Price played in the tormented narratives of Edgar Allan Poe is reflected in his adoption of Price's smoking jackets, cravats, cigarette holders

and facial expressions, all of which enable him to strike a believable transformative pose. Character and newly desired identity are embedded, therefore,
in clothing and props, which permit the Penguin, Vincent and Skellington to
perform convincingly.

If sartorial practices can establish an identity, then clothing signposts
individuality for Jack. He needs to be recognisably Santa and no longer the
pumpkin king. Clothing is integral in expressing his subjectivity because his
post-death skeletal form threatens the self. Such preoccupation with self-
adornment is understandable when fabric shrouds the absence of flesh (his
skeletal body is revealed only by his hands). Clothing literally provides form
and shape to his bones, a function that flesh would normally provide. Without
the natural textures and surfaces of flesh and skin that conceal a skeletal frame
within, Jack is reliant on clothing to perform this absence, fabric offering an
interplay of textures and surfaces that rematerialise his corporeal dissolution.
His command of clothing and overall ensemble decisions is symbolic of his
need not only to differentiate himself from others, to be instantly recognisable
as Jack, but also to exert a coherence that shapes subjective embodiment. Such
sartorial precision makes him appear whole, a complete entity, with clothing
restoring identity in the face of decomposition.

Effectively, fabric thereby performs an embalming procedure. Glenys
Howarth suggests that such a process 'humanise(s) the corpse [because it
provides] a representation of its former self' (2007: 187) and aesthetically
disavows the cadaverous form by diminishing decomposition. A potentially
unruly body is fleetingly quelled, and boundaries are regulated momentarily in
order to preserve recognisability. For Jack, therefore, his posthumous invest-
ment in fabric mitigates a potential loss of 'specificity' that Hurley maintains is
a recurring trope of the abject body of Gothic texts (1996: 113).

In *Corpse Bride*, the inhabitants of the afterlife also enact a process of
self-fashioning as they undergo different stages of physical decomposition.
Depending on how long they have lived in the Land of the Dead, characters
comprise of those whose facial features remain intact, exemplified by Paul the
head waiter, alongside others who parade their rotten flesh and skeletal frames.
In each deathly incarnation, clothing and props are integral to the characters'
spectral formation; for instance, naked skeletons proudly incorporate bowler
hats into their dance numbers. Some skeletons are more modest, covering their
naked bones by wearing jackets and other garments that establish individuality
in the face of an otherwise anonymised skeletal frame. Albert, for example, is
the personification of the Victorian dandy with coiffured moustache, cravat
and velvet dinner jacket. The dead are dressing up to differentiate themselves
from others. This is particularly evident in their foray to the Land of the Living
when their family instantly recognise their previous identities as deceased relatives because of their clothes. Fabric is literally the connective tissue to their

earlier selves. Further, by continuing to indulge in the dressing-up practices that define the Land of the Living, the dead are able to negotiate their relationship to their previous selves and thereby experience death with a reclaiming of embodied-ness; to 'read signs of the self' (Howarth 2007: 187) through embalming processes.

In keeping with *Corpse Bride*'s premise that there is more life in the dead than the living, expressed in the colourful *mise-en-scène* and animated figures, the dead's interaction with heightened adornment styling that asks to be noticed succeeds in constructing the skeleton as a liminal entity. If Jack uses fabric to shape his skeletal frame and restore coherence to somatic dissolution, not all the deceased in *Corpse Bride* subscribe to sartorial consistency. With the exception of the dandified Albert, skeletal bodies are not shrouded by clothing. Instead, they are aesthetically juxtaposed with fabric – the clean shiny surfaces of their bones are on display alongside garments and props.

In contrast, the Victorian Land of the Living is characterised by clothing's role in containing flesh, whereby bodies are regulated by tightly buttoned high collars, shirts and laced corsets. In addition, the Victorian body is erased by fabric, perpetuating the repressed sexuality stereotypical of the era. In the afterlife, however, clothes reveal rather than conceal. The result is a further interplay of textures that suture the skeletal colourless bones with an array of materials, recalling Dickens's ghost of Christmas past with its 'belt that sparkled and glittered' (in Smith and Hughes 2014: 1). The dead are often liberated by not offering sartorial coherence; rather, some revel in their self-fashioned textural inconsistencies in a celebration of liminality made possible by dress.

VISIBLE SEAMS: FABRICATING BODIES

While adopting different approaches to deal with physical decomposition, Jack Skellington and his *Corpse Bride* counterparts use sartorial practices as acts of defiance against the destabilising effects of death. In addition, Burton continues to consider the liberating relationship between fabric and embodiment in *The Nightmare Before Christmas* with reference to Sally, the rag doll responsible for Jack's dandified threads. However, whereas Jack's clothes encapsulate a literal and symbolic seamless coherence, Sally is far less interested in disavowing fragmentation. Instead, she adopts motifs of aesthetic deconstruction in her own attire with no desire to shroud any hint of somatic unruliness.

Sally is the seamstress of Halloweentown, liberated by the presence of a sewing machine in Dr Finkelstein's (William Hickey) castle where she is held captive. Needle and thread are essential props that she is rarely without, and these are hidden in her hair, ready to hand at all times for essential somatic maintenance. When her sewing skills are not being utilised in the bespoke tailoring service offered to Jack Skellington, she is instead reconstructing her own body parts that frequently require suturing. Sally resembles a rag doll; she is a variation on Dr Frankenstein's creation, moulded as a servant by an evil scientist. Her domestic duties involve cooking and cleaning the doctor's castle where she is confined in a tower, thus positioning her in the tradition of 'spatial incarceration and victimization' (Smith 2015: 126) attributed to many female heroines of Gothic fiction.

However, despite the nature of her origins and predicament, Sally overthrows the trappings of her literary antecedents and redefines and reclaims her patchwork assembled body. Her visibly stitched figure suggests an aesthetic fragmentation and a somatic scarring reminiscent of Gothic bodies that 'constantly threatens to unravel, to fail to hold together' (Halberstam 1995: 37). Recalling Dr Frankenstein's creation in Mary Shelley's novel (1818), a lack of corporeal integrity is apparent in the visibility of stitches that connote impending dissolution. Stitches are a reminder of Sally's constructed form; she is 'man-made', and this simultaneously highlights her potential to be physically unmade. Throughout *The Nightmare Before Christmas*, Sally's body routinely comes apart; her limbs fall off, stitches loosen and her physical form is unable to be securely contained. The needle and thread concealed in her hair is a response to the threat of her somatic dissolution. It is an empowering device that allows Sally to restore and subsequently control a remaking procedure and is a defiant act that contests a suggestion of victimisation. The vulnerabilities of an unruly abject body are reclaimed and, in the process, illustrate Sally's subjective awareness of her embodied self. It is also a conscious commitment to making her physical unruliness work in her favour. The body's ability to fall apart motivates her many instances of escaping the confines of the doctor's activity, and the impossibility of a body securely bound is liberated when hers is spatially enclosed. Sally is the conscious agent of her own dissolution when she escapes through narrow railings and flees the Gothic tower of the castle. To achieve this, she simply undoes her stitches and throws her body parts through the prison bars. Her malleable form is the agent of freedom, its ability to fall apart not being restrictive in the slightest: she merely stitches herself back together. This agency serves the narrative when she contributes to Skellington's plan to rescue Santa from the clutches of arch villain Oogie Boogie (Ken Page). Jack and Sally become partners-in-crime as she is enlisted to distract the incarcerator while Skellington releases the hostage. In a ruse worthy of a *film noir* femme fatale, Sally tantalises Oogie Boogie with her erotically charged leg, suggestively beckoning him away from Santa and towards the promise of devouring the rest of her body. As Oogie seizes her seductive ankle, he is confronted with Sally's command of her fragmented physique and is left frustratedly clutching a disembodied leg.

Sally's acceptance and innovative exploitation of her somatic vulnerability is evident in her clothing. While Jack uses well-dressed attire to shape and define his inner self, to provide a coherent unified appearance in the face of dissolution, Sally does the opposite. She uses fabric to make visible and directly correlate with her physical fragmentation. There is no concealment of an unruly form and, just as her body is defined by scars and assembled sections, so too her dress is comprised of mismatched fabric remnants disrupted by crass stitching. Considering her sewing skills applied meticulously to Jack's wardrobe, the amateur tailoring of her own clothing can arguably be construed as a deliberate gesture that celebrates her composite identity.

Burton himself identifies the creative correlation between Sally and Selina Kyle/Catwoman in the earlier *Batman Returns*, as one of 'being stitched together and constantly trying to pull yourself together' (in Salisbury 1995: 123). They are agents of their own self-fashioning evident in both being experts with a needle and thread. When Selina is thrown to her death, feral cats gnaw at her flesh in a vampiric fashion and resurrect her in a scene reminiscent of Shelley's *Frankenstein*. The transition into a new identity is illustrated in the construction of a new exterior layer that correlates with her interior self. The fact that a feline demeanour is constructed from a black PVC coat lurking in a predominantly pastel-coloured wardrobe suggests that this darker side has always been present within Kyle's psyche. According to Dominic Lennard (2013), her creative 'artistry' with a needle and thread facilitates an ironic statement on her previous entrapment within patriarchal submissive femininity.

Burton devotes an entire scene to signalling her character transformation using the trope of fabricating a new subjectivity through making a costume. While her PVC catsuit follows a standard association with dominant femininity through fetish connotations, it is also a fabric that encapsulates a motif of somatic containment. It is a surface that performs as a second skin in its sealing properties that cling to the flesh and is, significantly, a synthetic fabric that advertises its lack of organic naturalness in aesthetic qualities that reflect light and present a metallic sheen when worn. The catsuit therefore shrouds the fleshy matter of the body, offering an uninterrupted cohesive sealed surface that shields and protects. However, like Sally, Kyle advertises her own garment design in visible stitching that challenges the fabric's associations with containment. If PVC can erode somatic vulnerability in its highly polished hardened shell-like qualities that armour the body, Kyle undermines this with the suggestion of disintegration and unruliness through the unpicking of the stitches. The conscious decision to make visible this trope when both Kyle and Sally fabricate their garments themselves illustrates their defiant acceptance of a fragmented subjectivity.

Dissolving Seams: Disintegrating Bodies

Both Sally and Selina Kyle utilise fabric as a catalyst to express fragmentation, using stitching as a strategy for conveying the possibility of corporeal disintegration. Burton offers further insights on fabric and posthumous embodiment in the construction of Emily's wedding dress in *Corpse Bride*. In this example of somatic unruliness, the eponymous heroine's decomposing body triggers textile dissolution. Materials and surfaces of the body correspond as the perceived binaries between organic flesh and inorganic fabric are eroded.

Emily is in the process of decomposing, a feature made evident in a fleshiness that offers a clearly defined female form (breasts and cleavage) but with a skeletal interior emerging. Her right arm is completely intact while her left lacks any flesh. Fabric correlates directly to this asymmetric somatic liminality whereby one sleeve securely shapes the fleshy arm while the one on the left is completely withered, revealing bone. Her wedding dress, recalling that of Dickens's Miss Havisham in *Great Expectations* (1861), is in a state of deterioration; there are tears and discolouration of embellishments around the breasts and the once white garment has begun to mutate into sepia and earthier tones. The motif of decay is substantiated with a headpiece of rotting flowers that punctuate her matted hair.

Like Miss Havisham, Emily's nuptials have been tarnished with tragedy. She is a murder victim unjustly ensnared in the domain of the afterlife. The storyline of *Corpse Bride* juxtaposes characters in the Land of the Living with those of the deceased, with a central conceit of the dead possessing a far more colourful life than the deathly pallor of their living counterparts in a repressed Victorian milieu. In keeping with the film's aesthetic demarcation between these two worlds, Emily's bridal dress is in direct contrast to the wedding garment worn by Victoria (Emily Watson) in the Land of the Living.

Symbolically addressing the Victorian stereotype, the latter's bridal wear regulates her body by completely covering it with motifs of containment evident in the rigidly formed buttons that climb the torso to the strangulating collar. Her long hair is tied neatly in a bun lacking any decorative adornment. The crisp white dress is uniformly smooth without any embellishments or combinations of fabric to provide detail and texture. Victoria's conservative wedding appearance juxtaposes Emily's multifaceted garment with its array of textures achieved through several fabrics, jewellery, tactile flowers and decoration. As her decomposition process is underway, these features interact with the surface of the skin, and the patina of the materials begins to organically mutate and contribute additional textures and colours replicating deteriorating flesh. Paradoxically, the fabric is very much alive in its animated transformative condition. Inorganic matter is metamorphosing, and new forms are emerging from the dress in its withering dissolution. Fabric thereby directly correlates with the materiality of the body in its shape-shifting fluidity. Ironically, Victoria's symmetrical dress is symbolically fixed, static and lacking any dialogue between layers and textures. There is no aesthetic fluidity and therefore, arguably, fabric connotes a lack of substance, character and life. Fabric is especially alive when it moves autonomously, evident in the translucent veil which dances independently of Emily. A sense of somatic freedom of expression corresponds with the spectral hovering of the veil that mirrors her moves. This synergy between textiles and flesh is reiterated in the final scene, when the veil mutates into a whirlwind of moths/butterflies that frames the evaporation of corporeal matter. Her ultimate freedom is expressed as the fabric of her dress is intertwined with the fabric of her flesh, interconnected and permeable. It is this sequence that arguably reiterates the overarching premise of the film: that Emily's decomposing body 'attracts rather than horrifies' (Siegel 2013: 212).

Burton's conception of Gothic literary motifs connoting the spatial confinement of female characters (Smith 2015) is very present within this tale, whereby fabric highlights repression for Victoria and others in the suffocating Victorian milieu of the Land of the Living, recalling Spooner's suggestion of 'an aesthetic of containment' (2004: 3) apparent in Gothic costuming. When Victor experiences an alternative identity after encountering the afterlife, he returns to his bleached-out *mise-en-scène* with his sleeve torn, symbolically unravelling to reveal a less restrictive mindset. Similarly, Emily's deteriorating fabric signifies freedom, not constraint. Burton arguably reconfigures established suggestions that overembellished sartorial practices of characters in Victorian Gothic fiction indicate fakery and deceit (Halberstam 1995; Spooner 2004; Talairach-Vielmas 2014). The 'all surface' trope that signifies duplicity is dissolved in *Corpse Bride*, whereby the multiple textures and surfaces in the design of Emily are celebrated. Somatic formlessness conveyed through fabric provides substance after all.

This symbiotic connection between clothing and posthumous embodiment is heightened in the trope of the wedding dress during the séance sequence in *Beetlejuice* (1988). The Maitlands's untimely death in a car accident is the central plot motivator in this earlier Burton film. Consigned to the fate of ghosts roaming their beloved home, the couple embark on a series of schemes to transgress the afterlife and reinhabit their abode by expelling the current occupants residing there. One such tactic involves Barbara's (Geena Davis) nuptial attire becoming an instrument to enable her resurrection. As the séance begins, the fabric comes to life in anticipation of her arrival and hovers as Barbara's ghostly form gains materiality as it inhabits the dress, thereby giving it shape. The implication is that the body needs the dress to become present in the space and the fabric functions as a vessel to contain and control wayward borders. Naturally, without this ontological framing, the formless fabric hangs listlessly. This scene encapsulates Joanne Entwistle and Elizabeth Wilson's

(2001) assertion that 'dress is a fleshy practice involving the body' (2001: 4). However, while initially a medium for Barbara's somatic re-fabrication, the wedding dress restores the reality of her 'lifelike' physicality and her deathly decomposition is witnessed. On her return to the Land of the Living, dress is unable to embalm her. Instead, it replicates a burial shroud encouraging the natural disintegration of her flesh.

The wedding dress in *Corpse Bride* once again reminds the spectator of how fabric in Burton's work interacts with ontological forms. The other inhabitants of the afterlife in the film consciously celebrate their decomposing bodies by aesthetically advertising these, refusing to shroud their lack of somatic integrity. The correlation between putrefied flesh and deteriorating fabric foregrounds the symbiotic connections between materiality and corporeality, thereby dissolving the binary between inanimate textiles and bodies that wear them (Gill 1998). Burton's film makes visible the organic properties of the fabric in that Emily's dress, which is mutating and changing form and shape, corresponds to the fluidity of her somatic form. Textiles acquire a ruined patina that evolves as it deteriorates, with reconfigured textures emerging as newly formed layers and hues that disrupt the surfaces of the dress and body. There is no inorganic material here as flesh and fabric both respond to being exposed to the elements. In the terrain of the afterlife, animated bodies are adorned in textiles refusing stasis. Fabric's shape-shifting properties emulate decomposition of the flesh. As it decays, fabric is paradoxically full of life because the matter of materiality is the central emphasis.

SPLITTING SEAMS: FABRIC AND SOMATIC INTEGRITY

Oogie Boogie, the dastardly predator of *The Nightmare Before Christmas*, advertises his sadistic pleasures in terrorising others by threatening that he 'might just split a seam'. Rather than a side-splitting endeavour from laughing too much, he acknowledges his own lack of corporeality by, instead, referring to the suturing of fabric. Splitting his seams is of course wholly appropriate for Oogie Boogie. When Jack seizes on a loose thread dangling from his coarse hessian sheath and he unravels, he is literally undone and pulled apart to reveal no somatic entity. In the tradition of H. G. Wells's *The Invisible Man* (1897), Oogie Boogie's identity is entirely constructed by material – fabric does not interact with his body, rather he is all textile. He is therefore the symbolic cornerstone of the argument here: a character whose entire 'being' epitomises a dialogue between textiles and embodiment that hinges on somatic integrity. He is unable to control the cloth that shapes his threatening presence, a reminder that many of Burton's characters consciously rely on fabric for self-fashioning when they are faced with precarious bodies with a tendency to fall apart.

Byron claims that in the Gothic novel 'there is a desire to redefine and re-establish boundaries that the threatening other seems to disrupt' (2001: 133). Death and subsequent decomposition of the body is the ultimate 'threatening other' and the argument presented here suggests that for some of Burton's figures, corporeal vulnerability can be dealt with through textiles and adornment practices. Jeffrey Andrew Weinstock claims that the 'fascination with the fragility of the body' (2013: 14) is at the core of Burton's authorial signature, and such precarious embodiment is at its most evident in the narratives that locate characters within the liminal spaces between life and death. For Skellington particularly, fabric 'redefines' his physical disintegration, resembling an embalming procedure that restores the impression of cohesive contained flesh. Fabric thereby performs the role of taxidermy, disavowing 'the disrupted features of death' (Davies 2010: 14). Akin to the psychology of embalming the corpse (Aries 1994; Howarth 2007), individuality and subjectivity are maintained (for Jack and for the afterlife skeletons in *Corpse Bride*) when death threatens recognisability. Sartorial practices therefore rematerialise embodiment when the seams of the flesh are dissolving.

Not all of Burton's characters respond through recourse to seamlessness. Fabric is a conduit for subjective agency for both Sally and Selina Kyle in the reclaiming of the internal features of a garment and advertising its potential to unravel at any point. If, as Byron claims, the Gothic genre investigates the 'dissolution of the human subject' (2001: 133), then Burton allows Sally and Selina to revel in their fragmentation. Celebrating rather than disavowing somatic unruliness becomes a defiant act. Through interrogating bodies and fabric correlations, it is also apparent that Emily's wedding dress in *Corpse Bride* offers the antithesis of seamlessness. The presumed binary between organic flesh and inorganic textile is dispelled entirely. This example fore-grounds mortality when fabric, just like flesh, decays and assumes a patina that reveals its organic properties in its decomposition. Multiple textures and surfaces reveal captivating blemishes in the act of falling apart. This is Burton's ultimate celebratory nod to the Gothic tradition of fetishising romantic beauty in collapsing structures and forms. The Gothic novel's preoccupation with 'ruination' (Byron 2001; Hurley 1996; Steele and Park 2008) thereby frames the fabric/corporeal interaction in this film.

Hurley highlights that it is within the abject shape-shifting of bodies losing their recognisable forms that we are reminded of material substance, the onto-logical 'matter' of identity. In Burton's work, this is exacerbated by the use of fabric because clothing provides an additional materiality that interacts with the posthumous 'ruination of the human subject' (Hurley 1996: 3). Just as the glistening belt of Dickens's ghost of Christmas past heightens corporeal dissolution, Burton interrogates the ways in which sartorial practices inform our perceptions of the deteriorating body.

Spooner (2013) suggests that Burton's characters often use self-fashioning strategies as defiant statements that advertise their outsider status and desire for nonconformity. While 'I might just split a seam' consolidates Spooner's premise of a transgressive assertion through style for many of Burton's figures, this chapter illustrates that his work also contemplates an erosion of the 'binary relation of clothing and bodies' (Gill 1998: 48) and encourages further contemplation on fabric's role in documenting aesthetic representations of death. When Burton's narratives unravel the traditionally defined borders between life and death (Fowkes 2013), fabric channels discourses on mortality within the visual domain. Recalling the deceased Maitlands's attempts to visibly occupy their home by shrouding their ghostly bodies in a bed sheet in *Beetlejuice*, textiles provide material substance for the recurring liminal bodies in Burton's films and, in the process, fabricate death's presence within the *mise-en-scène*.

12. THE SEMIOTICS OF A BROKEN BODY: TIM BURTON'S USE OF SYNECDOCHE

Helena Bassil-Morozow

Synecdoche permeates every corner of Tim Burton's universe and comes in a variety of forms: as literal physical brokenness when a character is shattered into pieces and has to be rebuilt, and as emotional upset and psychological breakdown; it is also reflected in scars, and is often expressed in the visual or narrative focus on a body part such as eyes or hands. All of these images, and particularly those of the hands and the eyes, inhabiting Burton's metonymic space convey the combination of creativity and inability to be 'normal', and to feel socially acceptable, in a world where the ability to communicate 'properly' equals normality. This essay will examine the ways in which images of hands and eyes have been utilised by Burton in a range of his films, with a particular focus on *Charlie and the Chocolate Factory* (2005), *Sweeney Todd: The Demon Barber of Fleet Street* (2007) and *Big Eyes* (2014). It can be argued that the literal or narrative fragmentation of Burton's characters reflects the intrinsic conflict of modernity – that between individual identity and societal conformity.

Synecdoche has been defined in a number of ways, with the dictionary definition being 'a figure of speech in which a part is made to represent the whole or vice versa' (Anon. 2001). It is closely linked with metonymy, 'a word or expression used as a substitute for something with which it is closely associated' (Anon. 2001). Of the three tropes, synecdoche, metonymy and metaphor, synecdoche emphasises sameness of the two concepts while metonymy is more about borders and mapping (contiguity), and metaphor belongs to the order of similarity (Whitsitt 2013: 23). An example of synecdoche is the substitution of the car for 'wheels', with wheels being a defining part of the vehicle, their presence so essential that they can stand in for the rest of the phenomenon.

In art, metonymy often accompanies the grotesque, and likewise, Burton uses it to represent bodies that are incomplete, in transition: in short, bodies that are different. Broken and transgressive bodies in Burton's narratives are often juxtaposed with conformity and obedience, which his protagonists fail to recognise. Physical brokenness or exaggerated features occurring in characters such as Edward Scissorhands (Johnny Depp), Jack Skellington (Chris Sarandon), Emily as the Corpse Bride (Helena Bonham Carter), Willy Wonka (Johnny Depp), Alice (Mia Wasikowska), Sparky the Dog (Frank Welker) or Margaret Keane's (Amy Adams) big-eyed children reflect the psychological fragmentation that comes with the refusal to subscribe to a collective identity.

Burton draws particular attention to hands and eyes. These features serve as both metaphors and synecdoches in his films. As synecdoches, they point at their owners' struggles to communicate with the outside world. As metaphors, they also represent imperfection and creativity. The director's visual and narrative focus on exaggerated eyes and damaged hands paints a picture of creative children renouncing the realities of modernity in favour of individualistic fantasy and utopian authenticity.

These childlike, unique individuals also do not have a social mask – an artificial front – which would make them more acceptable. In *Tim Burton: The Monster and the Crowd* (Bassil-Morozow 2010) I explored this absence of the social mask by conceptualising the Burtonian protagonist as a child in all its incarnations, including the hero, the monster and the creative artist. The isolated and fragmented Burtonian child suspects that everyone else is simply covering their inner monster with a mask and pretending to be 'normal'.

The individual's unique vision and creativity, which partially originate in an unhappy or strange childhood overshadowed by abandonment, mistreatment or neglect, are out of place in the pastel world of bourgeois existence where appearances matter, and whose inhabitants hide their dark secrets under a superficial front of accepted social behaviour. Burton's anachronistic Gothic-Romantic protagonist lives in the shadow of modernity, simultaneously rejoicing in it and rejecting it, and escaping into fantasy and denial. His fragmentation is closely linked with the subject of industrialisation, with its cities and machines.

BURTON'S USE OF SYNECDOCHE: HANDS AND EYES

In his essay 'Two Aspects of Language and Two Types of Aphasic Disturbances', (reprinted in *Language and Literature*, 1987), Roman Jacobson cites the Russian literary critic Anatolij Kamegulov, (who perished in 1937 in the Stalin repression machine), describing an overuse of synecdoche as a trope in the description of people. Kamegulov draws attention to the semiotically challenging writing style and its disorienting effect on the reader of the Russian nineteenth-century author Gleb Uspensky: 'The reader is crushed by the multiplicity of detail unloaded on him in a limited verbal space, and is physically unable to grasp the whole, so the portrait is often lost' (in Jacobson 1971: 113).

Burton's literalisation of synecdoche, although multimodal rather than linguistic, can be said to be producing a similar effect on the audience. It applies, for instance, to individuals that can be dismantled and reassembled over and over again: heads that exist separately from bodies; eyes that escape or fall out; eyes that look like dark holes and occupy a prominent part of the face; and hands that fall off when shaken. Physical or figurative, the disintegration-reassembly play central to Burton's narrative has been an intrinsic part of his visual aesthetic since his humble beginnings at Disney in the 1980s.

These two images of disintegration and reassembly are typically integrated into larger, load-bearing structures in Burton's narratives such as the motifs of the monster and the assembly line. The use of synecdoche – literal or narrative focus on particular body parts – serves to emphasise the protagonist's fragmentation, his or her feelings of subnormality, an inability to integrate into society, and an incapacity to grow up. The protagonist's eyes and hands are important not only because they stand in for creative originality and misunderstood genius, but also because they signify incompleteness and deviancy in the eyes of society. The protagonist is deficient from the point of view of the bourgeois lifestyle with its mandatory artificial social front.

The image of the monster is closely related to the hands motif. Hands are synonymous with interpersonal communication, with making human connection as well as with being creative. The monster, for Burton, is the one who is simultaneously terrifying and helpless, and wants to touch yet is too scared to reach out. His characters, following in the footsteps of misunderstood cinematic monsters he admired as a child, avoid human contact, either because they have been hurt in the past or are afraid of hurting others. Burton explains his fascination with monster movies in one of his interviews:

> I've always loved monsters and monster movies. I was never terrified of them, I just loved them from as early as I can remember. [. . .] King Kong, Frankenstein, Godzilla, the Creature from the Black Lagoon – they're all pretty much the same, they just have different rubber suits or make-up. [. . .] I felt most monsters were basically misperceived, they usually had much more heartfelt souls than the human characters around them. (in Salisbury 2006: 3)

The human touch, physical or emotional, so natural in everyday communication, in Burton's world becomes the nightmarish vision of an individual unable to connect with others. Throughout James Whale's *Frankenstein* (1931) and *The Bride of Frankenstein* (1935), for instance, Boris Karloff's large hands are often the focus of the shot, gesturing helplessly or chaotically as the creature attempts to grasp the rules of the human world, communicate his intentions or express his frustration. Drawing attention to the hands emphasises the helpless otherness of the creature faced with the mass-made man of modernity whose social mask covers a myriad of imperfections. Similar to Whale, Burton exploits the conflict between the seen and the unseen in the modern individual in *Edward Scissorhands*:

> The idea actually came from a drawing I did a long time ago. It was just an image that I liked. It came subconsciously and was linked to a character who wants to touch but can't, who was both creative and destructive – those sort of contradictions can create a kind of ambivalence. It was very much linked to a feeling. The manifestation of the image made itself apparent and came to the surface probably when I was a teenager, because it is a very teenage feeling. It had to do with relationships. I just felt I couldn't communicate. It was the feeling that your image and how people perceive you are at odds with what is inside you, which is a fairly common feeling. [. . .] So the idea had to do with image and perception. (in Salisbury 2006: 87)

Instead of being relational, the human touch, metaphorically and metonymically represented by the hand, stands for disconnection, for disunity, for lack of communication, for things falling apart. It also feeds neatly into the (anachronistic) dichotomy that runs throughout Burton's entire body of work: its Gothic-Romantic sensibility, with its individualistic stance versus modernity's emphasis on importance of the social group, and on the similarity and the copy. The dichotomy is anachronistic because the Gothic-Romantic references that the director uses are all mediated through twentieth-century horror directors such as James Whale and Roger Corman, and iconic actors like Vincent Price (Salisbury 2006: 16–17). In Burton's own words, 'growing up watching these horror movies, for some reason I was always able to make direct links, emotionally, between that whole Gothic/*Frankenstein*/Edgar Allan Poe thing and growing up in suburbia' (in Salisbury 2006: 32).

Like Karloff's version of the Frankenstein creature, all of Burton's protagonists are wary of making contact with other human beings and, to emphasise this point, they often have hands that reflect this fear or inability: Edward Scissorhands has sharp scissors instead of hands, the Penguin (*Batman Returns* 1992) has flippers, Willy Wonka's hands are permanently gloved, and Benjamin

Barker (Johnny Depp) aka Sweeney Todd regards barber blades as an extension of his hand. The image of the hand is consistently linked to the idea of a broken trust. Each of these characters either fears human beings or hates them, and prefers to isolate himself from society rather than seek human contact.

Another image that dominates Burton's visual aesthetic is the eyes. Although it took the director a few decades to make a film which focuses specifically on the eyes (*Big Eyes*), as a prominent metaphor and synecdoche they have been a frequently used element in his narratives. For instance, large round eyes are one of the central features of his drawing style. Large eyes have been translated into his animated characters literally (*Vincent* [1982], *Corpse Bride* [2005], *The Nightmare Before Christmas* [1993], *Frankenweenie* [2012]), while the characters played by actors render this feature through make-up and special effects. For instance, both Michael Keaton's Beetlejuice and Danny DeVito's Penguin have black shadows around their eyes, which make them look large and round.

With eyes wide open and the hands that cannot touch, Burton's protagonists are unable to perform what the sociologist Erving Goffman calls 'facework' – the ritual presentation of oneself in social situations which represents people's 'willingness to abide by the ground rules of social interaction' (2005: 31) and to 'accept definitional claims made by others present' (1990: 21–2). Eyes are a key part of facework, often signalling an opening move, expressing 'clearance signs', showing 'openness to verbal statements' or, by contrast, controlling others' access by 'averting the gaze' or avoiding others (Goffman 1966: 91–5). Eyes thus work the hardest to maintain a decent impression and to ensure a smooth communication process. It is the eyes that present to the world the semblance of a complete individual and keep an external mask in place.

This is definitely not the case with Burton's protagonists who, not concerned with facework, eyework or other artificial communicative engagements, take the world at face value. These eyes – grotesquely big, made-up, accentuated by zoom, or even separated from the owner – become the definition of child-like naivety. Both hands and eyes also refer to creativity and uniqueness of (imperfect) vision – the very opposite of a suburban bourgeois sameness, bland conformity and compliance.

DISEMBODIED MODERNITY AND THE ASSEMBLY LINE

The image of the assembly line, which makes multiple appearances in Burton's films, evolves throughout his career. In his early films, the assembly line is a source and symbol of unbound creativity and entrepreneurial spirit: the sign of a genius, as in *Pee Wee's Big Adventure* (1985) and *Edward Scissorhands*. As Burton's protagonists mature or, rather, refuse to mature in the world of deceit and artificiality, representations of the assembly line take on a darker tone to express the protagonist's denial and escapism, like in *Charlie and the Chocolate Factory* and *Sweeney Todd: The Demon Barber of Fleet Street*.

Burton's use of the assembly line imagery goes hand in hand with his use of synecdoche as a trope defining degrees of imperfection, and degrees of conflict between external and internal realities. The assembly line's dual nature makes it, on the one hand, a symbol of inventiveness and entrepreneurialism and, on the other, of exploitation, repetition and boredom. In his essay 'The Work of Art in the Age of Mechanical Reproduction' (originally published in 1935), Walter Benjamin famously describes the demise of the original in the age of the copy, with accessibility and decontextualisation working at cross-purposes: 'even the most perfect reproduction of a work of art is lacking in one element: its presence in time and space, its unique existence at the place where it happens to be' (1969: 3). Meanwhile, authenticity and what Benjamin calls 'aura' – the non-reproducible elements of an artefact – 'withers' as the object's 'unique existence' is replaced with 'a plurality of copies' (Benjamin 1969: 4).

The image of the creative artist as the very embodiment of authenticity and 'aura' is central to Burton's narrative universe. Yet, paradoxically, the artist is also the one whose production of artefacts involves using an assembly line which constructs various objects including whole human beings (an obvious reference to the Frankenstein motif). This directly contrasts with Anthony Giddens's description of industrial work as 'the discipline of dull, repetitive labour' (2012b: 8).

In many of Burton's films, including both *Frankenweenie* versions (1984; 2012), *Pee Wee's Big Adventure, Edward Scissorhands* and *Charlie and the Chocolate Factory*, the assembly line stands for imperfection of the creative process: for example, the Abraham Lincoln statue at the end of Pee Wee's breakfast assembly line throws pancakes at the ceiling, the walking robots cutting cookies in *Edward Scissorhands* jump rather clumsily onto the flattened dough (not to mention that Edward is still left without hands at the end of the production process), and the collection of chocolate-making machinery in *Charlie and the Chocolate Factory* looks rather eclectic. The latter was literally a random selection from a scrapyard, as the production designer Alex McDowell testifies:

> Without really knowing what the machines were going to look like, we grabbed piles of junk from the aeronautic industry, old jet engines and things like that. We were picking things out of the piles and assembling the machines, just basically to fit in with the kind of profile of what we wanted them to do. We never really had construction drawings, we only had the vaguest idea of how it would all go together. Really, nobody, including my own team, knew what that set was going to look like until about two weeks before shooting.[1]

Removing perfection from the assembly line, a symbol of the optimistic objectivity of modernity, also means challenging the claim that the bourgeois individual is complete. Or, as Fredric Jameson would declare, 'the individualist subject is dead', along with the idea of personal identity (2009: 6). The individual, Burton implies, is a mess, falling apart, constantly having to reassemble themselves contrary to the myth of suburban happiness. In this sense, he 'agrees' with the critics of modernity such as Giddens, who argues:

> In the reflexive project of the self, the narrative of self-identity is inherently fragile. The task of forging a distinct identity may be able to deliver distinct psychological gains, but it is clearly also a burden. A self-identity has to be created and more or less continually reordered against the backdrop of shifting experiences of day-to-day life and fragmenting tendencies of modern institutions. Moreover, the sustaining of such a narrative directly affects, and in some degree helps construct, the body as well as the self. (2012a: 47)

Burton's images of hands and eyes, separated from their owner, render the conflict of modernity, namely, that of external perfection versus internal rupture, and the self-reflexive narrative with an emphasis on action and agency (Giddens 2012b: 77–9) versus the fragmenting multiplicity of experiences described by Georg Simmel in *The Metropolis and Mental Life* (2004: 51–2). Burton's synecdoche betrays the cracks in the smooth surface of a model individual; it challenges the idea of propriety, normality and perfection. In sum, the Burtonian protagonist does not seem to grasp the concept of a performed self, at least, in the sense society perceives it. Without the social performance which creates an impression of wholeness and seamlessness, his characters foreground their scars and broken-off parts of their bodies and souls. The monster is someone rejected by bourgeois propriety or, as David Punter argues, the Gothic 'questions how we are "clothed" in the human' (1998: 11).

Protecting the Self:
Gloves and Goggles in *Charlie and the Chocolate Factory*

Burton's metaphorical and metonymic use of hands and eyes in *Charlie and the Chocolate Factory* is more subtle than that in *Edward Scissorhands* or *Big Eyes*, both of which have hands and eyes respectively underlying the narrative and reflected in their titles.

Nonetheless, eyes and hands have a prominent visual place in Burton's rendition of Roald Dahl's tale. We see in a flashback that many years ago, after an industrial espionage ruined his trust in people, Wonka shut the door of his factory to outsiders. Now he is offering five lucky children, who find a golden ticket in one of the chocolate bars, a tour of the factory. What they do not know is that lonely Wonka wants to find an heir to his candy empire because he found a grey hair when having his 'bi-annual' haircut.

The image of the hands is woven into the story of Wonka's unhappy childhood: his father (Christopher Lee) is a dentist who makes the child wear giant orthodontic headgear, with the view that it will make his teeth perfectly straight. The child is not allowed to eat chocolate, and any sweets that accidentally end up in the surgeon's house are promptly confiscated and destroyed. Predictably, Willy Wonka rebels by abandoning his father's advice on dental hygiene and becomes a chocolatier. His rejection of the father is inevitably the rejection of everything associated with him, including attitudes and practices. Where the father is guided by regimens and stringent emotional boundaries, Willy Wonka is a colourful character whose creativity has no bounds, and whose bizarre behaviour often borders on sociopathic. As far as personalities go, they cannot be more different.

Yet, father and son also have a lot in common, and this commonality is expressed in the images of hands and eyes. Both wear gloves: surgical in the case of the father, or purple leather for the son. Equally they avoid communication: the father hides behind the cold objectivity of the medical gaze, and the son distances himself from people who may betray him again. Both are loners who invest in their career rather than human contact. Their gloves protect them from the pain that might come with trusting others and being betrayed by them – from the pain that comes with the imperfection of relationships, of being human. According to Giddens, 'trust in the objects [. . .] is based upon a more primitive faith in the reliability and nurturance of human individuals. Trust in others is a psychological need of a persistent and recurrent kind', while the opposite of trust is 'existential angst' (2012: 97–100). Unable to 'opt out of the abstract systems involved in modern institutions', the individual has to trust the expertise of human individuals and reliability of nonhuman objects, and base his or her ontological security and continuity of self-identity on their infallibility (Giddens 2012: 84–97).

Willy Wonka embodies the moral conflict at the heart of modernity in that he is both the one who has been traumatised by neglect and the one who is unreliable; the one who exploits his workers and the one who is creative and entrepreneurial. His production lines alter the bodies of the unruly children who break the rules inside the factory. One of his hobbies is melting wax dolls and then repairing them at the 'doll hospital'. Himself broken, he also breaks others, in the trademark combination of Burtonian creativity and destruction.

Charlie (Freddie Highmore), himself a victim of poverty and exploitation, attempts to heal Wonka's trauma. In the scene (presumably taking place in Willy Wonka's unconscious) in which Charlie takes Willy Wonka to visit his childhood home, the unsuspecting father greets them at the door and agrees to carry out a dental check-up. In the close-up of Willy Wonka's mouth (full of perfect teeth), his father's gloved hands hover over his son's face, the white rubber being the boundary protecting the father and son from each other and acting as a buffer to the intimacy of the touch. Hands in surgical gloves metonymically stand for a medical practitioner – for someone whose job is to be reserved and objective. He recognises his son by the 'bicuspids', with professional terminology being another buffer between himself and the world.

Yet, the very next sequence demonstrates that Willy Wonka's father is human albeit very protective of his emotions: Charlie is looking at the wall covered in media stories about Willy Wonka, from the opening of the factory and its success to the theft of trade secrets. The father has not been in touch in terms of the human touch, but he has been following his son's journey. His love expresses itself in ways which do not involve physical or emotional contact (apart from the gloved touch of the dentist), both of which are raw and difficult to control. The scene ends with the two carefully hugging each other accompanied by the sounds of squeaking rubber and cracking leather.

Eye imagery is also prominent in the film. The round eyes, still present in the original drawings, are replaced in the finished version by giant plastic goggles in a variety of frame colours which Wonka and the Oompa Loompas wear from time to time, and which the visitors are obliged to put on prior to entering the TV Room. Significantly, in a few of the original drawings the goggles are square and resemble the large square glasses Burton himself is wearing in some of his interviews. As part of the industrial narrative of health and safety, personal protective equipment is meant to protect the wearer in a hazardous environment. The chocolate factory is, indeed, an unpredictable and dangerous place where children can fall into chocolate rivers and garbage chutes or be blown up into giant blueberries.

Regardless, the goggles are more of a quirky element in Willy Wonka's bizarre universe. It is more that he mocks the idea of extreme precaution and safety measures as something that his father strictly observed. Latched onto the industrial metaphor of assembly-disassembly and the dangers associated with the production line, the goggles, much like the gloves, are here for protecting the wearer from 'the real world' with its relationships, imperfections, miscommunication and the human touch. Because of their size and grotesque appearance, with their thick purple or white frames and dark lenses, they dominate the wearer, seemingly popping out to the foreground of the frame. As tropes, they represent a reluctant, shy, defensive and fragile individual, reduced to the glasses and the gloves – the thick protective front covering a soft emotional core. The dark lenses' complete concealment of the eyes also demonstrates Wonka's disdain for facework; indeed, he is curt and irritable when speaking equally to children and adults, and when they get trapped by one of his machines, he is only happy for them to be 'processed' as part of the production process. The father's reconciliation sequence at the end of the film (added to the original narrative by John August[2]) reassembles the fragmented child from the synecdoches and makes him, if not whole, at the very least more complete.

THE DISASSEMBLY LINE AND FRAGMENTED BODIES IN *SWEENEY TODD: THE DEMON BARBER OF FLEET STREET*

In *Sweeney Todd*, the loss of trust in the world, and the subsequent existential angst, take on truly epic proportions. The humorous side of the 'disassembly line', which in *Charlie and the Chocolate Factory* still prevails despite the host's alarming penchant for feeding visitors into his industrial machines, is replaced in *Sweeney Todd* by the cold-blooded thirst for revenge for betrayal. The production line is a food processor which turns clients into meat pies. In fact, the film opens with a shadowy version of the symbol of capitalist innovation and entrepreneurialism, eclipsing the optimistic view of modernity and its machines. As the opening credits roll, blood flows onto a large wheel which starts moving, setting other wheels in motion. The blood glides onto them and seeps between them, filling out crevices and 'oiling' the mechanism. This is followed by the image of an industrial-size meat grinder churning out mince, ensued by fire burning inside the furnace, with rows of pies cooking inside it. The next shot in the sequence shows blood again, sliding into the sewerage system and making its way into the River Thames.

An adaptation of the penny dreadful *Sweeney Todd: The String of Pearls* (1846–7), *Sweeney Todd* tells the story of the barber Benjamin Barker, who renames himself Sweeney Todd after his family and his identity have been destroyed by the lecherous and corrupt Judge Turpin (Alan Rickman). Framed, falsely convicted and exiled, Benjamin returns to London to seek revenge on the judge. Burton has a tendency to move up and down the scale of modernity, from *Frankenstein* to the tales of Victorian city horrors to the middle of the twentieth century. Yet, despite his overambitious scale and anachronistic treatment of history, he is nevertheless consistently true to his central message: that modernity cannot be trusted, and that ontological security offered to the individual in the age of machines is an illusion. Sooner or later the individual will be disappointed, like Benjamin is when he realises that the machine is built for the privileged few, and that it is powered by blood – a sentiment Burton expresses in the musical number 'No Place Like London'.

Whereas the tale of Edward Scissorhands ends with the protagonist living alone in a castle, disappointed in the world and its inhabitants, Benjamin is Edward twenty years later. The razors in his hands become an extension, and an enhancement, of his flesh. His creativity lost and replaced by the urge to destroy, the hands, once more, take on a special meaning – and a special place in the film's line of images.

A hand holding a sharp object becomes a natural focus of attention for the audience. A hand with a knife is indexical of danger, and naturally metonymic because of the association with injury. It attracts even more attention if the object is not treated with care. Benjamin's hand movements are theatrical and careless and make no acknowledgement of the space they occupy, or the people around. For instance, when singing 'Epiphany', Benjamin falls on his knees on the street, his arms, holding blades, wide open, and sings that he is alive at last, and full of joy. He does the same move inside his 'office', which has a slanted ceiling (a reference to Edward's giant attic): holding out hands with blades, no longer innocently attempting to connect with other human beings, but in a bitter and gleeful anticipation of a bloodbath, he imagines how he would feed the bodies into his disassembly line, his personal trauma colluding with the deadly inevitability of the machine.

THE ESCAPED SYNECDOCHE IN *BIG EYES*

Burton's use of visual and narrative synecdoche, as a trope signifying the oxymoronic position of authentic self in modernity, even carries into the narratives which markedly lack many of the elements of his trademark moody Gothic melodrama. *Big Eyes*, which is replete with sunlit street, park and beach scenes, does not feel like a Burton film at all. Devoid of deep shadows, painterly blood or misunderstood monsters, *Big Eyes* is based on a true story of the artist Margaret Keane (Amy Adams), conned by her husband, Walter (Christoph Waltz), out of the authorship of her paintings. Familiar faces such as Johnny Depp and Helena Bonham Carter are also notably absent. Yet, the Burtonian synecdoche, typically emphasising the fate of the unique, creative individual in the age of the copy, lamenting the prevalence of sameness and reproducibility, while, simultaneously, in a masochistic twist, colluding with the machine, is still very much there. This time it is present in the large, sad, uncanny, grotesque eyes of the children in Margaret Keane's paintings. The protagonist's journey has other typical Burtonian narrative features, including the loss of innocence as a result of being betrayed by a greedy and unscrupulous individual, the childlike quality of the protagonist which makes her vulnerable in the cynical world, and the originality of the artistic vision which is rejected or exploited by society, or both. The protagonist is relatable, Burton explains in one of his interviews, since she is 'shy [and] non-communicative', and he 'used to be that way, not being able to talk but being able to speak through your art'.[3]

A struggling artist, Margaret is approached by Walter Keane, who poses as a painter and connoisseur of art. He praises her paintings of sad children which no one else seems to notice or like. Having lured Margaret into a relationship, he tries to sell and promote her paintings, but ends up claiming that they are his. Margaret goes along with the deception, but eventually becomes bitter and frustrated.

The film foregrounds its central image of large eyes until it becomes separated from everything else, much like the eyes that get separated from their owners in Burton's animated sequences, such as *Beetlejuice* and *Corpse Bride*. These eyes eventually acquire a life of their own, as shown in the scene in the mall when Margaret goes past numerous reproductions of her paintings on postcards and posters in a supermarket. These are a testament to the popularity of her vision as well as a reminder that she can no longer control her art which has turned into a production line, and become disembedded (as Giddens would call it) from her initial concept, from her feelings and intentions. The idea of disembedding, according to Giddens, is to 'open up manifold possibilities of change by breaking free from the restraints of local habits and practices' (2012: 20). The mass-produced cards are a cheap way of making a product and a far cry from the Romantic idea of uniqueness and individualism. Her own eyes resemble those of the children in her paintings, in that they are wide open, and unable to lie, to pretend, to do the 'facework' required of her in order to keep things quiet.

As she glances above the bookshelves, she meets the gaze of a female shopper with giant, surreal eyes. It is unclear whether the eyes are just grotesquely made up or are the product of Margaret's imagination. She then notices that other people around, including the cashier and shoppers in the queue, all have the same grotesque painted eyes. An assembly line is the opposite of synecdoche as it puts objects together rather than separating them. Burton is again playing with the opposing ideas of assembling and disassembling bodies and identities, of creating, recreating and fragmenting, of looking into the cracks and the seams in the finished, seemingly smooth and shiny product.

Margaret's art has escaped the confines of her small attic room and has become a fashion – it has been hijacked by her greedy husband and appropriated by the masses. It can be said that the eyes have acquired a life of their own similar to the nose in Nikolai Gogol's eponymous short tale (1836). In Gogol's tale the state bureaucrat's nose is a 'metonymy come to life and the supreme symbol of disintegration and collapse into chaos' (Fennell 1976: 95). Even though the eyes in Burton's film are foregrounded visually and narratively, and the nose in Gogol's tale is separated from the owner literally (making it a literalised synecdoche), their narrative role is fairly similar – to demarcate the boundary between external and internal realities. The individual in Burton's films collapses into chaos because of the intolerable position of maintaining a unique identity while being part of a mass society.

CONCLUSION

Fragmentation tropes in Burton's films question the very idea of individual completeness, and test the social front, which initially appears to be free of cracks, until it shows the conflict and turmoil happening underneath. Unable to relate, refusing to do the 'facework', to put up with 'the ways of the world', with the 'normal' ways of doing things, his protagonists assemble themselves from fragments, and show off their scars to the world. In particular, the images of hands and eyes, which often occupy a central position in Burton's narratives, render the protagonist's inability, and often refusal, to communicate with the external world. Hands – exposed or protected, holding blades or wearing gloves – symbolise the danger of touching, of building relationships. Meanwhile, the eyes, which are grotesquely enlarged, heavily made-up or protected by giant goggles, are windows into the characters' original, unmasked selves, the kinds of selves that are too open, too pure or too quirky to be accepted in a group.

Helpless and naïve, or betrayed, angry and embittered, Burton's characters attempt, and fail, to connect with others, and often end up scrambling to protect themselves from further pain. Their internal (and external) fragmentation is contrasted with the image of the assembly line, with its connotations of efficiency and flawlessness. Their plight epitomises the imperfection, the messiness, of human communication and encapsulates the scale of the individual's identity crisis against the backdrop of structures, processes and technologies of modern society. The individual falls apart precisely because wholeness does not exist – it is one of the most misleading, most attractive myths of modernity.

NOTES

1. Warner Bros. Entertainment (2015), 'Making of *Charlie and the Chocolate Factory*', Part 3, 11 January, https://www.youtube.com/watch?v=ZdBx-NLrv60 (last accessed 1 May 2020).
2. Warner Bros. Entertainment (2015), 'Making of *Charlie and the Chocolate Factory*', Part 1, 11 January, https://www.youtube.com/watch?v=ZdBx-NLrv60 (last accessed 1 May 2020).
3. '*Big Eyes*: Director Tim Burton Official Movie Interview', 7 December 2014.

13. ART AND THE ORGAN
WITHOUT A BODY:
'THE JAR' AS BURTON'S
ARTISTIC MANIFESTO

Fernando Gabriel Pagnoni Berns

In 'Activating the Differences: Expressionist Film and Earlier Weimar Cinema' and 'Weimar Cinema, Mobile Selves, and Anxious Males', Dietrich Scheunemann (2003) and Thomas Elsaesser (2003) argue against the pervading idea that all non-realist films made in the period of the Weimar can be classified as 'expressionist'. Both authors contend that only a small number of films can be grouped under the expressionistic umbrella: *The Cabinet of Dr Caligari* (Wiene 1920), *From Morn to Midnight* (Martin 1920) and the last episode from the portmanteau film *Waxworks* (Leni 1924). The other films considered as 'expressionistic' were works with roots firmly planted in the Romantic and/or the Gothic German past. Those Weimar films were made within an ideological and aesthetic framework which tried to dispense with realism and/or naturalism as the only feasible means for film. Indeed, films such as *The Golem* (Boese and Wegener 1920) or *Nosferatu* (Murnau 1922) answered the anti-realist aesthetics of the historical avant-garde movement rather than strictly following the dictates of expressionism. If the naturalist norm was generally established as the accepted mode of representation in earlier film, German cinema from just prior to the First World War into the 1920s feeds into a variety of aesthetic experimentations. These include elliptical storytelling, skewed camera angles and highly stylised sets and lighting. Expressionism was just another aesthetic within a larger corpus of anti-realistic styles.

Arguably, Tim Burton has been associated with aesthetic qualities directly lifted from expressionism (Bassil-Morozow 2013; Kunze 2016; Packer 2002).

His work, however, transcends the limitations of 'quoting' German expressionism; Burton's films are infused with a more general non-realist or anti-realist aesthetical experimentation. Already in two of his first films, *Hansel and Gretel* (1983) and *Aladdin and His Wonderful Lamp* (1986), viewers can glimpse blueprints of Burton's world. Indeed, *Hansel and Gretel*, a television special made for Disney some time before Burton gained his well-renowned reputation, was considered too dark for children and, thus, perfunctorily shelved after its initial airing on Disney Channel at 10:30 pm on Halloween 1983 (Wickman 2014). Filled with nightmarish scenarios, spirals, big eyes, odd German Expressionist angles and crawling creatures, this reimagining of the Brothers Grimm story was highly embedded in non-realistic aesthetics. *Aladdin and His Wonderful Lamp*, a live-action film, continued this interest in a universe where displaying the artifice is the main aesthetic. It is in those earlier television films that Burton slowly developed his taste for the grotesque, the Gothic, the Romantic and the avant-garde: in brief, non-realistic art.

This preference for experimental narrative also runs through the different ways in which Burton (re)imagines the human body. Even when working with actors rather than puppets, Burton reconfigures the body to dispense with realism. In *Aladdin and His Wonderful Lamp* there is a visual joke in which Aladdin (Robert Carradine) sits in a meditative way. He is trying to work out how to escape from a deep cave into which he has fallen. Aladdin's visual position, his chin resting on one hand while deep in thought, parallels the French sculptor, Auguste Rodin's *The Thinker* (1880). This way, the human body imitates high art. The camera zooms out to reveal a corpse close to Aladdin, sitting in the same position, which becomes Aladdin's double.

It is interesting to note that the body in this visual joke evokes, at first, realistic art. Indeed, Rodin's intention was that of creating something that closely resembled a human body: mimesis as passive representation. As Debora Silverman points out, 'Rodin presented his Thinker-Poet as engaged in a strenuous battle with the instinctual and the unconscious, a process in which the dream was transformed into art through restraint and repression' (1992: 267). Rodin's body is hard and impenetrable. The corpse, however, reveals what lies behind the surface of repression, the true art: the discarnate subject, free from the prison called flesh and embodiment. Correspondingly, the skeleton is the highest art because it allows a glimpse of the grotesque that lies behind the innocent surface. It is the minimal gesture without artifices and completely open for everyone to read; there is nothing to interpret.

In the episode of the new incarnation of *Alfred Hitchcock Presents* 'The Jar' (1986), Burton (who directed the episode) restages the same visual joke: Knoll (Griffin Dunne), an artist struggling with his art, sits in a chair imitating Rodin's *The Thinker*. The camera moves to reveal a headless sculpture close to him, sitting in the same position. If the whole body of Rodin's

Thinker-Poet 'has become head' (Silverman 1992: 267), this hierarchy is completely destroyed in the new staging of Rodin's ideas. Both TV films reveal a stance against the closed body, a visual statement of Burton's approach to art. Rather than art imitating reality – the human body reproduced as our senses perceived it, as a perfect machine – Burton's bodies are unchained from the traps of realism. The skeleton and the headless body are the most radical forms of art since, rather than replicate a defined system that privileges reason (the 'head') and reproduction of the sensible, both enthrone a deconstruction of the sign (the 'body').

In this sense, 'The Jar', a story which revolves around the world of artistic creation, may be read as Burton's artistic manifesto. It is with this little story that Burton informs viewers how he understands art or, at least, his own art. The episode tells about Knoll, an artist struggling to find his voice, who finds a mysterious jar and decides to incorporate it into his art exhibition. The object becomes the centrepiece of his exposition, but it also causes unexplained reactions. Through the film, a passage from a slightly anti-realist body in the form of the headless sculpture to a complete destruction of human embodiment takes place. This course marks Burton's thesis: to take art increasingly far away from realism right up to the point of complete destruction and deconstruction. It is not as simple as just infusing cinema with traces of expressionism (which still contains recognisable sensible forms): it is an attempt to deconstruct reality in a radical way.

This essay analyses Burton's 'The Jar' as a manifesto of things to come. Burton's ideas on artifice and the anti-realist body manifest again in films such as *Beetlejuice* (1988), *Sleepy Hollow* (1999) and *Big Eyes* (2014) and, rather than being just an earlier (and thus, not fully developed) Burton work, 'The Jar' contains seminal ideas on art and the body that the director will develop later in his career.

STRUGGLING WITH THE NEW BODY

In his book *Postproduction. Culture as Screenplay: How Art Reprograms the World* (2002), Nicolas Bourriaud states that the art of the late 1980s and 1990s follows the logic of the 'flea market', in which the fetishism for the object of art (the material production of a 'genius') has been replaced by pieces found in common places: 'It represents a collective form, a disordered, proliferating and endlessly renewed conglomeration' (2002: 28) of objects. As Bourriaud notes, 'A flea market, then, is a place where products of multiple provenances converge, waiting for new uses' (2002: 29). Discarded and/or mundane objects such as the jar, and even whole events, for instance, the act of eating, should be extrapolated to the sphere of art. This way, the great divide between artists (as some kind of geniuses living at the margins of common life) and common citizens (the praxis of life) could be surmounted. One and the other are the same.

According to Bourriaud, creativity today involves mixing and combining. He mentions the disc jockey (DJ) as the model for contemporary artistic manifestations. For him, 'The DJ's work consists both of proposing a personal orbit through the musical universe (a playlist) and of connecting these elements in a certain order, paying attention to their sequence as well as to the construction of an atmosphere' (Bourriaud 2002: 38). Like other artists do after scavenging a flea market, the DJ groups together diverse pieces into a unique body of work: 'The work of the DJ consists in conceiving linkages through which the works flow into each other, representing at once a product, a tool, and a medium' (Bourriaud 2002: 40). It is the aesthetic of remixing.

DJs do not cite or quote: they wander through the history of music and take whatever they want. This seems like postmodernism, but it is a different form of thinking. Postmodern citation implies reference to Old Masters and authority. The artist must engage in a hierarchal relation where the importance of all things past is exacerbated, quoted and reverenced. This work on quotation must be destroyed in the new art proposed by Bourriaud. Each piece does not take the viewers to past experiences and names but tells something completely personal. As he notes, 'High culture relies on the ideology of framing and the pedestal, on the exact delineation of the objects it promotes, enshrined in categories and regulated by codes of presentation. Low culture, conversely, develops in the exaltation of outer limits, bad taste, and transgression' (Bourriaud 2002: 41). Ironically, the main narrative device framing the episode of 'The Jar' contains a 'literal quote' from a master. The new iteration of *Alfred Hitchcock Presents* began each episode with an introduction performed by one of the most renowned directors of cinema, Alfred Hitchcock. Each introduction was made for his classic series. Now colourised, these introductions work as a postmodern pastiche that blends together the new with the old and this effect adds another layer of temporal disruption.

This introduction is the only direct quotation, while the flea market logic frames 'The Jar' as a whole. The TV episode begins in black and white, thus referring to classical Hollywood cinema. Filming in black and white, however, refers to a whole era and a form of production and style, rather than a concrete director, genre or studio. The episode opens with a Jewish woman, her religion identifiable through the David star stitched in her jacket, running away from a man (Paul Werner) who is chasing her and who is a Nazi, the swastika clearly recognisable on his uniform. In her flight, the woman hides in a laboratory, where the Nazi follows her. There, the man shatters all the glass vases but stops, fascinated, before the vision of a large jar containing what appears to be human remains or, even weirder, a mangled human body. Viewers can see an eye, with what appears to be a tiny hand and black hair attached to it, all floating in translucent liquid (in a later scene, Knoll's wife succinctly describes the contents as 'a stump with a wig'). It seems that the contents have what can be described as the minimal elements to recognise a human body – hair, hand, eye – and little else. The Nazi is fascinated by this vision and, after some seconds of watching the jar intently, the man retires. The woman takes advantage of his distraction and shoots the man with a rifle, presumably killing him, the death taking place offscreen.

Outside the laboratory, the streets are filled with fog and the illumination creates crisp contrasts of black and white against the burning lights, revealing the city with its gleaming wet pavements and a black car. This visual imagery refers unmistakably to *film noir*, a popular genre in classical American cinema. The sinister laboratory containing glass vases filled with liquids and human remains, on the other hand, evokes Universal horrors and cheap B films.[1] The Nazis hunting down scared people evoke war films and/or the mystery/thriller genre. Later in the episode, which is presented in colour after the prologue, Burton uses sharp hues of blue and pink to illuminate his *mise-en-scène* in key scenes, for example, when Knoll finds the vase or the second art exhibition. The blue and pink illumination parallels the colour schemes used by masters of Italian horror cinema such as Mario Bava and Dario Argento in their atmospheric works of the 1960s and 1970s.[2]

Burton is not making a direct quote lifted from a particular film or director. Instead, he creates an open network of aesthetic signifiers that connects recognisable styles and genres but without any concrete name behind this logic of pastiche. This is the DJ's style that Bourriaud declares as the dominant art of the latter half of the 1980s, when Burton created 'The Jar'. Using and abusing the conventions is part of a new art that Bourriaud labels as the art of postproduction.

This art of 'shopping and display' (Bourriaud 2002: 43) is replicated by Knoll throughout the episode and is also mirrored in the form in which the bodies are displayed. The Jewish woman in the prologue, after killing the man hunting her down, turns her gaze to the jar before the episode then makes an abrupt cut to an artistic exhibition in modern America (the episode now in colour). Here, the first piece is a human body made with what seems to be plaster. The figure is observing attentively an aquarium holding tiny goldfish but the human head has been replaced by a fishbowl, containing the same kind of fish.

What this simple act puts into crisis is the idea of an observer who is able to see, investigate and analyse the external world in a completely objective way. Both the viewer (the fishbowl) and the observed reality (the fishbowl) are one and the same. Also, the artistic display makes an ironic commentary about the ideal of a passive reality existing outside the subject waiting to be observed and scrutinised. Jacques Derrida introduces this topic in his text *The Animal That*

Therefore I Am (More to Follow) (2008), when he observes his cat 'looking' at him with intention. Derrida then makes an argument about how Western philosophy was historically sustained on the premise of some (active) observer and some (passive) out there which is not able to look back at the analysing subject. In other words, reality can be easily replicated through the art of mimesis. Derrida's ideas follow philosophical phenomenology that indicates that all reality is mediated through the senses, through our human body and, as such, complete objectiveness is simply impossible, an attempt doomed to fall into absurdity (Armstrong 2011: 194). Human intelligence and perceptions are incarnated in a material corporeality and, as a result, all reality is mediated.

In the artistic assemblage presented by Burton, the person who is looking is, in turn, observed. And those who look and are observed belong to the same species: animals (goldfish). If the animal has been 'thingified' to become commodity (the pet) and spectacle (the savage creature in zoos, circuses or film), here the human himself is coded as 'human/animal'. The human figure survives – as mentioned, the sculpture resembles Rodin's *The Thinker* – but the head, the shell for intelligence and reason, has been mutilated, replaced by a fishbowl; the body, thus, has suffered two acts of 'degrading'. Beheading is the first deed: if 'bodiless heads reflect a wish to transcend physical limitations in search of "a higher spiritual truth"' (Cornich and Sedgwick 2017: 36), the headless figure is inextricably linked to carnal desires, basic instinct, dumbness and bodily functions. The passive figure looking at/being looked at in the art exhibition is so attached to foolery (by lack of intelligence) that one art critic (Paul Bartel) is disgusted by its obviousness and simplistic allegorising. Second, the human figure is 'downplayed' to the animal level, thus destroying the seemingly 'essential' or 'natural' hierarchies that mark the human as vastly superior to the animal.

As a way to enhance this humanist crisis, the art exhibition is filled with headless human bodies. The one with a fishbowl for a head is just the first one. More human-like statues representing men and women are scattered throughout the place, all of them headless. Unlike the first one, the rest have lava lamps for heads. Lava lamps, objects denoting luxurious style in the 1960s, are now coded as kitsch, meaning objects considered of bad taste, cultural artefacts whose very awfulness makes them appealing for some. In fact, lava lamps were fashionable in the late 1980s, when 'everybody had one in their dorm room because they were trying to be all late '60s' (Harman 2009: 114). As Graham Harman notes, the lava lamps were once popular, then *passé*; later they became a novelty again to return to being *passé* (2009: 114). At the time of 'The Jar', the lava lamps were, for a second time, novelties on the brink of becoming tacky relics again. Knoll is using Bourriaud's logic of the flea market since he has scavenged through 'the debris of the bourgeoisie' – as the art critic interpreted by Paul Bartel mentions with a derogatory tone – to obtain his pieces; here, however, the ephemeral nature of the object is enhanced as the 'discarded object' is both a thing from the past and a novelty at the brink of becoming *passé*. Like Burton himself, Knoll seems to be probing within the world of art and artistic representation, looking for complete avant-garde reconstruction of sensible experiences. Burton stated in interviews that the tale was a 'tough one' (Umland 2015: 145) to film without clarifying why, and, allegedly, remembers the episode 'poorly' (Odell and Le Blanc 2005: 46). Knoll is still not yet there in terms of artistic identity, as he produces an art that remains bourgeois rather than being completely deconstructive of the shape of the human body. The 'good' forms still prevail and so does the institution 'art'. Independent filmmaker Bartel, himself an artist known to audiences for his works in camp and kitsch films, was associated with bad taste (Nash and Ross 1990: 196), the bizarre and an askew vision of the world. Thus, his role as an art critic can only be read as an exercise on irony on Burton's part.

The last works of art displayed in the exhibition are very telling. One is the silhouette of a human body sketched upon a sheet of paper: there are no eyes, hair, nose or genitalia: just an external figure crudely sketched. The human body is becoming deconstructed, but not fully so: the figurative remains. Closing the exhibition is a set of wind-up chattering teeth, the art critic looking disgusted at the sight of this sad attempt at art and/or body deconstruction. Knoll, who stands still next to the toy, seems deeply ashamed, to the point of being unable to make eye contact with the other guests. What troubles him is the fact that all his artistic ideas are stale, and he knows it. The art critic mentions that Knoll was an artist with a shining future but somehow lost his way. Rather than reinventing himself, Knoll is repeating his tricks. There is no explicit mention of what Knoll's goals are in the arena of art, but his exhibition indicates a common theme: the human body and how to deconstruct it. In this sense, the headless figures point to a desire to downplay reason while the wind-up chattering teeth indicate a desire to dispense with the human body understood as a closed system. Knoll wants to deconstruct the human body, turning it topsy-turvy, but he is unable to find the right ideas to do so. It is significant to note that Knoll's house, as shown in the final scene, is filled with mannequins: simulacra of the human body. Clearly, human corporeality is an obsessive theme for him.

After the critical failure of his last art exhibition, Knoll seems defeated, a point he makes to Periwinkle (Laraine Newman), the owner of the place and close friend. Knoll's girlfriend, Erica (Fiona Lewis), on the other hand, is uninterested in her partner's troubles as she is unable to grasp what he wants to achieve. Knoll's attempts to deconstruct the human body will be fully developed in his next art exhibition. Rather than just deconstructing the category of art by reuniting together different pieces, and the category of body through headless bodies and disembodied teeth, Knoll embraces the next step: the avant-garde extreme of the body without organs as argued by Gilles Deleuze and Félix Guattari (1983). Rather than a timid reconstruction, the shattering of categories and hierarchies will now be complete. The process of separating the Self from the physical body and an organism becomes a political as well as artistic issue.

THE ORGAN WITHOUT A BODY: NEW FORMS OF ART AND THE HUMAN

In their text *Anti-Oedipus: Capitalism and Schizophrenia*, philosophers Deleuze and Guattari (1983) dedicate chapter two to their argument about 'the body without organs', a concept that the authors leave provocatively ambiguous. The concept of a body without organs 'has nothing to do with a lack, and is part of the constitution of the field of desire crisscrossed by particles and fluxes' (Boundas 1993: 113). Neither a real organism nor a normal body, the body without organs is a series without concrete sequences or hierarchical systems of logic; it is a body with vague, undefined, transitory organs. As Constantin Boundas argues, its political function is being 'the site of anarchy' (1993: 13). What interests both Deleuze and Guattari about this particular image is the idea of a body whose organs are disjointed, emptied of concrete significance and proper place (something akin to the flea market). Rather than following a mechanical form comprised of the human body and its sequence of organs forming a perfect 'machine', the body without organs rejects normative categories and, specifically, hierarchies. It resists the fixed while favouring migrations and becomings to something not completely defined. All sense of order, utility and normalcy is destroyed: 'In order to resist organ-machines, the body without organs presents its smooth, slippery, opaque, taut surface as a barrier. In order to resist linked, connected, and interrupted flows it sets up a counterflow of amorphous, undifferentiated fluid' (Deleuze and Guattari 1983: 9). It is a multilinear system, with everything happening at once: each line breaks free from the point of origin. Unlike the capitalist body, which must serve economic ends of production, the body without organs is 'unproductive' and 'unconsumable' (Deleuze and Guattari 1983: 11). It is a body that does not emit sounds or thoughts. It is an undifferentiated, non-hierarchical arena for art and political thought as it is filled with potential for new junctures and conjunctions.

This is the kind of body that avant-garde artists such as Antonin Artaud might embrace. In fact, Deleuze first comes to the term 'body without organs' while investigating Artaud's writings (Deleuze and Guattari 1983: 8). This new model emanates from the desire to kill, exterminate or obliterate the bourgeois body that serves for something, that is obliged to say something communicable. Such bourgeois corporeality is what Knoll discards completely to embrace in turn the body without organs, the sterile materiality that does not signify anything, which does nothing, that does not resemble the human.

After the failure of his last art exhibition, Knoll returns to his favourite dump yard to see what he can rescue from the debris. There he buys a 1938 Mercedes-Benz car within which lies the jar displayed in the introduction, the vase containing what seems to be human parts/organs. After this finding, Knoll begins a new career with the vase as the *pièce de résistance* of his new exhibition. Erica, jealous of her partner's success, tries to downplay his artistic merit by mentioning that the jar was found in a dump yard. Periwinkle, however, retorts that these flea market proceedings constitute the new art. According to her, only an artist like Knoll is able to find beauty and/or revulsion in something discarded. The jar is an instant hit, with attendants deeply disturbed and shocked by the vision of this particular object. What the exact nature of its contents is remains a mystery for everyone, but people are enthralled, nevertheless. A friend of Knoll asks what exactly the thing floating in the blue liquid within the jar is. Knoll's answer is very telling: 'Why does it have to be something?' The destruction and deconstruction of the human body is now complete. It has lost its proper meaning. The answer is the matrix of Knoll and Burton's approach to art and the body. Rather than a faithful reproduction of an external, objective reality, both artists choose to celebrate art as an act of creation with its own rules and norms: art as an autonomous sphere rather than a 'slave' of an external logic. Art should deconstruct the external world (including the human body) rather than passively reflect it. Realism is a trap, while anti-realist art is a path to an incessant state of exploratory transformation. Further, there is no urgent necessity to produce something completely new, as the art critic played by Bartel asks from Knoll. When 'the grand narratives of progress and development have been thoroughly deconstructed, there is nothing left to be "ahead of"', and the pressure to produce something fundamentally different from preceding movements does not impose itself any longer' (Berghaus 2005: 215–16). Both Burton and Knoll extract from the already explored (in fact, as noted, 'The Jar' is a remake from an episode of the classic *Alfred Hitchcock Presents*) to deconstruct a sensible reality. It is not as simple as a return to the inventiveness of the expressionist aesthetic, but an art that predates the avant-garde, surrealism and the experimental. As a way to do so, Burton and Knoll both take their love for non-realistic art to new extremes. This is especially observable in the way in which bodies are (re)constructed. First, Knoll tries to 'destroy' the common, hegemonic body through a process of beheading. This is a somewhat inadequate step, as the body remains recognisable. Only the chattering set of teeth seem to indicate a nonhumanist (that is, the human as the centre and measure of all things) revolution: the human body is eliminated, turned into teeth and 'thingified' as a commodity. After finding the jar, however, Knoll is able to pursue a new path in his artistic career through the complete elimination of the Apollonian human body. The only thing remaining is a series of contents within a jar, traces of something vaguely resembling human corporeality.

Knoll's new art exhibition is, again, an arena of deconstruction: disembodied arms coming out from the walls and more human silhouettes are part of the new exhibit. The piece that creates the most attention, however, is the jar. Its contents seem to provoke different feelings and reactions from the attendants: they love it, hate it or feel repulsed, but all of them are fascinated by the deconstructed body floating in blue liquid. People even want to buy it. Further, Erica detects some kind of movement coming from the contents of the jar, indicating ambiguous traces of life.

It is no coincidence that the man in charge of the dump yard, Happy (Peter Risch), is of short stature. His corporeality does not answer the hegemonic, clean-cut, healthy, 'normal' body. The whole episode revolves around counter-hegemonic bodies and how to produce a rupture with traditional corporeality. The organ/body floating in the jar is the final art: the body without organs/the organ without body that does not respect hierarchies nor resemble anything. Like art itself, the jar is, according Erica, a disgusting 'fraud', something that Knoll found disposed of in the trash. For her, the jar cannot be art. For Knoll, Burton and Bourriaud, however, it is a different form of art that discards any reference to the figure of the Master and division between the genius and the common man, between high and low culture. The body/organ itself, undifferentiated as it is, parallels this artistic thinking. It blends lowbrow (a piece of trash) and high art (it is exhibited in an art gallery) and, while it may be human (and even alive), it is alien to human eyes at the same time. Following Artaud's dictates about art, it is a purely visual sensation in which the force would emerge from a collision exacted on the eyes (1978: 19). Indeed, people are deeply disturbed after observing the mysterious jar.

When Erica, tired of this 'disgusting' piece, attempts to eliminate the contents, she tries to do so using a kitchen knife. The choice of weapon is very telling, as Erica seems to be trying to kill a body. Through a fight with Knoll, who wants to stop Erica's murderous rage, the organ is torn apart piece by piece: immediately after, Knoll kills Erica, an act which takes place offscreen. In the episode's last scene, Knoll is again exhibiting the jar, a new element floating deep in the blue liquid: what seems to be Erica's head. The material support of this new piece is significant: rather than a simple column, the base evokes something organic, a sculptured piece resembling a tree or a cactus. It wears human clothes, thus coding it as human: nonetheless, it does not look like one. Like the contents of the jar, the new column is a step towards a revised materiality of the human body. Again, people are fascinated by the novel pieces of art. This exhibition is an extreme, even violent reaction against realism and imitation: the body is the main victim. Knoll has made all the required steps: first, breaking the hierarchy that separates high art from lowbrow and, second, destroying the body as a closed perfect machine. All these reconfigurations come together, converging in a new art installation that unites the flea market logic with the body without organs.

CONCLUSION

In *Aladdin and His Wonderful Lamp*, the Sultan (Joseph Maher) discovers, amazed, the pleasures of watching cinema. Indeed, the genie (James Earl Jones) offers him entertainment in the form of a little television set where the story's main villain is tortured by devils with cartoonish bodies. This is an earlier showcasing of Burton's cinema: the body should not be a split image of real bodies but, like film itself, corporeality should be deconstructed to produce shock and, thus, escape from the traps of realism: the passive reproduction of an external reality that presents itself as natural and a-historical and, thus, immovable.

Artistic objects and the concept of art itself should be rethought, privileging less the cerebral to celebrate, instead, the experimental and the transformational. In this scenario, realism must be destroyed and, with it, the human body. Thus, the main art piece in 'The Jar' is an ambiguous organ floating in a jar. The episode marks a passage from realism to artifice and, in parallel, from a body slightly modified to the complete obliteration of the 'normal' form.

'The Jar' is, basically, Tim Burton's artistic manifesto. Throughout the episode, Burton tells viewers that cinema allows experimentation and deconstruction. Following realism and/or naturalism is foolish, as it only repeats, to a lesser degree, what we sense in a daily way. The episode argues against the authority of 'high art' and the human body as the most perfect of systems. The body in the jar is translated into the languages of art: a piece of pure autonomy with no real purpose except inviting deconstruction and reactions. Burton, thus, declares his love for the different, the deconstructed and the marginal; as such, 'The Jar' was a blueprint of things to come.

NOTES

1. After the global success of *Frankenstein* (Whale 1931) and its sequels, laboratories filled with microscopes, chemical retorts and tubes quickly became a visual trope easy to imitate by the horror efforts of minor studios such as Republic or Monogram, to the point that a larger-than-life laboratory referred, in classical cinema, to 'mad scientists'.
2. Italian directors Mario Bava and Dario Argento are widely known in film studies for their striking, innovative use of bold, saturated colours as an integral part of the *mise-en-scène* (especially primary colours) of their horror films, such as *Suspiria* (Argento 1975) or *Sei donne per l'assassino* (Bava 1964). To general audiences, the vibrant use of colours became an integral part of classical Italian horror cinema (even if not all Italian horror directors used coloured lights in their films).

14. 'HELL HERE!':
TIM BURTON'S DESTRUCTION OF
MICHELLE PFEIFFER IN *BATMAN RETURNS*

Peter Piatkowski

For much of Tim Burton's career, his films tell the story of the abused misfit who undergoes trauma and transformation. As film critic Roger Ebert points out, 'All of Tim Burton's films [. . .] are about characters whose strange qualities place them outside the mainstream' (1992). In *Batman Returns* (1992), the follow-up to *Batman* (1989), his mistreated-misfit trope applies not only to the title character (Michael Keaton), but to the villains of the piece: the Penguin (Danny DeVito) and Catwoman (Michelle Pfeiffer). For most of his filmography, Burton has worked with a stable of performers, actors who have developed star personae that fit into his world of grotesques. This includes Johnny Depp, Helena Bonham Carter, Christopher Lee and Danny DeVito, Burton exploiting their eccentric, unconventional star images to help tell his story. In *Batman Returns*, he violates this method of casting by including Michelle Pfeiffer, a conventional film star, whose screen persona is defined by her looks and glamour. Unlike Depp or Bonham Carter, Pfeiffer's onscreen image is that of a traditional, classic Hollywood star. Because Burton's films concern themselves with the archetypal oddball, Pfeiffer's refinement makes her an unexpected addition to his acting troupe. Burton's treatment of Pfeiffer is similar to Hitchcock's conduct with Tippi Hedren in *The Birds* (1963), whereby he methodically dismantles and destroys Pfeiffer's glamorous image throughout the narrative. This chapter explores the ways in which Burton in *Batman Returns* uses Pfeiffer's star persona to advantage, but then gradually destroys it. She is made to appear dowdy, and then she is physically dismantled; as the film progresses, she also deteriorates mentally and emotionally. This degradation is not only evident in her actions, but sartorially as well: her Catwoman costume gradually disintegrates, until it is little more than just tatters and ripped stitching. While so much of Burton's oeuvre deals with the supernatural, what is important in his treatment of Pfeiffer is that he attacks her corporeal body; she is not a phantasm or a puppet, the injuries to her character are physical.

As noted, Burton often deals with themes of isolation and alienation. When he casts his films, he uses character actors who have distinctive traits that fit into his fictional worlds. In this respect, they are cast as misfits, outsiders or grotesques and, for most of his work, he identifies strongly with this characterisation, imbuing them with sympathy and poignancy. Indeed, as Johnson Cheu remarks, 'Tim Burton has always worked with the theme of Outsiders' (2016: 3). Similarly, Mark Salisbury opines that 'Burton's characters are often outsiders, misunderstood and misperceived, misfits encumbered by some degree of duality, operating on the fringes of their own particular society' (2006: xviii). There are villains in his productions, but these are often given tragic backstories that reveal a history of abuse and mistreatment. Burton seems to identify with these outsiders, and the actors he works with represent their characters as 'othered' and apart from society.

In casting Michelle Pfeiffer as Selina Kyle/Catwoman, *Batman Returns* is the first instance that she and Burton have collaborated (they would reunite in 2012 for his remake of the vampire soap *Dark Shadows*), and her casting is notable in that she does not fit into his usual stable of eccentric character actors. Furthermore, she lacks the distinct star persona that figures such as Johnny Depp or Helena Bonham Carter possess. By 1992, Pfeiffer was a popular leading female actor, well respected by critics and audiences for her versatility and diverse range of roles, including in *Dangerous Liaisons* (Frears 1988), *Married to the Mob* (Demme 1988) and *The Fabulous Baker Boys* (Kloves 1989). When she accepted the role of Catwoman, Pfeiffer was a two-time Academy Award-nominated actress with a reputation as a chameleon. Film critic Peter Travers praised Pfeiffer as 'one of those thin group of actresses (Angelica Huston, Meryl Streep) whose work keeps surprising us. Her powerful subtle acting can excite the funny bone or pierce the heart with equally mysterious skill' (1991).

However, that 'mysterious skill' that Travers lauds also means that Pfeiffer is largely a blank slate. She fills a character with the collaborative efforts of a director, screenwriter, costumer, not to mention her own input. She is not a character actor, nor does she get typecast (outside of glamour roles). Her wholly defining star quality is her beauty and this attribute is often the most notable and commented upon; it is part of her star image. Though reviewers frequently compliment her work – Edward Guthmann's assessment of her appearance in *One Fine Day* (Hoffman 1996) as 'spotless' (1996) is consistent with the kinds of reviews she receives – her looks are commonly highlighted. In a typical review, Pfeiffer's work would be deemed as laudatory but, more often than not, the reviewer will also make mention of her beauty. In his positive review of *Where Is Kyra?* (Dosunmu 2017), Justin Chang notes, '[Kyra] is beautiful – to put it another way, she's played by Michelle Pfeiffer' (2018). For her turn in the thriller *What Lies Beneath* (Zemeckis 2000), Lisa Schwarzbaum compliments Pfeiffer's character by remarking, 'she brims with the melancholy loveliness of Michelle Pfeiffer' (2000). Similarly, for her Oscar-nominated role in the 1993 civil rights drama *Love Field* (Kaplan 1992), Desson Howe characterised Pfeiffer's beauty as 'gratuitous' (1993). Therefore, unlike many of Burton's other stars, Pfeiffer is a 1990s version of 'the Golden Age of Hollywood' film star and recalls the glamorous beauties of the studio system. In assessing Pfeiffer's work in *The Fabulous Baker Boys*, Gerri Hirshey compares the actress to Lauren Bacall (1996: 261), while Roger Ebert likens her to Rita Hayworth and Marilyn Monroe (1989).

If Richard Dyer (2002) connects film stardom with notions of culture, pop culture, politics and economics, as well as societal and cultural norms on gender, race and sexuality, Pfeiffer's relative neutrality keeps her out of such discussions. As Dyer writes, 'the roles and/or the performances of a star in a film were taken as revealing the personality of the star' (2002: 20). Pfeiffer does not bring an established personality to her work as Catwoman. The only element she provides superficially is her glamour (it is telling that the role was first offered to Annette Bening, a similarly well-regarded actress known more for her work and looks than any sort of flamboyant persona).

In his study of stars, Dyer suggests that 'in certain cases, all the aspects of a star's image fit with all the traits of a character', thereby creating 'a perfect fit' (2002: 129). However, in other instances 'selective use of a star's image is problematic for a film, in that it cannot guarantee that the particular aspects of a star's image it selects will be those that interest the audience' (2002: 127). For Dyer, this constitutes a problematic fit and refers to Leo Braudy, who states that 'without an awareness of the aesthetic weight of a film star's accumulated image, a director can easily make mistakes that destroy the unity of his film' (in Dyer 2002: 129). Clearly, the box office returns suggest that Burton anticipated and counteracted this potential contradiction (the film grossed $267 million worldwide and was nominated for two Academy Awards).[1]

When examining how Burton works to undermine Pfeiffer's glamorous star image in his interpretation of Catwoman, one must look at how his reading of the character deviates from other canonical versions. In this respect, Burton's vision of Catwoman is quite different than the comic book version or the popular iteration of the character in the 1960s TV series *Batman* (1966–8). In the television version, Catwoman is played as a comedic vamp, a role that lends itself to the brightly coloured camp tone of the programme. She is a seductress who battles Batman (Adam West) with an arsenal of cat-themed gadgets and puns. For the show's first two series, the character was portrayed by Tony-winning actor/dancer Julie Newmar, whose statuesque and athletic physicality greatly contributed to the performance. The show was good-natured kitsch and Newmar's performance suited the generally light and humorous tone.

As indelible as Newmar's performance was, it is Eartha Kitt's work as Catwoman that is memorable. Though she only appears in the show's final season for two episodes, Kitt has become synonymous with Catwoman. Like Newmar, Kitt was able to bring her star persona to the role, but she did so in a far more obvious manner. Kitt – a popular nightclub/cabaret singer – was small and slight, unlike the Amazonian Newmar, but she made her mark as Catwoman by using her inimitable voice. She purred her lines in a unique growl and delivered her dialogue with a vaguely European affect, languishing extravagantly on the rolling of the letter 'r'. Her face was almost feline, with high cheekbones and deep, almond-shaped eyes. In comparison, Pfeiffer was a far blander choice – she had neither Newmar's nor Kitt's unique onscreen idiosyncrasies nor peculiarities. As Dyer points out,

> As regards the fact that a given star is in the film, audience foreknowledge, the star's name and her/his appearance (including the sound of her/his voice and dress styles associated with him/her) all already signify that condensation of attitudes and values which is the star's image. (2002: 126)

As mentioned, both Newmar and (especially) Kitt brought certain expectations from their respective audiences when playing Catwoman. Both actresses had followings from the theatre and nightclubs. In Dyer's example, he writes about Marlene Dietrich's work with Sternberg which essentially overwhelmed her oeuvre. Kitt's work as Catwoman, like Dietrich's Sternberg roles, informed everything else she has done – all her cabaret work, television work, chat show appearances, recall Catwoman more than anything else in her career. Newmar's work after *Batman* has also largely been defined and reduced by her Catwoman past. Both Newmar and Kitt would be seen as a 'perfect fit' according to Dyer's concept of the star image.

In addition, as mentioned earlier, the 1960s *Batman* TV show was light entertainment, far different from the grittier, stylised world of Burton's imagination. In his vision, Catwoman is one of his abused grotesques. Instead of being a petty jewel thief who indulges in puns, Burton presents Catwoman as a damaged, destroyed woman, a victim of toxic masculinity and unfettered patriarchy. In his creation, Selina Kyle is an extreme reaction to the systematic oppression of women. When Catwoman prowls the streets of Gotham City, she is setting out to upend the source of her pain and misery: men.

Because the central way that Burton conveys Catwoman's progressive deterioration is through her body and her costumes, it is important to closely examine the catsuit. In the comic book and, to a lesser extent, the television show, the cat costume makes Selina appear as an anthropomorphic cat. In Burton's version, he envisions Catwoman as he sees many of his creations: a Frankenstein-like creature, stitched shoddily with amateur skill. Once Selina becomes Catwoman, she throws together a hastily made suit of scraps of vinyl, leather and plastic that she sources from her home. Though she is referred to as Catwoman, she does not resemble a cat, but instead looks similar to his other characters such as Edward Scissorhands (Johnny Depp) or Sally from *The Nightmare Before Christmas* (Selick 1993). As Ken Hanke writes, 'Most interesting, though, is Burton's concept of Michelle Pfeiffer's Catwoman. If we take Edward Scissorhands as Burton's onscreen alter ego in that film, then we must also accept Catwoman as the most clearly defined personification of Burton in this film' (2007: 94).

As the film progresses and Catwoman engages in combat, the costume starts to fall apart, unravelling in places, with the stitching breaking, allowing for tufts of blonde hair to emerge or peeks of scarred and bruised skin to show. By the close of the film, when her ambiguous ending draws near, she is in complete disarray both physically and mentally, and any pretence of a cat costume is abandoned.

However, before Selina is destroyed, she requires an origin story, which is a recurring theme for superhero narratives (Rosenberg 2013). *Batman Returns* is set during the Christmas season, with Gotham City conveyed as a Fritz Lang-like creation of Deco and Neo-Gothic architecture enveloped in glittering swirling snow, as though in a shaken snow globe. Selina Kyle is a secretary for the Trump-like mogul, Max Shreck (Christopher Walken), whose empire is concentrated in a tower crowned by a grinning cat (a grim foreshadow): it is here that the spectator is first introduced to Selina Kyle.

From her first appearance, Burton does everything he can to destroy any semblance of film star glamour, which reinforces Dyer's notion of a problematic fit (2002: 129). Selina is dressed in an ill-fitting suit, and she assumes an awkward, nervous posture. She is fidgety and apologetic. Her messy blonde hair is carelessly pulled back into an untidy bun, and her face is obscured by large, unflattering spectacles. These details that Burton and Pfeiffer add to the performance serve as indications of her position as the archetypical underpaid, overworked, underrated secretary. She attends a board meeting in which Shreck is trying to convince the mayor of Gotham to approve his questionable business plans. Her demeanour is unconfident: she skulks and sneaks, trying to be inconspicuous. As she pours coffee, Shreck is presenting his proposal of a new energy plant in Gotham City to the powerful men in the room, and it is at this moment that Burton frames Selina and Shreck in a significant way. As she reaches to fill Shreck's cup, her outstretched arm seems to almost cut the frame in half. Shreck flashes an annoyed look which is essentially underlined by Selina's arm, while her face is obscured by the thick shoulder pad of her ill-fitting suit. Shreck's moment of irritation is underscored by Selina's arm and he must shift slightly to make eye contact with the mayor, whom he is trying to woo. This becomes a malevolent instant in which Selina occupies Shreck's personal space and makes him annoyed because he must acknowledge her presence. She has failed to remain invisible as she has desired and is expected to do.

The film moves forward as Shreck continues his future vision of Gotham with the mayor. At this juncture it is only the men in the room that are visible, with Selina blocked by Burton's framing of Shreck's body as he stands at the window. She asserts her presence with a stammered, 'I have a suggestion', and all eyes turn on her. Her interruption is met with hostility. The viewer witnesses only the back of Selina as she faces a panel of male judges, all of whom are conditioned to perceive help, particularly female help, as either merely decorative, expendable or invisible.

Intimidated by the sudden rapt attention, Selina is embarrassed. This is a moment in which her crumpled posture communicates the feelings of fear and intimidation she is experiencing. Like many Burton creatures, she has a panicky, edgy self-consciousness. In this instance, she manifests these emotions by shielding her body with a coffee urn and a tray. Her shoulders are hunched when she speaks up and she not only stammers, but she is also visibly shaking. There is no trace of the Hollywood glamour film star in this scene, with Pfeiffer successfully eschewing any semblance of sophisticated polish or hauteur.

While braving the contempt of the men she is serving, Selina stands in front of a large, upholstered wall which resembles a padded cell in an historic asylum. There are many layers to this allusion – one being Arkham Asylum, the fictional institution in which some of Batman's most notorious nemeses are committed; this *mise-en-scène* is also a clue to the future breakdown of Selina's own sanity. Finally, the padded wall recalls the practice of locking outspoken women in asylums for being, what was perceived as, unruly and deemed as failing to grasp their position in society. When faced with the unreceptive reaction to her interruption, Selina demurs from offering her suggestion. Shreck then focuses on her palpable discomfort and makes the degrading comment, 'I'm afraid we haven't properly housebroken Ms Kyle', comparing Selina to a domestic animal which, again, foreshadows what lies in store for both characters. After his dismissive and misogynistic comment, the meeting adjourns, and the men depart for a Christmas tree lighting ceremony, leaving Selina alone to clean up after them. Only now does the viewer obtain a glimpse into the dark duality of Selina's personality that will become more prominent later in the film. The moment she is by herself, her hesitant demeanour is dropped as she starts to utter words of self-loathing and disgust. She only stops verbally abusing herself when she spies that Shreck has forgotten his speech and, anticipating his anger, she flees to deliver it to him.

The boardroom scene leads to the first time that Batman and Selina meet. When Batman first sees Selina, he has just done battle with a marauding band of sideshow performers who interrupted the Christmas tree lighting ceremony. They descend on the City Hall plaza and the scene erupts into violent chaos as motorcycling pranksters and murderous stilt walkers lay claim to the city. As downtown Gotham is plunged into mayhem, Selina emerges from an alley, still anxious about Shreck's speech; again, she is rendered indiscernible to the other characters. Among the carnage, a killer clown grabs Selina from behind, threatening her life with a taser. This is the second instance in the narrative that Selina is intimidated and dominated by a man, but this time it is a physically violent act. The clown holds the taser close to her face but is quickly dispatched by a taciturn Batman who subdues him with one of his many bat-gadgets.

While Selina's treatment provides commentary on the dangers and inherent unfairness of a male-dominated world, her assault also represents a larger theme of female suffering in Burton's Gotham. Women in Burton's version of the Batman mythology do not play major roles outside of mother, victim or love interest, and Selina is the sole woman to have any kind of story or character depth in the film.

Once she is rescued, the script stages a grim parody of romantic comedies. Instead of sharing sparkling dialogue, though, the two protagonists are standing over the dead body of Selina's would-be attacker, while chaos reigns around them. Rather than witty dialogue, Selina is the only one talking, blathering nervously and incoherently, trying to make pathetic little jokes about dating, while Batman simply floats away, as he has other people to save. The brief exchange then becomes another opportunity for Selina to degrade and demean herself. Her self-pitying monologue is the script's way to act as a reminder that she is homely and sad. Burton takes pains to submerge Pfeiffer's looks in plain-girl clothes and present a pitiful character. As Tim Hanley notes, 'Initially, Selina was a stereotypical helpless, downtrodden woman, bespectacled and frumpy and a failure at every aspect of her life' (2017: 103).

There is further evidence of Selina's despondency when the viewer is given access to her apartment. Herein a range of banal signifiers, some of which tip into stereotype or cliché, project the image of a dejected, lonely single woman. After her ordeal, Selina trudges tiredly into her miserable little abode. As well as talking to her cat, she speaks to herself – betraying a sly wit that is lacerated with self-hate. Her home is suffused with pink and has vestiges of conventional femininity, including dolls, cute-cat posters and stuffed animals. Here, her only companion that talks back to her – or at her – is her answering machine, its messages neatly encapsulating the pathos of her life: her hectoring, disapproving mother, an errant boyfriend who unceremoniously dumps her and a scolding message she left for herself as a reminder to prep Shreck for his meeting with Bruce Wayne (Michael Keaton). The scene of Selina alone in her home is very effective in projecting her loneliness: her apartment has a bed she pulls down from the wall; a neon sign greets her with an optimistic 'Hello There' and she acknowledges her empty flat with a hollow joke of 'Honey I'm home! Oh, I forgot, I'm not married'. By the end of this scene, the portrait of Selina is complete: Burton has transformed beauty queen Pfeiffer into one of his depressing sad loners. As film critic Nathan Rabin notes:

> [Selina] begins the movie as the meekest of milquetoasts. Pfeiffer spends much of the film's first act talking to herself, because within the world she inhabits, she's not just powerless, but invisible. She captures the existential despair of someone who is so used to being ignored that she all but disappears. (2016)

The act of Selina becoming Catwoman is a difficult part of the story to reconcile because it is unclear whether the script is implying that this transformation is supernatural or metaphorical. Because none of the aspects of the film are supernatural – Batman's powers are due to him having immense wealth as well as honed skills in hand-to-hand combat, the Penguin's appearance is explained as a childhood deformity – it is challenging to accept this one injection of the supernatural into the narrative: a question which also leads to how Selina becomes a preternaturally adept streetfighter. Before she is Catwoman, there is no hint that she has any athletic acumen at all. She is easily overpowered by Shreck and the killer clown, and she does not display any skill or agility. Once she emerges as Catwoman, however, she fights men twice her size and performs impressive feats of gymnastics.

The compelling aspect about the sequence of Selina's transformation is that it highlights Burton's interest in origin stories, reanimation and resurrection. For example, his film *Frankenweenie* (1984) tells the story of a little boy who brings his dead dog back to life. Burton has also woven the Frankenstein theme into other films which repeatedly explore the pathetic aspect of creatures being resurrected, only to be rejected. Edward Scissorhands is another Frankenstein figure, sad and wistful, animated by his creator (Vincent Price), only to be left alone, misunderstood and ostracised, when the old man dies. The Catwoman origin story repeats these tropes: a lonely figure who is ignored and underestimated by society and who must find her way and place in the world after being brought back to life. As Ian Nathan observes, 'Monsters, [Burton] has always thought, are misunderstood. They have more heart than any of the humans you're supposed to root for' (2016: 10).

Burton's Catwoman origin story starts with Shreck returning to his office after the melee at the tree lighting ceremony, where he spots Selina snooping through his files. As Shreck enters the darkened office, Selina is shown through his point of view, her back to the camera. She is peering into a filing cabinet, rummaging through paperwork. From behind, she looks like the archetypical Burton character, but one of his stop-motion animation creations. This is due to Pfeiffer's awkward and stilted posture when she is playing up Selina's weakness. The ill-fitting clothing, which is a marker of socio-economic status, is bunched up in odd places on her body, and she appears lopsided and almost crooked. When confronted by her boss, Selina starts to chatter ceaselessly again, similar to when she first encountered Batman, though in this instance she is disguising her nerves. As she continues to speak, she guilelessly regurgitates some of the information she has gleaned from his files, including incriminating evidence of Shreck's nefarious business practices.

At this point the office is dark, and the main source of light is a desk lamp. When Selina, seen in close-up, stumbles back to her desk, continuing her chatter, she is illuminated from below by the lamp, which casts shadows on her face in an eerie manner. In a further close-up of her face, the shadows thrown from her large spectacles mimic the eyeholes of her Catwoman mask.

The scene reaches a shocking climax when Shreck murders Selina, brutally defenestrating her. As she smashes through the glass, the grinning feline from the tower gruesomely smiles down at her like a deranged Cheshire Cat as she drops through several awnings, the final one bearing the cat logo; Selina's body tears through its mouth as if it were devouring her. She lands on the snow-covered pavement with a sickening crunch.

In a startling high-angle shot, Selina's dead body is displayed. Her limbs are splayed at odd angles, like a marionette that has been tossed to the ground. The sequence is accompanied by the enigmatic score of long-time Burton collaborator Danny Elfman, with its tense, string-laden soundtrack accompanying the gathering of stray cats which cluster around Selina's lifeless body. Another close-up frames her now ashen white face, a blueish tint accentuating her features, and a ruby red trail of blood is smeared across her forehead. As the cats scamper around her body, they begin to gnaw at her fingers and, in response, her body begins to twitch. Just as the music reaches a crashing crescendo, Burton employs an extreme close-up: Selina's eyes flutter and snap open, her gaze blank, still dead. Just like Frankenstein's monster, Selina is reborn.

When Selina returns to her apartment, Burton completes her revival. In fact, it is in the post-revival scene that Burton enjoys his most Burton-esque character in *Batman Returns*. She has a deathly pallor, dark circles under her eyes, and her hair is a bedraggled mess resembling a female version of Edward Scissorhands. Wearing a devastatingly haunted look on her face and having a listless drone of a voice, Burton has literally destroyed Selina's body and in doing so has transformed her into one of his grotesques, abused by a cruel world.

In a catatonic state, she returns to her flat, moving slowly, mimicking her actions from earlier that night, though these now take on an uncanny note because she is essentially a zombie. When she finally suffers a breakdown, she trashes her small abode, angry and hoping to exorcise any remnants of the weak Selina. A new Selina has replaced her, and she is intent on completing Shreck's job, killing any vestiges of her former self. This means destroying all indicators of her past life: the stuffed animals are fed to the garbage disposal, her dolls' house is demolished, her cheery neon sign is smashed, and she changes the optimistic greeting of 'Hello There' to the cynically appropriate 'Hell Here'. As she works through her home, abolishing any evidence of her former self, she stumbles upon a black vinyl raincoat and suddenly has an epiphany. By the window of her bedroom she sets to work sewing, as cats congregate on her window ledge. In this scene, Selina is at once Frankenstein the monster and the creator. When her work is complete, a medium shot frames Selina's window, the 'Hell Here' sign glowing in the background, before she emerges, a figure in liquid black. She then purrs, 'I don't know about you, Miss Kitty, but I feel so much yummier'.

A changeling achieved through her clothes and demeanour, the figure of Catwoman now projects a troubled and mixed personality. She is instrumental in saving a woman who is dragged into an alley by an assailant about to rape her. Catwoman suddenly appears and taunts the man with the sneering, 'I just love a big strong man who's not afraid to show it with someone half his size'. As he charges towards her, she says, 'Be gentle, it's my first time', before quickly disabling him with several swift kicks and duly killing him by smashing his face with her homemade claws. Before the woman can express gratitude for Catwoman's intervention, she is thrown against a wall by Catwoman who sniffs contemptuously, 'You make it so easy, don't you? Always waiting for some Batman to save you'. The scene is a perverse parallel to the sequence in which Selina and Batman first met; in much the same way, Selina was a potential victim, until a human-animal hybrid came to the rescue. Though Selina has transformed into Catwoman, her self-loathing is still lodged in her psyche, evidenced by the disgust she feels towards the young woman she saves.

In this sequence, Burton is finally sharing with his audience his vision of Catwoman, who embodies many of the aesthetic qualities that he prizes when imagining characters. Her costume is a crude assemblage of household items and, like Edward Scissorhands, there is a dishevelled, improvised look to it. Though the catsuit is sleek, it is puckered in places, the stitching obvious and not the work of an accomplished seamstress. Her appearance borrows heavily from sadomasochistic fashion, with its knee-high, laced-up stiletto boots and corset. To approximate a tail, she wears a bullwhip laced around her neck and torso, with its end left dangling. She is a version of the Frankenstein monster, a key motif in Burton mythology, constructed from a figure that is crudely stitched together which speaks to the 'creepy-crawly style in keeping with Edward Gorey and Charles Addams' (Nathan 2016: 18).[2]

Selina's transformation spills over to her work life as well. As Selina Kyle, she no longer resembles the trembling, mousy loner who was introduced in the beginning of the film. In contrast to that mincing figure, Selina strides into the office with a swagger to join a stunned Shreck in his meeting with Bruce Wayne. She is sporting bandages from her fall to her death, but otherwise there is little evidence that she suffered any trauma. Assertive and confident, she addresses the men around her, even allowing for gallows humour, quipping 'Couldn't you just die?' when pretending not to remember how she was injured. She is no longer hunched over but is instead relaxed, languishing almost decadently against the furniture. As she speaks to the men, she strolls the room with a studied nonchalance and revels in Shreck's discomfort, teasing him when he splutters her name repeatedly with the insouciant 'That's my name, Maximillian. Don't wear it out or I'll make you buy me a new one'.

When Batman and Catwoman meet for the first time (albeit he had rescued her in her previous incarnation), it is after she has blown up Shreck's signature department store. Just as Batman confronts the Penguin, Catwoman approaches the two, cartwheeling towards them, stopping with just enough time to utter 'meow' before being backlit by an enormous explosion from inside the store. As the Penguin flies off on a novelty umbrella-turned-helicopter, Batman pursues Catwoman to a rooftop, and the two engage in a battle in which she delivers a series of relentless blows that he manages to fend off before he grounds her with a swift punch. 'How could you?' she beseeches, 'I'm a woman'. Stunned, he apologises, but his misplaced chivalry is repaid with a renewed set of attacks that drive him off a ledge, before she saves his life with her bullwhip, taunting him as he dangles on the side of the building. He quickly regains the upper hand by injuring her with a vial of acid, sending her off the roof, and then promptly saves her. As they stand on the ledge of a building, facing each other, they are framed in front of what appears to be the window of a penthouse apartment; cream-coloured satin curtains adorn the window, and an elegant lamp emits a warm glow in what would be a seeming place for a romantic evening. This is not the first time that Burton plays with notions of romance in the film; as already mentioned, earlier, when Batman first encounters Selina, there are humorous touches that bleakly recall a romantic comedy.

As the two characters stand facing each other, Burton creates a twinning: two bodies, encased in form-fitting black. Both figures are wearing masks and pointed ears, each identified with and hiding behind the form of a creature: he is a bat, she is a cat. In the fight sequence, Catwoman and Batman are essentially on an even keel, and though he is larger and stronger, she can best him at times because of her agility and adroit grasp of hand-to-hand combat. Significantly, in a film that is so concerned with identities around animals, having two nemeses that are dressed as natural opponents in the wild makes for a noteworthy conflict.

The scene on the ledge proves to involve seduction that is all about masks and the human body. Though both Batman and Catwoman are comparable in that they are wearing costumes, it is important to note the differences between their outfits: Batman's is essentially armour while Catwoman is wearing a home-made catsuit. When she runs her claws on his breastplate, she is effectively searching for his soft underbelly, like a consummate predator; when she finds it, she strikes, prompting him to hit back, sending her off the rooftop again and into a passing lorry of sand. She responds to this 'death' with a funny, rueful pun about being saved by 'kitty litter'.

As mentioned earlier, when Catwoman attacks Batman and he responds in kind, she plays to his gallantry and exploits it. What is so important to note in this scene is that Batman has never fought against a woman in Burton's interpretation of the character. His interactions with women have either been sexual, or when he saved them. The only woman of note in Burton's mythology of Batman is Vicki Vale (Kim Basinger), his love interest from Burton's earlier *Batman*.

In the *Batman* TV series, when Batman confronted Catwoman, she would never engage in physical violence against the Caped Crusader. Her henchmen – often also wearing some variation of cat costume – would jump into action, fighting with Batman, delivering blows that would explode in cartoon letters splashed across the screen. Catwoman would stand off in the background, urging her goons, and maybe reacting to the violence, but she never jumped in herself to fight. The reason for this is Batman is a superhero, a good guy, and morality in 1960s family television has often been reduced to 'good guy' versus 'bad guy'. Having Batman hit a woman would have been unacceptable, especially on a show that is targeted towards young viewers. Thus, he is unnerved at having to fight a woman, especially one who can match him.

However, Burton's fairy tale is not directed towards young viewers (despite the accompanying merchandise such as dolls, action figures and t-shirts that were sold) and his version of *Batman* is not as interested in peddling a reductive version of masculinity. Instead, the film presents a complicated play on gender; Catwoman uses seduction and feminine wiles to her advantage and Batman's old-fashioned courtliness makes him vulnerable. When she lies curled up on the floor after being hit, Batman immediately regrets it, coming to her aid, whereupon she delivers an instant kick to his groin which incapacitates him, allowing her to drive him off the ledge. It would be tempting to see this as a woman emasculating a man, but Burton does not seem to harbour anxieties about masculinity. Instead, what emerges is a woman who finds weaknesses in her opponent, both physical and tactical, and uses them to her advantage.

The fight between Catwoman and Batman is also key in discussing the character of Catwoman because it is the first significant step in her gradual degradation. In a following scene, Catwoman appears at the Penguin's lair, which acts as his campaign office as he is improbably running for mayor in a convoluted parallel plot. She is already showing physical signs of wear and tear. Her arm is left scarred and her costume is starting to fray, its amateurish stitching beginning to give. The right eyelet from her mask is ripped to the hair line, and the costume is tattered in places, her skin now exposed.

From this moment, Catwoman begins to fall into a steep decline. When she joins forces with the Penguin in a scheme to frame Batman, she spurns his advances because she is disgusted that he has murdered an innocent woman. Enraged, the Penguin responds and 'kills' Catwoman by wrapping one of his novelty propeller-umbrellas around her neck, sending her flying high above the Gotham City skyline until she manages to free herself, thereby crashing into a rooftop greenhouse. She sits up among the broken glass and smashed pottery, her mask now in tatters, her blonde hair spilling out. Nonetheless, instead of reacting to this 'death' with a wry one-liner, she lets out an anguished scream that shatters the remaining glass. This death is particularly traumatic to Catwoman because it closely resembles her initial demise at the hands of Shreck, who also caused her to fall through glass.

Though Burton takes great pains to present Pfeiffer as a broken soul and successfully diverts his audience from her film star glamour, in a later ballroom scene he nonetheless exploits this facet. Bruce and Selina run into each other, not realising that they had spent the previous evening trying to kill each other. Selina is eye-catching in a sequinned evening gown and Bruce is dapper in his tuxedo, both opting out of the fancy dress, even though they are attending Shreck's annual Christmas fancy dress party. Over the moody strains of Siouxie & the Banshees' *Face to Face*, Bruce and Selina unite and, through some flirtatious banter, they unwittingly discover each other's alter egos. In a film that returns to the themes of masks, it is significant that Burton has his two main characters without masks revealing their secrets in a room full of people wearing disguise. At one point, Selina wearily sighs, 'I guess I'm tired of wearing masks'. But more importantly, when she divulges her plan to kill Shreck with a small pistol she has secreted in her garter, an appalled Bruce asks her, 'Who do you think you are?' A crumbling Selina honestly answers, 'I don't know anymore', before dissolving into peals of mirthless laughter. It is at this moment that the fragile border between the two halves of Selina's personality is revealed – and how she is failing to maintain that separation.

Masks are important in *Batman Returns* as so many characters wear them, and when Selina expresses wariness about masks, she is clearly exhausted attempting to maintain her two identities. For Burton, masks 'symbolise hiding, but when I used to go to Hallowe'en parties wearing a mask it was actually more of a doorway, a way of expressing myself. There is something about being hidden that in some weird way helps you to be more open because you feel freer '(in Salisbury 2006: 106). The mask has given Selina an outlet to become an avenging anti-heroine and to distance herself from the meek victim she was before she became Catwoman, but by this point in the film she cannot maintain the duality anymore and the heavy strain is causing her to crack.

Her closing scene is a tragic end, one in which she finally confronts Shreck over the harm he has caused her. After Shreck improbably escapes the Penguin's imprisonment, he is quickly captured by Catwoman, who follows him to the Penguin's crumbling lair. At this point, her costume is in complete tatters, torn and destroyed, much like her physical and mental state. Just as she fell into a catatonic state when Shreck and then the Penguin killed her, she now settles into a homicidal rage, intent on destroying Shreck. Batman arrives, hoping to rescue Shreck and prevent his lover from becoming a murderer. He appeals to her emotions, highlighting their similarities. 'We're the same', he says, 'Split down the middle'. This exchange is similar in some ways to her seduction scene on the rooftop, except this time it is Batman who is searching for Catwoman's vulnerability that is hidden in her protective emotional body armour. The alter egos collapse at this point and Bruce and Selina are seen at their most emotional. Bruce proposes to her and begs for Shreck's life to be spared. He pulls off his mask, revealing himself to both Selina and Shreck. There is no point in hiding who he is: he is no longer Batman, the avenging superhero, but Bruce Wayne, a man who is hoping to appeal to his lover's better side. He understands that Selina is no longer able to maintain the separation between her two selves and removing his mask is his way to appeal to her aversion to disguise. However, when she pulls off her cover, whatever happens, Shreck will not survive this, as Selina does not bother hiding her identity anymore.

When Selina kills Shreck, it is a spectacularly violent end to both characters. Just as Shreck brutalised Selina's body, she uses it to kill Shreck. He tries to kill her in vain, shooting her with a gun that he has spirited, and, despite the injuries he inflicts on her, she continues to come towards him. Her body is crouched, and she is doubled over in pain. She can barely speak, her voice coming out in rasps, and her body takes several bullets. Her make-up is smeared, and her unruly hair is an untidy mop. As she staggers, dying, she pulls Shreck close and gives him a kiss of death, slipping the taser in both their mouths and plunging her talons into an electric generator, causing large explosions as she electrocutes them both. Bruce struggles through the wreckage, only to unearth Shreck's charred corpse, while Selina is nowhere to be found. Her ending remains ambiguous, although before the rousing Elfman theme plays over the end credits, there is a shot of Catwoman looking up to the sky as the Bat Signal flashes.

The tragic ending of Catwoman makes sense because, more than anyone else in *Batman Returns*, Catwoman is the ultimate Burton monster who suffers because she does not fit in. Pfeiffer's casting is key when discussing the character because Burton uses her body and figuratively abuses it to tell his tale about the intrinsic dangers in mistreating outcasts. Like Frankenstein, Catwoman becomes a monster and her creator must put an end to her: tragically, she is her own creator. When Bruce tries to appeal to Selina's emotions and feelings for him, he believes that it will be possible for Selina to somehow manage a balance between her two identities: she is unable to and is aware of that.

With Pfeiffer in the role, Burton took on a leading glamorous Hollywood figure and completely disassembled her. When Dyer (2002) writes about film stardom and its relationship to film studies, he looks at audience expectations of what they will bring to a viewing of the film, particularly when it comes to the construction of a character. Dyer posits that audiences go into a film with a preconceived notion based on what they have already learned or know about the character as well as the actor, whether through film publicity or other roles or biographical material. By 1992, Catwoman was a significant figure in popular culture, primarily because of Newmar and Kitt. It was both women's distinctive performances that helped define what that character meant to the public. Both Newmar and Kitt also created the iconic Catwoman look which Burton strayed from, imbuing the role with his own unique stamp that calls to mind the aforementioned Gorey and Addams. He purposely avoided any resemblance to the enduring programme of the 1960s, eschewing its camp and good-natured humour. For the most part, audiences likely approached *Batman Returns* with an expectation that Burton would take the existing creative property and interpret it in his distinct way, but the casting of Pfeiffer distorts these expectations. In 1992, she was not a member of his acting troupe, nor was she known as anything other than a popular and beautiful actress. Her presence in a Tim Burton film should have not worked, as she was far too conventional a film star to mesh with his quirkier outlook. But Pfeiffer and Burton succeeded because he was able to fracture and remould Pfeiffer's Hollywood gloss and transform her into one of his grotesques, albeit with sexualised undertones, making the point that anyone can be a misfit, no matter what their star image.

Notes

1. https://www.imdb.com/title/tt0103776/
2. Edward Gorey (1925–2000), American writer and artist, known for his pen-and-ink illustrations, influenced by a Victorian/Gothic aesthetic. Charles Addams (1912–88), American cartoonist, known for his cartoon *The Addams Family*, which mined dark and macabre humour.

PART FOUR

GOTHIC, MONSTROUS AND PECULIAR BODIES

15. THE GROTESQUE SOCIAL OUTCAST IN THE FILMS OF TIM BURTON

Michael Lipiner and Thomas J. Cobb

Throughout his career, Tim Burton has created imaginative films which depict the social 'outcast' in ways critical of contemporary society. This analysis focuses on how Burton's cinematic treatment of the 'grotesque' – including its elements of macabre, comic, ridiculous, strange parody and satire (Thomson 1972) – shaped this figure to mirror mainstream American culture in the form of a Gothic or 'cultural body' often metaphorical of popular lore, and which appears in the various recognisable forms of a persecuted monster. Beginning with a brief examination of the grotesque, the essay follows with an analysis of Burton's reification of this literary concept, using the films *Beetlejuice* (1988), *Edward Scissorhands* (1990), *Batman Returns* (1992) and *Miss Peregrine's Home for Peculiar Children* (2016). It suggests that Burton's manifestation of the grotesque offers universal and multifaceted implications, subverting the homogeneity of American suburbia.

THE COMIC GROTESQUE

To understand Burton's delineation of the social outcast, it is worth considering his debt to the classic grotesque invoked by Frances Barasch. She discusses the origins of this literary concept in the Renaissance period, a time which encompassed usage of 'unruly characters, common folk, grotesque monsters, giants, magicians, hags and spirits for allegorical purposes' (Barasch 1983: 62).

Mikhail Bakhtin's (1984: 19) exploration of this period also embeds 'grotesque realism' within a universalism representing all people, connecting death and life, as well as creating a sense of degradation. Aspects of this fusion of comedy and tragedy are furthered by Richard Dunn, who analyses the works of Charles Dickens and contends that there exists in his works a tragi-comic fusion of grotesque character types. Dunn states that Dickens 'refined his characterization by grotesquely blending terror and comedy in grotesque tragi-comedy and intensified his themes by dramatizing the terror, absurdity, and alienation he found in mid Victorian England', which is cited as 'essential to grotesque art' (1969: 147). These syntheses play a central role in Burton's oeuvre and are especially evident in two films, released at opposite ends of the director's career, and examined in the following section.

INVERSIONS OF DOMESTICITY: FOUNDATIONS OF EQUILIBRIUM IN *BEETLEJUICE* (1988) AND *MISS PEREGRINE'S HOME FOR PECULIAR CHILDREN* (2016)

Although released nearly three decades apart, both *Beetlejuice* and *Miss Peregrine's Home for Peculiar Children* feature overlapping elements in their reification of the grotesque outcast and the 'comic grotesque'. Both films champion characters who embrace their otherworldliness and find satisfactory equilibria between exclusion and conformity. The two films display settings which approximate the quotidian and indicate ambiguity around iconographic orthodoxy; this is emblematic in the fight against the modish changes made to the Connecticut mansion in *Beetlejuice* and the dour, yet dualistic, Wales and Blackpool locales of *Miss Peregrine*. Finally, these films manifest a form of the comic-grotesque which offers a catharsis for the viewer and complicates Michael Steig's dichotomous description of 'extreme types of the grotesque' which either comprise 'liberation from fear [or] liberation from inhibition' (1970: 260).

Despite being famed for its portrayal of the flamboyant titular character, *Beetlejuice* only introduces Michael Keaton's rendition of the comic grotesque after focusing on disquieting examples of the grotesque outcast. Tangible dimensions of this low-level horror emerge when spouses Barbara (Geena Davis) and Adam Maitland (Alex Baldwin) perish in a car accident outside their idyllic Connecticut country home. Their deaths elicit plot arcs indicative of a comic-grotesque sensibility suffused by strains of pathos. Following the accident, Adam and Barbara materialise onscreen as ghosts and assume the trappings of their previous domestic regime. At first, unaware that they are merely spirits invisible to the living world, the Maitlands are forced to watch the trashing and remaking of their home by its new inhabitants, the Deetz family. They consist of Reaganite real estate developer Charles (Jeffrey Jones), sculptress wife Delia (Catherine O'Hara) and depressive daughter Lydia (Winona Ryder). Their luridness is complemented by Otho (William Glenn Scott), a sardonic interior designer who supports Delia's aim of turning the old-fashioned house into a modern art piece, symptomatic of what is attractive in the Deetz family's original home of New York City.

Adam and Barbara's protestations at this colonisation of small-town Americana outlandishly simulate the comic grotesque. This is shown when Barbara hangs herself in a closet and pulls her face off to reveal a skull with gruesome protruding eyes in front of Delia and Otho. It is evident later when Barbara stands deadpan in front of Otho and Delia, holding Adam's severed head. The Deetz family, however, seem oblivious to these acts and instead behave as what Alan Siegel calls 'tasteless yuppies' (2018). Siegel further elicits dimensions of class conflict in Burton's 'playfully macabre aesthetic' and an 'opus [filled with] campy, terrifying special effects, teen angst, nouveau riches bashing, New England charm, a vision of death as an inescapably dysfunctional bureaucracy and Harry Belafonte songs' (2018).

The emphasis on a culture war contained within these descriptions possesses similarity with the theories of Bakhtin and his view of a 'grotesque realism' located in the 'popular-festive travesties of carnival' (1984: 28). Bakhtin's underlining of a grotesque which 'degrades and materializes' (1984: 20) conveys a phenomenon which confronts class privilege. Adam and Barbara's behaviour fits the idea of a grotesque which serves to defy a social hierarchy typified in the 'church, school, the corporation, the nation, and the various policing agencies whose gaze regulates speech and bodies' (Bakhtin 1984: 188).

These dynamics in *Beetlejuice* further relate to the work of Roger Berger (1989: 7), who captures and builds on the rebelliousness evident in Bakhtin's account of 'grotesque realism' (1984: 19). Analysing the 'comic vision' contained in the work of Kenyan writer Ngugi wa Thiong'o, Berger detects the strain of grotesque realism in a 'carnival utopian spirit' used to oppose the 'bourgeois neocolonial authorities' (1989: 2). Berger argues that the author's literary output employs the grotesque to serve narratives concerned with the 'betrayal of African aspirations following political independence' (1989: 1). A novel such as *Petals of Blood* (1977) consequently suggests 'the seemingly grotesque life of the Kenyan peasants in opposition to the bourgeois life of the ruling elite' (Berger 1989: 9).

This 'universalised' and class-based emphasis on grotesque realism abounds in the vicarious routines and experience of non-existence thrust on Adam and Barbara. They further connect this aspect of the grotesque with Burton's invocations of the consummate outsider. Katherine A. Fowkes discusses the consensus that Burton's films present 'variations on themes and characters related to his attraction to loners and misfits and the macabre' (2013: 231). *Beetlejuice* typifies these motifs, but it also finds ways of anchoring them in ways distinctly unsensational and universal.

The alienation of the depressed Lydia most purveys this banal take on the grotesque outcast. Lydia's reference to her whole life as 'one big dark room' provides a quotidian mirror of the Maitlands's time in spiritual limbo. Fittingly, Lydia is the only one of the Deetz family who comes to recognise the Maitlands's presence. When queried by the Maitlands on how she can see them, Lydia states that she has read the 'handbook for the recently deceased' given to the couple upon their deaths and understands that 'live people ignore the strange and unusual . . . I myself am strange and unusual'.

The mysticism of Lydia in this exchange contrasts with the aggressive kind of intelligence possessed by the rest of the Deetz family in capturing a world-view which includes the grotesque outcast as part of a milieu grounded and capable of reflection. These tensions of vulgar normal versus sophisticated abnormal are further tied up with how tropes of the real threaten the potential for gravitas in the afterlife. Jacob Stolworthy acknowledges this dynamic in the production design of Bo Welch, who, in Burton's words, 'wanted it to be specific enough to invoke fear that the afterlife might not be much different than real life' (2018). In the article, Burton recounts how Welch 'was the one responsible for transforming the Maitlands' creaky old rural house into Deetz matriarch Delia's nouveau riche nightmare' (in Stolworthy 2018). The use of two sound stages for set design, one in the modern city of Los Angeles, the other in the genteel New England of East Corinth, Vermont (Stolworthy 2018), likely mirror this transition. Moreover, it overlays this culture war with the spectre of a clash between new and old worlds, raising questions over the fundamental fluidity of American identity.

Numerous plot developments encapsulate such cultural dislocation. When the Maitlands use their handbook to travel to a netherworld waiting room, they find that making progress in the afterlife hinges on a complex bureaucracy run by overworked caseworkers and beleaguered by mass demand from the dead. The grotesques sitting alongside Adam and Barbara are less intimidating for the characters than the inordinate waiting time, an anxiety which counters conventional demonology with the horror of mundanity. When relating the first act of *Beetlejuice* to Steig's account of a grotesque art which 'evokes a world in which the dreamlike and the real are no longer distinguished' (1970: 253), it is clear that Burton depicts the real as more deleterious than the dream-like through poking fun at routines associated with modern life. The boredom of the waiting room and the soulless one-upmanship of the Deetz takeover imply that the banal can surpass the oppressiveness of the ghoulish.

Nevertheless, as *Beetlejuice*'s narrative develops, Burton declines to embrace a model of the grotesque which provides wholesale catharsis. If the Deetz parents personify the dangers of too much 'normality', the freelance bio-exorcist ghost Beetlejuice (Michael Keaton) emblematises the destructiveness of an unadulterated grotesque. From the character's first meeting with the Maitlands, Beetlejuice purveys Steig's notion of an animus expressing 'infantile fears, fantasies and impulses' and mirrors the theorist's dichotomy of grotesque models which could be 'primarily threatening' or adopting 'means of ridicule' (1970: 258–60).

Beetlejuice, who sexually harasses Barbara and changes form wildly, vaunts the victory of the id over the superego by celebrating the means of ridicule and Steig's understanding of 'liberation from inhibition' (1970: 260). He also, however, muddies Steig's dichotomy by encapsulating the stereotypical model of the 'threatening' grotesque. Subsequent to his transgressive behaviour towards the Maitlands, Beetlejuice transforms into a snakelike creature and terrifies every member of the Deetz family. This pushes the new homeowners towards attempting an exorcism and convinces Lydia that Adam and Barbara are directly responsible for the serpent's manifestation, compromising the initial affinities between her outcast status and the Maitlands's purveyance of the comic grotesque.

The solution Burton proposes to the disequilibrium thrives on reconciliation, absent of the misanthropy which could emerge from an unremitting fulfilment of grotesque tropes. In the film's climax, in which Lydia saves the Maitlands from exorcism and Beetlejuice is sent back to the netherworld, Burton draws attention to a new order where the grotesque has become domesticated, capable of assimilation by both the dead and the living.

During the final scene, the exuberant sounds of Harry Belafonte's *Jump in the Line* play over several important plot resolutions. The serpent monster, formerly incarnated by Beetlejuice, is now a sculpture modelled by Delia Deetz. She jokingly scares her husband Charles with the artwork, a light-heartedness echoed by the conciliatory relationship the family have consolidated with the Maitlands. The house is now shared equally, an accord which proposes a classless and happily egalitarian solution to the divides earlier conjured by the grotesque. Yet this higher state ultimately depends on the marginalisation of the uncouth Beetlejuice. The transcendent state of Lydia and her surreal ascent towards the mansion ceiling manifests an inverse to the torpid experience of the erstwhile bio-exorcist ghost, who is trapped in the afterlife waiting room for eternity, tormented through a perennial state of boredom.

Lydia's overcoming of her outcast status and the punishment wrought on the grotesque Beetlejuice suggest a worldview hinging on rapprochement between the normal and the eccentric, an affinity only achievable if the unsavoury elements of the latter are ironed out. *Miss Peregrine's Home for Peculiar Children* furthers this dynamic by unifying the macabre and whimsical, demonstrating that the pathologised outcast requires equilibrium to pursue their alternative lifestyle.

The first act of Burton's post-millennium film, which is an adaptation of a novel written in 2011 by Ransom Riggs, goes beyond the culture wars of *Beetlejuice* by delineating a landscape where the grotesque outcast is hemmed in by forces alternately quotidian and historically totemic, necessitating the provision of a safe haven. It begins in the Sunbelt setting of Florida circa spring 2016: a nouveau riche paradise emblematic of the capitalist vulgarity initially embodied by the Deetz family. The film's protagonist, Jake Portman (Asa Butterfield), though certainly not grotesque, is implied to be a social outcast and left out of the hedonism and frivolity enjoyed by his peers. As he works in a supermarket, a voice-over by the character recalls the depressiveness of Lydia by bemoaning the consensus that 'your teenage years are for having fun and making friends'. Jake's social failings become obvious when a female student he recognises from school colludes with classmates who mock him, an ostracisation succeeded with Burton's familiar preoccupation with the supernatural.

A phone call by Portman's grandfather, Abe (Terence Stamp), juxtaposes the anxieties of Jake's adolescence with overtly sinister threats, again reprising the alternation between the soulless normal and dangerous abnormal so prevalent in *Beetlejuice*. On the journey to Abe's house, Jake sees a ghostly figure with a vacant expression standing alone in the street, an alarming portent of the trauma about to be inflicted. Subsequently, he finds his grandfather lying down in the woods with his eyes removed. Abe tells Jake to head to the 'loop'[1] of 3 September 1943 before expiring. The opening sequence finishes with Jake glimpsing a monster in the forest, prefiguring a nightmare more existential than the problems of adolescence previously established.

Indeed, the starker thematic antinomies of *Miss Peregrine* become transparent after Abe's departure, and emerge when Burton outlines the role the grandfather's stories played in Jake's maladjustment. Flashbacks to Jake's life as a pre-pubescent child show Abe telling him stories about his retreat to a Welsh island during the Second World War. He celebrates a school led by a headmistress known as Miss Alma Peregrine (Eva Green) and filled with paranormal children known as 'Peculiars'. These Peculiars include individuals with powers such as invisibility and the ability to create fire, but their whimsical stories, however, also prove to be the source of much of Jake's marginalisation. This is noticeable in flashbacks where Jake naively gives class presentations on the diverse abilities and manifestations of the Peculiars to laughter and derision.

Burton piles an intimidating allegory on top of these incidents of the ostracised eccentric, overshadowing Jake's humiliations with incomparably evil persecutions of 'difference'. The fantastical tales have justification in the emotional and historical authority emphasised when Abe reveals to Jake as a child that he came to Miss Peregrine's school from Poland, a country he jokingly claims had monsters with 'huge arms and tentacles'.

The 1940s context of Abe's arrival on Cairnholm means that the notions of peculiar here mine history for commentary on mainstream stigmatisations of 'difference'. Jake tacitly acknowledges the real-life allegory of Nazi persecution underlying Abe's outlandish descriptions of his former schoolmates, musing,

'The children were special . . . but not the way you said'. Here, the oppression of the comic grotesque takes on existential connotations, becoming a threat to all forms of human variation. The fact that Abe euphemises the Nazis as 'monsters with tentacles', thus sharing grotesque characteristics, perhaps suggests that the pathologising of those not 'normal' merely takes the perpetrators of the stigma full circle, hypocritically embracing the very divergence from norms they wished to demonise.

The allegorical and fantastical role of the grotesque here is recounted by numerous scholars in relation to treatments of the Holocaust. Maurizio Viano detects 'grotesque comedy' (1999: 170) in Appelfeld's *Badenheim 1939* (1980) and Art Spiegelman's *Maus*'s (1997) rendition of the Holocaust. These treatises 'dared to stray variously from realism [and] introduce the comic', serving 'another tool for the dissemination of its memory' (Viano 1999: 170–1). Similarly, Sue Vice sees Jerzy Kosinski's 1965 novel *The Painted Bird* as fitting a pattern of 'non-realist, grotesque works about the Holocaust', crystallised in an 'intersection between the allegorical and the fabular-realist plots' (2003: 69).

The grotesque invocation of the Holocaust in *Miss Peregrine* is, however, fleeting compared to these works. Jake's eventual investigation of the school at Cairnholm, which is justified by a psychiatrist treating him for trauma, returns the viewer to tropes of the comic-grotesque that fashion equilibrium and equality, in some ways revisiting the accords achieved at the conclusion of *Beetlejuice*. The explorations of Cairnholm, which are initially overseen by Jake's father, pose eerie combinations of the macabre and whimsical.

The former is evident in the ramshackle hotel Jake and his father stay in upon arrival on the island, a decaying building filled with beer-swilling locals. Moreover, it becomes conspicuous when Jake encounters a mocking Welsh youth who entertains dreams of becoming a rapper and mines material from his father's time 'on the dole'. This gallows sensibility, as antithetical to the Sunbelt ostentation of Florida as the Maitlands's creaking house was to the avant-garde tastes of Delia Deetz, also exists on the same landmass as the 1940s loop containing Miss Peregrine's picaresque school, highlighting that the macabre and genteel are frequently two sides of the same coin. Although Jake soon discovers that Miss Peregrine's school was bombed during the Second World War, he finds a parallel world within the site, established in the loop of 3 September 1943 foregrounded by Abe.

The *mise-en-scène* of the Peculiars discovered by Jake is well illuminated and signals a carefree egalitarianism. Miss Peregrine's community live in a grand mansion and start each day on 3 September 1943 in the style of *Groundhog Day* (Ramis 1993), capturing the sense of disinhibition and liberation fostered in *Beetlejuice*'s epilogue. Because the same day begins anew and is wholly detached from previous events, the schoolchildren can get away with antics and chance disturbances of the local island community. The equilibrium outlined at the end of Burton's 1988 film is similarly redolent in Jake's romance with Emma Bloom (Ella Purnell), an aerokinetic teenager who can breathe underwater. She encourages the Floridian to see past his 'ordinary' background and harness his special power of being able to see 'Hollowgasts', invisible disfigured Peculiar scientists that resulted from an experiment in attaining immortality led by a sinister dissenter known as Mr Barron (Samuel L. Jackson).

The uncomfortable invoking of the Holocaust, again evident in the appellation of 'Hollowgast', repeats the idea that the solipsism of the grotesque outcast can culminate in a circular pattern of evil, merely bringing the figure down to the same level as his most heinous persecutors. This symmetry of grotesque dissension and conformist oppression, which was raised on a less ideologically charged level by the vulgarity of Beetlejuice and the Deetz family, becomes clear in exposition which reveals that the Hollowgasts steal the eyes of children to maintain life and regain human form, generating an image of a grotesque which is predatory and parasitic.

Miss Peregrine's climax provides a model of a grotesque hinging on revitalisation and rapprochement, capable of alleviating decline and extremes of inequality. Barron's kidnapping of Miss Peregrine, a development which occurs amid a host of other plot convolutions, compels Jake and the Peculiars to exit the 1943 loop and head for a 2016 loop in the English seaside town of Blackpool. This town is famous for its role as a holiday resort in Britain's early post-war era. It fell out of favour among the British because of the advent of cheap flights and the increasing economy of European holidays abroad in the final decades of the twentieth century, fostering a sense of declinism perhaps elemental in Blackpool's 67.5% vote to leave the EU in 2016 (Pidd 2016). The fact that Burton chooses to set the battle between the Peculiars and Barron in 2016, and not during the town's heyday of the 1940s and '50s, speaks to the director's treasuring of the unfashionable and his revelling in the perversity of an 'outcast status'.

His selection of Blackpool had precedent. In 2012, Burton filmed a music video for the American rock band The Killers in the town. The video featured Winona Ryder, who played Lydia in *Beetlejuice*, and markedly contrasted with the *mise-en-scène* of The Killers's Las Vegas origins (Martinovic 2012). Burton's history with, and appreciation for, the town was reinforced when, in the midst of the filming of *Miss Peregrine* in 2015, he was reminded that he had 'stayed in Blackpool when working on stop-motion films in Manchester' (Anon. 2015) and was happy to participate in the town's famous annual lights show, known as the Blackpool Illuminations. Blackpool reciprocated the publicity gained by Burton's shoot in 2016 with the promotion of 'Miss Peregrine's Blackpool Trail', which encompassed a tour of all the locations used in the film (Anon. 2016). Councillor Gillian Campbell, Deputy Leader of Blackpool

Council, felt 'extremely proud that Tim Burton chose to shoot elements of the Miss Peregrine film here in Blackpool' (in Anon. 2016).

It is the dour imagery of this town, and not the Sunshine State, which complements the 'Peculiar' personality. The defeat of Barron in Blackpool, which takes place in the loop of January 2016 and occurs months prior to Abe's death in the spring of 2016, allows Jake to find his grandfather alive and well in contemporaneous Florida. Jake's search for Emma, however, takes precedence in the conclusion of *Miss Peregrine*. Emma, who is left behind with the other Peculiars in the world of 1943 as a result of leaving the 2016 loop, meets Jake in the film's final scene.

Explaining a map of international 'loop' locations given by his grandfather, Jake reveals that he left 2016 Florida and embarked on a series of bizarre misadventures, including joining the Navy in the throes of the Second World War, to reach her. Jake's exit from the Sunbelt caters to Burton's sense of whimsy and the equilibrium attainable for those deemed outcasts, grotesque or simply maladaptive. As noted in the next section's analysis, *Edward Scissorhands* depicts the threats to this transcendence in the hegemony of American suburbia that Jake escapes from, shifting from an emphasis on equilibrium and focalising the orthodox expectations thrust on the grotesque outcast.

THE GROTESQUE SOCIAL OUTCAST IN *EDWARD SCISSORHANDS*

In *Edward Scissorhands*, Burton modernises a retelling of Mary Shelley's classic Frankenstein's monster. His production begins with a montage depictive of the machines used to create the film's bedraggled and otherworldly protagonist, followed by an introduction to the elder Kim Boggs (Winona Ryder) and her relaying of Edward Scissorhands's (Johnny Depp) story.

Siobhan Lyons notes how 'a Tim Burton film is instantly recognizable through its dark yet cartoonish aesthetics, its skeletal, pale heroes and heroines, and its steadfast rejection of the norm' (2017: 195). This is exemplified at the beginning of the film with the juxtaposition of Edward's dark and Gothic mansion situated within proximity of the (seemingly) peaceful and tranquil suburbs redolent of America's post-war era. Craig Hammond contrasts the local suburbanites who dress in bright pastel colours and live in 'uniform and pastel-shaded exteriors, of symmetrically perfect and sprawling suburban homes' (2015: 227). Indeed, one of the first shots of *Edward Scissorhands* is of a suburban community where the inhabitants possess identical pastel-coloured houses and wear clothes to match their homes, a uniformity at odds with Edward's baroque abode.

The conventional suburbia, which Edward's Gothic mansion overlooks, is based on Burton's hometown of Burbank, California, a place described as 'a suburb of Los Angeles' which 'symbolizes mainstream America during the 1950s and 1960s, oft remembered as the Eisenhower-era world of mass conformity with its standardized houses and lockstep mentality', where all were 'expected to do and believe and behave the same way' (Hanke 2000: 26).

Peg Boggs (Dianne Wiest), an Avon sales representative desperate to make a sale, catalyses the pathologisation of Edward by attempting to bring him into mainstream American society. When Peg enters his mansion, she sees newspaper clippings about 'freaks', including a boy who 'reads with his hands' and 'feels heat of the words', as well as an advertisement that satirises suburbia with the caption, 'modern furniture that lives up to its "Nice-to-Live-With look"'. Peg, who finds Edward cowering in a corner, tries to assure him that she is 'as harmless as cherry pie' and his 'local Avon representative', a vanguard of American culture and suburbia.

To Helena Bassil-Morozow, Edward's scissors possess a class dimension, functioning like 'Boris Karloff's [who portrayed Frankenstein's monster in the classic film *Frankenstein* (Whale 1931)] large working-class hands [which] take centre stage not only because language fails this particular monster' (2010: 74). They also mirror the character's lack of congruence with the hegemony of American suburbia. When Edward takes up Peg's offer to leave the mansion and stay with the Boggs family, he attempts to please suburbanites by using his scissors for hairdressing and sculpture but is nevertheless viewed as a 'freak' to the suburban majority (Lyons 2017: 197).

Edward's social awkwardness is only accepted when he contributes to the mainstream. As Bassil-Morozow comments, 'bourgeoise culture is willing to consume the products of the artist's creativity, and even absorb his rebellion because it, too, is suitable for consumption, but does not like the actual sharpness of his demeanour' (2010: 69). This dynamic, as manifested in *Edward Scissorhands*, means that 'the curious, bored villagers are ready to tolerate Edward provided that his idiosyncrasies and deviations are under their control [. . .] they are happy to use "the fruits" of his unusual personality, but are not prepared to accept its less safe side' (Bassil-Morozow 2013: 68). Edward's 'less safe side', however, is frequently an imaginary product of the suburbanites he encounters.

When Peg's neighbour, Joyce (Kathy Baker), tries to seduce him, he immediately becomes terrified and rejects her predatory advances, resulting in a false and malicious rumour that Edward tried to rape her. Edward is further abused when the young daughter of the Boggs family and the narrator introduced at the beginning of the film, Kim, allows her boyfriend Jim (Anthony Michael Hall) to exploit him. Jim wants to rob a high-security room in his own father's house for money and uses Edward for this task, suspecting that his scissors can easily open the front door. When Edward is arrested and acquitted on grounds of naiveté, Kim confronts Jim and he simply tells her, 'I did what I could. My old man thinks he's retarded, so he's free'.

To Renee Middlemost, the mean-spiritedness of these suburbanites draws on the 'longing for an authentic connection' Burton experienced in Burbank, which 'suggests that it is the behaviour sanctioned by "normal society" that is truly monstrous' (2017: 217). This cruelty is heightened by the 'normalcy' of American capitalistic mores, a hegemony which deems Edward's otherworldliness impractical and alien. Burton reinforces this when Edward is refused a bank loan on the grounds that he has no employment history or social security number. A later scene exemplifies Edward's maladaptive relationship with a society built on free markets and private property rights. In the wake of the botched robbery organised by Jim, the Boggs family attempts to give Edward an ethics lesson over dinner. The patriarch of the Boggs family, Bill (Alan Arkin), asks Edward what he would do if he found a suitcase on the street containing money. Edward responds that he would 'buy things for my loved one', a response which prompts exasperation from most of the household.

Edward's perceived functional impairments derive from an ironic and tragic effort at creating the perfect human. Like Frankenstein's monster, he remains unfinished or rather 'flawed or faulty' by his inventor who, himself, 'is not an ideal person because, by having a heart attack, he undermines his status as an omnipotent, magnificent god' (Bassil-Morozow 2010: 74), thus leaving an abandoned monster unprepared for the real world. Because of this dynamic, Burton's employment of the grotesque creates a number of thematically rich dichotomies redolent of Geoffrey Harpham's citing of clashes between 'artist vs. the bourgeoisie, capitalism vs. fascism, and the enlightened soul vs. the benighted mob' (1976: 466–7).

The American Christmas holiday season's centrality within *Edward Scissorhands* compounds this vein of ideological conflict. This is depicted by Burton as a capitalistic tyranny of department stores, conservative ideologies and merchandised products (Born 2017: 82–3). The season's commercialism is also rationalised by its suburban proponents. In one scene, while decorating a Christmas tree, Kim asks Peg, 'Mom, do you really think we should be having this party?' Peg replies, 'It's just what we need to calm things down, and everything will go back to normal'.

Instead, dysphoria and disequilibrium reign in *Edward Scissorhands*'s climax. After Edward accidentally cuts Kim's hand, Jim hunts and harasses him before drinking alcohol. Although Edward saves the younger Boggs child, Kevin (Robert Oliveri), from being run over by an intoxicated Jim, outside observers perceive the rescue as an attack. A crowd of suburbanites follow Edward to his mansion (amid a 'Happy Holidays' sign in the background), invoking what Elizabeth Scherman describes as 'a mob reminiscent of another intolerant kill-the-creature story, Mary Shelley's *Frankenstein*' (2016: 44).

A final showdown between Edward and Jim, which results in the latter's death, prompts the creature to say goodbye to Kim and choose isolation over what Bassil-Morozow calls the 'joys of socialisation' (2010: 46). *Edward Scissorhands*'s rendition of the grotesque outcast is bittersweet. Nevertheless, Burton attributes fault not to the outcast who struggles to conform to majoritarian notions of suburban conformity, but instead to Adam Barkman and Antonio Sanna's understanding of a society that is 'ill-equipped in embracing more nuanced, unique figures' (2017: xxiv).

THE GROTESQUE SOCIAL OUTCAST IN *BATMAN RETURNS* (1992)

In the sequel to Burton's *Batman* (1989), the tragic antihero of the Penguin (otherwise known as Oswald Cobblepot and played by Danny DeVito) poses 'yet another outgrowth of the disillusioned boy with scissors' and who, 'of all Burton's antagonists [. . .] is the most poignant, and most hurt' (Bassil-Morozow 2013: 77). The film opens with a montage depictive of the grotesque outcast's creation, delineated in the Penguin's mother (Diane Salinger) screaming during childbirth. Subsequently, his parents stand beside a Christmas tree (reminiscent of *Edward Scissorhands*) watching their child use his flipper hands to grasp the bars of his boxed, cage-like crib. From the start of *Batman Returns*, Burton emphasises the plight of the rejected 'other' and the congenital alienation of a nonconformist who expresses his independence but meets collective hostility.

The Penguin's aristocratic, bourgeois parents, moreover, lend their class a psycho-social dimension. When the Cobblepots take the Penguin out for a buggy ride near a frozen lake, they callously reject him from upper-class society by throwing him into the icy water. Through the loss, respectively, of their creator and parents, both Edward Scissorhands and the Penguin become 'characterized by a form of arrested development leading to the eternalization of their childhood world' (Elferen 2013: 66).

Much like Edward, the Penguin is fixated on what Bassil-Morozow calls the 'identity problem' wrought by 'birth and parental rejection [. . .] a more regressive Edward who wants his toy back and who will butcher the world for the sins committed by his evil parents' (2010: 77). The Penguin's giant plastic duck transportation vehicle literalises this sinister infantilism through resembling a toy that hangs in front of his crib in the film's exposition. To Bassil-Morozow such tropes played a thematic role through hinting that Penguin's 'make-up, his mask, his toys are all allegorical, hyperbolical, grotesque, hysterical offshoots of his childhood complexes' (2013: 77).

Burton expresses this dynamic by subverting the Gothic imagery of horror movies that he grew up with. The 'normalcy' beleaguering the Penguin is most embodied by what Simon Born describes as the 'affluent consumer society that rejected him as a monster', thus reminding viewers of 'the by-products of a ruthless capitalism' (2017: 82–3). As in *Edward Scissorhands*, Burton satirises and reflects on the hegemony of American capitalistic greed by once again returning to Christmas, the most profitable and marketable time of the year for Americans.

The isolation of the Penguin is furthermore exemplified psychically, as well as ideologically, eliciting further comparisons with the thematic underpinnings of Burton's previous film; Edward and the Penguin have scars and dark hair, dress in traditional Gothic attire, and have extremely pale skin. Burton's use of black, however, elicits a more positive meaning here, in contrast to more traditional associations depicted in genres such as the Western and horror. In this film, as in much of Burton's oeuvre, black expresses the 'ultimate freedom in art', which contrasts with the sheer paleness of the Penguin's face, 'an "artistic anemia" that suggests long hours spent in his study or other places of isolation, far from the rest of civilization' (Karácsony 2017: 31).

Even more normative things are reversed in *Batman Returns*; black (Batman, played by Michael Keaton) is 'good', and white (the corrupt business mogul and aspirant tyrant Max Shreck, played by Christopher Walken) is 'bad'. In a key plot development, the Penguin tells Shreck, 'You and I have something in common; we're both perceived as monsters', referring to his own freak status and the corrupt businessman's deleterious effect on Gotham City. The Penguin notes, 'But somehow, you're a well-respected monster and I am, to date, not . . . And, like you, I want some respect! A recognition of my basic humanity'. The Penguin threatens to expose Shreck's illicit business dealings if he does not agree to help him become acclimated and accepted into the higher echelons of Gotham City. Thus, like Edward, the Penguin is willing to try to assimilate in society (although the methods to achieve this assimilation in *Batman Returns* are, unlike Edward's, malevolent).

As the abandoned orphan searches for his birth parents in the Gotham City Hall Office of Birth Records, reporters gather, and residents observe the Penguin. Alienated from society, akin to Frankenstein's monster, he reacts with resistance, thus illustrating Peter Kunze's citing 'of the hypocritical tendency of American society to depend on the othering of minority groups while simultaneously laying claim to ideals of life, liberty, and the pursuit of happiness' (2016: 206–7).

Much like when Peg shows Edward pictures of her loving family and his expressions communicate longing and poignancy, the Penguin's sadness connotes alienation. He tells the watching crowd, 'A penguin is a bird that cannot fly! I am a man! I have a name! Oswald Cobblepot!' The media respond by printing headlines honouring the Penguin's respectable character and one passer-by even says, in a perverse nod to Edward Scissorhands, 'Don't need hands as long as you got heart'.

Soon after the Penguin shares his desire to be respected in the eyes of Gotham City urbanites, Shreck manipulates him to run for mayor in a scheme to administer the city from behind the scenes. In actions which resemble the Boggs's attempt to help Edward adapt to societal 'norms', Shreck's cohorts try to cajole the Penguin into abandoning his 'freakiness'. An 'image consultant' encourages Penguin to cover his flippers with gloves because 'Our research tells us that voters like fingers'. The problems inherent in this makeover become clear when another spin doctor mocks the Penguin's upbringing in the sewers, only to be met with violence. The shallowness of these machinations and the Penguin's refusal to embrace conventional notions of electability resonate with Bakhtin's foregrounding of the grotesque's political nature by serving to demystify hierarchy and the institutions 'whose gaze regulates speech and bodies' (1984: 188). This affinity with Bakhtinian notions of class tension suggests that the Penguin possesses more commonality with the antagonist Beetlejuice than the protagonist Edward Scissorhands, a synergy crystallised in his anarchic and purportedly radical status.

In another scene, Batman and his loyal butler, Alfred (Patrick Gough), hijack a speech by the Penguin and expose his hatred of Gotham's citizens on a recorded videotape revealing that the 'freak' lacks the blameless vulnerability tangible in Edward's character. When the Penguin flees back to his safe sewers to escape the wrath of Gotham's mob, there is a circumstantial resemblance to Edward's fleeing from Burbank residents (both mirroring the Monster in Whale's *Frankenstein* who flees while being hunted by an unforgiving and angry mob). Yet, the self-inflicted nature of the Penguin's downfall fails to corroborate Born's idea that 'Burton's monsters are inherently innocent' and that 'it is the confrontation with a xenophobic society that makes them evil' (2017: 99). Much as the grotesque outcast Beetlejuice compounds the problems experienced by the Maitlands, the Penguin's character is simply too unadulterated to generate the equilibrium required for Gotham City's febrile body politic.

As in *Beetlejuice*, however, an equal amount of disarray derives from the grotesqueness of 'normalcy' and those emblematic of the American capitalist system. This is conspicuous in Schreck, who decides to abandon the Penguin after the hijacked speech. Kunze reflects how the character's perturbing qualities manifest in his incongruous white hair, 'rendering him both unusual and sinister' (2016: 206–7). This ambiguity around the grotesque's true nature is reinforced when Alfred stresses Shreck's danger to Batman by informing him, 'Our prime concern is this ghastly grotesque'.

Such fluidity recalls Sylvie Debevec Henning's description of early Renaissance grotesque art as 'an attack on the principles of identity and difference and with it the law of contradiction', presenting scenarios where 'the grotesque involves a sustained disruption of conventional logic that manifests itself particularly in the de-formation of traditional categories' (1981: 109). Central to Henning's analysis is the questioning of dichotomies of 'ludicrous/fearsome' and 'familiar/

uncanny' and the complication of these divides through the 'indeterminacy' of the grotesque character (1981: 109).

Similar to the unforgiving suburban community that Edward must contend with, *Batman Returns* explores the blurriness of defining the grotesque through an unpleasant and tyrannical corporate milieu where 'freaks' and 'monsters' are supposedly condemned. This schismatic quality of the grotesque emerges when the Penguin crashes an upscale party and tells the bourgeois elite his plan to kidnap their first-born sons whom they 'left defenceless at home so you could dress up like jerks, get juiced and dance badly'. When the Penguin threatens to kidnap Shreck's son, Chip (Andrew Bryniarski), the former tells him, 'If you have any human feeling, take me instead [. . .] I'm the one you want. Isn't it Max Shreck who manipulated and betrayed you?' Shreck therefore confirms that he indeed is the real villain, a 'normal' human being who moulds mainstream society and its corrupt, hypocritical rules, creating parallels between what Scherman describes as the 'outcast and the deviant; that which in our society may find its parallel in disabled or disfigured individuals' (2016: 48).

In both *Edward Scissorhands* and *Batman Returns*, Burton draws on the classic grotesque to expose 'normal' society's hypocrisy and corruption, critiquing mainstream society's stigmatisation of nonconformity and childlike wonder (Lackner 2013: 163). Because of this quality, the death of the Penguin in the final scenes carries the air of tragedy, even though his murderous plans and destabilisation of Gotham's body politic have been thwarted. His lethal plummet to death in the icy water of his lair mirrors the ending of Shelley's novel, *Frankenstein* [1818] (2003).

As in the epilogue of *Edward Scissorhands*, where the elder Kim believes the snow prevalent in her suburban town to be a product of Edward still being alive and in his mansion crafting ice sculptures, the Penguin's farewell retains poignancy and gives the impression of a grotesque legacy for Gotham City. His body is flanked by his loyal penguins who are, as Susan Bernardo comments, 'as close as Penguin gets to a family' (2016: 80). Immortalised as a perennial outcast, the Penguin expires as his true self, relieved of the falsity required for his brief foray into the grotesqueness of Gotham politics.

Conclusion

Burton's social outcasts are constructed within a multitude of genres and follow Harpham's (1976: 464) description of the grotesque as consisting of subdivisions split between 'caricature', 'comic grotesque', 'fantastic grotesque' and 'Gothic-macabre'. Burton mixes these subdivisions, and also depicts his tragic grotesque characters' alienation through physical deformity.

Burton's model of the grotesque is therefore multifaceted. To quote the ideas of Guy Westwell (2014: 94), much of its application thrives on a 'hegemonic reconciliation', while bridging gaps between conservative Americana and those left out of its fashionable democratic capitalist model. In other cases, the representation is more dysphoric, connoted in figures such as Penguin and Edward Scissorhands. The reification of the grotesque is complex and frequently ambiguous: a rendition potentially invoking and playing on the original dichotomous understanding of Steig (1970: 258–60), while alternating between threat and self-deprecating ridicule. Collectively, Burton's films encompass unique collaborative bodies that fall between the cracks of our real world.

NOTE

1. Refers to a time loop that constantly replays the day leading up to the bombing and thus prevents the home's destruction.

16. 'A GIANT MAN CAN'T HAVE AN ORDINARY-SIZED LIFE': ON TIM BURTON'S *BIG FISH*

José Duarte and Ana Rita Martins

For more than forty years Tim Burton has been telling (extra)ordinary tales by means of a particular visual style, but also via narrative content. The adjective 'Burtonesque', which defines Burton's cinematic approach and techniques, is used by critics and academics to explain how the director 'employs a number of recurring themes that create a cohesive and personal vision' (Odell and Le Blanc 2005: 14).

Visually, Burton's cinematic world is often influenced by German Expressionism, horror movies, particularly the ones by Hammer Studios, and B-science-fiction films. Thematically, he is inspired by Gothic and horror fiction, with authors such as Edgar Allan Poe and Mary Shelley having a prominent effect on certain films, while fairy tales, magic and inverted worlds, or the monstrous are also a common presence. In this sense, Burton inverts the rules of the world as we know it: for him, the normal is weird and the weird is normal. The director's constant subversion, and inevitable undermining of 'normal' worlds, is a continuous reminder of the potential of stories to embrace and understand difference, especially of those who, like Burton himself, are inclined towards the uncommon. As he says:

> I've always loved monsters and monster movies. I was never terrified of them, I just loved them from as early as I can remember. My parents said I was never scared, I'd just watch anything [. . .] there was something about that identification. Every kid responds to some image, some fairy tale image, and I felt most monsters were basically misperceived, they

usually had much more heartfelt souls than the human characters around them. (in Salisbury 2000: 2)

Burton's remarks in an interview with Mark Salisbury highlight an important element that reinforces the idea of subversion already mentioned. Interested mainly in those who are misperceived, the director's unusual characters are explored both as a provocation to the audience – as disruptive figures – but also as a representation of the way we tend to react to what we do not understand, thus 'translating the uncanny experience into something concrete and communicable to others' (Adams 2001: 132).

Within this context, Burton's characters, whether monsters, 'freaks' or others, usually reveal a truer nature than their 'normal' counterparts: although the spectator is confronted with disfigured, disproportional bodies, they are also genuine, kind and understanding. This perspective lends a unique meaning to the bizarre and macabre world of the director: in spite of a cinema often dominated by a sombre atmosphere, muted, expressionist *mise-en-scène* and a disruption of normalcy, Burton's vision celebrates the extraordinary or anomalous body as a major characteristic of one's individuality. Thus, characters such as Victor (Charlie Tahan), Edward Scissorhands (Johnny Depp), Jack Skellington (Chris Sarandon) and Ichabod Crane (Johnny Depp), for instance, represent an alternative way of telling a story about the human condition, the power of stories and of different ways of telling them. Along these lines, understanding (and potentially believing) becomes a key word in Burton's films.

Several authors (Bassil-Morozow 2011; Le Blanc 2001; McMahan 2005; Pheasant-Kelly 2017; Salisbury 2000; Weinstock 2013) have already underlined some of these issues by pointing out specifically how the idea of monstrosity is central in Burton's films, with Jeffrey Weinstock and Frances Pheasant-Kelly's studies focusing on the use of space to explore the abject and weird bodies that inhabit the director's world.

Usually regarded as a minor film in Burton's filmography, *Big Fish* follows the story/stories told by Edward Bloom (Albert Finney/Ewan McGregor) who, on his deathbed, and through a series of flashbacks, recounts his numerous extraordinary adventures. The film opens with Edward's son Will (Billy Crudup) and his wife Josephine (Marion Cotillard) returning from Paris to Ashton, Alabama, to see his dying father. Will has a tense relationship with Edward, as he does not believe in the wondrous tales he tells about his life.

However, as Will fights to distinguish fact from fiction, he soon learns that his father's stories are more than a mixture of both and are a way for him to understand his father, himself and other curious beings that may not be fully appreciated. Adapted from the work *Big Fish: A Novel of Mythic Proportions* (1998), written by Daniel Wallace, the film enables Burton to explore the 'many elements of fantasy' (Le Blanc and Odell 2000: 124), which allow him to continuously redefine the world, its boundaries and its preconceptions as they are commonly comprehended.

In this context, scholarship regarding *Big Fish* (Bonilla 2013; Hada 2014; Perdigao 2016; Plate 2017; Weinstock 2013) mostly centres on the importance of its diegetic storytelling and narrative. In the film, the world of fantasy, as opposed to or as an extension of the real world, provides a unique opportunity to tell stories of unruly and weird bodies. Indeed, it is via the many tales recounted by Edward Bloom that the spectator is confronted with different perspectives that take us to a creation of 'mythic proportions', as the title of the novel suggests. This is evident not only in the way Bloom relates his stories, whereby he adds as many fantastic layers as possible to project his self and others (Hada 2014), but also in the way the director explores the thin veil between reality and fantasy as a commentary on the human condition.

Thus, and as Ken Hada further notes, Edward is the one who tells the fantastic stories and, by doing so, it is how 'he understands and posits the significant moments of his life' (2014: 10) and of the lives of the ones who inhabit his world. The fact that he uses a world of fantasy, either as an extension of or as a clash with the real world, is crucial in appreciating the importance of storytelling in the diegesis; it is through this interrelation between real and fantasy that Burton accomplishes his own vision, one that, as Lisa Perdigao explains, presents 'the transformation of reality' (2016: 96) via the fantastic. Therefore, at the end of the film, viewers are confronted with the existence of all the characters Edward mentioned in his stories and, albeit not as fantastic as depicted by him, they are real and celebrate Edward's life symbolically by, in turn, relating tales about him, thereby participating in a discourse that underscores the importance of storytelling.

Nonetheless, while this theme is crucial to the force of the film, it is also relevant to perceive how *Big Fish* reflects other 'Burtonesque' themes. Distinct from the aforementioned approaches, this study focuses on the film's portrayal of freaks and monsters in relation to cinematography, figure behaviour and physical qualities as well as considering the spaces they inhabit and the times of day that they appear. Grounding an analysis on research by Salisbury (2000), Adams (2001) and Weinstock (2013), this chapter considers notions of freaks as monsters (as proposed by Adams and developed by Cohen [1996 and 1999], Mittman [2016] and Carroll [2020]) in relation to the monstrous and weird bodies portrayed in *Big Fish*, which are intimately connected with the other 'bodies' the director has created.

The chapter first enquires into the importance of weird and monstrous bodies, while also considering a particular visual inspiration for *Big Fish*, namely, the work of Diane Arbus, an American photographer who was able to integrate 'the freakishness in normalcy and the normalcy in freakishness' (Bosworth 2005: 248). Secondly, it analyses the weird bodies presented by

Edward Bloom's 'larger than life' story/stories, in particular those of the giant, the werewolf and the conjoined twins. By examining these bodies, the essay suggests Will's recognition of the 'Other' as recognition of himself and his self. As such, Edward Bloom's 'unique perspective of the world' (Bonilla 2013: 168), and indeed that of Burton, propose a chance to consider changes in how anomalous bodies are viewed in the 'real' world.

'The Freakishness in Normalcy and the Normalcy in Freakishness'

The terms monster and freak are usually used to categorise specific bodies. While the latter is as a rule a derogatory term historically applied to human beings with real bodily differences, 'a self-evident physical anomaly with which someone is born' (Tromp and Valerius 2008: 4), the first can have a multitude of meanings. It has been argued that one of the features of monsters is that they 'resist attempts to include them in any systematic structuration' (Cohen 1996: 6) and thereby 'def[y]the human desire to subjugate through categorization' (Mittman 2016: 7). Yet, some common features are discernible. On the one hand, the term monster might be used to identify humans who may have bodily surplus, whether that means an excess of flesh or an absence (Gil 2006: 75). On the other, it is also applied to human-animal hybrids, such as the cyno-cephalus,[1] who have 'mixed-up bodies [that] manifest confusion about what might constitute the boundaries of human society and the limits of acceptable human being' (Wright 2020: 174).

On this point, though addressing the 'horrific monster' in particular, Nöel Carroll has suggested that one of the structures used to construct monstrous bodies is 'fusion' – the other one being 'fission' – that 'hinges upon conflating, combining, or condensing distinct and/or opposed categorical elements in a spatiotemporally continuous monster' (2020: 139), which is precisely what one finds when looking at the bodies of beings like the cynocephalus. The term monster may also be employed to distinguish wondrous mythological creatures, like the chimera, which fits into what might be called 'classical monsters'. Furthermore, there is a traditional association between the concept of monstrosity and malevolence. A common feature of the monster in monster narratives in general is often its willingness to commit cruel and gruesome acts, though, as others have pointed out, 'not all monsters are evil' (Asma 2009: 11). This is a key point when thinking about monstrosity, especially when it comes to identifying the monster and, given its multiple meanings, one might suggest that the best way is to look at its impact or effect.

Although the physical aspect undeniably marks monstrous (and freakish) bodies, since it signals their otherness, allowing the spectator to quickly recognise their abnormality, it is not the only – nor the most important – factor to be taken into account. As argued by Asa Simon Mittman:

Above all, the monstrous is that which creates this sense of vertigo, that which calls into question our (their, anyone's) epistemological world-view, highlights its fragmentary and inadequate nature, and thereby asks us (often with fangs at our throats, with fire upon our skin, even as we and our stand-ins and body-doubles descend the gullet) to acknowledge the failures of our systems of categorization. (2016: 8)

One might therefore contend that 'monster is as monster does'. Intent, action and outcome(s) seem to be more reliable indicators of monstrosity than mere appearance. In addition, thinking about the monster as a concept or idea, as Mittman does, becomes a means through which one can gain a privileged outlook on human society. In other words, looking at the extraordinary bodies imagined, produced and/or reclaimed by a culture can be a useful method of reading that same culture. Although the notion of what constitutes monstrosity has changed both diachronically and geographically, how monstrosity or freakishness is constructed is tied to how we perceive ourselves. A sense of what is normal (and what is not) is ultimately what is at stake, for reassurance is in part why we create monsters and freaks; in other words, to prove that we are not like them. For this reason, some authors have suggested that humankind produces monsters for the sole purpose of thinking about itself, its place in the world and its relationship with it (Gil 2006).

As a result, imagining the 'Other' also 'necessarily involves constructing the borderlands, the boundary spaces that contain – in the double sense, to enclose and to include – what is antithetical to the self' (Uebel 1996: 265). Exceptional, perplexing and uncanny bodies in particular are often pushed to the farthest corners of one's known world or, in this case, screen; they are positioned at the borders, wherein all kinds of (mis)creations are possible and hence become a suitable location for exorcising both societal and individual fears. This concept is employed by Burton, who tends to locate some of his unusual characters in parallel worlds, such as Halloween Town in *The Nightmare Before Christmas* (1993), or in isolated and estranged places, illustrated, for example, by the abode of the Witch (Helena Bonham Carter) in *Big Fish*; despite living close enough to civilisation to be visited by children in the middle of the night, she lives alone in a decaying house in an inhospitable swamp. Space is thus a significant element in relation to monstrous and freakish bodies that are also distinguished by the places they inhabit. Time is equally important since the strange and the inexplicable tend to make their appearance at specific periods of the day, namely when there is dwindling or absent light.

The night has conventionally been regarded as the time for monstrosity, as the part of the day when all sorts of deviant fantastic beings come not quite out of the shadows, but move within them. There are several reasons for this but, given the impossibility of addressing them all in this chapter, it is key to bear in mind the biblical and Christian imagery developed in the Middle Ages that intrinsically linked the concept of 'light' to God and his (also uncanny) son Christ and, therefore, goodness while simultaneously opposing it to 'darkness'; therefore, 'By following the divine light of Christ, his followers became sons of light; [whereas] his enemies were cast as sons of darkness' (Youngs and Harris 2003: 136). As a period distinguished by the absence of sunlight, the night then 'became home to imagined horrors' (Youngs and Harris 2003: 135), a status it still has today.

Furthermore, the night can be a transformative agent, the time when bodies are able to change and commit acts they cannot during the day. One such transmutation is the werewolf, a man (or woman) cursed to turn into a wolf, or a part human/part wolf being, when the moon is a complete circle, though only at night. In *Big Fish*, Calloway Circus's proprietor and ringmaster, Amos (Danny DeVito), one of the characters in Bloom's tales, is in effect transmuted by night-time, becoming a seemingly ravenous werewolf that simply turns out to love playing 'fetch' (and so is not monstrous at all). The unexpected outcome of wolf-Amos's interaction with Edward Bloom (Ewan McGregor) makes the latter realise 'that most things you consider evil or wicked are simply lonely, and lackin' in the social niceties' (*Big Fish*). This is a key point when understanding the role of monstrous and freakish bodies in Burton's films, as what the filmmaker seems to be implying with productions like *Edward Scissorhands* (1990), *The Nightmare Before Christmas*, *Big Fish* and *Frankenweenie* (2012) is that these extraordinary beings are not in fact cruel or inherently dark, but in need of sympathy.

Burton's work, therefore, participates in the shift witnessed in recent decades in what it means to be monstrous or freakish. Even though, as noted, these two terms are generally used in academic parlance to categorise distinct figures, it is suggested here that they can be correlated, since the freak's body might be read as monstrous while the monstrous form may be seen as freakish. Similarly, the fictional freak is indubitably capable of committing malevolent acts and, as pointed out by Marlin Tromp and Karyn Valerius, like the monster, the freak too is 'a social construct' (2008: 4). Ultimately, and for the sake of this argument, it is suggested that both terms point to being 'Other', that is, to being *different*, and to outwardly threatening, incongruous and peculiar bodies.

Taking this into account, what is critical in *Big Fish* is that Edward Bloom understands and accepts the difference portrayed by most of the uncommon characters he meets in his many journeys and adventures. In them, Bloom performs various spectacular feats, faces a witch and a giant, works in a circus, falls in love with a girl, visits the surreal town of Spectre, defies a poet to change his life and meets conjoined twins, among many other peculiar characters.

As noted, Burton's influence for this particular film appears to have been the work of Arbus, who, much like Bloom (and Burton) himself, knew how to accommodate difference, exploring the contradictions and ambivalences of the world in her photography. Indeed, Arbus's photographs had the ability to affirm bodily differences as something positive and, above all, natural. The fact that she photographed mostly 'freaks' and 'monstrous' people 'not as an object of curiosity' (Adams 2001: 10) but by celebrating their difference, as she describes in the *Aperture Monograph*, is relevant to the argument here:

> There's a quality of legend about freaks. Like a person in a fairy tale who stops you and demands that you answer a riddle. Most people go through life dreading they'll have a traumatic experience. Freaks were born with their trauma. They've already passed their test in life. They're aristocrats. (Arbus 1972: 3)

Arbus's own vision reinforces that the concepts of freak or monster are constructs established by society to avoid dealing with the 'Other' and with the unusual, which is also a way of coping with one's own traumas, anxieties and issues. Focusing on 'the deviant body' (Adams 2001: 131), the photographer's influence on Burton, however, is mostly discernible in visual terms. Photographs such as *Identical Twins* (Roselle, NJ, 1967), *A Jewish Giant at Home with his Parents in the Bronx* (NY, 1970) or the 'circus photos', like *Tattooed Man at a Carnival* (MD, 1970), point out the uniqueness of each being, creating a noteworthy and relevant rhyme between Arbus and Burton.

In these, the photographer is interested in the 'eerie visual quality' (Bosworth 2005: 27) of her characters, as well as in honouring their difference. Recording them mostly in a snapshot structure, as Bosworth demonstrates (2005: 27), Arbus's technique presents the viewer with the awkward and strange figure in front of them, which creates 'a space of identification in which the viewer projects her own most hidden perverse fantasies onto the freak and discovers them mirrored back in the freak's gaze' (Adams 2001: 8). By doing so, the audience is confronted with an alternative way of reading the image (and the 'Other') that accentuates the normalcy of their difference, because it inverts the way we understand the Other's nature which ultimately is also our own.

However, Arbus's photographs are not without contention. As David Hevey notes, they 'paradoxically had the effect of problematising or opening up the issue of the representation of disabled people' (2013: 435). Nonetheless, her imagery, like that of Burton, is perceived by key scholars to be important in the celebration of difference, with Susan Sontag stating that 'her work shows people who are pathetic, pitiable, as well as repulsive, but it does not arouse any compassionate feelings [. . .] the photos have been praised for their candor and for an unsentimental empathy with their subjects' (1979: 33).

Like Arbus, Burton invites empathy with his oddball characters who similarly take centre stage in his productions. Indeed, there are distinct similarities in their presentation of such anomalous beings, with *Big Fish* seeming to directly emulate some of Arbus's compositions and approaches. Parallels lie, for example, in Burton's depiction of Karl the Giant (Matthew McGrory), Jing and Ping (Ada Tai and Arlene Tai) the Siamese Twins, as well as other physically different bodies that inhabit the world of *Big Fish*. The film's plot is eclectic as it traces Edward Bloom's (Albert Finney) life story, or a slightly exaggerated version of it, through his tales. As noted, these are told through flashbacks as he lies ill in bed and, through them, the spectator encounters various othered bodies. The first of these is Karl the Giant, who is initially presented as a threatening figure, in one scene depicted as a vast shadow passing over sheep looking upwards as if about to meet their fate. The implication is that the giant is eating the livestock, leading an angry town mob to congregate, in a scene recalling James Whale's *Frankenstein* (1931), a reference that is multiplied many times throughout Burton's canon.

However, in the flashback, a young Edward seeks out and confronts the giant, only to discover a rather dejected individual with whom he remains lifelong friends. The way that Karl is represented suggests analogies with Arbus's photograph *A Jewish Giant at Home with his Parents in the Bronx* (NY, 1971), whereby she frames a giant standing adjacent to his parents in their home. Her use of long shot to frame the threesome exacerbates their size difference and highlights the enormous stature of the giant, who is hunched over in order to fit into the room.

Karl's stature too is likewise accentuated by the use of long shot. In other scenes, Burton chooses to frame fragments of his body to achieve analogous effects. For instance, when Edward and Karl depart the town of Ashton to go on their travels, a close-up of Karl's hand shaking Edward's hand makes the latter seem tiny. In the same sequence, Bloom is awarded a key by the townspeople of Ashton; he is framed in long shot while the foreground is dominated by the torso of Karl who, because of his enormity, is only partially visible. The consistent use of extreme high and low angles throughout the film continues to accentuate the size differential so that the spectator assumes either Karl's point of view from a physically elevated position (which makes others appear distant and small) or from the perspective of those looking up towards him, equally drawing attention to his stature. Moreover, much like the giant in Arbus's image, Karl frequently dominates or fills the frame while shot-reverse-shots display others as much less prominent. The overall effect is to emphasise his size. Nonetheless, also like Arbus's subjects, such characters become Edward's friends, and their physical difference is insignificant and ultimately discounted. This connection between Arbus's photography and Burton's imagery in *Big Fish* shows that, in a certain way, the giant, the circus people and the twins are replicated from the world of still images to the one of moving pictures.

'A GIANT MAN CAN'T HAVE AN ORDINARY-SIZED LIFE':
BIG FISH'S CURIOUS BODIES

Taking this into account, the concept that better defines *Big Fish* is that of the double. This can be explained by the numerous duplications in the film, between the real and the fantastic, between the normal and the uncommon. Bloom's stories are a reflection of the human condition, always divided in two: the story as it happened and the story as told by Bloom, which is a way for the protagonist to evade reality, including that of his imminent death. Likewise, the power of the stories told by Bloom alerts the spectator to the fact that the world is no longer open to changes and to what is exceptional and, therefore, different.

Since Edward himself is an exceptional man – the stories he tells are the account of 'fantastic' and unusual travels – he needs to expand his self beyond the boundaries imposed by the town from which he originates, thus refusing to settle for a single vision of the world. Hence, the idea of a double life is engendered: the one he lives in the real world and the other via the stories he creates, the latter being a way of enriching his (and the spectator's) life. Nonetheless, and although it is possible to interpret the stories from the real world as negative and the stories from the fantastic world as positive, they do not annul one another. On the contrary, they contribute to a better understanding of the bodies that inhabit the film, functioning as a reflexive metaphor for how the power of stories can lead to a change in the way the world and the 'Other' are perceived.

While Bloom himself may use some of the tales as a gateway for his absence as a father, as well as to 'conceal [his] human weaknesses' (McMahan 2005: 76), he also believes with absolute faith in what he is telling, showing, much like Burton, that 'a change of mentality in the individual will lead him/her and his/her society from the imprisonment of normality and routine to the openness of future economical, social and spiritual possibilities' (Bonilla 2013: 170). Joe Montenegro Bonilla's statement indicates a crucial idea in *Big Fish*, which is the fact that, as an individual, Bloom acknowledges there is much more potential in following an alternative way of living – a dual identity that does not fit within standard society – than submitting to what is mundane and real.

Consequently, the intertwining of the two narratives (the fantastic and the real) suggests the world is a better place when both reality and fiction are embraced, hence celebrating 'the creative impulse that makes life more than mindless repetition' (Hada 2014: 25). On the one hand, the 'monstrous characters' that inhabit the fictional side of the story replicate, in a way, Bloom's desire to be much more than just an ordinary person. At the outset the spectator knows that Bloom, from an early age, needs to see and learn about the world that lies beyond his town, which is also a way of understanding his true identity. On the other hand, the encounter with many different realities and subjects, in particular the curious and extraordinary bodies, is only possible because Bloom himself feels different from the rest of the town, which allows him to both pursue his adventures and better understand himself and others.

Here again, Karl the Giant is a useful example. His appearance provides Bloom the ideal justification to leave his 'perfect' suburban middle-class town and see the world. Since 'giants are what most people mean by "monsters," with gaping orifices and indistinct boundaries' (Prescott 1996: 78), Bloom initially offers himself to Karl as human sacrifice, only to realise the latter is 'just too big', but certainly neither a cannibal nor inherently evil. Because he is a giant and, therefore, 'a figure whose indomitable corporeality suggests the difficulty of being merely human' (Cohen 1999: xiv), Karl struggles to find a place to fit in, and while Bloom comments that he 'is a big man and should be in a big city', Karl's difference will not be so easily effaced. After leaving Ashton, which is after all simply too small for both characters – for Karl because of his prodigious-sized body and for Bloom because of his ambitious nature – the two are able to find a place where Karl can be himself: the circus.

Yet, even though the circus is composed of entertainers and performers and has been typically associated with sideshows where (human) rarities, including freaks and curiosities, were displayed, the stature and incongruity of Karl's body is still highlighted. In the scene of his first appearance in the circus tent, Karl is seen towering over the audience and the circus's colossus, who next to him seems like a rather average man. A wide shot of Karl, framing him literally with the audience on both sides, shows his magnitude when compared to the colossus who, upon getting closer, is framed at a canted angle, thus revealing not only his awe, but also his disquiet before someone who is twice his size. Indeed, 'because there is no place that can accommodate the massive expanse of his body' (Adams 2001: 127), Karl's freakish nature cannot be completely set aside. This enables the onlooker to be simultaneously shocked and drawn by an insatiable curiosity, reflecting how monstrous bodies at the same time allure and repulse, therein lying the voyeuristic attractions of their exposed flesh. Even so, the circus as a space that both displays and safeguards those with strange and unusual bodies becomes the place where Karl seems to find contentment and acceptance and can 'fulfil his destiny' (*Big Fish*).

Karl's size is especially pinpointed in relation to another anomalous body, that of Amos Calloway, the physically short circus owner, as well as one of its performers, who has dwarfism. Calloway's tiny human body (literally) contains a monstrous nature that cannot be confined. This becomes apparent after Bloom espies a young woman with whom he becomes obsessed. Amos withholds her name from Bloom, but when Bloom can wait no longer he visits Amos's trailer, only to discover that Calloway's body has been 'turned over to the wolf' (Carroll 2020: 139). The camera frames wolf-Amos with an extreme close-up – showing his ferocious animal-like side – while attacking Bloom, which prompts the circus clown, Mr Soggybottom (Deep Roy), to pull out a gun to shoot Amos. This action itself is revealing of the way in which Amos sees himself when he changes into a wolf: as a menace both to himself and others, as monstrous body that contrasts with his tiny physical figure. Nonetheless, and upon Bloom's intervention in the scene, his ferocious self, which is potentially the reason why he understands the other circus members, becomes merely an extension of his physical self: a gentle, tolerating being who runs a circus that is home to many like him.

Bloom's alternative way of looking at things allows him to accept Amos's other nature, so he manages to help him avoid harming anyone. But Amos and Karl are not the only ones that Edward assists in *Big Fish*. In fact, Calloway's circus features a number of 'different' bodies, each of their aberrations both drawn attention to and then overridden with seemingly direct connections to Arbus's photographs. For example, during one circus performance, as Amos introduces another giant to the onlooking spectators, the camera pans across the crowd to momentarily stop and frame what we initially perceive to be identical twins. Similar to Arbus's *Identical Twins* (Roselle, NJ, 1967), they are frontally framed, sit adjacent and are dressed identically. Just as scrutiny of Arbus's image starts to reveal differences between the two, so too do the centrally framed Burton 'twins' begin to look 'unidentical' and we come to realise that they are not twins at all. As Graham Clarke notes about Arbus's image: 'we are left with such a pervasive sense of difference as to belie the certainty of the title [. . .]. Far from identical, these are individuals in their own right' (1997: 30). In a related vein, the appearance of Siamese twins in *Big Fish* highlights identity and individuality.

Bloom encounters the Siamese twins in his conscription to the army when he parachutes into a North Korean military show where the twins are about to sing (they too are performers). The sequence begins with a slow pan up one of the twins' legs in a side-on shot. The initial impression is that there is only one individual, who appears exotic and beautiful before 'she' turns to face the audience in a frontal centrally framed shot to reveal Siamese twins. The reveal is deliberately surprising but, as in Arbus's images, it encourages the spectator to first witness the beauty of the individual before the disability. As Sontag further notes: 'The authority of Arbus's photographs derives from the contrast between their lacerating subject matter and their calm, matter-of-fact attentiveness' (1979: 35). The frontality that Burton employs in these various scenarios also echoes the work of Arbus and is especially applicable to the performance of the Siamese twins in the film. In this respect, Sontag also observes: 'What makes Arbus's use of the formal post so arresting is that her subjects are often people one would not expect to surrender themselves so amiably and ingenuously to the camera' (1979: 38).

Although the twins' role is a minor one, their appearance serves to signal the importance that anomalous bodies have in Bloom's (and Burton's) imagination and, again, to echo the imagery that Arbus promoted. Ping and Jing's 'double body', perhaps even more so than Karl and Amos's bodies, is from the outset a locus to be gazed at and admired, a fact made clear as they perform to the song *Twice the Love* in front of an army of male soldiers. Unlike the other extraordinary bodies, Ping and Jing are able to explore their exceptional nature to their own advantage by highlighting their sexuality both through the way they dance and display their body/ies and through the song they sing. As noted, the camera frames the twins directly, centring on a single body through a side-on shot, before the body becomes double and, thus, twice pleasurable to the eye. The song reflects this idea: Danny Elfman's lyrics to *Twice the Love* point to the concepts previously explored here, as it mentions that for this type of love 'an unusual man' is needed.

Burton once again plays with the audience's mixed feelings when facing the 'Other'. With these examples, what distinguishes Bloom from everyone else is that he sees kindness and greatness in the characters he meets under very unusual circumstances. As Michelle Le Blanc and Colin Odell explain:

> The most sympathetically portrayed protagonists are those who differ from the norm – be they awkward, gauche, naive or simply misunderstood. *Big Fish* subverts the misanthropic hero pattern, as the affable and gregarious lead acts as a catalyst to bring those who are on the fringes of society into his fold, rather than being an outcast himself. (2000: 16)

The director achieves this by framing most of these characters in a certain manner: either with mid- to high-angle camera shots together with light and warm colours or by means of close-ups in order to underline the characters' emotional state, particularly in fantastic moments. This is further emphasised through the narrative told by Bloom (and by Burton), specifically, in the way he narrates the 'monstrous' figures in the film by not describing them as monsters at all. For Bloom – as for Burton – the witch, Amos, Karl the Giant or Ping and Jing, among others, are not monsters, it is only a matter of perspective. That is why, although the characters that appear in Bloom's 'alternative' version of his life are projected via his stories, they exist in the 'real' world of the diegesis, but with slightly different features from the ones he described.

As noted by S. Brent Plate (2017: 22), *Big Fish* is a film about the power of constructing identities either narratively or via audiovisual techniques. The final scene is an example of this, demonstrating how stories (and perspectives) can be exaggerated and then brought to reality. Similarly, and as Brent Plate further notes (2017: 23), there is never any mention in the film that these characters are indeed giants, a wolf or conjoined twins and, indeed, for the author the funeral scene exemplifies this argument: Karl is not a giant, but taller than the average; the twins are not conjoined, but identical. They are both fantastic and real because Bloom and Burton make them so, but they are also different and, by being so, exceptional. It is Will's own investigation into his father's past that shows us the existence of these figures. While Will, who thinks his father is a liar, wants a glimpse of the truth, at the very end of *Big Fish* he seems to learn a valuable lesson, as Hada points out (2014: 26), by 'accepting his father's life' and his own identity as his son, but also as a future father.

At the heart of *Big Fish*, thus, lies the idea that the real (but also the fictional) – hence the importance of the double – is always more than what we imagine. That is why Will agrees to tell a final story to his dying father which is a narration of how he became the 'big fish'. Rather than showing Edward's death, Burton chooses to endow him with mythological proportions, turning him into a huge catfish and putting him in the same mythical plan as other curious bodies. This is a metaphor with multiple meanings: the circle of life; Will's understanding of the power of stories; and the numerous identities, roles and features that change throughout time, or even immortality (one that only fiction/film can provide). The tales as told by Edward are testimony of the strange and bizarre (marginal) bodies that he encounters in his journey. In its turn, the final story as told by Will is also evidence of Edward's similar condition, in the sense that he is not that different from the other characters he meets.

At Edward's funeral, Karl the Giant, Amos and some of the circus members, Ping and Jing, Winslow and Spectre's townspeople are all there to celebrate not only the main character's life, but also to serve as a living proof that magic and the real can coexist: that fiction and reality are better when told together. It also suggests, through Burton's very particular vision along with Arbus's perception, that strange (and bizarre) bodies can exist side by side with other bodies, and that embracing the 'Other' is also a way of changing a community.

Conclusion

In a recent interview upon the release of *Dumbo* (Burton 2019), Danny DeVito, an actor who has been working with the director in several of his projects, commented that the film represented 'the completion of the Circus Trilogy' (Roffman 2019). This was an expression used by Burton himself to describe a trilogy that includes *Batman Returns* (1992), *Big Fish* and *Dumbo*. In these films, the circus plays an important role as a space of acceptance of otherness: the Arctic circus company composed of freak characters controlled by the Penguin, himself a mixture of human and animal; the circus in *Big Fish* – a place for giants, werewolves, dwarves but also for all kinds of dreams; and, finally, the circus in *Dumbo*, where animals, especially those with unusual characteristics like Dumbo, are forced to perform for the sake of pure entertainment. Burton's 'Circus Trilogy' can be seen as a key example of how the director uses certain (other) spaces to 'juxtapose [. . .] the everyday and the living' with 'different beings' (Pheasant-Kelly 2017: 16).

Although the circus plays an important role in *Big Fish*, it is significant that this space is presented to us by Bloom, who is the one telling the stories and thus introducing the spectator to the curious bodies that he encounters along the way. As Weinstock notes, stories 'enchant reality by highlighting the essence of things' (2017: 10). At the same time, this 'essence of things' the author mentions can only be grasped when one is willing to embrace what is different. The intertwining of the real and the magic, the normal and the different, the ordinary and the unusual is probably one of the most important lessons of the film and one that Will finally learns in the end.

The importance of the story (as told by Bloom) within the story (as told by Burton) points out the many perspectives on life and people. In Burton's singular vision, *Big Fish* is a film on embracing difference and about participating in that difference, thus finding ways of 'accommodating the broad swathe of human variability' (Adams 2001: 9), much like Arbus herself, who '[i]nstead of trying to coax her subjects into a natural or typical position, encouraged [them] to be awkward' (Sontag 1979: 39). Hence, both Arbus and Burton commemorate these 'figures long after the curtains have closed on their final performance' (Adams 2001: 121), implying that it is only by accepting alternative visions (as it happens with the stories and, consequently, with the characters that inhabit them) that we truly get to know others and ourselves.

NOTE

1. A man with the head of a dog.

17. TIM BURTON'S CURIOUS BODIES IN *MISS PEREGRINE'S HOME FOR PECULIAR CHILDREN*: A CONTEMPORARY TALE OF THE GROTESQUE

Marie Liénard-Yeterian

With *Miss Peregrine's Home for Peculiar Children*, Tim Burton artfully inter-twines the conventions of the fairy tale, the Gothic mode, the *Bildungsroman* and the creation of an array of peculiar grotesques to deal with major themes – freedom and agency, temporality and mortality – in a posthuman context. Uncanny bodies and tropes are superimposed in a kaleidoscopic dynamic of 'show and tell', characters morph in and out of different identities and forms, and time shifts or freezes. The cinematic spatial and temporal magic lantern projects fantastic and realistic elements, propelling the viewer into a space of endless possibility. This chapter explores the cultural work (as described by Lauter 2001: 11) performed by the various 'curious' and monstrous bodies featured in the film's imaginary world while addressing Burton's ability to interweave different generic traditions.

Because Burton's films are often peopled by strange and puzzling creatures and incongruous situations, his work provides insightful expressions of the grotesque onscreen. The grotesque combines comedy and terror, and defines situations and characters, the grotesques. These are characterised by their distortions (physical or other), excessive and inappropriate behaviour, and exemplary or emblematic qualities. The grotesques, as 'freaks' or monsters, fascinate or repel, keep the narrative poised between the real and the supernatural, and usher the peculiar mood of Burton's cinematic universe, which is a blend of play and fright. The film title combines, in a quasi-programmatic way, the notions of peculiarity and homeliness, conjuring the Uncanny and the Gothic, which is frequently associated with the grotesque, and with which it shares the common element of terror: the economy of the Gothic revolves around the tragic whereas that of the grotesque revolves around the comic. The film stages a main protagonist, Jake (Asa Butterfield), who launches on a quest following his grandfather Abe's (Terence Stamp) strange request just before he died. He travels to the Welsh island of Cairnholm and discovers a mansion where children with peculiar gifts live under Miss Peregrine's (Eva Green) benevolent care. Jake soon realises that they inhabit a different time period, known as a loop, which functions as a form of shelter against the predatory grip of invisible monsters who hunt them to procure their eyes as a means of attaining immortality. A violent chase follows between the different protagonists as Jake ends up acting as the saviour of the group.

Burton sketched and elaborated, from a series of pictures that had inspired author Ransom Riggs (2011) for the novel from which the film is adapted, a gallery of 'peculiars' who constitute, through their unusual physical, mental and ontological dimension, curious bodies. 'Curious' evokes the notion of otherness and intuits the fascination that these weird bodies trigger, while 'bodies' invokes the material presence of these grotesques whose shapes and abilities depart from the norm. The children's alterity – monstrosity – is channelled in the service of good until they are compelled to use their 'gifts' to defend themselves and includes the following characters: Emma (Ella Purnell), an aerokinetic teenager who can manipulate air and can breathe under water; Enoch O'Connor (Finlay Macmillan), a teenager who can reanimate the dead; Olive Abroholos Elephanta (Lauren McCrostie), a pyrotechnic girl; Millard Nullings (Cameron King), an invisible boy; Bronwyn Bruntley (Pixie Davies), a teenager endowed with supernatural strength; Hugh Apiston (Milo Parker), a boy who has bees in his stomach; Fiona Frauenfeld (Georgia Pemberton), a girl who has power over plants and vegetables; Claire Densmore (Raffiella Chapman), a girl who has an additional jaw in the back of her neck; Horace Somnusson (Hayden Keeler-Stone), a boy who can project his dreams; Victor Bruntley (Louis Davison), who has been killed, but had superhuman strength; and finally, the Twins (Joseph and Thomas Odwell), who can turn people they see into stone. The children are preyed upon by 'real' monsters, creatures whose human features have been lost and who exemplify inhuman behaviour. In addition, the human grotesques are 'supplemented' – in the Derridean sense – by a grotesque bestiary where birds are human, and humans are bird-like. As Jacques Derrida explains, 'whether it adds or substitutes itself, the supplement is exterior, outside of the positivity to which it is super-added, alien to that which, in order to be replaced by it, must be other than it' (2016: 158). One such example includes Miss Peregrine, whose ability to morph in and out of the shape of a bird figures a state of in-betweenness between the curious body as human-shaped and as animal-shaped.

Initially, this chapter explores the notion of 'monster' embedded in the motif of these curious bodies, poised as they are at the intersection of the Gothic and grotesque in their staging of an encounter with terror. Like the Gothic, the grotesque has a moral function and performs cultural work, including operating as a form of alternative and transgressive political discourse. The film script follows the Gothic formula of pitting bodies of light and life (the peculiar children, whose otherness is a good-giving gift) against bodies of darkness and death (the Hollows, whose monstrosity is an evil-inflicting curse). Benevolent and malevolent peculiars are thus engaged in a chase and moral warfare in different haunted spaces, all of which constitute formulaic Gothic elements. The essay considers the reality behind the gallery of characters formed by the curious bodies and the cultural work performed by these grotesques.

ENTER THE GROTESQUE

'The bird will tell you' (Abe to Jake)
The origin of the term and concept of the grotesque is anchored in the domain of the visual arts. As a mode, it does not propose a passive representation but constitutes a dynamic evocation of reality, initiating a semiotic game that has a performative role. Its force relies on the power of the image, or 'agency' as a recent book by Horst Bredekamp (2018) titled *Image Acts: A Systematic Approach to Visual Agency* has theorised.

Derived from the Italian term *grottesco*, meaning cave, the term is first referred to in the strange motifs found in the collapsed and partly underground ruins of Nero's *Domus Aurea* in the fifteenth century that combined human, animal and vegetal motifs. Because of the uneven surface of the ceiling, the figures seemed distorted. The word 'grotesque' came to be associated with both what it represented and the effect it triggered – comic but also terrifying in its uncanniness. Its main features, enriched over the centuries, include the following: exaggeration, deformity (the physical distortion often symbolises the mental or emotional one, and/or the dysfunctional societal elements), incongruity, name humour and puppet-like characters, dark humour, irony, hyperbole and excess, the fusion of categories (in particular the animate/inanimate) and tonal shifts. Grotesque is used as an adjective (as in a grotesque effect or situation) and as a noun (as in a grotesque or a gallery of grotesques, meaning a grotesque creature or character), and its qualities range from the bizarre and the unpredictable to suddenness, surprise and shock.

Over the years, the term has extended to other artistic forms beyond the visual arts. It often functions as a form of countercultural discourse whereby the aesthetic dimensions of the grotesque have political resonances that have cultural significance. As Ralf Remshardt explains in *Staging the Savage God: The Grotesque in Performance*, 'In so far as it perceives hierarchies and inverts them or erases them, the grotesque maintains a link to the deconstructive project' (2004: 286). The grotesque indeed involves revising established assumptions about reality by staging an alternative representation of it through different strategies, notably the following: the conflation of different elements, the exaggeration of certain features and the fragmentation of the considered entity. Overall, it tutors the spectator to envision reality differently as it transgresses canonical ways and norms. In addition, it is endowed with emblematic and didactic dimensions: the material level ushers a moral reflection on societal and cultural dysfunctional elements. Frequently, it blends comedy (especially through the staged physical distortions) and terror (through recognisable political references). In *The Grotesque in Art and Literature*, Wolfgang Kayser (1981) argues that the grotesque is an attempt to invoke and subdue the demonic aspect of the world. For him, the grotesque is an expression of an estranged and alienated world. The familiar is seen from a perspective which suddenly renders it strange, be it comic, terrifying or both. Likewise, in his study *On the Grotesque: Strategies of Contradiction in Art and Literature*, Geoffrey Galt Harpham (1982) stresses its disunity – the fact that the grotesque fuses things that should be kept apart.

Recent scholarship on the grotesque has emphasised its political dimension, particularly in the context of the American South. For instance, Patricia Yaeger indicates, 'I want to describe the grotesque's political fierceness as well as its transitivity [. . .] I am convinced that the grotesque reproduces the possibility for confronting the strangeness of southern culture' (2000: 25). Through its alternative mode of representation, the grotesque often functions as a form of countercultural discourse. It includes a didactic element as it focuses on dysfunctional social codes and habits, moral contradictions, psychological distortions and emotional conflicts. Grotesque bodies are, in Yaeger's words, 'emblems both of the region's incarcerating ideologies of race, class, and gender, and of the inevitable disruption and eventual dissolution of those ideologies' (2000: 13). In terms of gender, the 'female grotesque' has inspired a growing body of work in the wake of Mary Russo's (1994) groundbreaking book titled *The Female Grotesque: Risk, Excess and Modernity*. The handling of the female body in Southern fiction reveals how fiction can convey such politics. As Yaeger describes it: 'Women's open, wounded bodies become political intensifiers, spaces for mapping an entire region's social and psychic neuroses' (2000: 293). The character of the female giant identified in Southern American literature as the Southern Gargantua by Yaeger has been seen as a figure of transgression. Such distortions and exaggerations inherent to grotesque aesthetics become figures of political criticism with 'the volume turned up' in Yaeger's suggestive image when she explains: 'when the grotesque body marches onto the page, the ideology that controls Southern bodies explodes in the most unexpected ways [. . .] Southern women's writing is filled with bizarre narrative images that seem unnecessarily cruel or out of control, and yet this cruelty has a function: it tears at the social fabric and leaves it in shreds' (2000: 293). My previous work has focused on the link between the margin(s)/marginal and the grotesque, on the grotesque as a form of cultural counterculture, especially in the work of writers such as Eudora Welty, Flannery O'Connor and Carson McCullers, and on the poetics of a political grotesque in literature and in film.[1] The approach in this chapter focuses on an analogous political use of the grotesque, in particular on the heuristic economy of the marginal in relation to a normative centre.

The film credit sequence owes its style to grotesque aesthetics, establishing the importance of the mode as an interpretive framework. It combines different elements in a collage fashion – a sort of visual *Tale of the Grotesque and Arabesque* (Poe 1840) where arabesque, as in Edgar Allan Poe's title, designates an intricate pattern of intertwined figures: in this case, human faces, photographs of cities and places, texts (scribblings on a page and newspaper excerpts) and flowers. Together they offer the viewer an intriguing body of texts and visual cues beyond the fragmented images. They also illustrate the incongruous dimension of the grotesque whereby unexpected images are made even stranger through editing and their juxtaposition with the actors' names. Gaps between the word and the image are opened, introducing visual and cognitive ruptures so that the images do not fit within any coherent line and do not match the words superimposed upon them. The viewer is invited into reading peculiarity beyond appearances – all the more so since no particular editing principle seems to preside over the kaleidoscopic succession of the fragments. Proceeding through synecdochic associations, the imagery continues with a close-up of a white rose that morphs into white smoke and then a beard, ushering the spectator into a space where beauty can turn into ugliness. The sequence is characterised by a hallucinatory quality, poised between a nightmare and a dream, and the generic mix (film, photo album, credit sequence) signals the ambivalent and ambiguous nature of reality. At times, it extends into the referential world of crime and murder through inserts of newspaper excerpts, hinting at a violent world beyond.

The opening sequence establishes sight as an important sense, and the film transpires as a story of eyes: white eyes or no eyes, or regular eyes, or eyes that can see what others cannot see. Such emphasis on sight is a tribute to the importance of sight for cinema and reiterates the overall importance of the grotesque mode in the film. It also reflects one of Burton's key themes, echoed across several films, such as *Big Eyes* (2014) and *Charlie and the Chocolate Factory* (2005). Because of the distortion it proposes, the grotesque creates an 'assault' and a shock through its visual impact. The concept of doubling images also owes to the grotesque and its logic of mimicry – to borrow Homi Bhabha's concept (2004: 122) – that of a repetition with a difference which highlights the way the grotesque revisits reality to expose its arbitrary, conventional and reversible nature. The credit sequence presents a series of doubled images that reappear in the film. These include the crabs on the beach in the opening sequence/Enoch's fantastic claw-endowed puppets and Jake's twin cousins who show up at his birthday party/the peculiar Twins of the house. Other pairs include Jake's family home/Miss Peregrine's mansion and natural birds (the real ones and those which appear on the television watched by Jake's father)/ human birds (the Umbryns). In addition, the picture of a creature that looks like a Hollow on the wall of the pub where Jake is staying with his father on the island/the encounter with the real monsters when they launch their assault on Miss Peregrine's house, acts as a further example of replicated images.

The abrupt cut from the last image of the credit sequence – a place in the British Isles with a date – to the very first image of the film jump-starts a shift in time and space and triggers an overall impression of strangeness and displacement: the device of the voice-over and the direct address to the viewer, which is never repeated, anchors the film in a dialectic dynamic with the spectator. Two questions (rhetorical or not) are raised by a voice-over we will later recognise as Jake's: 'Do you ever feel like nothing you do matters?'. The voice-over continues: 'You leave footprints on the beach and tomorrow they are gone'. Thereafter, the film frames crabs scurrying on the beach, a scene which fleshes out the uncanniness ushered in the credit sequence as there seems no obvious link between the images and the comment offered by the voice-over. The final statement, 'Like it's just today over again', sounds like a riddle at this point in the narrative, but in fact it paves the way for the temporal process soon to be experienced in the device of the time 'loop' experienced by the peculiar children as an unending repetition of a single day.

HOMELY CURIOUS BODIES: THE PECULIAR CHILDREN

'What is your gift?' (Fiona to Jake)
The term 'curious' connotes something different, abnormal and extraordinary. The discussion around normality and abnormality is rehearsed from the beginning with the opening debate about Abe's mental health. The grandfather's apparent irrationality is framed within the medical diagnosis of 'dementia', with his final request to Jake sounding like a riddle: 'go to the island, find Emerson, the bird will explain' – where Emerson indeed refers to a book, and the bird turns out to be a person. On locating the island, Jake encounters the strange array of children who are 'peculiar' because they have a gift that enables them to 'enhance' reality in a way that benefits the community they form in the loop. They are grotesques who typify the aforementioned distortions and departures from the norm, whether it is in terms of physical, behavioural or mental abilities. We encounter them one

by one: Miss Peregrine, both human and bird, and her ability to manipulate time; Olive and her ability to manipulate heat and fire; Hugh and his beehive; Emma and her ability to float in the air ('air is my peculiarity, it does what I want'); Enoch and his ability to make hearts beat again and manipulate life and death; Fiona and her ability to pull things out of nature (the carrot, the branch) and impact the vegetal world by activating growth or giving it a different size. Claire and Bronwyn displace traditional models of femininity: Bronwyn's ability to lift heavy burdens proposes a grotesque revisitation of female gentility akin to the previously described character of the female Gargantua in Southern literature, and Claire's frightening set of teeth and monstrous jaw undermine canons of female beauty as emblematised in her doll-like features and blonde curly hair. Indeed, both girls offer a peculiar variation on canonical female appearance. Moreover, the twins wear masks and are thus deprived of human features; they function as visual reminders that the children have hidden potential. In a similar way to the Twins, Millard's gift (his invisibility) functions as a cautionary tale regarding peculiarity: it can be concealed yet it is real.

Some of the peculiars are directly based on the characters of the eponymous novel by Ransom Riggs that Burton adapted for the screen. While the filmmaker sketched and elaborated from a series of pictures of real children that the author had seen and that had inspired him for his novel, Burton also conjures up some well-known fairy-tale elements. As a result, the children appear uncanny: they are recognisable, but they exceed their formulaic models. The fairy-tale backdrop provides the context for exploring how peculiarities can be seen as gifts. The children's supernatural versatility creates wonder and a dreamlike ambience; their awe-inspiring ability to break conventional assumptions about gentility, strength and beauty constitutes a variation on some of the generic conventions of the fairy tale, where characters are endowed with supernatural powers. For example, at times, the characters of 'Mary Poppins' and 'Sleeping Beauty' come uninvited as potential doubles to some of Burton's protagonists (Emma Oliver and Miss Peregrine in particular) in the film. We can also imagine Alice's rabbit in relation to Miss Peregrine's obsession with clocks and time in another wonderland – and the giant carrot (a peculiar vegetal body indeed) that Fiona pulls out of the ground.

Jake is gradually initiated into the children's 'difference'. Influenced by his teacher, who had dismissed the photographs of the children contained in a cardboard box given to him by his grandfather as 'trick pictures', and his own father, Franklin (Chris O'Dowd), who said that the 'children were special but not in the sense your grandfather intended', he is tempted to dismiss Abe's stories as pure madness too. But when he is introduced into the loop he acknowledges their existence and identity by naming them: 'You are Hugh, and Emma and Bronwyn'. Jake's stubborn resistance to admit that he himself is a peculiar child persists until he realises that his own gift lies in his ability to discern the presence of the Hollows and detect evil. As Emma tells him: 'The thing that killed Victor, you can see it'. He thus comes to understand that his grandfather had prepared him to inherit his gift through storytelling. As Miss Peregrine explains to him, 'he had hoped that his bedtime stories would pave the way'. Jake had already seen the curious bodies in his imagination, prompted by the pictures his grandfather had commented on and mimicked in a pantomime of sorts where shadows had cohered to inspire Jake's imagination.

The grandfather's early 'show and tell' to Jake as a child is a *mise-en-abyme* of the way the film functions as a larger show and tell for a range of peculiarities and conjures the world of the circus or travelling fair, and the freak show: curious bodies intrigue and fascinate, like 'freaks', and if it were not for the Umbryns' goodwill, the children could be instrumentalised as exposed attractions (Fiedler 1978). Indeed, the world of the circus and fair appear later in the film as well as in other productions in the director's canon, most recently *Dumbo* (2019). In these spaces, the children perform their freakish persona in a carnivalised replay of the deadly struggle against the Hollows: they act and act out, and work through the trauma of being peculiar by retaliating against the evil pressing on them in a reverse and empowering confrontation.

Abe had given Jake a cardboard box in which he had kept the pictures of the children. This cardboard box functions in the narrative strategy of the film as a micro stage for the peculiars' performance. It indeed rehearses on a miniature scale the all-important circus scene that takes place in the final part of the film. In order to be meaningful, the pictures must be taken out of the book to be looked at and commented upon, an element that provides a supplementary dimension to the narrative as such an exposing process enhances their curiosity and singularity. The pictures themselves can be misappropriated, mishandled or mis-narrated (they could be 'trick pictures'), conjuring the notion of a master narrative. Peculiarity indeed hinges on a dialectic, with the potential to usher a real interest in the Other, or to inspire a voyeurism that turns the Other into a commodity. The alterity connoted by the word 'peculiar' often triggers envy or fear, resulting in persecution. As Miss Peregrine explains to Jake, 'some people are peculiar, peculiars have been persecuted. We create a loop and live safe from the outside world'; the box symbolises that shelter and isolation.

The reversible nature of the children's gifts rehearses the basic ambivalence encoded in the term peculiar, as illustrated by the episode when Enoch endows his puppets with uncanny life. He boasts to Jake, who is horrified at the crude and lethal violence displayed by a couple of puppets, that 'it's more fun with people', adding: 'the epic battles they used to have at my parents' funeral parlour . . .'. Monstrosity is offstage, suggested in the image of raw violence already seen onscreen in the bird scene on television in the programme that Franklin watches as Abe is telling Jake about his stories: the birds feeding on their prey demonstrate the brutal violence that later extends to include the Hollows' feeding on the children's eyes, or slaughtering sheep. Such monstrous violence is also visible in the wake of the attack on Abe, occurring at the film's outset, through the torn-up screen and fence. In addition, Abe, like the crabs on the beach and Enoch's puppet, brandishes some kind of claw (a huge fork), which functions as the synecdochic sign of the visceral fight.

PECULIAR BODIES OF ANOTHER KIND: HOLLOWS AND OTHER MONSTERS

'The thing that killed Victor' (Emma to Jake)

Jake's peculiarity bridges the gap between the two sets of bodies staged in the film, namely, the children and the Hollows. As Miss Peregrine recounts to Jake, 'A splinter faction rose among the disaffected peculiars' who expressed boredom at their fate and left. They conducted some 'scientific' experiment to become immortal which went wrong and turned them into monstrous creatures whose physical distortion points to their lack of morality. The Hollowgasts, or 'Hollows, for short', as Miss Peregrine further explains to Jake, can only retrieve their original bodily shape by consuming the eyes of other peculiars, in particular children, and raiding the loops. Their leader, Mr Barron (Samuel L. Jackson), has managed to fully reverse the process; his peculiarity is the ability to assume different personae, masquerading as the birdwatcher John Lamont (Rupert Everett) or the psychiatrist Nancy Golan (Allison Janney). With the character of Barron, who is black, the fairy tale intersects with the concept of passing (passing for white/passing for a woman). As a grotesque, Barron fluctuates between genders and races, his character resonating with the figure of the trickster or the conman, and their attendant cultural and political dimensions as transgressors of normative systems.

This darker aspect of the peculiar body as monster is a leitmotiv from the outset. Early in the film, Abe describes to Jake the monsters he faced as a child in Poland in the following way: 'they are huge, they have long arms, they have tentacles'. He explains how he had to hide in a tunnel and later went to a home with other children, children who had 'special abilities'. The war context allows the viewer to translate the terrifying content that Abe encodes for the child, such that the fairy-tale subtext itself comes with a supplemental back-drop: warfare and its destructive monsters and effects, as in this case, falling bombs. The gas masks worn by the children and Miss Peregrine during the 'reset' (the moment when they are brought back to the beginning of the day, trapped as they are in the one day they are given to experience over and over again) serve as a chilling reminder of the defacing and dehumanising effect of war. With their masks on, humans become monsters indeed.

If the Gothic stages the conflict between good and evil, the Hollows thus dramatise haunting monsters, including historical fiends, while their desire to eat children's eyes revisits the Promethean quest for power as configured in the Western classical tradition. In addition, they conjure up other leading figures in contemporary Gothic and grotesque cultural expressions, namely zombies and vampires, that pervade the post-9/11 literary and cinematic imagination.[2] Behind the horror of their ghastly appearance, they suggest a particular mode of terror, evoking the predatory world of greed 'vampirising' the vulnerable elements of society, as symbolised by the children in the film. The film's cannibalistic tropes also echo those in recent Gothic imagination, as illustrated in Cormac McCarthy's *The Road* (2006).[3] In addition, the quest for immortality resonates with the posthuman agenda and the vision proposed by the Singularity, the code name for enhanced intelligence.[4]

CURIOUS INTERTEXTUAL BODIES AND THE ART OF CINEMA

'Find Emerson' (Abe to Jake)

Burton's intertextual references to cinema (such as the films of James Cameron) and literature (the writings of Ralph Waldo Emerson) provide other 'bodies' of texts that mobilise curiosity and challenge memory. The inter-filmic dimension frequent in his work takes on a peculiar turn with the character of Horace, whose special power allows him to project moving pictures for others to see, namely, silent films derived from his dreams, nightmares or forebodings, which constitute Burton's own tribute to cinema, and to its power as an art endowed with foresight. Horace's dream factory provides a meta-referential moment by offering a statement about the work that film does. In a related vein, the giant carrot that Fiona pulls from the ground evokes the ability of the moving image to distort and reshape, and the magic of cinematic creations (it is a prop that Ransom Riggs chose as a gift after the film). Of note is the iconic shot of James Cameron's *Titanic* (1997) lovers, along with the empowering prospect of having the liner emerge from the sea, as if indeed historical events themselves could be recovered and averted or reversed. Rescuing the *Titanic* out of the stillness of its own time loop might become the ultimate happy ending in a world so enamoured with virtual and alternative reality(ies).

The reference to Emerson's *The Complete Essays and Other Writings* (1950) constitutes a curious body of text amid so much terror. Emerson's ideal of harmony between humans and nature, and his vision of man's call for a higher order of consciousness, sounds incongruous. In a corresponding way, the perfection of the garden around the home of the peculiar children mirrors the harmonious tending of man over nature and offers a counter narrative to the Hollows' destructive grip over the world, where transcendentalism and the legacy of the Enlightenment have been forgotten. Jake is entrusted with the book and Abe's map of the loops, a map charting a course of humanity and self-sacrificial love in direct opposition to the Hollows's deadly appetite. His gift of seeing what others cannot see so that he can protect them, models a new kind of heroism which is individual and collective: as a group, he and the children overtake the Hollows – fulfilling the Emersonian vision.

Moreover, the cinematic experience also involves re-contextualising the elements within the cultural issues addressed by the film at the time of its release. The well-known trope of the time machine, for example, is reinvented through the notion of the time loop that engages with current perceptions of mortality and attendant desires for immortality. The obsession with clocks goes beyond the allusion to Lewis Carroll's *Alice's Adventures in Wonderland* (1865), even if the giant carrot triggers a synecdochic allusion to the famous rabbit of the fairy tale. Mastery of time and eternal youth comes with a terrible trade-off – the surrender of free will to mindless predictability and repetition: human robots in a world of paradox and oxymoron ushered by fiction and fantasy. The overall warped sense of time and place resonates with our current dwelling in temporalities and spaces we can choose or opt out of.

CONCLUSION

'He could see the monsters, that was Abe's greatest gift' (Emma to Jake)
One might ask where the reality ends and the fiction begins. In a way, the articulation between the two sets of 'peculiar bodies' plays on the border crossing of what art, and film in particular, does, and especially through the singular notion of monstrosity rehearsed in the film. Monsters are the typical fare of fairy tales and other childhood stories; they call forth the product of fantasy or nightmares, as dramatised by Abe and his range of playful staging. Yet, as transpires later, Abe had real monsters in mind, and his narrated monsters were meant to hold in check his fears of the all too authentic ones in a form of displacement or rewriting of reality, thus carnivalising the terrifying historical context of his own childhood. When Abe tells Jake about escaping monsters with tentacles, he rewrites reality in a way that the child can understand it without downplaying the truth of the Nazi horror behind it. In this metafictional moment, Burton addresses what the work of art is and its performative function. The film itself could be compared to Abe's stories: it stages monsters, real and frightening, in a way that they can be understood, through bodies that display peculiarity indeed. They embody contemporary and topical questions through their grotesquery and rehearse the surprising guise that truth sometimes takes.

NOTES

1. For further reading, see the work of Marie Liénard-Yeterian in the Bibliography.
2. See Agnieszka Soltysik Monnet and Marie Liénard-Yeterian (2015), 'The Gothic in an Age of Terror(ism)', *Gothic Studies*, 17(2), pp. 1–11.
3. See Marie Liénard-Yeterian (2016), 'Gothic Trouble: Cormac McCarthy's *The Road* and the Globalized Order', in Agnieszka Soltysik-Monnet (ed.), Special Issue 'Gothic Matters', *Text Matters: A Journal of Literature, Theory and Culture*, (6), pp. 144–58.
4. Posthumanism connotes an era where mankind as we know it will have disappeared. The Singularity designates the threshold when machines will overcome – and overtake – human beings, intelligence-wise.

18. ASEXUALITY AND SOCIAL ANXIETY: THE PERILS OF A PECULIAR BODY

Alexandra Jayne Hackett

Two attributes not usually associated with Tim Burton's characters are asexuality and associated social anxiety. It is argued here that the 'outsiderness' of certain of Burton's characters is not limited to their appearance but is also reflected in their sexual identity and insecurity. Asexuality is an often-misunderstood sexual identity, while anxiety may also be misread or stigmatised, and it is in these senses that Burton, on occasion, arguably creates 'peculiar bodies'. This chapter considers how these two factors contribute to the idiosyncrasy of his protagonists and suggests that it is not in fact their appearance that makes them outsiders but, rather, their misconstrued way of communicating their sexuality or anxieties. Specifically, it will analyse the physical manifestation of Edward Scissorhands (Johnny Depp), the eponymous character of *Edward Scissorhands* (1990), and examine his sexuality which is deemed unacceptable by the traditional suburban community he inhabits. *Charlie and the Chocolate Factory* (2005) will also be considered, particularly Willy Wonka's (Johnny Depp) fear and avoidance of intimate communication and female sexuality as a result of his father's authority during childhood. The essay will engage with Sigmund Freud's (2001) theory of psychosexual development and Jacques Lacan's (Rabaté 2001) concept of the mirror stage as well as non-verbal communication theory (Andersen 1999) to consider the development of self-identity in the characters of Edward Scissorhands and Willy Wonka.

Carol Siegel (2013) has discussed sexuality in a range of Burton's films, including *Edward Scissorhands*. Her contention is that although 'film reviewers and critics adhere to a "don't ask, don't tell" policy regarding sexuality in Burton's work', a number of characters exhibit 'blatant sexualised depictions of perversity' (2013: 197). Siegel goes on to say that some audiences refuse to acknowledge the 'S&M' symbolism of the tight leather outfits that characters such as Edward wear because they are uncomfortable with such imagery. As she notes,

> One audience is composed of children who delight in the fairy-tale aspects of the films, identify with their often childlike protagonists, and are apparently presumed by adults to be ignorant of the overlaps between their imagery and the artefacts and practices of sexualities deemed perverse by the dominant culture. Another audience is made up of viewers who are clearly old enough to know that, for instance, tight black leather or vinyl outfits identical to Edward's and Catwoman's are commonly used in S&M rituals, but who refuse to recognize such correlations, perhaps because they prefer to avoid thinking about sexualities that depart from the norm. (Siegel 2015: 169)

Siegel subsequently describes Edward Scissorhands as a sadist because 'his caresses slice and injure' (2015: 172), and she even concludes that 'Edward, as a sadist, is perhaps the most radically represented of Burton's perverts' (2015: 175). While her claim that his costume and capacity to cut correlates with contemporaneous S/M culture, and she acknowledges the 'sensitive, suffering face of Edward' (Seigel 2013: 206), a closer study of Edward's figure behaviour and non-verbal communication reveals otherwise. Indeed, his body language wholly contradicts the idea that he is a sexual sadist. In fact, he is the opposite and arguably not a sexual being at all: Edward is asexual and lacks sexual feeling and intuition entirely. In this respect, Jack Curtis Dubowsky briefly touches upon Edward's lack of sexual awareness by stating that 'Edward does not understand sexual advances' (2016: 179). Instead he argues that Edward experiences a sexual awakening (Dubowsky 2016: 178) and goes on to categorise him as a 'queer monster'. In so doing, Dubowsky focuses on the monstrous characteristics that Edward shares with Frankenstein and less on his sexuality. Overall, while sharing similar ideas regarding Edward's innocence, Dubowsky's work considers Edward as 'monster' and argues that he is 'queer' rather than asexual.

In contrast to these limited examinations of sexuality, while some of Burton's characters undoubtedly exhibit S/M inferences, others, such as Edward Scissorhands and Willy Wonka, display characteristics of asexuality and anxiety. According to Catriona Jones, Mark Hayter and Julie Jomeen, 'Contemporary definitions of asexuality vary; however, an asexual is commonly defined as one who does not experience sexual attraction. Lack of sexual behaviour or activity has also been used to define asexuality' (2017: 3812). Asexuality can be interpreted as the complete lack of sexual feelings or associations, although asexual individuals can desire romantic relationships; this is applicable to Edward and Kim (Winona Ryder) (diegetically, Kim is the romantic interest of Edward and daughter of Mr and Mrs Boggs [Dianne Wiest and Alan Arkin], whom Edward stays with for the duration of the narrative). It is possible to have romantic emotions without sexual feelings, as it will be argued in Edward's case whereby the conflict of his asexuality with his romantic feelings for Kim causes anxiety.

Edward Scissorhands is commonly defined as a Gothic fairy tale. John Yorke identifies the perils of eponymous characters of fairy tales, noting, 'Whether real or imagined, great characters are consciously or subconsciously at war with themselves [. . .] There is contradiction within us all' (2013: 128). This essay will examine such inner conflict in Edward (along with another Burton protagonist, Willy Wonka), by analysing how his physical representation, namely, his figure expression and appearance, embodies asexuality and social anxiety. It will argue that the characters are imperilled, that is, suffering anxiety, in part due to their peculiar bodies and associated asexuality.

FREUD AND THE FIVE STAGES OF SEXUALITY

Both Edward Scissorhands's and Willy Wonka's lack of sexuality may be explained with reference to Freud's (2001) concept of psychosexual development. Here, Freud argues that infants seek gratification via a number of routes and in a specific sequence whereby 'the sexual aim of the infantile instinct consists in obtaining satisfaction by means of an appropriate stimulation of the erotogenic zone which has been selected in one way or another' (2001: 184). He describes three successive stages, namely the oral, anal and phallic phases, which correspond to a child's respective preoccupations with the mouth (through sucking and biting), the anus (by experiencing control of the excretory organs) and the genitals (via masturbation) (2001: 185–7). Subsequent stages include a latent phase which involves the repression of sexual feelings, and a final genital phase whereby sexual orientation is matured. However, individuals may not undergo all these stages and may become arrested at a particular moment. For example, in the aforementioned claim by Siegel, she suggests that Edward is a sadist – this corresponds to the anal stage and an obsession with control. According to Freud, a lack of adult sexuality, together with a propensity for cruelty, accords with the anal stage. As he states, 'it may be assumed that the impulse for cruelty arises from the instinct for mastery and appears at a period of sexual life at which the genitals have not yet taken over their later role' (Freud 2001: 193). However, in contending that the characters of Edward and Willy Wonka are asexual beings, it is suggested that they do not undergo this sequence of psychosexual development. Rather, because Edward is created in adult form rather than born, he does not have the opportunity to develop a coherent sexual identity, whereas Willy Wonka remains fixated at the oral stage because of paternal persecution.

The Lacanian Mirror Phase

Lacan also proposed a sequence of childhood development whereby at around the age of eighteen months, usually when the child attains language, it concurrently recognises itself in the mirror as an individual, distinct from its parents. Lacan's mirror phase is outlined by Nitzan Ben-Shaul, who notes, 'The psychoanalyst Lacan introduced the hypothesis that our first notion of identity, occurring between the age of six to eighteen months, is based upon a mere reflection of ourselves' (2007: 109). This means that a child begins to have a sense of its own identity when it sees its reflection in a mirror. Richard Appignanesi notes that this concept of reflection is extended to mimicking what infants learn of themselves from their parents (2005: 23). Lacan's concept has been widely utilised in screen theory to explain the process of identification of spectators with onscreen characters, whereby 'the child lacks any sense of its body as a unitary object, and that it is therefore literally uncoordinated. However, this state is overcome by the process through which the child learns to see itself as a unitary and coherent whole through its identification with the image of other bodies. The imaginary is therefore about identification with an image, and gives a sense of wholeness' (Hollows, Hutchings and Jancovich 2000: 193). In relation to Burton's films, Lacan's mirror concept becomes relevant diegetically in the formation of a coherent identity for the two protagonists under discussion.

Non-verbal Communication Theory

Another way of analysing asexuality and social anxiety is to consider the way that characters physically express communication through body language and figure behaviour. Textual analysis of these aspects of the two protagonists will take into account three key forms of non-verbal communication defined by Peter Andersen (1999) and Mark G. Frank, Hyi Sung Hwang and David Matsumoto (2013): kinesics, adaptors and proxemics. Kinesics refers to hand and arm movement, eye contact, gestures, facial expressions and posture. Matsumoto and Hwang explain that 'adaptors' allow the individual to adapt to internal or external stimuli (2013: 87), while proxemics evaluate how space and distance is used to communicate (Burgoon et al. 2016: 19). By analysing these key elements of non-verbal communication, one might argue that through gestures such as adaptors, Edward's preferences for other characters, and his proxemic interaction with other characters, Johnny Depp lends nuances of anxiety to Edward's character.

EDWARD SCISSORHANDS (1990)

The notion that Edward is asexual is evidenced in his contrasting relationships with two key women, Kim and Joyce (Kathy Baker). Kim is young, fair and acts with a conscience whereas Joyce shows typical traits of being predatory with excessive make-up and overly tight-fitting clothes; she also has sexually aggressive tendencies, pursuing numerous men throughout the narrative. For example, she flirts with the handyman who is fixing her kitchen as well as with Edward. She leans over the handyman closely, flutters her eyelashes, pouts her lips and hints that 'housewives get lonely too'. When Joyce sees Edward for the first time, she looks him up and down with her lips apart, and gossips about him with the other women in a sexual manner, making comments such as 'just imagine what a single snip could do'. She pursues him by flirting, flicking her hair and batting her eyelids. In terms of Freudian psychosexual development, there is provisional engagement with the oral phase when she feeds Edward at a barbecue. In contrast, Kim is the object of Edward's romantic attention, but she also has a boyfriend, Jim (Anthony Michael Hall), who is possessive and controlling. Edward is attracted to Kim and even voyeuristic towards her; every time he gazes at her, a romantic atmosphere is created through a slow soundtrack and measured camera zooms. In Siegel's aforementioned 'sadistic' scenario, one might therefore argue that this correlates with a fixation at the primal stage of development, an aspect that Laura Mulvey exploits in her association between sadism and scopophilia (2000: 245).

Indeed, there are multiple occasions where Edward directs a voyeuristic gaze towards Kim; usually, the camera movements decelerate, and music transforms the scene into a fantasy indulgence as he watches her from a distance, visualised in a long shot of the crowd. For instance, in the scene where Edward sees a photo of Kim for the first time, he smiles timidly. A slow-moving panning camera carefully and hesitantly explores the room from Edward's point of view, the spectator sharing his perspective, and non-diegetic fairy-tale music becomes noticeably louder when he sees a photo of Kim, with whom he seems enthralled. In a later scene, Edward sees Kim with her friends out shopping. Again, the camera tracks slowly through the crowd, with Kim centrally framed. The music is relaxed and dreamy as Edward moves towards her slowly and steadily, the camera framing his face in a close-up and allowing the audience to share his perspective and fantasy. A light reflected in his eyes makes them appear almost tear-filled, suggesting sadness, but as he draws closer, Kim and Jim embrace then leave, and the music becomes melancholic. Edward's enjoyment of gazing is thus interrupted by the reminder that Kim already has a partner, and by extension he is reminded of his incapacity for romantic intimacy with her.

However, Edward does not understand these feelings, and in this respect Edwin Page notes that 'Edward cannot cope with everyday life and needs guidance in order to survive in the "real" world. He does not know how to handle his feelings towards Kim and her boyfriend' (2007: 88). One might therefore suggest that, because Edward is physically an adult yet is unable to understand his feelings towards Kim, he displays signs of delayed psychosexual development. He appears afraid to explore these feelings and he is shy around her and visibly afraid at the beginning. In one scene, she arrives back from her camping trip in the middle of the night. Edward has never encountered a social situation like this, and so remains very still, holding his scissor hands up protectively in front of his chest as though trying to hide. When Kim sees him, incidentally through a mirror reflection, he panics and frantically flicks his scissors, which punctures the waterbed. Edward flails in panic, and changes from being merely tense to being completely out of control with anxiety.

Barbara Creed (2005) suggests that male characters with symptoms of interrupted psychosexual development such as impotence, exert power by substituting vaginal penetration for object penetration motivated by frustration and anger. This might be by stabbing women (for example, Jack the Ripper), whereby 'bloodlust and the tearing of flesh replace proper civilized sex' (Creed 2005: 94). However, Edward rarely acts out in anger or frustration and never indicates a desire to exert physical or psychological power. Rather than his blades being penetrative weapons, as described by Creed, they are an instrument of caution. Importantly, he has no innate desire to stab and penetrate with his scissor hands; in fact, when he does accidentally cut and cause harm, he is afraid and shocked. It is as if he has no understanding of penetration as a consequence, let alone as desire. Therefore, arguably, Edward experiences sexual anxiety because he has effectively bypassed the various stages of psychosexual development. Rather than exhibiting the manifestation of such anxiety through a harmful and violent penetrative outlet as Creed suggests, the anxiety has subverted itself and Edward portrays a complete lack of sexual inclination altogether.

Michael Kahn's (2002) discussion of Freud and parental response to sexuality in children supports an implication that the inventor created Edward without sexual organs. He notes that 'Freud and his followers quickly discovered that it had been a major concern of their parents, one that had enduring consequences' (Kahn 2002: 48). Parents may either punish or neglect their children when they approach the phallic stage of psychosexual development. Because it is unpleasant for a parent to acknowledge their child's sexuality, it is plausible that the inventor, as a father figure, might construct Edward without genitals and instead replace them, albeit here with something deadly and dangerous (the scissor hands) to maintain a childhood innocence: a quality frequently attributed to Edward. Indeed, many of Burton's characters are likewise innocent and childlike. For example, Edward takes joy in simple things and is curious, he obeys other adults and is ashamed when reprimanded. Furthermore, he does not understand witticisms and is hesitant and timid; in a similar vein, Wonka is immature and engages in sarcastic banter with other children. Correspondingly, the inventor takes joy in teaching Edward poetry and etiquette and in perpetuating Edward's innocence, a notion substantiated by Johnny Depp's interpretation of the character: 'Edward is not a human being, he's not an android, he's not an alien. To me he was like a new-born baby, with that kind of innocence' (in Page 2007: 86). Therefore, the inventor may have deliberately 'castrated' Edward and provided him with scissors for hands to allow him to remain perpetually innocent. Freud's notion of castration anxiety in male children ascribes a related subconscious fear of losing his penis. As Kahn explains, 'The anatomical form of the penis lends itself to the fantasy of castration. If, for example, the child is doing something forbidden with a hammer, the hammer will certainly be taken away from him' (2002: 49). Edward is inhibited by his scissor hands, and arguably has no sexual organs at all. While Edward cuts and causes damage with his scissor hands, which, as Siegel (2013) proposes, might determine the scissor hands as phallic, the damage he causes with his hands is accidental and not an exertion of power or dominance, attesting to his potential asexuality.

In this regard, Burgoon et al. (2016) outline non-verbal communication and discuss how to interpret communications such as adaptors, illustrators, vocalics and kinesics. As the authors note, '*Adaptors* are behaviours that satisfy physical or psychological needs. [. . .] adaptors satisfy personal needs (e.g. need for comfort), respond to internal states (e.g. anxiety, relaxation, perceptions of crowding, feelings of submissiveness or defensiveness) [italics in original]' (2016: 127). Edward channels anxiety through figure behaviour which, at the same time, conveys a lack of interest in sex and by extension his asexuality. There are moments where he imitates the arm and hand gestures of other characters without fully understanding why, which shows a limitation to his communication skills and perception. Adaptors may be uncontrollable movements that channel anxiety, including fidgeting or nervous ticks such as nail-biting. Edward often keeps his blades moving back and forth, and the more nervous he seems to be, the faster they move. On the subject of adaptors (adaptors may also be referred to as manipulators), Matsumoto and Hwang state that '*changes* in the frequency, duration, or intensity of these may have important meaning to the mental state of the individual. Individuals under duress, for example, may show an increase in their manipulators [. . .] or in actions that appear fidgety [italics in original]' (2013: 87). The movement of the scissor hands' blades might therefore serve as an adaptor for Edward. If twitching his scissors is an adaptor and the scissors are constantly moving, this suggests he is in a constant state of mild anxiety, and in more stressful situations the scissor-twitching becomes increasingly frantic and the sound of the blades against one another becomes louder and faster. Such scenes illustrate how adaptors increase in correlation with increasing discomfort (Frank and Svietieva 2013: 131). In regard to his appearance, Edward's make-up also lends itself to the idea that he is constantly apprehensive. The pinkish hue beneath his eyes resembles those that are sore from crying. His eyebrows are poised with a crease between them to show a constant state of worry and concern. Other adaptors such as self-touching, for example, twirling hair or scratching one's head, indicate nervousness with possible flirtatious connotations. Touching gestures infer anxiety because of arousal, for example, if a person is attracted to another individual they may experience mild unease because they want to please them. Edward's scissor hands prohibit him from touching himself and others and therefore he can never express this kind of communication. He cannot flirt or release flirtation anxiety through self-touch and he does not display sexualised body language, indicating he does not feel disquiet associated with arousal.

Edward, not having experienced infancy, would not have undergone the stages of psychosexual development. Although the spectator does see him explore the oral phase, it has become apparent that he does not need food to survive as he has spent many years in isolation without access to it, and when he dines with the Boggs family for the first time, it is evident that he is learning how to eat – he balances a pea on one blade and repeatedly drops it in recurring medium shots. In addition, it is implied that the anal phase is limited due to the physical restraints of his costume. His leather suit is never taken off, nor do we see a means of removing it. Instead, he wears clothing over the suit. This infers that the suit is his body, encasing his organs. Not only would his leather-bound body inhibit access to sexual activity, his scissor hands would also prevent him from exploring the phallic stage, which itself would evoke a threat of castration. If Edward has not experienced these stages of development, he cannot be aware of sexual fulfilment or his incapacity for it, and therefore he is asexual because he cannot feel sexual desire.

In terms of the Lacanian mirror phase, Edward sees his own reflection, which is slightly warped, thereby giving him an adverse image of himself. This occurs in his hilltop Gothic mansion when he looks upon his reflection in the attic. However, the mirror is broken, indicating that he perceives himself to be broken and ugly, creating a lasting impression of anxiety and timidity in how he presents himself to other people for the rest of the story. Another key scene that illustrates Lacan's mirror theory and examines Edward's anxiety arises when he pierces the wallpaper in the hallway with his scissor hands and proceeds to stare at himself in the mirror, repeatedly slashing the walls on either side of it. This episode occurs immediately after Kim leaves Edward to go to Jim and he realises that any intimacy he shares with her cannot be sustained. He is frustrated with himself and experiences anxiety about his identity and what he is. Edward has not grown up, so he does not have the emotional intelligence to deal with his feelings maturely and therefore this physical manifestation of anxiety and self-dislike is a metaphorical display of self-harm. He continues to scratch the walls as he glares at himself. Thereafter, Edward remains centrally framed as he walks down the hallway until he reaches the bathroom mirror. Again, he scratches the walls downward in vertical lines repeatedly while his face appears as if he is about to cry but his expression is mixed with anger, a new emotion for him to experience. The scene then cuts to Edward with his head hung in shame and sadness while Mr Boggs attempts to teach him morals and ethics, thus illustrating how he is not developed or aware of societal regulation.

It is worth noting that this anxiety only manifests when Edward is in context with other characters, therefore not necessarily representing identity anxiety. When he is alone he is quite happy and creative, implying that it is social situations that trigger repressed anxieties about himself. Among others, Edward does not know who he is; he is nervous about meeting the neighbours so Mrs Boggs tells him to be himself, to which he replies 'myself?' as though he does not know who he really is and how to act. His mimicking behaviour also indicates he does not completely understand how to conduct himself in a social setting. The residents discover Edward's artistic talents only because Edward imitates Mr Boggs while he is trimming the hedges; thus he begins to learn who he is through imitation. In the hair salon, he follows Joyce around and copies her arm movements, indicating that he does not completely comprehend what she is trying to communicate through her figure expression. It is therefore unlikely that he understands her motives when she makes sexual advances towards him.

Indeed, through non-verbal communication, Edward shows a lack of sexual attraction to Joyce in the salon scene. Joyce is extremely forthcoming with her behaviour, but Edward again cannot reciprocate by touching her. Instead his entire demeanour is timid, as it is for the duration of the film, and his body is stiff and rigid as though he is uncomfortable. Only his hands spasm, which could be an indicator of the previously mentioned adaptive nervous twitching. In support of this, exploring the times that Edward's personal space is infiltrated gives insight to his asexuality. According to Edward Hall, personal space is considered to be between 1.5 and 4 feet, while intimate space is within 1.5 feet (in Matsumoto and Hwang 2013: 84). Edward rarely has his personal space invaded unless by Mrs Boggs, a maternal figure, or someone he feels emotionally close to, such as Kim. Therefore, when Joyce enters his zone of intimate proximity, it is jarring and uncomfortable for both Edward and the spectator. During the hair salon scene, Joyce uses the salon chair and smocks as a ruse to flirt and make sexual advances towards Edward. Edward, like a child, needs to be told by Joyce not to touch the electricity panel because he does not understand it is dangerous. Having drawn the spectator's attention to Edward's innocence, Joyce's sexual advances towards him are therefore akin to making such an approach towards a child or someone as equally innocent and vulnerable. When Joyce asks if he would like her to model the smocks, he says yes, much in the same way a child would because he knows this is what she wants to hear. Indeed, Edward will do things to make people happy without fully understanding the consequences. A single unflattering light hangs above the salon chair, forming a spotlight effect on Edward and creating an interrogative atmosphere. Joyce positions herself on top of him after pushing him hard back into the chair. She does this with aggression, elevating herself to a stance of power while Edward is vulnerable and childlike beneath her. From this point the camera only shows fractions of Edward from behind the chair or behind Joyce, suggesting he is trapped. When the camera cuts to Joyce, all that is visible of Edward are his scissors convulsing; the light catches them as they move and flicker and begin to twitch faster. When asked which smock he prefers, he says the drab boring unattractive one as opposed to the seductive lacy one that Joyce favours, and his scissors start to spasm faster, suggesting adaptive anxiety behaviour. This is because he has no intuition for flirting or understanding of how the lacy smock might be considered sexy or attractive; rather, Edward values being covered up and practicality. Joyce says 'You're trembling, so am I', but Edward is trembling with anxiety and confusion.

Upon leaving, Edward avoids eye contact and his body is rigid, indicating his discomfort. It is clear that he does not understand the situation in the same way that Joyce does when he meets the Boggs family afterwards, and says blankly with no expression of happiness or excitement, 'Mrs Monroe showed me where the salon is going to be . . . and then she showed me the back room where she took all of her clothes off'. He speaks innocently and openly as though it is a normal occurrence because he does not understand what may be wrong, much like a child who unwittingly incriminates an adult, leaving the Boggs family in a state of shock. In contrast, when Kim enters his immediate vicinity, he is obliging but does not initiate sexual contact. Kim gently places his arms around her, but his hands do not touch her. Edward has a romantic inclination towards Kim; they embrace, but they do not kiss passionately or touch, and their physical contact is not sexualised. Rather, it is careful and romantic.

Edward's body language communicates his self-perception even more so than that of Wonka (to be discussed). He walks timidly in small steps, is hesitant and sometimes hunched over, and holds his 'hands' either up close to his chest guarding his intimate proximity or spread out protecting his personal space. For example, in the final scenes when the suburban residents turn against Edward, he runs away, scared and ashamed that he has hurt Kevin (Robert Oliveri). Edward runs down the street with his arms stretched out, the camera panning outward, emphasising his need to flee. This non-verbal communication indicates that he regards his personal space and intimate proximity as something he fears is about to be infiltrated. Throughout the film, Edward's personal space is not often entered by other characters except by those he trusts, such as Mrs Boggs, who is a maternal figure and cares for Edward.

Edward has a disrupted psychological development. Losing his father figure before he has learnt much as an infant means he loses the source from which a boy learns about his own masculinity. As discussed by Ronald F. Levant and William Pollack, having a present father figure enhances a sense of self, 'leading to a more stable sense of self through the boy's identification with his father's masculine role' (1995: 42). Furthermore, he loses his parental figure in a traumatic way. Lacan's mirror phase refers to children also learning about themselves from mimicking their parents. Edward witnesses the inventor die in front of him, and also sees blood on his hands from accidentally cutting his face while trying to wake him up. From this he learns to fear himself and fear hurting others. The severance from his parental figure is cruel, and Levant and Pollack continue to discuss how unconscious fears can be triggered by traumatic experiences with parents:

> The point is not to condemn mothers and fathers – but rather to highlight that men may either feel or unconsciously experience a sense of having been abandoned, betrayed, or hurtfully separated. Most men have no conscious memory of this earlier trauma, though their vulnerabilities (especially to shame) in adult life may be the evidence of the unhealed wound. (1995: 43)

Overall, one might suggest that Edward suffers anxiety because of who he believes he is and the damage he thinks he causes, or from not fully understanding what he is. This is because prior to the point in time where the film starts, he did not complete the stages of psychosocial development for an identification of self.

WILLY WONKA IN *CHARLIE AND THE CHOCOLATE FACTORY* (2005)

Another Burton character to exhibit interrupted psychosexual development is Willy Wonka. Willy Wonka, a world-famous chocolatier, allows five children to visit his factory with the motive of finding an heir. In doing so, Wonka is forced to confront his childhood and his relationship with his father. Burton relates Wonka's childhood to his subsequent problems as an adult. During flashback scenes we see a young Willy Wonka cruelly and metaphorically castrated by physically invasive, cage-like braces that cover his head and hold his jaw open. The braces prevent him from eating with ease or freedom, and they, and his father's hatred of chocolate (he is a dentist), effectively inhibit oral pleasure and therefore serve the purpose of arresting psychosexual development at the oral phase. In fact, oral satisfaction is entirely prohibited by his father, who forbids Wonka from eating chocolate. When Wonka secretly indulges in this forbidden act, he becomes obsessed; indeed, his preoccupation with forbidden chocolate becomes a lifelong commitment and he travels to different countries to achieve this. He is thus fixated at the oral stage and is unable to continue to the next phases, causing an incomplete psychosexual progression to manifest as social and sexual anxiety in adulthood. This makes him unable to deal with sexual confrontation from Mrs Beauregarde (Missi Pyle). Wonka first escorts the group of children into the 'chocolate room', a room resembling grass and trees and plants and a river of chocolate in which everything is edible. The group are about to board the boat (a giant hardboiled sweet) when Wonka tells them that chocolate releases endorphins that give people the feeling of being in love, to which Mrs Beauregarde responds by looking at Wonka in a desiring manner before she smiles flirtatiously and says 'You don't say'. Wonka responds by ignoring her remark and laughing nervously, ushering the group on.

Wonka's inability to forge close relationships or engage with sexual activity such as flirting or intimate touch is derived from his negative relationship with his father, whose authority he is afraid to engage with. Freud related certain forms of anxiety to the repression of sexual impulses, stating, 'If any of those fears were strong, a likely way of dealing with them would be to repress the dangerous impulse in the hopes of eliminating the fear' (in Kahn 2002: 108). Wonka seemingly tries to erase his childhood from memory and, as a result, never moves onto other stages of psychosexual development. Throughout the narrative his suppressed childhood resurfaces through flashbacks and causes him to confront the source of his anxiety, which occurs in the final part of the film. Wonka is stuck in a state of anxiety associated with his father's authoritarian reign over the pleasure the boy craved as a child, causing repressed sexuality that manifests as asexuality.

Wonka shows such behaviour in the scene where Mrs Beauregarde flirts with him. Joyce and Mrs Beauregarde are both presented as overly provocative in body language, and with exaggerated make-up, fake tan, heavy eye shadow and excessive bouffant hairstyles. They both examine men as if to calculate their next move, and stand close to their 'victims', smile and accentuate their hourglass shape with their posture. Mrs Beauregarde and Joyce are often framed in two ways: long shots, which accentuate their height and showcase their figures and upright posture, and profile shots of their face that emphasise their pageant smiles and perfect teeth. Both Edward and Wonka are especially socially awkward when confronted with this mode of presentation. Once inside the factory, the children introduce themselves to him one by one. Violet Beauregarde (AnnaSophia Robb) hugs him and Wonka gasps, Veruca Salt (Julia Winter) and Augustus Gloop (Philip Wiegratz) step in front of him and introduce themselves, and Wonka takes a step back while issuing a sarcastic retort. Burgoon et al. examine a person's physical reaction to unwanted intimate special interaction, stating, 'When people feel threatened physically or psychologically, or when the amount of social involvement is excessive, they may attempt to compensate by increasing nonimmediacy, which increases psychological distance' (2016: 381). There are numerous occasions where Wonka displays this behaviour and reaction to social interaction. He recoils at social confrontation, grimaces at gluttony and pride, and becomes rigid when touched. This suggests that he feels anxiety when confronted with others in close proximity, especially intimate exchanges such as hugging. It would also indicate an inability to forge intimate relationships and by extension sexual relationships. He protects himself from touch by encasing his body in tight, form-fitting clothing. His skin is inaccessible to human touch because he wears layers of clothes, a high neckline and gloves. Like Edward, his body is protected from touch and he himself does not initiate this sense. In this way, through non-verbal communication, Wonka physically manifests asexuality.

Yet Wonka displays social awkwardness in a different way to Edward. He struggles with knowing how to present himself in a social situation and needs prompts. For example, when he welcomes the children and their parents into the factory, he literally reads from prompt cards to guide him through conversation. He is framed alone while the children and their parents, who are located directly opposite him, are framed together, strengthening the feeling of his isolation and discomfort in a social setting. However, Wonka throws aside the prompt cards when he sees that they are not entertaining. This suggests that he can read social cues but does not know how to engage himself and react. The same applies when Mrs Beauregarde hints at being attracted to Wonka. He knows what she is suggesting because he becomes awkward and avoids the situation by changing the subject. Unlike Edward, he is aware of Mrs Beauregarde's intentions and avoids them at all costs.

Similarly, Willy Wonka knows he is different and does not communicate well with others. His lack of social skills particularly manifests with the opposite gender because of his deficient interest in flirting and sex. This creates anxiety, and manifests in flamboyant behaviour, erratic decisions and the way he presents himself: he dresses pristinely but is fully covered in order to avoid skin to skin contact with anyone. The moment of his revelation occurs when he undergoes a physical change through a haircut; he recognises himself thereafter, which triggers the development of his journey to an understanding of his inner conflict. Wonka holds up a mirror and notices a grey hair. He experiences a clichéd 'midlife crisis' when he finds this hair, and he realises he is getting older and has no relatives to pass on his life's work. Seeing himself in this reflection changes his perspective of himself and his relationship with others, so much so that, based on this experience, he decides to welcome children to the factory to find an heir and business partner. This decision points to self-discovery throughout the narrative, a series of flashbacks ultimately leading Wonka to confront his childhood. Having suffered an authoritarian trauma at the hands of his father, this is difficult for Wonka, and he struggles to say the word 'parents', so much so that Mr Salt (James Fox) has to finish the sentence for him. Subsequently the word 'Dad' triggers Wonka's first dissociative episode, where he stares into space and disassociates from his surroundings. It is as if, at heart, he is still a repressed child coming to terms with his identity.

Conclusion

Through an analysis of Edward Scissorhands's non-verbal communication, a theoretical use of Freud's essays on sexuality, and an application of Lacan's mirror phase to Edward's development of self-identity, this chapter suggests that he is asexual and correlates this to his social anxiety. Firstly Edward, having been constructed by the inventor as an adolescent, has not experienced the primary stages of psychosexual development, a factor evident throughout the narrative. Attempts at eating are awkward, and even this is forced upon him rather than him seeking it out. He is prevented from experiencing the phallic stage because of his scissor hands which, if he were experiencing sexual frustration, may have been an instrument of phallic rage, and therefore could have been a penetrative substitute. Instead the scissors act as a guard for his anxiety; he often positions them protectively up close to his chest, or holds them out shielding a zone of intimate proximity. The theory that these kinesthetics represent sexual anxiety in Burton's characters is reinforced by Willy Wonka, who flinches when in close proximity to others and who, like Edward, is clothed neck to toe, concealing any skin from human touch. These analyses infer an innate lack of sexuality in Edward, and an aversion to sexuality in Wonka: 'asexuality'. Edward is either disinclined or disinterested in sexual behaviours presented to him, and he lacks competitive drive with other male figures, even when presented with intimidating dominance from Jim, for example. Edward has also subverted the castration anxiety derived from his affection for Kim, who is forbidden to him, into asexuality and social submission and anxiety. He rarely speaks, and when he does, he is quiet, timid and often portrayed as innocent and childlike. The climax of the narrative is initiated with Edward running away. The challenges his body presents him with centre on asexuality in a sexually fuelled society, and the anxiety that this brings. These perils of peculiarity provide just one example of many throughout Burton's portfolio of peculiar bodies.

19. BURTON'S BENEVOLENTLY MONSTROUS FRANKENSTEINS

Robert Geal

Like many filmmakers, Tim Burton is drawn to certain pre-existing narrative and thematic tropes that are repeated and reworked into much of his oeuvre. Burton combines these tropes in various complex ways, but a defining feature of these combinations is a rehabilitation of the ostensibly monstrous. Scholarship has generally analysed how this rehabilitation functions as a politically progressive celebration of non-hegemonic 'outsiders' of various kinds (Hills 2013; Scherman 2016; Sullivan 2014; Sweeney 2016). This chapter, however, explores how the rehabilitated monstrosity in *Edward Scissorhands* (1990) and *Frankenweenie* (2012), which both loosely adapt Mary Shelley's novel *Frankenstein* ([1818] 1974), blunts some of the progressive proto-feminist political potential otherwise associated with the source text.

Burton's intertextual engagements thereby run counter to the current orthodoxy in the field of adaptation studies. This dominant approach explores how texts mutate as they travel across time and cultures. Texts are understood as inevitably dialogic in the sense that they commune with existing texts in ways that express something not only about each related (inter-)text but also about the ambient cultural discourses prevailing during each particular articulation of the (inter-)text.

The dialogic paradigm conceptualises the historical trajectory of such texts as fundamentally politically progressive. Taking the same issue addressed in this chapter – gender – for example, Robert Stam, one of the key proponents of the dialogic method, claims that contemporary 'revisionist adaptations [release] the latent feminist spirit of the novels and of the characters, or even of the author, in a kind of anachronistic therapy or adaptation rescue operation' (2005: 42). This concept, termed 'excanonation' (Geal 2019: 23), is a politically progressive process in which 'canonical culture's false choice between, for example, Shakespeare and Dickens can be transcended by adaptation's dialogic customisation of those texts' (Geal 2019: 24). So, for instance, Holly Hassel (2011: 49) can argue that retrogressive attitudes about female passivity in the fairy tale *Sleeping Beauty*, repeated in the animated Disney adaptation (Geronimi 1959), are subverted by representing princesses according to the narrative and visual conventions of traditionally male action heroes in *Shrek the Third* (Miller and Hui 2007); I have discussed (Geal 2016) how *Frozen* (Buck and Lee 2013) adapts the malicious antagonist from *The Snow Queen* (Hans Christian Andersen 1844) into a conflicted but ultimately benevolent and empowered/empowering protagonist, and Jack M. Downs (2014: 74) notes the progressive repercussions of replacing the male elf-lord Glorfindel, in a key action sequence in the novel *The Fellowship of the Ring* (Tolkien 1954), with the female elf Arwen (Liv Tyler) in Peter Jackson's film adaptation (2001).

This chapter argues that Burton's intertextual engagements with Shelley's *Frankenstein* do not conform to such a politically progressive trajectory. Or, more precisely, Burton's Frankensteinian filmmaking, exemplified in *Edward Scissorhands* and *Frankenweenie*, includes elements that are ostensibly progressive, but undercuts these aspects with more politically conservative, even misogynistic revisions that invert some of the source novel's proto-feminist potential.

There has been much debate about the novel *Frankenstein*'s proto-feminism. The term 'proto-feminism' as opposed to 'feminism' is appropriate here because Shelley's novel points diachronically forwards to political movements and socio-cultural attitudes which were only in their embryonic form in the early nineteenth century. In Stam's aforementioned approach to adaptation, more recent films might activate 'the latent feminist spirit of the novel' (2005: 42), although the argument here is that Burton displaces rather than activates this latent feminism.

The full details of the debate about the novel's proto-feminism (Baldick 1987; Bloom 2000; Mellor 1988) are beyond the scope of this essay, but the salient point is that the doctor-creator in the novel makes something monstrous and destructive not only because he violates God's control over metaphysical creation (making life from non-living matter), but because he also violates woman's control over biological creation (making life from outside the womb). Thus, for Anne K. Mellor, '[t]he destruction of the female implicit in Frankenstein's usurpation of the natural mode of human reproduction symbolically erupts in his nightmare following the animation of his creature' (1988: 115). The animation part of Mellor's argument will be revisited later, given how it refers to Burton's reflexively Frankenstein-like filmmaking as well as his Frankenstein-like narratives and characters. However, most importantly an integral element of the novel *Frankenstein*, and of most other texts engaging with it,[1] is a form of destructive monstrosity specifically associated with a male attempt to usurp the female creative act.

Edward Scissorhands and *Frankenweenie* repeat Frankenstein's male progenitor of a creation with certain ostensibly monstrous qualities. The eponymous Edward (Johnny Depp) was at first a mechanical cutting machine bestowed a heart, and then various other body parts, by a quirky (and always benevolent) inventor (Vincent Price) who dies just before he can replace Edward's scissors with real hands. In the animated film *Frankenweenie*, a young boy, Victor Frankenstein (Charlie Tahan), brings his beloved dog Sparky back to life after it is killed in a car accident. Burton's revisions, however, rehabilitate the novel's monstrosity, removing the malevolence and destructiveness that Shelley previously attached to it. To a degree the created 'monsters' in these two films repeat the creation's complaint in the novel that 'am I not alone, miserably alone? You, my creator, abhor me; what hope can I gather from your fellow-creatures, who owe me nothing? They spurn and hate me' (Shelley 1974: 95). Both Edward and Sparky inherit this societal alienation. Their creators might not abhor them, but the wider world, at various stages, in both films, does 'spurn and hate' them. Shelley's and Burton's creations, therefore, are similarly shunned by society. What is different, however, is the degree of pathos that Burton provides his creations, and the way that these films shift violent destructivity from the apparently (that is, principally, visually) monstrous onto the apparently (visually) non-monstrous, with this shift reversing the novel's proto-feminist critique of man's scientific quest for power over life.

Frankenweenie employs an aesthetic that makes all characters somewhat visually grotesque, but *Edward Scissorhands* renders clear visual distinctions between the ostensibly monstrous and non-monstrous, and these differences completely reverse various conventions going back at least as far as German Expressionist films like *Nosferatu* (Murnau 1922) and a more diffuse Victorian (neo-)Gothic style. Thus, the mansion where Edward lives, shown at the beginning and end of the film, is framed from low angles and geographically positioned on a high 'mountain', so that it looms menacingly over both the spectator and the locals in the narrative. This location has a *mise-en-scène* employing conventionalised low-lit echoing stone chambers with a spiralling staircase, jagged lines, menacing statues, cobwebs and cast shadows. Edward's metal hands glint with reflected light from the darkness and will be shown cutting and red with blood. His black costume and pallid make-up are strikingly chiaroscuro, evoking both Boris Karloff's monster from the Universal *Frankenstein* (Whale 1931) and more especially the murderous somnambulist Cesare (Conrad Veidt) from *The Cabinet of Dr Caligari* (Wiene 1920). These intertextual cues all typically equate visual monstrosity with narrative destructiveness, and, on first encountering Edward, Peg Boggs (Dianne Wiest) responds with fear and alarm as he emerges from the generically foreboding shadows.

Edward calms Peg with his childlike loneliness and innocence, and these features encourage the spectator to see beyond the apparently monstrous in order that, as the film poster's tagline has it, 'His story will touch you, even though he can't'. Burton takes a long-standing generic equation of images and meanings and ascribes different implications to those images, whereby the visually monstrous is made benevolent rather than malevolent. Shelley's monster announces that he became destructive because he is alone and abhorred, whereas previously he was 'benevolent; [his] soul glowed with love and humanity' (Shelley 1974: 95). Even when Edward is rejected, however, the spectator is under no doubt that the creation's motivations do not waver from 'love and humanity'.

For example, Edward is taken in to live with Peg's family. The teenage daughter Kim's (Winona Ryder) bullying jock boyfriend, Jim (Anthony Michael Hall), refuses to accept the outsider and accuses Edward of deliberately cutting Kim's hand. However, this accident occurs during a sequence in which Burton uses slow-motion and wondrous non-diegetic music to frame Kim's joyous dance in response to snowflakes falling from an ice sculpture that Edward is making. Burton thereby encourages a spectatorial response that shares Edward's (and, here, Kim's) innocent benevolence. Similarly, the community definitively turns on Edward when he jumps onto Kevin (Robert Oliveri), cutting him in the process. However, the spectator is again clearly aligned with Edward's sympathies, as his point-of-view shots reveal that a van being driven by a drunk Jim is swerving dangerously towards the oblivious Kevin. The spectator therefore knows that Edward benevolently saves Kevin from being killed, whereas the community think that Edward malevolently attacks the boy. Even when Edward finally kills Jim, it is only to protect Kim; Jim is the aggressor who begins the fight by shooting a gun, which looms menacingly in the foreground, directed at Edward. During this conflict Jim is violently dominant, positioned threateningly over Edward, with his enemy prostrate on the floor, and with Jim now framed from low angles that demonstrate his power and danger.

Unlike Shelley's creation, being left 'alone, miserably alone' (1974: 95) is not enough to make Edward destructive. Minor moments of rage, when he cuts at the wallpaper in the Boggs's house, and slashes the legs off one of the figures he has sculpted into a hedge, are subsumed into a broader and more permanent acceptance of isolation. This acceptance culminates in the final scene where Edward carefully tends his topiary statues, and repeats his creation of snow by cutting fragments of ice from figures he is carving. These sculptures, moreover, represent joys like dancing and playing ball games which are associated with the society from which he is excluded.

Edward's created snow is used to repeat the juxtaposition between the benevolently monstrous and the malevolently non-monstrous. The film's opening sequence, accompanied again by suggestively awe-inspiring non-diegetic music, provides a white blanket of snow which covers over the suburban environment that is otherwise contrasted with Edward's Gothic home, costume and make-up. Without this snow cover, the suburban world is not only explicitly not Gothic, but is banal in a manner specifically associated with the female. Although the principal character who destructively confronts Edward is male, the suburban world that turns against him is principally female. Flashbacks reveal the Gothic mansion as a place of quirky and ostensibly monstrous male creativity – the opening scene features anthropomorphised machines, with cogs and gauges positioned like eyes and noses, playfully making cookies. A heart-shaped cookie will inspire the inventor to craft one of these machines into the creation, Edward, and this process, despite the fact that it takes place within a traditionally monstrous *mise-en-scène*, is always benevolent, with the inventor smiling at his ingenuity, and encouraging his creation to laugh at comic poetry. The suburban world, in contradistinction, is impersonal, fake and banal. Once the opening scene's snow is gone, Burton represents the community via a muted pastel colour palette, each house a slightly different but equally insipid shade. This opening shot of the community also has one house covered in a similarly pastel fumigation tent, demonstrating a world divorced from nature.

From the outset, this banal suburban world is predominantly female. High-angle shots of the street show the men all emerging from their houses at the exact same time, so that they too appear un-individualised, and they drive off to work and leisure events, like golfing, in unison. But this leaves suburbia to the women, and Burton feminises the suffocating conformity of small-town America. It is not only that the women are depicted as ugly and petty beneath their overdone make-up, with Peg introduced as an Avon saleswoman calling on women stereotyped through unappealing hair in rollers, gossiping phone conversations and inauthentic relationships. In addition, the banality of these women is intimately connected with the same biological sexuality and creation that is entirely removed from Edward's non-biological creation. The *mise-en-scène* of the first phone conversation about Peg's new guest opens with the framing of a child's playpen situated beside the mother, Marge (Caroline Aaron), who is distracted by the gossip. Joyce (Kathy Baker) has no time for Peg because she is busy trying to seduce a dishwasher repairman. Her comically exaggerated flirtations will soon extend to Edward, and become decidedly vindictive when her advances are rejected, leading the women to incorrectly conclude that 'he practically raped Joyce, you know, threatening her with those knives of his'. By this point, the sexual impulse behind female biological creation has become explicitly malevolent.

Frankenweenie may not include such clearly defined visual distinctions between the benevolent ostensibly monstrous and the malevolent non-monstrous, but it does repeat *Edward Scissorhands*'s association of the female with the mundane and with biological sexuality that is juxtaposed with the wondrousness of male non-biological creation. After the dog Sparky is killed in a car accident, the tools that his young owner, Victor, gathers to bring his beloved pet back from the dead include numerous items from the kitchen. These objects are directly associated with the female because his mother (Catherine O'Hara) notices they are missing while baking. Victor is able to collect these implements, moreover, because Mrs Frankenstein is distracted by reading a paperback with an image of an embracing heterosexual couple on the cover. Burton connects this biologically sexual romance novel with domestic drudgery when Mrs Frankenstein is later shown with a vacuum cleaner in one hand and the book in the other. With her visual focus on the novel and the sound of the vacuum impairing her hearing, she is unable to definitively hear the barking of the recently reanimated Sparky. She pauses momentarily, but remarks 'no, it couldn't be', and returns to the non-wondrous female distractions that lead her to this conclusion.

In a similar vein to *Edward Scissorhands*, *Frankenweenie* also codes the mothering of small children as banal, and, as with Marge's telephone gossiping, motherhood is represented as sufficiently dull to require stereotyped distractions which are themselves only a little less facile. When the reanimated Sparky temporarily escapes his confinement, he encounters two mothers with children in buggies, seated at a bench. Burton considers their conversation unworthy of attention, so that only minor snatches of non-specific complaining can be heard. Nonetheless, the mothers' distraction from their children means that Sparky's quasi-monstrous but non-malevolent interaction with one of the children – slobbering on a discarded dummy which is then shoved into the crying child's mouth – goes unnoticed. Just as with Mrs Frankenstein, the distractions of female biology and social banality mean that the wondrousness of Victor's male non-biological creation is unimaginable, unseen and unheard.

As Joyce's aforementioned vindictive sexual revenge against Edward demonstrates, the mundanity which Burton associates with the female can be accompanied by a malevolence that reverses Shelley's equation of male non-biological creation and destructiveness. In both films, the mobs which hunt down the creations are dominated by female figures (Figures 19.1 and 19.2), with Joyce's ubiquitous cigarette functioning as a metonymic flaming torch which, together with her central positioning, marks her out as the mob's leader. The femaleness of these mobs is especially conspicuous in *Edward Scissorhands*, where the principal male antagonist, Jim, attempts a form of destructiveness more definitive than that of the mob, when he tries to kill Edward. However, in *Frankenweenie* the main male antagonist, Mayor Burgemeister (Martin Short),

Figure 19.1   *Frankenweenie*, 2012.

Figure 19.2   *Edward Scissorhands*, 1990.

is the community's supreme political authority, and therefore more centrally associated with the mob. Indeed, *Edward Scissorhands*'s supreme political authority, Police Officer Allen (Dick Anthony Williams), half-heartedly attempts to prevent the mob from pursuing Edward. The suburban women who had previously welcomed Edward therefore eventually lead the community against him.

In *Frankenweenie* the malevolent male authority of Burgemeister is tempered with the benevolent male authority of Victor's science teacher, Mr Rzykruski (Martin Landau). Rzykruski exemplifies a number of the male-centred reversals of Shelley's (and generic) associations between the monstrous and the malevolent. Visually, he is portrayed according to grotesque conventions, with his head, pointed nose and limbs all impossibly elongated. He is given a somewhat menacing non-specific East European accent, and he is a victim of the same fear and distrust which the community has for Burton's non-biological creations. This distrust demonstrates his benevolence, his ostensible monstrosity and the banality of the biological parents – explaining his attempts to nurture their children's scientific curiosity, he tells the parents, 'To you, science is magic and witchcraft because you have such small minds. I cannot make your heads bigger, but your children's heads, I can take them and crack them open. This is what I try to do, to get at their brains!'

Rzykruski is also closely associated with male non-biological creation because it is his demonstration of how electricity can animate the muscles of a dead frog that inspires Sparky's resurrection. After being fired for his benevolently monstrous approach to education, Rzykruski is replaced by the unnamed female Gym Teacher (Catherine O'Hara). The replacement is much less visually monstrous than Rzykruski, but she is also significantly less benevolent, refusing her predecessor's nurturing approach and, instead, shouting her instructions to the class. Whereas Rzykruski is associated with Sparky's resurrection, his female replacement is associated with the dog's death, having overseen the baseball match during which the car accident happened, when Sparky ran into the road to retrieve a ball.

Frankenweenie also has other characters who repeat Victor's life-bestowing experiment. These are mostly performed by other male pupils, but the most monstrous and most malevolent of the new creations is made by the only girl to perform the experiment, and one of the male-created monsters is also vicariously associated with femaleness. The other male students are attempting to win the school science competition, and repeatedly mention this, so their motivations are strictly neither benevolent nor malevolent. But Weird Girl (Catherine O'Hara) expresses no motivation for her experiment, so that the monstrosity stemming from it has a stereotypically negative female association of something inadvertent and inevitable rather than a stereotypically positive male association of something intended and instrumental. In attempting to resurrect a dead bat, she accidentally hybridises the creature with her cat, producing a genuinely malevolent creation. This hybrid outlives the other monstrous creations, and comes closest to genuinely harming people, causing both Elsa (Winona Ryder) and Victor to plummet dangerously from the windmill to which the hybrid had dragged Elsa's dog.

This female-created monster is therefore more destructive, malevolent and long-lived than the male-created monsters, but even one of these is associated with the female by virtue of a verbal pun. The dead tortoise that is resurrected is named Shelley, referring both to the animal's carapace and the female author of the novel. Sparky, the central male-created monster, is, in contrast, explicitly benevolent. This benevolence is depicted through a playfulness that is juxtaposed with the creepy immobility of Weird Girl's cat, as Sparky, having had a drink, chases spurts of water that shoot out from the holes in his stitched-together body. Most explicitly, Sparky's benevolence is demonstrated through his heroic attempts to save Elsa, her dog and Victor from the cat-bat hybrid. The final confrontation thereby pits the male-created Sparky and the female-created hybrid as binary opposites. Sparky's heroism in this contest also leads to his acceptance in the community which had hitherto found him monstrous. As a result, *Frankenweenie* is even more of a rehabilitation of the ostensibly monstrous than *Edward Scissorhands*.

These films' rehabilitations thus displace Shelley's critique of male attempts to usurp woman's biological form of creating life. But it is also the case that Burton's celebrations of benevolent monstrosity have another form of politically progressive potential in terms of celebrating the 'outsider' status of the creations (and creators). It might therefore be the case that Burton's Frankensteinian filmmaking is simultaneously politically regressive, in terms of gender, but also politically progressive, in terms of representing individuals typically rejected by wider society as deviant 'Others'.

Both scholarship (Scherman 2016; Sullivan 2014; Sweeney 2016) and fandom (Hills 2013) have addressed Burton's celebration of the outsider as a defining feature of his work, demonstrating that it is possible for audiences to draw parallels between the ways that society rejects and persecutes characters like Edward, Victor and Sparky, and their own experiences of isolation and alienation. This aspect of Burton's rehabilitation of the ostensibly monstrous outsider might be particularly politically progressive in the context of a tendency in Hollywood filmmaking to associate the persecution of the monstrous with persecution of minorities. Harry M. Benshoff (1997), for example, examines how 1930s horror films in particular link monstrosity with homosexuality. Indeed, Benshoff interprets Edward as a 'monster queer' (1997: 266) in a reversal of the earlier homophobic horror convention, so that the diegetic community's acceptance and rejection of the outsider mirrors wider acceptance and rejection of homosexuals: 'Like gay hairdressers and flamboyant entertainers, Edward is accepted as long as he keeps working (and stays in the closet). However, when he will not or cannot play into their heterosexual fantasies, he becomes an outcast once again' (1997: 267). Subverting generic equations between monstrosity and malevolence can therefore be politically progressive, in these terms.

To some extent, Burton's Frankensteinian filmmaking might be a scenario of socio-political conservatism on the one hand (gender), and socio-political progression on the other (outsiders, including homosexuality). However, it is also the case that Burton's rehabilitation of the outsider repeats his narrative celebration of male creativity with a reflexive celebration of male creativity. Part of this repetition is signalled by the way that Daniel Sullivan links Burton's narratives, his audiences and his own artistic enterprise which, Sullivan suggests,

> reflect the anxieties and wonders he often experienced as a lonely child, some of which he seems to have never outgrown. [. . .] [C]hildhood is often characterized by what philosophical psychiatrist R. D. Laing [. . .] referred to as *ontological insecurity*: a state of felt alienation, loneliness, or anxiety. [. . .] Burton [. . .] channelled [his] insecurities into dark fantasies, and similarly insecure children resonate with these 'therapeutic' works [which] reflexively examine [. . .] Burton's own use of art as an escape from insecurity [italics in original]. (2014: 48)

Burton's filmmaking is not only a series of narratives about persecuted insecure outsiders but is also a reflexive meditation on the process of how obsessive activities can express a beauty that most of society rejects. Edward's inventor,

Edward and Victor are characters who re-enact Burton's own obsessive creation of something that society cannot recognise as being beautiful, and this double form of creation is positioned as a male activity that makes something infinitely more wondrous than anything created by the biological female.

Both *Edward Scissorhands* and *Frankenweenie* explore such reflexivity by aesthetically replicating much older forms of androgenic creativity that are also considered (and subverted) in Shelley's novel. This form of male creativity goes back at least as far as the Old Testament, where the patriarchal God asserts an aggressive monopoly over creation that narrativises monotheism's usurpation over earlier matriarchal religions, which had associated biological procreation with the sacred feminine (Miles 1993: 35–58). The male God detached the creation of life from (particularly female) biology and situated it in a practice which, when performed by humans, produces something resembling life – artistic mimesis. So, 'the LORD God formed man of the dust of the ground, and breathed into his nostrils the breath of life; and man became a living soul' (Genesis 2:7). To defend this magical exaggeration of human sculpture, the new patriarchal socio-religious order demanded that '[t]hou shalt not make unto thee any graven image, or any likeness of any thing that is in heaven above, or that is in the earth beneath, or that is in the water under the earth' (Exodus 20:4).

If Shelley's novel is a proto-feminist critique of this male mimetic usurpation of the feminine procreative principle, then Burton's filmmaking is a reflexive celebration of that same male usurpation. Both Edward and his inventor are God-like sculptors. The inventor's machines, as discussed above, are simulacra of human bodies, and are used to create further simulacra of life, in the form of cookies shaped into animals, people and the heart that will inspire the creation of Edward. The machines, moreover, are positioned on a conveyor belt, producing wonders that culminate in Edward. Burton thereby reflexively suggests that his filmmaking operates in an industrial context elevated beyond its usual banality by the same (male) creative impulse driving the diegetic inventor, which mirrors Burton's own auteurist transcendence of Hollywood's conveyor belt-like conformity and mediocrity. Through the magic of the inventor's and the filmmaker's ingenuity, the simulacra of anthropomorphic machines, human-shaped cookies and generically industrial Hollywood filmmaking can all be given the kind of miraculous life that non-outsider society does not understand.

These two acts of male creation, one diegetic and one directorial, are also juxtaposed with the feminine by the dissolve that Burton uses to move from the mundanity of suburbia to the wondrous moment of Edward's non-biological inception. Preparing for a (dull) suburban barbecue, Peg uses a can opener. The camera moves in closer on the can's lid, and dissolves into a close-up of Edward's face. Another dissolve to a different can being opened signals that the first can has activated Edward's memory in what amounts to a strangely desexualised version of Sigmund Freud's primal scene. This second can is positioned at the beginning of the inventor's conveyor belt. At the end of the conveyor belt the inventor picks up the heart-shaped cookie and holds it up to the machine that will be Edward, so that Edward's memory here is from before he was bestowed human consciousness (or a time when he did possess that consciousness but not the human body associated with it). To emphasise the specifically male nature of this usurpation of female procreation, Peg is confined to a humdrum stereotypically female activity in the kitchen, still talking, her voice fading out, as Burton reveals the marvel of Edward's non-biological inception, of which she is left oblivious. Thus, when Burton is most reflexive about how his filmmaking mirrors his narrative, he continues to encode the female as non-wondrous.

In another strangely desexualised replication of Freudian ideas about how children adopt sexuality from their parents, Edward is drawn to repeat his sculpted form of creation, pruning hedges into numerous simulacra of life, including the heteronormative Boggs family. His topiary sculptures, however, are not as lifelike or as wondrous as his ice sculptures which, as mentioned above, are coded with an awe that outdoes the beauty of (natural) snow. Edward's sculpting, like Burton's filmmaking, makes something more enchanting and ephemeral than reality. The film concludes by juxtaposing the timelessness of Edward's and Burton's creative acts with the temporal limitations of mortal biological creations. An aged Kim tells her granddaughter that she does not visit Edward because 'I'm an old woman now. I would rather he remember me the way I was'. The snow from Edward's mansion is then revealed to arise from his sculpting a figure of the young Kim dancing. A subsequent dissolve reveals a slow-motion close-up of the 'real' (as opposed to sculpted) young Kim dancing, so that the biologically created and female Kim decays towards death, but the non-biological simulacra created by both Edward and Burton permanently retain all their undimmed wonder. Non-biological male creativity here transcends the impending death that haunts biological female creativity.

Frankenweenie is even more reflexive. In biblical times, sculpture was the medium that most directly challenged God's creativity – a mimetic sculpture looks like something real, in its three-dimensionality, even if it does not move. Another especially mimetic medium, although one not yet invented in biblical times, is film. Film might be (mostly) two-dimensional rather than three-dimensional, but movement is a fundamental component (and various filmmaking conventions also invoke the illusion of three-dimensional space). Animation is particularly reflexive in terms of movement, because live-action film captures real pro-filmic movement and turns this movement into still images which appear to move when projected, whereas animation creates this impression of movement from still images.

Animation, therefore, is a medium that replicates God's non-biological creation of something that moves without any genuine biological reason for so moving. Shelley's novel also focuses on another form of non-biological movement. As Mellor claims, '[t]he destruction of the female implicit in Frankenstein's usurpation of the natural mode of human reproduction symbolically erupts in his nightmare following the *animation* of his creature [author's italics]' (1988: 115). Merely animating Shelley's narrative, therefore, is inherently reflexive.[2]

In keeping with Burton's doubling of his diegetic male characters' creativity with his own filmmaking creativity, however, *Frankenweenie* extends this reflexivity with explicit connections between the wondrous benevolence of the diegetic creator and the filmmaker. The film begins by establishing Victor as an animated filmmaker. He activates an analogue film projector and shows a diegetic stop-motion animated film of his toys which soon includes a live-action component in the form of the still-alive Sparky. From the outset, Burton associates his protagonist with his own filmmaking – both aesthetically animate the inanimate.

After Sparky's death, Burton establishes that the dog should now be inanimate. Victor draws an inanimate image of the dog in his school textbook, which Burton then suggests might be able to move – Mr Rzykruski passes electricity through the legs of a dead frog, making its legs move, and Victor adds jagged electrical waves around his drawing of Sparky, suggesting both that electricity might make the body mobile and producing a limited suggestion of kinesis, in line with how a comic book uses motion lines around a character. When Victor brings Sparky back to life, he channels electricity across an upturned bicycle (Figure 19.3) in such a manner that the two brightly lit wheels replicate the two reels of the film projector that is positioned behind Victor as he sews Sparky's body back together (Figure 19.4). Victor's animation of the inanimate dead is thereby visually linked with his previous animation of inanimate images, and both these forms of benevolent male creativity are reflexively associated with Burton's own animated filmmaking.

Figure 19.3 *Frankenweenie*, 2012.

In sum, Burton's rehabilitation of the ostensibly monstrous outsider displaces Shelley's critique of man's myopic quest for scientific power. Burton associates female biological creation with the banal and constraining social world that judges

Figure 19.4   *Frankenweenie*, 2012.

the non-biological 'monsters' by their bodies' grotesque 'otherness'. Both *Edward Scissorhands* and *Frankenweenie*, moreover, elevate this benevolent form of monstrosity to the level of filmic reflexivity. Edward demonstrates film's ontological ability to construct the semblance of life out of non-living components by restaging his own creation through topiary and ice sculpture, with the snow-like fragments from this last process a beautiful illusion of something real, similar to Burton's cinema. In *Frankenweenie*, the animation medium replicates the narrative's reanimation of the inanimate, with the diegetic male creator, Victor, both scientist and filmmaker, and both creator of reanimated life and reanimated film images. Burton's filmmaking processes, then, as well as his narratives, celebrate the transgressive creation of the illusion of life, but in so doing valorise a male form of benevolent monstrosity which displaces Shelley's original proto-feminist conflation of male power and destructive monstrosity.

NOTES

1. I discuss how numerous films code male usurpations of female biological creativity as monstrous in Geal 2018a.
2. For a fuller discussion of how films reflexively engage with animating the inanimate, see Geal 2018a and Geal 2018b.

BIBLIOGRAPHY

Aaron, Michele (ed.) (1999), *The Body's Perilous Pleasures: Dangerous Desires and Contemporary Culture*, Edinburgh: Edinburgh University Press.

Aaron, Michele (ed.) (2004), *New Queer Cinema: A Critical Reader*, Edinburgh: Edinburgh University Press.

Adams, Rachel (2001), *Sideshow U.S.A – Freaks and the American Cultural Imagination*, Chicago and London: University of Chicago Press.

Adams, Rachel (2016), 'Freaks of Culture: Institutions, Publics and the Subjects of Ethnographic Knowledge', in Peta Tait and Katie Lavers (eds), *The Routledge Circus Studies Reader*, London: Routledge, pp. 237–68.

Akita, Kimiko and Rick Kenney (2016), 'Mixing Man and Monkey in *Planet of the Apes*', in Johnson Cheu (ed.), *Tim Burton: Essays on the Films*, Jefferson, NC: McFarland, pp. 102–16.

Alexander, Bryan (2012), 'Burton's *Frankenweenie* Pays Tribute to a Beloved Dog', *USA Today*, 5 October 2012, https://eu.usatoday.com/story/life/movies/2012/10/04/tim-burton-dog-tribute/1608471/ (last accessed 25 July 2019).

Allen, Steven (2010), 'Bringing the Dead to Life: Animation and the Horrific', in Stephen Hessel and Michele Huppert (eds), *Fear Itself: Reasoning the Unreasonable*, Amsterdam: Rodopi, pp. 87–95.

Allen, Steven (2013), *Cinema, Pain and Pleasure: Consent and the Controlled Body*, London: Palgrave.

Alward, Lori (2016), 'Why Circuses are Unsuited to Elephants', in Peta Tait and Katie Lavers (eds), *The Routledge Circus Studies Reader*, London: Routledge, pp. 469–88.

Andersen, Hans Christian (1844), 'The Snow Queen (Snedronningen)', in *New Fairy Tales. First Volume. Second Collection. 1845 (Nye Eventyr. Første Bind. Anden Samling. 1845)*, Copenhagen: C. A. Reitzel (n.p.).

Andersen, Peter. A. (1999), *Nonverbal Communication: Forms and Functions*, Mountain View: Waveland Press.

Anon. (2001), *Oxford Dictionary, Thesaurus and Wordpower Guide*, Oxford: Oxford University Press.

Anon. (2015), 'Tim Burton: Why I love Blackpool', *The Blackpool Gazette*, 5 September, https://www.blackpoolgazette.co.uk/news/tim-burton-why-i-love-black-pool-1-7445783 (last accessed 11 July 2019).

Anon. (2016), 'Follow in Footsteps of Peculiar Stars', *The Blackpool Gazette*, 17 October, https://www.blackpoolgazette.co.uk/whats-on/tv-and-film/follow-in-foot-steps-of-peculiar-stars-1-8184961 (last accessed 13 March 2019).

Anthony, David (2005), 'Gone Distracted: Sleepy Hollow, Gothic Masculinity, and the Panic of 1819', *Early American Literature*, 40(1), pp. 111–44.

Appelfeld, Aharon (1980), *Badenheim 1939* (trans. Dalya Bilu), Boston: David R. Godine Publisher Inc.

Appignanesi, Richard (ed.) (2005), *Introducing Lacan*, Cambridge: Totem Books.

Arbus, Diane (1972), *An Aperture Monograph*, New York: Aperture Foundation.

Aries, Philippe (1994), *Western Attitudes Toward Death from the Middle Ages to the Present*, London: Marion Boyars Publishing Ltd.

Armstrong, Philip (2011), 'The Gaze of Animals', in Nik Taylor and Tania Signal (eds), *Theorizing Animals: Re-thinking Humanimal Relations*, Boston: Brill, pp. 175–99.

Artaud, Antonin [1927] (1978), *Oeuvres Complètes*, Vol. III, Paris: Éditions Gallimard.

Asma, Stephen (2009), *On Monsters: An Unnatural History of Our Worst Fears*, Oxford: Oxford University Press.

Auerbach, Jonathan (2007), *Body Shots: Early Cinema's Incarnations*, Berkeley: University of California Press.

AVEN (2001), *The Asexual Visibility and Education Network*, https://asexuality.org/ (last accessed 23 April 2020).

Badmington, Neil (ed.) (2000), *Posthumanism*, London: Palgrave.

Baker, Steve (2001), *Picturing the Beast: Animals, Identity, and Representation*, Urbana and Chicago: University of Illinois Press.

Bakhtin, Mikhail (1984), *Rabelais and His World* (trans. Helene Iswolsky), Bloomington: Indiana University Press.

Baldick, Chris (1987), *In Frankenstein's Shadow: Myth, Monstrosity, and Nineteenth-Century Writing*, Oxford: Clarendon Press.

Barasch, Frances K. (1983), 'Definitions: Renaissance and Baroque, Grotesque Construction and Deconstruction', *Modern Language Studies*, 13(2), pp. 60–7.

Barkman, Adam and Antonio Sanna (eds) (2017), *A Critical Companion to Tim Burton*, New York: Lexington Books.

Barrier, Michael (2003), *Hollywood Cartoons: American Animation in its Golden Age*, Oxford and London: Oxford University Press.

Barthes, Roland (2006), *The Language of Fashion*, Oxford: Berg Publishing.

Bassil-Morozow, Helena (2010), *Tim Burton: The Monster and the Crowd: A Post-Jungian Perspective*, London and New York: Routledge.

Bassil-Morozow, Helena (2011), 'Individual and Society in the Films of Tim Burton', in Christopher Hauke and Luke Hockley (eds), *Jung & Film II The Return: Further Post-Jungian Takes on the Moving Image*, London and New York: Routledge, pp. 206–24.

Bassil-Morozow, Helena (2013), *Tim Burton: The Monster and the Crowd: A Post-Jungian Perspective*, London and New York: Routledge (Kindle edition).

Batkin, Jane (2017), *Identity in Animation: A Journey into Self, Difference, Culture and the Body*, London and New York: Routledge.

Baudrillard, Jean [1970] (1998), *The Consumer Society: Myths and Structures*, London: Sage Publications.

Bekoff, Marc (2006), 'Wild Justice, Social Cognition, Fairness, and Morality: A Deep Appreciation for the Subjective Lives of Animals', in Paul Waldau and Kimberley Patton (eds), *A Communion of Subjects: Animals in Religion, Science and Ethics*, New York: Columbia University Press, pp. 461–80.

Bell, David and Barbara Kennedy (eds) (2000), *The Cybercultures Reader*, London and New York: Routledge.

Benjamin, Walter and Hannah Arendt (eds) (1969), *Illuminations*, New York: Schocken Books.

Ben-Shaul, Nitzan (2007), *Film: The Key Concepts*, Oxford, New York: Berg.

Benshoff, Harry (1997), *Monsters in the Closet: Homosexuality and the Horror Film*, Manchester: Manchester University Press.

Berger, John (2009), *About Looking*, London: Bloomsbury.

Berger, Roger A. (1989), 'Ngũgĩ's Comic Vision', *Research in African Literatures*, 20(1), pp. 1–25.

Berghaus, Günter (2005), 'From Futurism to Neo-Futurism: Continuities and New Departures in Twentieth-Century Avant-Garde Performance', in Dietrich Scheunemann (ed.), *Avant-Garde/Neo-Avant-Garde*, New York: Rodopi, pp. 195–224.

Bernardo, Susan (2016), 'Capitalism and its Discontents: Gender, Property and Nature in *Batman Returns*, *Sleepy Hollow* and *Corpse Bride*', in Johnson Cheu (ed.), *Tim Burton: Essays on the Films*, Jefferson, NC: McFarland, pp. 70–85.

Bhabha, Homi (2004), *The Location of Culture*, London and New York, Routledge.

Birch, Gaye (2010), 'Burton's *Frankenweenie*: A Love Action Short with An Animated Future', *Den of Geek*, 1 June, https://www.denofgeek.com/movies/15850/tim-burton%e2%80%99s-frankenweenie-a-live-action-short-with-an-animated-future (last accessed 25 July 2019).

Birke, Lynda, Mette Bryld and Nina Lykke (2004), 'Animal Performances: An Exploration of Intersections between Feminist Science Studies and Studies of Human/Animal Relationships', *Feminist Theory*, 5(2), pp. 167–83.

Bloom, Michelle E. (2000), 'Pygmalionesque Delusions and Illusions of Movement: Animation from Hoffman to Truffaut', *Comparative Literature*, 524, pp. 291–320.

Bodson, Liliane (2000), 'Motivations for Pet-Keeping in Ancient Greece and Rome: A Preliminary Survey', in Anthony Podberscek, Elizabeth Paul and James Serpell (eds), *Companion Animals And Us: Exploring the Relationships Between People And Pets*, Cambridge and New York: Cambridge University Press, pp. 27–41.

Bonilla, Joe Montenegro (2013), 'The Carnivalesque Construction of a World: The Case of *Big Fish*, a Novel and a Film', *Revistas de Lenguas Modernas*, 19, pp. 161–83.

Boon, Timothy (2008), *Films of Fact: A History of Science in Documentary Films and Television*, London: Wallflower.

Born, Simon Philipp (2017), 'Shadows of the Bat: Constructions of Good and Evil in the Batman Movies of Tim Burton and Christopher Nolan', *Journal for Religion, Film and Media*, 3(1), pp. 75–104.

Boss, Pete (1986), 'Vile Bodies and Bad Medicine', *Screen*, 27(2), pp. 14–25.

Bosworth, Patricia (2005), *Diane Arbus: A Biography*, London: Vintage.

Botting, Fred (1996), *Gothic*, London and New York: Routledge.

Botting, Fred (2002), 'Aftergothic: Consumption, Machines and Black Holes', in Jerrold Hogle (ed.), *The Cambridge Companion to Gothic Fiction*, Cambridge: Cambridge University Press, pp. 277–300.

Bouissac, Paul (1976), *Circus and Culture: A Semiotic Approach*, Bloomington: Indiana University Press.

Boulle, Pierre [1963] (2011), *Planet of the Apes*, eBook (trans. Xan Fielding), London: Vintage, http://www.amazon.co.uk (last accessed 21 April 2020).

Boundas, Constantin (ed.) (1993), *The Deleuze Reader*, New York: Columbia University Press.

Bourriaud, Nicolas (2002), *Postproduction Culture as Screenplay: How Art Reprograms the World*, New York: Lukas & Stenberg.

Bovingdon, Edward (2012), 'Tim Burton: How Disney Fired Me', *Yahoo Movies*, 18 October 2012, https://uk.movies.yahoo.com/blogs/movie-editors/tim-burton-disney-fired-181740632.html (last accessed 25 July 2019).

Braidotti, Rosi (2013), *The Posthuman*, Cambridge and Malden, MA: Polity.

Bredekamp, Horst (2018), *Image Acts: A Systematic Approach to Visual Agency* (trans. Elizabeth Clegg), Berlin and Boston: De Gruyter.

Breskin, David (1997), *Inner Views: Filmmakers in Conversation: Expanded Edition*, New York: Perseus Books Group.

Brophy, Philip (1986), 'Horrality – The Textuality of Contemporary Horror Films', *Screen*, 27(2), pp. 2–13.

Brown, Jennifer (2013), *Cannibalism in Literature and Film*, New York: Palgrave Macmillan.

Burgoon, Judee, Laura Guerrero and Kory Floyd (2016), *Nonverbal Communication*, London: Routledge.

Burke, Edmund [1759] (1998), 'A Philosophical Enquiry into the Origin of our Ideas of the Sublime and the Beautiful', in Andrew Ashfield and Peter de Bolla (eds), *The Sublime: A Reader in British Eighteenth-Century Aesthetic Theory*, Cambridge: Cambridge University Press, pp. 131–43.

Burlingame, Jon (2016), 'Danny Elfman Looks Back at Tim Burton's Cinematic Adventures', *Melody Variety Magazine*, 8 September, https://variety.com/2016/film/awards/tim-burton-danny-elfman-music-cinematic-adventures-1201854151/ (last accessed 26 May 2020).

Butler, Judith (1993), *Bodies that Matter: On the Discursive Limits of Sex*, London and New York: Routledge.

Butler, Judith (2004), *Precarious Life: The Powers of Mourning and Violence*, London and New York: Verso.

Butler, Judith (2009), *Frames of War: When Is Life Grievable?*, London: Verso.

Byron, Glennis (2001), 'Gothic in the 1890s', in David Punter (ed.), *A Companion to the Gothic*, Oxford: Blackwell Publishing, pp. 132–41.

Canemaker, John (1994), 'Life Before Mickey', *The New York Times*, 10 July, p. 14.

Cantor, Paul A. (2014), '*Mars Attacks!*: Burton, Tocqueville, and the Self-Organizing Power of the American People', in Jennifer L. McMahon (ed.), *The Philosophy of Tim Burton*, Lexington: The University Press of Kentucky, pp. 85–109.

Carroll, Lewis [1865] (2016), *Alice's Adventures in Wonderland and Through the Looking Glass: And What Alice Found There*, London: Macmillan.

Carroll, Nöel (2020), 'Fantastic Biologies and the Structures of Horrific Imagery', in Jeffrey Weinstock (ed.), *The Monster Theory Reader*, Minneapolis and London: University of Minnesota Press, pp. 136–47.

Carter, Angela and Corinna Sargood (1990), *The Virago Book of Fairy Tales*, London: Virago Press.

Cartwright, Lisa (1995), *Screening the Body: Tracing Medicine's Visual Culture*, Minneapolis: University of Minnesota Press.

Carver, Steven (2013), '"He wants to be just like Vincent Price": Influence and Intertext in the Gothic Films of Tim Burton', in J. Weinstock (ed.), *The Works of Tim Burton: Margins to Mainstream*, London: Palgrave Macmillan, pp. 117–31.

Catmull, Edwin (2014), *Creativity, Inc.: Overcoming The Unseen Forces That Stand in The Way Of True Inspiration*, London: Bantam Press.

Chang, Justin (2018), Review of *Where Is Kyra?*, *Los Angeles Times*, 12, https://www.latimes.com/entertainment/films/la-et-mn-where-is-kyra-review-20180412-story.html (last accessed 1 June 2020).

Charlton, Michael (2020), '*Dumbo* and the Circus of Childhood', in Teresa Cutler-Broyles (ed.), *The Big Top on the Big Screen: Explorations of the Circus in Film*, Jefferson, NC: McFarland, pp. 103–13.

Cheu, Johnson (ed.) (2016), *Tim Burton: Essays on the Films*, Jefferson, NC: McFarland

Christol, Florent (2017), 'A Colonial Tapestry: Race and Ideology in *Pee-wee's Big Adventure*', in Adam Barkman and Antonio Sanna (eds), *A Critical Companion to Tim Burton*, Lanham, MD: Lexington Books, pp. 161–72.

Clarke, Graham (1997), *The Photograph*, London and Oxford: Oxford University Press.

Clarke, James (2014), *The Cinema of James Cameron: Bodies in Heroic Motion*, London: Wallflower.

Clemens, Valdine (1999), *The Return of the Repressed: Gothic Horror From the Castle of Otranto to Alien*, New York: State University of New York Press.

Cohen, Jeffrey (1996), 'Monster Culture (Seven Theses)', in Jeffrey Cohen (ed.), *Monster Theory: Reading Culture*, Minneapolis: University of Minnesota Press, pp. 3–25.

Cohen, Jeffrey (1999), *Of Giants: Sex, Monsters and the Middle Ages*, Minneapolis and London: University of Minnesota Press.

Cole, Lucinda (2011), 'Introduction: Human-Animal Studies and the Eighteenth Century', in Lucinda Cole (ed.), *Animal All too Animal*, Special Issue, *Eighteenth Century*, 52(1), pp. 1–10.

Cole, Lucinda, Donna Landry, Bruce Boeher, Richard Nash, Erica Fudge, Robert Markley and Cary Wolfe (2011), 'Speciesism, Identity Politics, and Ecocriticism: A Conversation with Humanists and Posthumanists', in Lucinda Cole (ed.), *Animal All too Animal*, Special Issue, *Eighteenth Century*, 52(1) pp. 87–106.

Cooter, Roger (2010), 'The Turn of the Body: History and the Politics of the Corporeal', *Arbor*, 186, pp. 393–405.

Cornich, Ian and Laura Sedgwick (2017), *Gothic Dissections in Film and Literature: The Body in Parts*, New York: Palgrave Macmillan.

Crafton, Donald (2012), *Shadow of a Mouse: Performance, Belief, and World-Making in Animation*, Berkeley: University of California Press.

Creed, Barbara (1993), *The Monstrous-Feminine: Film, Feminism, Psychoanalysis*, London and New York: Routledge.

Creed, Barbara (2005), *Phallic Panic: Film, Horror and the Primal Uncanny*, Carlton, Victoria: Melbourne University Press.

Cutler-Broyles, Teresa (ed.) (2020), *The Big Top on the Big Screen: Explorations of the Circus in Film*, Jefferson, NC: McFarland.

Dahlquist, Marina, Doron Gaili, Jan Olsson and Valentine Robert (2018), *Corporeality in Early Cinema*, Bloomington: Indiana University Press.

Dalle Vacche, Angela (2014), *The Body in the Mirror: Shapes of History in Italian Cinema*, Princeton: Princeton University Press.

Danner, Mark (2004), *Torture and Truth: America, Abu Ghraib, and the War on Terror*, New York: New York Review of Books.

Davies, Cath (2010), 'Technological Taxidermy: Recognising Faces in Celebrity Death', *Mortality*, 15(2), pp. 138–53.

Dawkins, Richard (2006), *The Selfish Gene*, Oxford: Oxford University Press.

De Baecque, Antoine (2005), *Tim Burton*, Paris: Cahiers du Cinéma.

Deleuze, Gilles (1983), *L'image-mouvement*, Paris: Les Éditions de Minuit.

Deleuze, Gilles [1981] (2003), *Francis Bacon: The Logic of Sensation* (trans. Daniel Smith), New York: Continuum.

Deleuze, Gilles and Félix Guattari (1983), *Anti-Oedipus: Capitalism and Schizophrenia*, Minneapolis: University of Minnesota Press.

Delorme, Stéphane (2005), 'Pédophobe et deppophile', *Cahiers du Cinéma*, 604, pp. 31–2.

Denham, Jess (2016), 'Tim Burton sparks anger with bizarre defence for lack of diversity in his films', *The Independent*, 30 September, https://www.independent.co.uk/arts-entertainment/films/news/tim-burton-diversity-films-black-actors-miss-peregrines-home-for-peculiar-children-johnny-depp-a7338881.html (last accessed 3 June 2020).

Derrida, Jacques (2008), *The Animal That Therefore I Am (More to Follow)*, New York: Fordham University Press.

Derrida, Jacques (2016), *Of Grammatology* (trans. Gayatri Spivak), Baltimore: Johns Hopkins University Press.

Dickens, Charles [1843] (2003), *A Christmas Carol*, London: Penguin.

Dickens, Charles [1861] (1996), *Great Expectations*, London: Penguin.

Diffrient, David S. (2004), 'A Film is Being Beaten: Notes on The Shock Cut and the Material Violence of Horror', in Steffen Hantke (ed.), *Horror Film: Creating and Marketing Fear*, Jackson: University of Mississippi Press, pp. 52–83.

Dixon, Wheeler Winston (1992), 'Review: *Unspeakable Images: Ethnicity and American Cinema*', *Film Criticism*, 17(1), pp. 60–5.

Donald, James (ed.) (1989), *Fantasy and the Cinema*, London: British Film Institute.

Downs, Jack M. (2014), '"Radiant and Terrible": Tolkien's Heroic Women as Correctives to the Romance and Epic Traditions', in Lori M. Campbell (ed.), *A Quest of Her Own: Essays on the Female Hero in Modern Fantasy*, Jefferson, NC: McFarland, pp. 55–75.

Dubowsky, Jack Curtis (2016), *Intersecting Film, Music, and Queerness*, London: Palgrave Macmillan.

Dunn, Richard J. (1969), 'Dickens and the Tragi-Comic Grotesque', *Studies in the Novel*, 1(2), pp. 147–56.

Dyer, Richard (1986), *Heavenly Bodies: Film Stars and Society*, London and New York: Routledge.

Dyer, Richard (2002), *Stars*, London: British Film Institute.

Dyer, Richard (2004), *Heavenly Bodies: Film Stars and Society*, London and New York: Routledge.

Ebert, Robert (1989), Review of *The Fabulous Baker Boys*, *Roger Ebert*, 13 October, https://www.rogerebert.com/reviews/the-fabulous-baker-boys-1989/ (last accessed 1 June 2020).

Ebert, Roger (1992), Review of *Batman Returns*, *Roger Ebert*, 19 June, https://www.rogerebert.com/reviews/batman-returns-1992 (last accessed 19 July 2019).

Eco, Umberto (1986), *Travels in Hyper-reality*, London: Picador.

Edmundson, Mark (1997), *Nightmare on Main Street: Angels, Sadomasochism, and the Culture of Gothic*, Cambridge, MA: Harvard University Press.

Eisenstein, Sergei (1986), *Eisenstein on Disney* (trans. Alan Upchurch), Chicago: Seagull Books.

Eisner, Michael (1995), 'Letter from The Chairman', *The Walt Disney Company 1995 Annual Report*, http://corporate.disney.go.com/investors/annual_reports/1995/chairman.html (last accessed 25 July 2019).

E-Learning Support Initiative (2013), *Communication in the Real World: An Introduction to Communication Studies*, University of Minnesota Libraries Publishing [Online], http://open.lib.umn.edu/communication/chapter/4-2-types-of-nonverbal-communication/ (last accessed 9 February).

Elferen, Isabella van (2013), 'Danny Elfman's Musical Fantasyland, or, Listening to a Snow Globe', in Jeffrey Weinstock (ed.), *The Works of Tim Burton: Margins to Mainstream*, London and New York: Palgrave, pp. 65–82.

Elsaesser, Thomas (2003), 'Weimar Cinema, Mobile Selves, and Anxious Males: Kracauer and Eisner Revisited', in Dietrich Scheunemann (ed.), *Film: New Perspectives*, Woodbridge: Camden House, pp. 33–71.

Emerson, Ralph Waldo [1844] (1950), *The Complete Essays and Other Writings*, New York: Modern House Press.

Entwistle, Joanne and Elizabeth Wilson (eds) (2001), *Body Dressing*, Oxford: Berg Publishing.

Everett, Anna (1995), 'The Other Pleasures: The Narrative Function of Race in the Cinema', *Film Criticism*, 20(1/2), pp. 26–38.

Fanon, Frantz (2020), *Black Skin, White Masks*, London: Penguin.

Fennell, John (1976), *Nineteenth Century Russian Literature: Studies of Ten Russian Writers*, Berkeley: University of California Press.

Feuerstein, Anna and Carmen Nolte-Odhiambo (eds) (2017), *Childhood and Pethood in Literature and Culture: New Perspectives on Childhood Studies and Animal Studies*, London and New York: Routledge.

Fiedler, Leslie (1978), *Freaks: Myths and Images of the Secret Self*, London: Penguin.

Forshaw, Barry (2013), *British Gothic Cinema*, Basingstoke: Palgrave Macmillan.

Fowkes, Katherine (2013), 'Tim Burton and the Creative Trickster: A Case Study of Three Films', in Jeffrey Weinstock (ed.), *The Works of Tim Burton: Margins to Mainstream*, London: Palgrave, pp. 231–44.

Fraga, Kristian (ed.) (2005), *Tim Burton Interviews*, Jackson: University Press of Mississippi.

Frank, Mark, Hyi Sung Hwang and David Matsumoto (eds) (2013), *Nonverbal Communication Science and Applications*, London: Sage.

Frank, Mark and Elena Svetieva (2013), 'Deception', in Mark Frank, Hyi Sung Hwang and David Matsumoto (eds), *Nonverbal Communication Science and Applications*, London: Sage, pp. 121–44.

Fraser, Mariam and Monica Greco (eds) (2005), *The Body: A Reader*, London and New York: Routledge.

Freud, Sigmund (1977), *7 On Sexuality*, London: Penguin.

Freud, Sigmund [1953] (2001), *The Standard Edition of the Complete Psychological Works: A Case of Hysteria, Three Essays on Sexuality and Other Works*, Vol. 7 (trans. James Strachey), London: Penguin.

Freud, Sigmund (2003), *The Uncanny* (trans. David McLintock), London: Penguin.

Friedman, Lester (ed.) (2004), *Cultural Sutures: Medicine and Media*, Durham, NC and London: Duke University Press.

Furze, Robert (2015), *The Visceral Screen: Between the Cinemas of John Cassavetes and David Cronenberg*, London: Intellect.

Gabbard, Krin (2000), 'Race and Reappropriation: Spike Lee Meets Aaron Copland', *American Music*, 18(4), pp. 370–90.

Gardner, Colin and Patricia MacCormack (eds) (2017), *Deleuze and the Animal*, Edinburgh: Edinburgh University Press.

Geal, Robert (2016), '*Frozen*, Homosexuality, and Masochism', *Film International*, 14(2), pp. 99–111.

Geal, Robert (2018a), 'Animated Images and Animated Objects: Reflexively and Intertextually Transgressive Mimesis in the *Toy Story* Franchise', *Animation: An Interdisciplinary Journal*, 13(1), pp. 69–84.

Geal, Robert (2018b), 'Anomalous Foreknowledge and Cognitive Impenetrability in *Gnomeo and Juliet*', *Adaptation*, 11(2), pp. 111–21.

Geal, Robert (2019), *Anamorphic Authorship in Canonical Film Adaptation: A Case Study of Shakespearean Films*, Basingstoke: Palgrave Macmillan.

George, Amber E. and J. L. Schatz (2016), *Screening the Nonhuman: Representations of Animal Others in the Media*, Lanham, MD: Lexington Books.

Gerke, Jeff (2010), *Plot Versus Character: A Balanced Approach To Writing Great Fiction*, Cincinnati, OH: F+W Media.

Giddens, Anthony (2012a), *Modernity and Self-Identity: Self and Society in the Late Modern Age*, Stanford, CA: Stanford University Press.

Giddens, Anthony (2012b), *The Consequences of Modernity*, Cambridge and Malden, MA: Polity Press.

Gil, José (2006), *Monstros*, Lisbon: Relógio D'Água.

Gill, Alison (1998), 'Deconstructing Fashion', *Fashion Theory*, 2(1), pp. 25–49.

Gillotta, David (2013), *Ethnic Humor in Multi-ethnic America*, New Brunswick, NJ and London: Rutgers University Press.

Gilman, Sander (2003), *Jewish Frontiers: Essays on Bodies, Histories and Identities*, London: Palgrave.

Goffman, Erving (1966), *Behaviour in Public Places: Notes on Social Organization of Gatherings*, New York: The Free Press.

Goffman, Erving (1990), *The Presentation of Self in Everyday Life*, London: Penguin.

Goffman, Erving (2005), *Interaction Ritual: Essays in Face-to Face Communication*, New Brunswick, NJ and London: AldineTransaction.

Gogol, Nikolai (1836), 'The Nose', *The Contemporary*, n.p.

Golomb, Elan (1992), *Trapped in the Mirror: Adult Children of Narcissists in their Struggle for Self*, New York: Quill William Morrow.

Gorman, Tessa (1997), 'Back on the Chain Gang: Why the Eighth Amendment and the History of Slavery Proscribe a Resurgence of Chain Gangs', *California Law Review*, 85(2), pp. 441–78.

Graham, Elaine (2002), *Representations of the Post/Human: Monsters, Aliens and Others in Popular Culture*, New Brunswick, NJ: Rutgers University Press.

Greene, Eric (2006), *Planet of the Apes as American Myth: Race and Politics in the Films and Television Series*, Jefferson, NC: McFarland.

Gregersdotter, Katarina and Nicklas Hållén (2015), 'Anthropomorphism and the Representation of Animals as Adversaries', in Katarina Gregersdotter, Johan Höglund, and Nicklas Hållén (eds), *Animal Horror Cinema: Genre, History and Criticism*, Basingstoke: Palgrave Macmillan, pp. 206–23.

Gregersdotter, Katarina, Johan Höglund and Nicklas Hållén (eds) (2015), *Animal Horror Cinema: Genre, History and Criticism*, Basingstoke: Palgrave Macmillan.

Griffin, Donald (2006), 'From Cognition to Consciousness', in Paul Waldau and Kimberley Patton (eds), *A Communion of Subjects: Animals in Religion, Science and Ethics*, New York: Columbia University Press, pp. 481–504.

Gropepel-Wegener and Jenny Kidd (2019), *Critical Encounters With Immersive Storytelling*, London and New York: Routledge.

Grosz, Elizabeth (1994), *Volatile Bodies: Towards a Corporeal Feminism*, Bloomington: Indiana University Press.

Gruen, Lori (2011), *Ethics and Animals: An Introduction*, Cambridge: Cambridge University Press.

Guthmann, Edward (1996), Review of *One Fine Day*, *San Francisco Gate*, 20 December, https://www.sfgate.com/films/article/One-Fine-Day-Is-Forgettable-Fun-2955515.php (last accessed 29 May 2020).

Hada, Ken (2014), 'Fishing for the [Mediating] Self: Identity and Storytelling in *Big*

Fish', in Jennifer McMahon (ed.), *The Philosophy of Tim Burton*, Lexington: University Press of Kentucky, pp. 9–31.

Hailes, N. Katherine (1999), *How We Became Posthuman: Virtual Bodies in Cybernetics, Literature, and Informatics*, Chicago and London: University of Chicago Press.

Halberstam, Judith (1995), *Skin Shows, Gothic Horror and the Technology of Monsters*, Durham, NC: Duke University Press.

Halberstam, Judith and Ira Livingston (eds) (1995), *Posthuman Bodies*, Bloomington: Indiana University Press.

Hall, Melinda (2016), 'Horrible Heroes: Liberating Alternative Visions of Disability in Horror', *Disability Studies Quarterly*, 36(1), https://dsq-sds.org/article/view/3258/4205 (last accessed 4 June 2020).

Hammond, Craig (2015), 'Monstrosity and the Not-Yet: Edward Scissorhands via Ernst Bloch and Georg Simmel', *Film-Philosophy*, 19(1), pp. 221–48.

Hanich, Julian (2012), *Cinematic Emotion in Horror Films and Thrillers: The Aesthetic Paradox of Pleasurable Fear*, London and New York: Routledge.

Hanke, Ken (2000), *Tim Burton: An Unauthorized Biography of the Filmmaker*, Folkestone: Renaissance Books.

Hanke, Ken (2007), 'Tim Burton', in Paul Woods (ed.), *Tim Burton: A Child's Garden of Nightmares* – UltraScreen Series, London: Plexus Publishing, pp. 81–95.

Hanley, Tim (2017), *The Many Lives of Catwoman: The Felonious History of a Feline Fatale*, Chicago: Chicago Review Press.

Haraway, Donna (1990), *Primate Visions: Gender, Race, and Nature in the World of Modern Science*, London and New York: Routledge.

Haraway, Donna (1991), *Simians, Cyborgs, and Women: The Reinvention of Nature*, Free Association Books: London.

Haraway, Donna (2007), 'Cyborgs to Companion Species: Reconfiguring Kinship in Technoscience', in Linda Kalof and Amy Fitzgerald (eds), *The Animals Reader: The Essential Classic and Contemporary Writings*, Oxford and New York: Berg, pp. 362–74.

Harman, Graham (2009), 'The McLuhans and Metaphysics', in Jan Kyrre Berg Olsen, Evan Selinger and Søren Riis (eds), *New Waves in Philosophy of Technology*, New York: Palgrave Macmillan, pp. 100–22.

Harmetz, Aljean (1984), 'Touchstone Label to Replace Disney Name on Some Films', *The New York Times*, 16 February 1984, p. 19.

Harpham, Geoffrey (1976), 'The Grotesque: First Principles', *The Journal of Aesthetics and Art Criticism*, 34(4), pp. 461–8.

Harpham, Geoffrey Galt (1982), *On the Grotesque: Strategies of Contradiction in Art and Literature*, Princeton: Princeton University Press.

Harryhausen, Ray (2012), 'Tim Burton Sits Down with Ray Harryhausen', https://www.youtube.com/watch?v=uMLMi-zQvL4 (last accessed 9 June 2020).

Hassel, Holly (2011), 'Susan Murphy, Ginormica, and Gloria Steinem: Feminist Consciousness-Raising as Science Fiction in *Monsters vs. Aliens*', in R. C. Neighbors and Sandy Rankin (eds), *The Galaxy Is Rated G: Essays on Children's Science Fiction Film and Television*, London: McFarland, pp. 31–52.

Heholt, Ruth and Melissa Edmundson (2020), 'Introduction', in Ruth Heholt and Melissa Edmundson (eds), *Gothic Animals: Uncanny Otherness and the Animal With-Out*, London and New York: Palgrave Macmillan, pp. 1–17.

Hendershot, Cyndy (1998), *The Animal Within: Masculinity and the Gothic*, Ann Arbor: University of Michigan Press.

Henning, Sylvie Debevec (1981), '"La Forme In-Formante", A Reconsideration of the Grotesque', *Mosaic: An Interdisciplinary Critical Journal*, 14(4), pp. 107–21.

Hevey, David (2013), 'The Enfreakment of Photography', in Lennard Davis (ed.), *The Disability Studies Reader*, London and New York: Routledge, pp. 432–46.

Hills, Matt (2013), '"Tim is Very Personal": Sketching a Portrait of Tim Burton's Auteurist Fandom and Its Origins', in Jeffrey Weinstock (ed.), *The Works of Tim Burton: Margins to Mainstream*, Basingstoke: Palgrave Macmillan, pp. 179–96.

Hirschmann, Nancy J. (2013), 'Queer/Fear: Disability, Sexuality and the Other', *Journal of Medical Humanities*, 34(2), pp. 139–47.

Hirshey, Gerri (1996), 'Catwoman Michelle Pfeiffer', in Peter Travers (ed.), *The Rolling Stone Reader: The Best Film Writing from Rolling Stone Magazine*, New York: Pocket Books, pp. 258–63.

Hockenhull, Stella (2015), 'Horseplay: Equine Performance and Creaturely Acts in Cinema', *NECSUS: European Journal of Media Studies*, 4(1), pp. 181–98.

Hockenhull, Stella (2016), 'Horseplay: Beastly Cinematic Performances in Steven Spielberg's War Horse', in Amber George and J. L. Schatz (eds), *Screening the Nonhuman: Representations of Animal Others in the Media*, London and New York: Lexington Books, pp. 47–58.

Hockenhull, Stella (2017a), 'Celebrity Creatures: The "Starification" of the Cinematic Animal', in Sabrina Qiong Yu and Guy Austin (eds), *Revisiting Star Studies: Cultures, Themes and Methods*, Edinburgh: Edinburgh University Press, pp. 279–94.

Hockenhull, Stella (2017b), 'Ride 'Em Cowboy', in Sue Matheson (ed.), *A Fistful of Icons* Jefferson, NC: McFarland, pp. 99–112.

Hockley, Luke (2014), *Somatic Cinema: The Relationship Between the Body and the Screen – A Jungian Perspective*, London and New York: Routledge.

Höing, Anja (2020), 'Devouring the Animal Within: Uncanny Otherness in Richard Adams's *The Plague Dogs*', in Ruth Heholt and Melissa Edmundson (eds), *Gothic Animals: Uncanny Otherness and the Animal With-Out*, London and New York: Palgrave Macmillan, pp. 57–74.

Højbjerg, Lennard (2014), 'The Moving Image: Body Language and Media Context', *Kosmorama* #258, http://www.kosmorama.org/Artikler/The-Moving-Image---Body-Language-and-Media-Context.aspx (last accessed 2 February 2018).

Holliday, Christopher (2018), *The Computer-Animated Film: Industry, Style and Genre*, Edinburgh: Edinburgh University Press.

Hollows, Joanne, Peter Hutchings and Mark Jancovich (2000), 'Screen Theory 1: From Marxism to Psychoanalysis', in Joanne Hollows, Peter Hutchings and Mark Jancovich (eds), *The Film Studies Reader*, London: Hodder, pp. 189–96.

Holmlund, Chris (2002), *Impossible Bodies: Femininity and Masculinity at the Movies*, London and New York: Routledge.

hooks, bell (2008), *Reel to Real: Race, Sex and Class at the Movies*, London and New York: Routledge.

Horner, Avril and Sue Zlosnik (1998), *Comic Gothic*, Salford: ESRI University of Salford.

Horrocks, Roger (1995), *Male Myths and Icons: Masculinity in Popular Culture*, New York: St Martin's Press Inc.

Horsley, Jason (2009), *The Secret Life of Movies: Schizophrenic and Shamanic Journeys in American Cinema*, Jefferson, NC: McFarland.

Howarth, Glenys (2007), *Death and Dying: A Sociological Introduction*, Cambridge: Polity Press.

Howe, Desson (1993), 'Review of *Love Field*, *Washington Post*', 12 February, https://www.washingtonpost.com/wpsrv/style/longterm/films/videos/lovefieldpg13howe_a0af6b.htm (last accessed 1 June 2020).

Hurley, Kelly (1996), *The Gothic Body: Sexuality, Materialism, and Degeneration at the Fin de Siècle*, Cambridge and New York: Cambridge University Press.

Hurley, Kelly (2007), 'Abject and Grotesque', in Catherine Spooner and Emma McEvoy (eds), *Companion to Gothic*, London and New York: Routledge, pp. 137–46.

Hynes, James (2014), *Writing Great Fiction: Storytelling Tips and Techniques*, Chantilly, VA: The Teaching Company: The Great Courses.

Ince, Kate (2017), *The Body and the Screen: Female Subjectivities in Contemporary Women's Cinema*, London and New York: Bloomsbury.

Irving, Washington [1820] (2014), 'The Legend of Sleepy Hollow', in *The Legend of Sleepy Hollow and Other Stories*, New York: Penguin, pp. 312–41.

Itzkoff, Dave, (2012), 'Tim Burton, at Home in His Own Head', *The New York Times*, 19 September, https://www.nytimes.com/2012/09/23/movies/tim-burton-at-home-in-his-own-head.html (last accessed 19 July 2019).

Jacobs, Jason (2003), *Body Trauma TV*, London: BFI.

Jacobson, Roman (1987), *Language in Literature*, Cambridge, MA and London: Harvard University Press.

Jameson, Fredric (2009), *The Cultural Turn: Selected Writings on the Postmodern, 1983–1998*, London and New York: Verso.

Jeffords, Susan (1993), *Hard Bodies: Hollywood Masculinity in the Reagan Era*, New Brunswick, NJ: Rutgers University Press.

Jenkins, Jennifer L. (2014), 'A Symphony of Horror: The Sublime Synesthesia of Sweeney Todd', in Jennifer L. McMahon (ed.), *The Philosophy of Tim Burton*, 1st edition [Kindle edition, n.p.], Lexington: University Press of Kentucky.

Jentsch, Ernst (1997), 'On the Psychology of the Uncanny (1906)', *Angelaki: Journal of the Theoretical Humanities*, 2(1), pp. 7–16.

Johnston, Ollie and Frank Thomas (1995), *The Illusion of Life: Disney Animation*, New York: Hyperion.

Jones, Catriona, Mark Hayter and Julie Jomeen (2017), 'Understanding Asexual Identity as a Means to Facilitate Culturally Competent Care: A Systematic Literature Review', *J Clin Nurs*, 26(23–4), pp. 3811–31.

Jonson, Annmarie (2007), 'Porky's Stutter: The Vocal Trope and Life/Death in Animation', in Alan Cholodenko (ed.), *The Illusion of Life II: More Essays on Animation*, Sydney: Power Publications, pp. 424–55.

Just, Martin-Christoph (1997), *Visions of Evil: Origins of Violence in the English Gothic Novel*, New York: Peter Lang.

Kahn, Michael (2002), *Basic Freud*, New York: Basic Books.

Karácsony, Orsolya (2017), 'The Dark and the Darker: The Meaning and Significance of Dark and Light Colors in Tim Burton Films', in Adam Barkman and Antonio Sanna (eds), *A Critical Companion to Tim Burton*, Lanham, MD: Lexington Books, pp. 29–38.

Kashner, Sam (2014), 'The Class That Roared', *Vanity Fair*, March, https://archive.vanityfair.com/article/2014/3/the-class-that-roared (last accessed 10 June 2020).

Kaufman, Kenneth and Nathaniel Kaufman (2006), 'And Then the Dog Died', *Death Studies*, 30(1), pp. 61–76.

Kavka, Misha (2002), 'The Gothic on Screen', in Jerrold Hogle (ed.), *The Cambridge Companion to Gothic Fiction*, Cambridge: Cambridge University Press, pp. 209–28.

Kayser, Wolfgang (1981), *The Grotesque in Art and Literature*, New York: Columbia University Press.

Keil, Charlie and Kristen Whissel (2016), 'Glossary – Go Motion', in Charlie Keil and Kristen Whissel (eds), *Editing and Special/Visual Effects*, New Brunswick, NJ: Rutgers University Press, pp. 229–36.

Klein, Norman (2000), 'A Brief Disappearing Act: Animation and Animorphs', in Vivian Sobchack (ed.), *Meta Morphing: Visual Transformation and the Culture of Quick-Change*, Minneapolis: University of Minnesota Press, pp. 21–40.

Korkis, Jim (2012), 'The Making of The Original *Frankenweenie*', *Mouseplanet*, 13 June, https://www.mouseplanet.com/9942/the_making_of_the_original_franken weenie (last accessed 25 July 2019).

Kosinski, Jerzy (1965), *The Painted Bird*, Boston: Houghton Mifflin.

Kristeva, Julia (1982), *Powers of Horror: An Essay in Abjection* (trans. Leon Roudiez), New York: Columbia University Press.

Kunze, Peter (2016), 'The Use of German Expressionism and American Exceptionalism', in Johnson Cheu (ed.), *Tim Burton: Essays on the Films*, Jefferson, NC: McFarland, pp. 198–211.

Lackner, Eden Lee (2013), 'A Monstrous Childhood: Edward Gorey's Influence on Tim Burton's *The Melancholy Death of Oyster Boy*', in Jeffrey Weinstock (ed.), *The Works of Tim Burton: Margins to Mainstream*, London: Palgrave Macmillan, pp. 151–64.

Lasseter, John (2008), 'Foreword' in *Walt Disney Animation Studios – The Archive Series: Story*, Glendale: Disney Editions, pp. 7–9.

Lasseter, Peter (1995), *Toy Story: The Art and the Making of an Animated Film*, Glendale: Disney Editions.

Lauté, Jérôme (2010), 'No Exit', *Eclipses*, 47, pp. 134–41.

Lauter, Paul (2001), *From Walden Pond to Jurassic Park: Activism, Culture and American Studies*, Durham, NC and London: Duke University Press.

Lawrence, Michael and Karen Lury (eds) (2016), *The Zoo and Screen Media: Images of Exhibition and Encounter*, London and New York: Palgrave.

Lawrence, Michael and Laura McMahon (eds) (2015), *Animal Life: The Moving Image*, London and New York: Palgrave.

Le Blanc, Michelle and Colin Odell (2000), *Tim Burton*, Harpenden: Pocket Essentials.

Lehman, Peter (2007), *Running Scared: Masculinity and the Representation of the Male Body*, Detroit: Wayne State University Press.

Lennard, Dominic (2013), '"This is My Art and it is Dangerous!": Tim Burton's Artist-Heroes', in Jeffrey Weinstock (ed.), *The Works of Tim Burton: Margins to Mainstream*, London: Palgrave Macmillan, pp. 217–30.

Lester, Catherine (2016), 'The Children's Horror Film: Characterizing an "Impossible" Subgenre', *The Velvet Light Trap*, 78, pp. 22–37.

Levant, Ronald F. and William Pollack (eds) (1995), *A New Psychology of Men*, New York: Basic Books.

Lévi-Strauss, Claude (2016), *We Are All Cannibals and Other Essays* (trans. Jane Todd), New York: Columbia University Press.

Liénard-Yeterian, Marie (2010), 'Ecriture du marginal et genre grotesque: l'exemple de la literature sudiste', in Anne Garait (ed.), *De la norme à la marge: écriture mineures et voix rebelles*, Clermont-Ferrand: PU Blaise Pascal, pp. 43–68.

Liénard-Yeterian, Marie (2011), 'The Female Grotesque: Mapping Out a New Space in the Southern Imagination', in Brigitte Zaugg and Gérald Préher (eds), *Women and Space*, Metz: PU Université de Metz, pp. 29–41.

Liénard-Yeterian, Marie (2012), 'The Grotesque: A Tale of Southern Defiance and Dissent', in Marie Liénard-Yeterian and Gérald Préher (eds), *Nouvelles du Sud: Hearing Voices, Reading Stories*, Palaiseau: Éditions École Polytechnique, pp. 81–7.

Liénard-Yeterian, Marie (2016), 'Gothic Trouble: Cormac McCarthy's *The Road* and the Globalized Order', in Agnieszka Soltysik-Monnet (ed.), Special Issue, 'Gothic Matters', *Text Matters: A Journal of Literature, Theory and Culture*, 6, pp. 144–58.

Lindner, Oliver (2012), '"An Entirely Different and New Story": A Case Study of Tim Burton's *Planet of the Apes* (2001)', in Pascal Nicklas and Oliver Lindner (eds), *Adaptation and Cultural Appropriation: Literature, Film, and the Arts*, Berlin: Walter de Gruyter, pp. 117–31.

Littmann, Greg (2014), 'Charlie and the Nightmare Factory. The Art of Children's Horror Fiction', in Jacob M. Held (ed.), *Roald Dahl and Philosophy: A Little Nonsense Now and Then*, 1st edition, Lanham, MD: Rowman and Littlefield, pp. 173–89.

Longhurst, Robyn (2001), *Bodies: Exploring Fluid Boundaries*, London and New York: Routledge.

Lyons, Siobhan (2017), 'Fools on the Hill: Tim Burton's Nietzschean Outcasts and Heidegger's das Man', in Adam Barkman and Antonio Sanna (eds), *A Critical Companion to Tim Burton*, Lanham, MD: Lexington Books, pp. 195–206.

MacCannell, Juliet. F. (2014), *Figuring Lacan: Criticism and the Cultural Unconscious*, London: Routledge.

Magliozzi, Ronald S. and Jenny He (2009), *Tim Burton*, New York: The Museum of Modern Art.

Marks, Laura (2000), *The Skin of the Film: Intercultural Cinema, Embodiment and the Senses*, Durham, NC and London: Duke University Press.

Martinovic, Paul (2012), 'The Killers Shoot New Video with Tim Burton in Blackpool', *Digital Spy*, 17 November, https://www.digitalspy.com/music/a438943/the-killers-shoot-new-video-with-tim-burton-in-blackpool/ (last accessed 4 June 2019).

Masson, Alain (2008), 'Charlie et la chocolaterie: L'oeil digestif', in Pierre Eisenreich (ed.), *Tim Burton*, 1st edition, Paris: Collection Positif, pp. 74–7.

Matsumoto, David and Hyi Sung Hwang (2013), 'Body and Gestures', in Mark Frank, Hyi Sung Hwang and David Matsumoto (eds), *Nonverbal Communication Science and Applications*, London: Sage, pp. 75–96.

Mattfield, Monica (2017), *Becoming Centaur: Eighteenth-Century Masculinity and English Horsemanship*, University Park: Pennsylvania State University Press.

Mayo, Michael (1985), '*Frankenweenie*', *Cinefantastique*, 15(2), pp. 4–5.

McCarthy, Cormac (2006), *The Road*, New York: Alfred A. Knopf.

McCort, Jessica (2016), 'Why Horror? (Or, The Importance of being Frightened)', in Jessica McCort (ed.), *Reading in The Dark: Horror in Children's Literature and Culture*, Jackson: University Press of Mississippi, pp. 3–26.

McDonald, Brian (2017), *Invisible Ink: A Practical Guide to Stories That Resonate*, Omaha: Tin Drum.

McGavin, Paul A. (2011), 'Celibacy and Male Psychosexual Development', *Journal of Pastoral Care and Counselling*, 65(4), pp. 1–11.

McHugh, Susan (2004), *Dog*, London: Reaktion Books.

McIlroy, Brian (2019), 'The Big Top on Screen: Towards a Genealogy of Circus Cinema', Conference Paper at The Film Studies Association of Canada, 5 June.

McKee, Robert (1999), *Story: Substance, Structure, Style and the Principles of Screenwriting*, London: Methuen.

McKenna, Kristine (2005), 'Playboy Interview: Tim Burton', in Kristian Fraga (ed.), *Tim Burton Interviews*, 1st edition, Jackson: University Press of Mississippi, pp. 155–75.

McLean, Adrienne (2008), *Dying Swans and Madmen: Ballet, The Body and Narrative Cinema*, New Brunswick, NJ: Rutgers University Press.

McMahan, Alison (2005), *The Films of Tim Burton: Animating Live Action in Contemporary Hollywood*, New York: Bloomsbury Publishing.

McMahon, Jennifer L. (2014a), 'Introduction', in Jennifer L. McMahon (ed.), *The Philosophy of Tim Burton*, Lexington: University Press of Kentucky, pp. 1–8.

McMahon, Jennifer L. (2014b), 'It's Uncanny: Death in Tim Burton's Corpus', in Jennifer McMahon (ed.), *The Philosophy of Tim Burton*, Lexington: University Press of Kentucky, pp. 215–41.

Meeuf, Russell (2017), *Rebellious Bodies: Stardom, Citizenship, and the New Body Politics*, Austin: University of Texas Press.

Mellamphy, Deborah (2016), '"I'm Not Finished": Gender Transgression and Star Persona in *Edward Scissorhands*', in Johnson Cheu (ed.), *Tim Burton: Essays on the Films*, Jefferson, NC: McFarland, pp. 212–27.

Mellor, Anne K. (1988), *Mary Shelley: Her Life, Her Fiction, Her Monsters*, New York: Methuen.

Mendik, Xavier and Graeme Harper (2000), *Unruly Pleasures: The Cult Film and Its Critics*, Guildford: FAB Press.

Michie, Elsie B. (2007), 'Horses and Sexual/Social Dominance', in Deborah Denenholz Morse and Martin A. Danahay (eds), *Victorian Animal Dreams: Representations of Animals in Victorian Literature and Culture*, Aldershot: Ashgate, pp. 145–66.

Middlemost, Renee (2017), '"Most Whole Life is a Dark Room": Nostalgia and Domesticity in Beetlejuice and *Edward Scissorhands*', in Adam Barkman and Antonio Sanna (eds), *A Critical Companion to Tim Burton*, Lanham, MD: Lexington Books, pp. 207–20.

Miles, Rosalind (1993), *The Women's History of the World*, London: HarperCollins.

Mills, Kirstin A. (2020), 'Hellish Horses and Monstrous Men: Gothic Horsemanship in Washington Irving and Edgar Allan Poe', in Ruth Heholt and Melissa Edmundson (eds), *Gothic Animals*, London: Palgrave, pp. 223–40.

Mitchell, Donna (2017), 'Doll Doubles: Female Identity in Tim Burton's Stop-Motion Films', in Adam Barkman and Antonio Sanna (eds), *A Critical Companion to Tim Burton*, New York: Lexington Books, pp. 231–40.

Mittman, Asa Simon (2016), 'Introduction. The Impact of Monsters and Monster Studies', in Asa Simon Mittman and Peter J. Dendle (eds), *The Ashgate Research Companion to Monsters and the Monstrous*, London and New York: Routledge, pp. 1–14.

Mizejewski, Linda (2014), *Pretty/Funny: Women Comedians and Body Politics*, Austin: University of Texas Press.

Molloy, Claire (2011), *Popular Media and Animals*, Basingstoke: Palgrave Macmillan.

Molloy, Claire (ed.) (2012), *Beyond Human: From Animality to Transhumanism*, London: Continuum.

Morris, B. David (1985), 'Gothic Sublimity', *New Literary History*, 16(2), pp. 299–319.

Moseley, Rachel (2016), *Hand-Made Television: Stop-Frame Animation for Children in Britain, 1961–1974*, London: Palgrave Macmillan.

Muir, John K. (2004), *Horror Films of the 1980s*, Jefferson, NC and London: McFarland.

Mulvey, Laura (2000), 'Visual Pleasure and Narrative Cinema', in Joanne Hollows, Peter Hutchings and Mark Jancovich (eds), *The Film Studies Reader*, London and New York: Arnold, pp. 238–47.

Munsterberg, Hugo (2005), *The Photoplay: A Psychological Study*, The Project Gutenberg eBook.

Nash, Jay Robert and Stanley Ross (1990), *The Motion Picture Guide 1990 Annual: The Films of 1989*, New York: Cinebooks.

Nathan, Ian (2016), *Tim Burton: The Iconic Filmmaker and his Work*, London: Aurum Press.

Nelmes, Jill (ed.) (2011), *Analyzing the Screenplay*, London and New York: Routledge.

Newman, Kim (2000), 'The Cage of Reason', *Sight and Sound*, 10(1), pp. 14–16.

Newman, Kim (2001), 'The Cage of Reason', in Paul Woods (ed.), *Tim Burton: A Child's Garden of Nightmares*, London: Plexus Publishing, pp. 156–60.

Ngugi, wa Thiong'o (1986), *Decolonising the Mind: The Politics of Language African Novel*, Frankfurt am Main: Peter Lang.

Nyamnjoh, Francis B. (ed.) (2018), *Eating and Being Eaten: Cannibalism as Food for Thought*, Bamenda: Langaa Research and Publishing Common Initiative Group.

O'Hehir, Andrew (2000), 'Review: *Sleepy Hollow*', *Sight and Sound*, 10(2), pp. 54–5.

Odell, Colin and Michelle Le Blanc (2005), *Tim Burton*, Harpenden: Pocket Essentials.

Oldfield Howey, Mary (2002), *The Horse in Myth and Magic*, Mineola, NY: Dover Publications Inc.

Olson, Debbie (2014), 'Little Burton Blue: Tim Burton and the Product(ion) of Color in the Fairy-Tale Films *The Nightmare Before Christmas* and *Corpse Bride*', in Jennifer L. McMahon (ed.), *The Philosophy of Tim Burton*, Lexington: University Press of Kentucky, pp. 267–86.

Packer, Sharon (2002), *Dreams in Myth, Medicine, and Movies*, Westport: Greenwood.

Page, Edwin (2006), *Gothic Fantasy: The Films of Tim Burton*, London: Marion Boyars Publishers Ltd (Kindle edition).

Page, Edwin (2007), *Gothic Fantasy: The Films of Tim Burton*, London: Marion Boyars Publishers Ltd.

Pallant, Chris (2011), *Demystifying Disney: A History of Disney Feature Animation*, New York: Bloomsbury Publishing.

Palmer, Clare (2010), *Animal Ethics in Context*, New York: Columbia University Press.

Parkinson, Claire (2019), *Animals, Anthropomorphism and Mediated Encounters*, London and New York: Routledge.

Parks, Lori (2016), 'Corporeal Mediation and Visibility in *Sleepy Hollow*', in Johnson Cheu (ed.), *Tim Burton: Essays on the Films*, Jefferson, NC: McFarland, pp. 54–69.

Peberdy, Donna (2013), *Masculinity and Film Performance: Male Angst in Contemporary American Cinema*, Basingstoke and New York: Palgrave Macmillan.

Pelle, Susan (2010), 'The "Grotesque" Pussy: "Transformational Shame", in Margaret Cho's Stand-up Performances', *Text and Performance Quarterly*, 30(1), pp. 21–37.

Pender, Stephen (1996), '"No Monsters at the Resurrection": Inside Some Conjoined Twins', in Jeffrey Cohen (ed.), *Monster Theory: Reading Culture*, Minneapolis and London: University of Minnesota Press, pp. 143–67.

Perdigao, Lisa K. (2015), 'Becoming the Stories: Indefinite Play in *Big Fish*', in Johnson Cheu (ed.), *Tim Burton: Essays on the Films*, Jefferson, NC: McFarland, pp. 86–102.

Petersen, Anne Helen (2017), *Too Fat, Too Slutty, Too Loud: The Rise and Reign of the Unruly Woman*, New York: Plume.

Pettigrew, Neil (1999), *The Stop-Motion Filmography: A Critical Guide to 297 Features Using Puppet Animation*, Jefferson, NC: McFarland.

Pheasant-Kelly, Frances (2017), 'The Abject, Carnivalesque, and Uncanny', in Adam Barkman and Antonio Sanna (eds), *A Critical Companion to Tim Burton*, London: Lexington Books, pp. 15–28.

Piatti-Farnell, Lorna (2010), 'A Tour of the Cannibal Quarters: Industrial Fantasies and Carnivorous Appetites in Roald Dahl's Fiction' [online] *Semanticscholar*, https://www.semanticscholar.org/paper/A-Tour-of-the-Cannibal-Quarters%3A-Industrial-and-in-Piatti-Farnell/d57c2040fbe3378f8f7b7e8ac81f5e031a5edbbc (last accessed 2 May 2020).

Pick, Anat (2011), *Creaturely Poetics: Animality and Vulnerability in Literature and Film*, New York: Columbia University Press.

Pidd, Helen (2016), 'Blackpool's Brexit Voters Revel in Giving the Metropolitan Elite a Kicking', *The Guardian*, 27 July, https://www.theguardian.com/uknews/2016/jun/27/blackpools-brexit-voters-revel-in-giving-the-metropolitan-elite-a-kicking (last accessed 17 April 2019).

Piette, Adam and Mark Rawlinson (eds) (2012), *The Edinburgh Companion to Twentieth-Century British and American War Literature*, Edinburgh: Edinburgh University Press.

Pile, Steve (1996), *The Body and the City: Psychoanalysis, Space and Subjectivity*, London and New York: Routledge.

Plate, S. Brent (2017), *Religion and Film: Cinema and the Re-creation of the World*, New York: Columbia University Press.

Poe, Edgar Allan (1840), *Tales of the Grotesque and Arabesque*, Philadelphia: Lea and Blanchard.

Pomerance, Murray (2013), 'Burton Black', in Jeffrey Weinstock (ed.), *The Works of Tim Burton. Margins to Mainstream*, London: Palgrave Macmillan, pp. 33–46.

Prescott, Anne Lake (1996), 'The Odd Couple: Gargantua and Tom Thumb', in Jeffrey Cohen (ed.), *Monster Theory: Reading Culture*, Minneapolis and London: University of Minnesota Press, pp. 75–91.

Prince, Stephen (2000), *A New Pot of Gold: Hollywood Under the Electric Rainbow, 1980–1989*, Berkeley: University of California Press.

Probyn, Elspeth (2000), *Carnal Appetites: FoodSexIdentities*, London: Routledge.

Punter, David (1998), *Gothic Pathologies: The Text, the Body and the Law*, London: Macmillan Press Ltd.

Punter, David (2007), 'The Uncanny', in Catherine Spooner and Emma McEvoy (eds), *The Routledge Companion to Gothic*, London: Routledge, pp. 129–36.

Punter, David and Glennis Byron (2004), *The Gothic*, Oxford: Blackwell Publishing.

Purves, Barry (2014), *Stop-motion Animation: Frame by Frame Film-making with Puppets and Models*, London: Bloomsbury Publishing.

Purvis, Barry (2008), *Stop Motion: Passion, Process and Performance*, London: Focal Press.

Quinlivan, Davina (2014), *The Place of Breath in the Cinema*, Edinburgh: Edinburgh University Press.

Rabaté, Jean-Michael (2001), *Jacques Lacan: Psychoanalysis and the Subject of Literature*, Basingstoke: Palgrave.

Rabin, Nathan (2016), 'Why *Batman Returns* . . .', *Rotten Tomatoes*, 20 December, https://editorial.rottentomatoes.com/article/why-batman-returns-deserves-its-cult-following/ (last accessed 15 July 2019).

Ray, Brian (2010), 'Tim Burton and the Idea of Fairy Tales', in Pauline Greenhill and Sidney Eve Matrix (eds), *Fairy Tale Films: Visions of Ambiguity*, Logan: Utah State University Press, pp. 198–218.

Redmalm, David (2015), 'Pet Grief: When Is Non-Human Life Grievable?', *The Sociological Review*, 63, pp. 19–35.

Remshardt, Ralf (2004), *Staging the Savage God: The Grotesque in Performance*, Carbondale: Southern Illinois University Press.

Reyes, Xavier Aldana (2014), *Body Gothic: Corporeal Transgression in Contemporary Literature and Horror Film*, Cardiff: University of Wales Press.

Reyes, Xavier Aldana (2016), *Horror Film and Affect: Towards a Corporeal Model of Viewership*, London and New York: Routledge.

Rhimes, Shonda (2015), *A Year of Yes: How to Dance it Out, Stand in the Sun and Be Your Own Person*, New York: Simon and Schuster.

Richardson, Niall (2016), *Transgressive Bodies: Representations in Film and Popular Culture*, London and New York: Routledge.

Ritvo, Harriet (1987), *The Animal Estate: The English and Other Creatures in the Victorian Age*, Cambridge, MA: Harvard University Press.

Roffman, Mark (2019), 'Danny DeVito on Tim Burton's *Dumbo*: "I believe this is the completion of the Circus Trilogy"', *CoS*, 30 January, https://consequenceofsound.net/2019/01/danny-devito-dumbo-circus-trilogy/ (last accessed 7 May 2019).

Romano, Aja (2019), 'Tim Burton has built his Career around an Iconic Visual Aesthetic. Here's how it Evolved', *Vox*, 17 April, https://www.vox.com/culture/2019/4/17/

18285309/tim-burton-films-visual-style-aesthetic-disney-explained (last accessed 7 May 2019).

Rony, Fatimah Tobing (1996), *The Third Eye: Race, Cinema, and Ethnographic Spectacle*, Durham, NC: Duke University Press.

Rosenberg, Robin (2013), 'The Psychology behind Superhero Origin Stories, *Smithsonian Magazine*, February, https://www.smithsonianmag.com/arts-culture/the-psychology-behind-superhero-origin-stories-4015776/ (last accessed 25 May 2020).

Rowe, Kathleen (1995), *The Unruly Woman: Gender and Genres of Laughter*, Austin: University of Texas Press.

Rowe, Kathleen (2011), *Unruly Girls, Unrepentant Mothers: Redefining Feminism on Screen*, Austin: University of Texas Press.

Russo, Mary (1994), *The Female Grotesque: Risk, Excess and Modernity*, New York: Routledge.

Salisbury, Mark (ed.) (1995), *Burton on Burton*, London: Faber and Faber.

Salisbury, Mark (ed.) (2000), *Burton on Burton*, New York: Farrar, Straus and Giroux.

Salisbury, Mark (2001), 'Graveyard Shift', in Paul Woods (ed.), *Tim Burton: A Child's Garden of Nightmares*, London: Plexus Publishing, pp. 150–5.

Salisbury, Mark (2005), *Tim Burton's Corpse Bride: An Invitation to the Wedding*, London: Titan Publishing Group Ltd.

Salisbury, Mark (ed.) (2006), *Burton on Burton*, eBook, revised edition, London: Faber and Faber, http://www.amazon.co.uk (last accessed 21 April 2020).

Salisbury, Mark (ed.) (2006), *Burton on Burton*, London: Faber and Faber.

Salisbury, Mark (ed.) (2008), *Burton on Burton*, London: Faber and Faber (Kindle edition).

Sammond, Nicholas (2011), '*Dumbo*, Disney and Difference: Walt Disney Productions and Film as Children's Literature', in Julia Mickenberg and Lynne Vallone (eds), *The Oxford Book of Children's Literature*, Oxford: Oxford University Press, pp. 147–66.

Scherman, Elizabeth Leigh (2016), 'Mixed Assortment: The Typical and Atypical Body in *Charlie and the Chocolate Factory*', in Johnson Cheu (ed.), *Tim Burton: Essays on the Films*, Jefferson, NC: McFarland, pp. 36–53.

Scheunemann, Dietrich (2003), 'Activating the Differences: Expressionist Film and Earlier Weimar Cinema', in Dietrich Scheunemann (ed.), *Expressionist Film: New Perspectives*, Woodbridge: Camden House, pp. 1–32.

Schoonover, Karl (2012), *Brutal Vision: The Neorealist Body in Postwar Italian Cinema*, Minneapolis: University of Minnesota Press.

Schwartz, Margaret (2011), 'The Horror of Something to See: Celebrity "Vaginas" as Prostheses', in Su Holmes and Diane Negra (eds), *In the Limelight and Under the Microscope: Forms and Functions of Female Celebrity*, New York: Continuum, pp. 224–41.

Schwartz, Vanessa and Jeannene M. Przyblyski (eds) (2004), *The Nineteenth-Century Visual Culture Reader*, London and New York: Routledge.

Schwarzbaum, Lisa (2000), Review of *What Lies Beneath*, *Entertainment Weekly*, 28 July, https://ew.com/article/2000/07/28/what-lies-beneath-4/ (last accessed 2 June 2020).

Scott, Sharon M. (2010), *Toys and American Culture: An Encyclopedia*, Santa Barbara, CA: Greenwood.

ScreenSlam (2014), '*Big Eyes*: Director Tim Burton Official Movie Interview', 7 December, https://www.youtube.com/watch?v=lp2R7hhyHM (last accessed 1 May 2020).

Sedgwick, Eve Kosofsky (1980), *The Coherence of Gothic Conventions*, New York: Methuen.

Seltzer, Mark (1997), 'Wound Culture: Trauma in the Pathological Public Sphere', *October*, 80, pp. 3–26.

Shaviro, Steven (1993), *The Cinematic Body*, Minneapolis: University of Minnesota Press.

Shelley, Mary [1823] (2003), *Frankenstein or The Modern Prometheus*, London: Penguin.

Shelley, Mary [1818] (1974), *Frankenstein; or, The Modern Prometheus: The 1818 Text*, London: University of Chicago Press.

Siegel, Alan (2018), 'How "Beetlejuice" Was Born', *The Ringer*, 30 March 2018, https://www.theringer.com/movies/2018/3/30/17178786/beetlejuice-30-years-tim-burton-michael-keaton (last accessed 8 May 2019).

Siegel, Carol (2013), 'Tim Burton's Popularization of Perversity: *Edward Scissorhands*, *Batman Returns*, *Sleepy Hollow*, and *Corpse Bride*', in Jeffrey A. Weinstock (ed.), *The Works of Tim Burton: Margins to Mainstream*, Basingstoke: Palgrave Macmillan, pp. 197–216.

Siegel, Carol (2015), *Sex: Radical Cinema*, Bloomington: Indiana University Press.

Silverman, Debora (1992), *Art Nouveau in Fin-de-siècle France: Politics, Psychology, and Style*, Los Angeles: University of California Press.

Silverman, Kaja (1988), *The Acoustic Mirror: The Female Voice in Psychoanalysis and Cinema*, Bloomington: Indiana University Press.

Simmel, Georg [1903] (2004), 'The Metropolis and Mental Life', in Vanessa Schwartz and Jeannene M. Przyblyski (eds), *The Nineteenth-Century Visual Culture Reader*, London: Routledge, pp. 51–5.

Singer, Peter (1994), *Rethinking Life and Death*, Oxford: Oxford University Press.

Singer, Peter (2015), *Animal Liberation*, London: Bodley Head.

Smelik, Anneke (ed.) (2010), *The Scientific Imaginary in Visual Culture*, Goettingen: V&R Unipress.

Smith, Andrew (2014), 'Victorian Gothic Death', in Andrew Smith and William Hughes (eds), *Victorian Gothic: An Edinburgh Companion*, Edinburgh: Edinburgh University Press, pp. 156–69.

Smith, Andrew and William Hughes (eds) (2014), *Victorian Gothic: An Edinburgh Companion*, Edinburgh: Edinburgh University Press.

Smith, Angela (2011), *Hideous Progeny: Disability, Eugenics, and Classic Horror Cinema*, New York: Columbia University Press.

Smith, Julie (2015), 'Masculine Spatial Embodiment in Dracula', *English Academy Review*, 32(1), pp. 124–39.

Smith, Jim and Clive Matthews (2002), *Tim Burton*, London: Virgin Books.

Sobchack, Vivian (ed.) (2000), *Meta Morphing: Visual Transformation and the Culture of Quick-Change*, Minneapolis: University of Minnesota Press.

Sobchack, Vivian (2009), 'Animation and Automation, or, the Incredible Effortfulness of Being', *Screen*, 50(4), pp. 375–91.

Soltysik Monnet, Agnieszka and Marie Liénard-Yeterian (2015), 'The Gothic in an Age of Terror(ism)', *Gothic Studies*, 17(2), pp. 1–11.

Sontag, Susan (1979), *On Photography*, London: Penguin.

Sontag, Susan (2003), *Regarding the Pain of Others*, London: Penguin.

Spiegelman, Art (1997), *The Complete Maus*, New York: Pantheon Books.

Spooner, Catherine (2004), *Fashioning Gothic Bodies*, Manchester: Manchester University Press.

Spooner, Catherine (2013), 'Costuming the Outsider in Tim Burton's Cinema or, Why a Corset is like a Codfish', in Jeffrey Weinstock (ed.), *The Works of Tim Burton: Margins to Mainstream*, London: Palgrave Macmillan, pp. 47–64.

Spooner, Catherine (2015), 'A Gothic Mind', in Claire Wilcox (ed.), *Alexander McQueen*, London: V&A Publishing, pp. 141–54.

Spooner, Catherine and Emma McEvoy (eds) (2007), *The Routledge Companion to Gothic*, London: Routledge.

Squier, Susan (2004), *Liminal Lives: Imagining the Human at the Frontiers of Biomedicine*, Durham, NC and London: Duke University Press.

Stacey, Jackie (2010), *The Cinematic Life of the Gene*, Durham, NC and London: Duke University Press.

Stacey, Jackie and Lucy Suchman (2012), 'Animation and Automation – The Liveliness and Labours of Bodies and Machines', *Body & Society*, 18(11), pp. 1–46.

Stam, Robert (2005), 'Introduction: The Theory and Practice of Adaptation', in Robert Stam and Alessandra Raengo (eds), *Literature and Film: A Guide to the Theory and Practice of Film Adaptation*, Oxford: Blackwell Publishing, pp. 1–52.

Steele, Valerie and Jennifer Park (2008), *Gothic: Dark Glamour*, New Haven, CT: Yale University Press.

Steig, Michael (1970), 'Defining the Grotesque: An Attempt at Synthesis', *Journal of Aesthetics and Art Criticism*, 29(2), pp. 253–60.

Stephens, Elizabeth (2011), *Anatomy as Spectacle: Public Exhibitions of the Body from 1700 to the Present*, Liverpool: Liverpool University Press.

Stier, Oren (2015), *Symbolizing the Shoah in History and Memory*, New Brunswick, NJ: Rutgers University Press.

Stoddart, Helen (2000), *Rings of Desire: Circus History and Representation*, Manchester: Manchester University Press.

Stolworthy, Jacob (2018), 'Day-O: How *Beetlejuice* Conquered its Strangeness to Become a Cult Classic', *The Independent*, 26 October, https://www.independent.co.uk/arts-entertainment/films/features/beetlejuice-30-years-michael-keaton-tim-burton-winona-ryder-cinema-release-film-a8602251.html (last accessed 26 February 2019).

Sullivan, Daniel (2014), 'The Consolations and Dangers of Fantasy: Burton, Poe, and *Vincent*', in Jennifer L. McMahon (ed.), *The Philosophy of Tim Burton*, Lexington: University of Kentucky Press, pp. 47–66.

Sweeney, Gael (2016), '"Why Spend Your Life Making Someone Else's Dreams?": *Ed Wood* Comes Out and Makes his Own Dreams in a Fluffy Pink Angora Sweater', in Johnson Cheu (ed.), *Tim Burton: Essays on the Films*, Jefferson, NC: McFarland, pp. 8–20.

Tait, Peta (2005), *Circus Bodies: Cultural Identity in Aerial Performance*, London and New York: Routledge.

Tait, Peta and Katie Lavers (eds) (2016), *The Routledge Circus Studies Reader*, London and New York: Routledge.

Talairach-Vielmas, Laurence (2014), 'Sensation Fiction: A Peep Behind the Veil', in Andrew Smith and William Hughes (eds), *Victorian Gothic: An Edinburgh Companion*, Edinburgh: Edinburgh University Press, pp. 29–42.

Tasker, Yvonne (1993), *Spectacular Bodies: Gender, Genre and the Action Cinema*, London: Routledge.

Thain, Alanna (2017), *Bodies in Suspense: Time and Affect in Cinema*, Minneapolis: University of Minnesota Press.

Thompson, Douglas (1993), *Pfeiffer: Beyond the Age of Innocence*, London: Smith Gryphon Publishers.

Thomson, Philip (1972), *The Grotesque: The Critical Idiom*, London: Methuen.

Thomson, Rosemarie Garland (ed.) (1996), *Freakery: Cultural Spectacles of the Extraordinary Body*, New York: New York University Press.

Thomson, Rosemarie Garland (1997), *Extraordinary Bodies: Figuring Physical Disability in American Culture and Literature*, New York: Columbia University Press.

Tolkien, J. R. R. (1954), *The Fellowship of the Ring*, London: George Allen and Unwin.

Travers, Peter (1991), 'Review of *Frankie and Johnny*', *Rolling Stone*, 31 October, https://www.rollingstone.com/reviews/film/5947379/review/5947380/frankie_and_johnny (last accessed 14 June 2010).

Tromp, Marlene and Karyn Valerius (2008), 'Introduction: Toward Situating the Victorian Freak', in Marlene Tromp (ed.), *Victorian Freaks. The Social Context of Freakery in Britain*, Columbus: The Ohio State University Press, pp. 1–18.

Tuan, Yi-Fu (2007), 'Animal Pets: Cruelty and Affection', in Linda Kalof and Amy Fitzgerald (eds), *The Animals Reader: The Essential Classic and Contemporary Writings*, Oxford and New York: Berg, pp. 141–53.

Turner, Bryan (1996), *The Body and Society*, London: Sage.

Uebel, Michael (1996), 'Unthinking the Monster: Twelfth Century Responses to Saracen Alterity', in Jeffrey Cohen (ed.), *Monster Theory: Reading Culture*, Minneapolis and London: University of Minnesota Press, pp. 264–91.

Umland, Samuel (2015), *The Tim Burton Encyclopedia*, Lanham, MD: Rowman and Littlefield.

Van Dartel, Michel (2010), 'Enactive Media: A Dialogue between Psychology and Art', in Anneke Smelik (ed.), *The Scientific Imaginary in Visual Culture*, Goettingen: V&R Unipress, pp. 117–32.

Varma, Devendra P. (1987), *The Gothic Flame: Being a History of the Gothic Novel in England: Its Origins. Efflorescence, Disintegration, and Residuary Influences*, Lanham, MD: Scarecrow Press.

Vernallis, Carol (2013), *Unruly Media: YouTube, Music Video, and the New Digital Cinema*, Oxford: Oxford University Press.

Viano, Maurizio (1999), 'Life is Beautiful: Reception, Allegory and Holocaust Laughter', *Annali d'Italianistica*, 17, pp. 155–72.

Vice, Sue (2003), *Holocaust Fiction*, Abingdon: Routledge.

Wallace, Daniel (1998), *Big Fish: A Novel of Mythic Proportions*, New York: Algonquin Books.

Walpole, Horace [1764] (2002), *The Castle of Otranto*, London: Penguin.

Warner Bros Entertainment (2015), 'Making of Charlie and the Chocolate Factory', Part 3, 11 January, https://www.youtube.com/watch?v=ZdBx-NLrv60 (last accessed 1 May 2020).

Warner, Marina (1995), *From the Beast to the Blonde: On Fairy Tales and their Tellers*, London: Random House.

Wasko, Janet (2005), *Understanding Disney: The Manufacture of Fantasy*, Cambridge, MA: Polity Press.

Weinstock, Jeffrey (ed.) (2013), *The Works of Tim Burton: Margins to Mainstream*, London: Palgrave Macmillan.

Weinstock, Jeffrey (2013), 'Mainstream Outsider: Burton Adapts Burton', in Jeffrey Weinstock (ed.), *The Works of Tim Burton: Margins to Mainstream*, London: Palgrave Macmillan, pp. 1–32.

Weinstock, Jeffrey (2016), 'American Vampires', in Joel Faflak and Jason Haslam (eds), *American Gothic Culture: An Edinburgh Companion*, Edinburgh: Edinburgh University Press, pp. 203–21.

Weinstock, Jeffrey (2017), 'Burton's Bowl: Constructions of Space in the Films of Tim Burton', in Adam Barkman and Antonio Sanna (eds), *A Critical Companion to Tim Burton*, Lanham, MD: Lexington Books, pp. 3–15.

Weishaar, Schuy R. (2012), *Masters of the Grotesque: The Cinema of Tim Burton, Terry Gilliam, the Coen Brothers and David Lynch*, Jefferson, NC: McFarland. (Kindle edition).

Weldon, Ryan (2014), 'Catwoman and Subjectivity: Constructions of Identity and

Power in Tim Burton's *Batman Returns*', in Jennifer L. McMahon (ed.), *The Philosophy of Tim Burton*, Lexington: The University Press of Kentucky, pp. 31–46.

Wells, H. G. [1897] (2005), *The Invisible Man*, London: Penguin.

Wells, Paul (1998), *Understanding Animation*, London: Routledge.

Wells, Paul (2009), *The Animated Bestiary: Animals, Cartoons, and Culture*, New Brunswick, NJ and London: Rutgers University Press.

Wells, Paul (2011), 'Boards, Beats, Binaries and Bricolage: Approaches to the Animation Script', in Jill Nelmes (ed.), *Analyzing the Screenplay*, London and New York: Routledge, pp. 89–105.

Wells, Paul (2015), '"You Can See What Species I Belong to, but Don't Treat Me Lightly": Rhetorics of Representation in Animated Animal Narratives', in Michael Lawrence and Laura McMahon (eds), *Animal Life: The Moving Image*, London and New York: Palgrave, pp. 95–107.

Westwell, Guy (2014), *Parallel Lines: Post-9/11 American Cinema*, New York: Columbia University Press.

Whitsitt, Samuel Porter (2013), *Metonymy, Synecdoche, and the Disorders of Contiguity*, Padova: Libreriauniversitaria.

Wickman, Forrest (2014), 'Watch Tim Burton's *Hansel and Gretel*, Long Thought to Be Lost', *Slate.com*, 18 June, https://slate.com/culture/2014/06/tim-burtons-hansel-and-gretel-disney-short-long-thought-lost-surfaces-on-youtube-in-full-video.html (last accessed 12 April 2020).

Williams, Jessica L. (2017), *Media, Performative Identity, and the New American Freak Show*, New York: Palgrave Macmillan.

Wilson, Laura (2015), *Spectatorship, Embodiment and Physicality in the Contemporary Mutilation Film*, London: Palgrave.

Wilt, Judith (2003), '"And Still Insists He Sees the Ghosts": Defining the Gothic', in Diane Hoeveler and Tamar Heller (eds), *Approaches to Teaching Gothic Fiction: The British and American Traditions*, New York: Modern Language Association of America, pp. 39–45.

Wood, Aylish (2007), *Digital Encounters*, London: Routledge.

Woods, Paul (ed.) (2002), *Tim Burton: A Child's Garden of Nightmares*, London: Plexus Publishing.

Woods, Paul (ed.) (2007), *Tim Burton: A Child's Garden of Nightmares*, London: Plexus Publishing.

Wright, Alexa (2019), 'Monstrous Strangers at the Edge of the World: The Monstrous Races', in Jeffrey Weinstock (ed.), *The Monster Theory Reader*, Minneapolis and London: University of Minnesota Press, pp. 173–91.

Yaeger, Patricia (1997), 'Beyond the Hummingbird: Southern Writers and Southern Gargantua', in Anne Goodwyn Jones and Susan V. Donaldson (eds), *Haunted Bodies: Gender and Southern Texts*, Charlottesville: University Press of Virginia, pp. 287–318.

Yaeger, Patricia (2000), *Dirt and Desire: Reconstructing Southern Women's Writing, 1930–1990*, Chicago: University of Chicago Press.

Yorke, John (2013), *Into the Woods: How Stories Work and Why We Tell Them*, Milton Keynes: Penguin.

Young, Lola (1996), *Fear of the Dark: 'Race', Gender and Sexuality in the Cinema*, London and New York: Routledge.

Youngs, Deborah and Simon Harris (2003), 'Demonizing the Night in Medieval Europe: A Temporal Monstrosity?', in Bettina Bildhauer and Robert Mills (eds), *The Monstrous Middle Ages*, Toronto and Buffalo: University of Toronto Press, pp. 134–54.

Zipes, Jack (2011), *The Enchanted Screen: The Unknown History of Fairy-tale Films*, New York: Routledge.

Zoglin, Richard (1984), 'Gremlins in the Rating System', *Time*, 25 June, p. 46.

FILM AND TELEVISION

8mm, Joel Schumacher, 1999
20 Million Miles to Earth, Nathan Juran, 1957
The Adventures of Ichabod and Mr Toad, Jack Kinney, Clyde Geronimi and James Algar, 1949
Alfred Hitchcock Presents 'The Jar', television, season 1, episode 19, Tim Burton, 1986
Alice in Wonderland, Tim Burton, 2010
Avatar, James Cameron, 2009
A Zed and Two Noughts, Peter Greenaway, 1985
Baby: Secret of the Lost Legend, Bill Norton, 1985
Batman, television series, William Dozier, 1966–8
Batman, Tim Burton, 1989
Batman Returns, Tim Burton, 1992
Battle for the Planet of the Apes, J. Lee Thompson, 1973
Beetlejuice, Tim Burton, 1988
Beneath the Planet of the Apes, Ted Post, 1970
Big Eyes, Tim Burton, 2014
Big Fish, Tim Burton, 2003
The Birds, Alfred Hitchcock, 1963
Boxing Helena, Jennifer Lynch, 1993
Bram Stoker's Dracula, Francis Ford Coppola, 1992
The Cabinet of Dr Caligari, Robert Wiene, 1920
Charlie and the Chocolate Factory, Tim Burton, 2005
Clash of the Titans, Desmond Davis, 1981
Conquest of the Planet of the Apes, J. Lee Thompson, 1972
Coraline, Henry Selick, 2002
Corpse Bride, Tim Burton, Mike Johnson, 2005
Dangerous Liaisons, Stephen Frears, 1988
Dark Shadows, Tim Burton, 2012

Dead Ringers, David Cronenberg, 1988
Die Hard, John McTiernan, 1988
Diner, Barry Levinson, 1982
Doctor of Doom, Tim Burton and Jerry Rees, 1980
Dumbo, Ben Sharpsteen, 1941
Dumbo, Tim Burton, 2019
Edward Scissorhands, Tim Burton, 1990
Ed Wood, Tim Burton, 1994
The Elephant Man, David Lynch, 1980
Escape from the Planet of the Apes, 1971
The Exorcist, William Friedkin, 1973
The Fabulous Baker Boys, Steve Kloves, 1989
Faerie Tale Theatre: 'Aladdin and His Wonderful Lamp', television, season 5, episode 1, Tim Burton, 1986
Fantasia, James Algar et al., 1940
The Fox and the Hound, Ted Berman, Richard Ric, Art Stevens, 1981
Frankenstein, James Whale, 1931
Frankenweenie, Tim Burton, 1984
Frankenweenie, Tim Burton, 2012
Freaks, Tod Browning, 1932
From Morn to Midnight, Karlheinz Martin, 1920
Frozen, Chris Buck and Jennifer Lee, 2013
Gamera, The Giant Monster, Noriaki Yuasa, 1965
Ghostbusters, Ivan Reitman, 1984
Glengarry Glen Ross, James Foley, 1992
The Golem, Carl Boese and Paul Wegener, 1920
The Goonies, Richard Donner, 1985
Gremlins, Joe Dante, 1984
Groundhog Day, Harold Ramis, 1993
Hansel and Gretel, television, Tim Burton, 1983
Indiana Jones and the Temple of Doom, Steven Spielberg, 1984
The Island of Dr Agor, Tim Burton, 1971
Jason and the Argonauts, Don Chaffey, 1963
King Kong, Merian C. Cooper and Ernest B. Schoedsack, 1933
Labyrinth, Jim Henson, 1986
Life and Death: 'The Autopsy', television, Gunther von Hagens, 2002
Little Monsters, Richard Alan Greenberg, 1989
The Lord of the Rings: The Fellowship of the Ring, Peter Jackson, 2001
The Lion King, Jon Favreau, 2019
The Lost Boys, Joel Schumacher, 1987
Love Field, Jonathan Kaplan, 1992
Luau, Tim Burton, 1982
M, Fritz Lang, 1931
Married to the Mob, Jonathan Demme, 1988
Mars Attacks!, Tim Burton, 1996
Missing Link, Chris Butler, 2019
Miss Peregrine's Home for Peculiar Children, Tim Burton, 2016
Monster House, Gil Kenan, 2006
The Monster Squad, Fred Dekker, 1987
Monty Python's Flying Circus, 'Full Frontal Nudity', television, series 1, episode 8, 1969
Muto, Blu, 2008

Nanook of the North, Robert J. Flaherty, 1922
The Nightmare Before Christmas, Henry Selick, 1993
Nosferatu, F. W. Murnau, 1922
One Fine Day, Michael Hoffman, 1996
The Owl Who Married a Goose, Caroline Leaf, 1974
ParaNorman, Sam Fell and Chris Butler, 2012
Pee-wee's Big Adventure, Tim Burton, 1985
Pinocchio, Norman Ferguson, T. Hee, Wilfred Jackson, Jack Kinney, Hamilton Luske,
    Bill Roberts, Ben Sharpsteen, 1940
Planet of the Apes, Franklin J. Schaffner, 1968
Planet of the Apes, Tim Burton, 2001
Rambo: First Blood, Ted Kotcheff, 1982
The Red Shoes, Michael Powell and Emeric Pressburger, 1948
The Shining, Stanley Kubrick, 1980
Shrek the Third, Chris Miller and Raman Hui, 2007
Sleeping Beauty, Clyde Geronimi, 1959
Sleepy Hollow, Tim Burton, 1999
The Skeleton Dance, Walt Disney, 1929
Snow White, Dave Fleischer, 1933
Snow White and the Seven Dwarfs, David Hand et al., 1937
Stainboy, Tim Burton, 2000
Stand By Me, Rob Reiner, 1987
The Street, Caroline Leaf, 1976
Suspiria, Dario Argento, 1977
Sweeney Todd: The Demon Barber of Fleet Street, Tim Burton, 2007
Teen Wolf, Rod Daniel, 1986
The Terminator, James Cameron, 1984
Titanic, James Cameron, 1997
Toy Story, John Lasseter, 1995
Un Chien Andalou, Luis Buñuel and Salvador Dalí, 1929
Vertigo, Alfred Hitchcock, 1958
Vincent, Tim Burton, 1982
Your Face, Bill Plympton, 1987
Waxworks, Paul Leni, 1924
What Lies Beneath, Robert Zemeckis, 2000
Where Is Kyra?, Andrew Dosunmu, 2017
'The World of Stainboy', television series, Tim Burton, 2000–1

INDEX

adaptors, 248, 251, 252
Alfred Hitchcock Presents: The Jar (1986), 2, 3, 174–84, 294
Alice in Wonderland (2010), 1, 8, 9, 16, 24, 25–6, 294
animals, 3, 4, 9, 10, 11, 44, 75, 81–93, 94–104, 105, 117, 118–32, 179, 191, 194, 196, 232, 269
  and transgression, 10, 82, 86; *see also* transgression
  as food, 85, 102, 103, 104
  as pets, 10, 81–93, 94–104
animation, 15–26, 27–41, 42–53, 54–66, 81, 89, 91, 97, 125, 261, 270–2
  and the uncanny, 9, 57–8, 63–4
  computer-generated, 6, 16, 24, 49, 50, 51, 52, 58, 125, 132
  metamorphosis in, 9, 15–26, 28, 49
  of *Corpse Bride*, 27–41, 54–66
  stop-motion, 9, 17, 50, 54, 57, 58, 95
  twelve principles of, 19, 26
  unruly, 42–53
anthropomorphism, 58, 119, 120, 126
anti-realism, 174, 175
apes, 10, 69–80, 119
Arbus, Diane, 12, 221
asexuality, 245–59
assembly line, 163, 165–7, 172, 173
authorship, 38, 43, 44

Bakhtin, Mikhail, 48, 120, 203, 205, 216
Batman (character) 119, 185–99, 214–17
Batman (1989), 74, 97, 147, 294
Batman Returns (1992), 11, 72, 73, 95, 97, 105, 147, 150, 151, 155, 185–99, 214–17, 231, 294
becoming centaur, 105–17
Beetlejuice (character), 22–3, 26, 165, 207, 216
Beetlejuice (1988), 6, 9, 11, 12, 16, 21, 23, 24, 25, 119, 157, 160, 172, 176, 204–8, 210
benevolent monstrosity, 260–72, 294
Berger, John, 121, 123, 126, 129, 130
Big Eyes (2014), 8, 11, 147, 161, 165, 167, 171–2, 176, 237, 294
Big Fish (2003), 12, 147, 219–32, 294
Blackpool, 210–11
bodies
  abject, 4, 5, 6–7, 56, 61, 62, 65, 89, 149, 152, 154, 159
  affective, 5
  and organs, 174–84, 247, 250, 251, 252
  and teeth, 111, 142, 144, 168, 169, 180, 182, 239
  animal, 3, 4, 7, 10–11, 69–132, 179, 190, 194, 222
  animated, 9. 10, 14–66, 131, 270
  anomalous, 3, 118–32, 226, 228, 230

bodies (*cont.*)
  circus, 3, 4, 118–32, 179, 224, 225, 226, 228–32, 240
  corporeal, 2–3, 4, 5, 6, 48, 64, 90, 135–99
  creaturely, 10, 69–132
  curious, 227–32, 233–44
  disabled, 229
  fragmented, 148, 149, 150, 154, 155, 162, 170–1
  freak, 3–4, 122–3, 124, 126, 212, 215, 216, 217, 219–32, 233, 240
  gendered, 5, 45, 47, 105–17, 131, 196, 236, 241, 257, 260–72
  Gothic, 54–66, 81–93, 94, 105, 111, 148–60, 203, 235; *see also* animals
  grotesque, 12, 18, 23, 45, 49, 56, 61, 162, 175, 203–18, 233–44, 266, 272
  hard, 5
  in war, 4, 125, 147, 174, 208, 209, 211
  intertextual, 242–3; *see also* intertextuality
  monstrous, 5, 45, 51, 61, 62, 64, 84, 88, 89, 91, 101, 103, 104, 105–17, 149, 219–32, 233, 239, 241, 246
  peculiar, 44, 203, 211, 224, 233–44, 245–59
  performing, 3–4, 119, 122, 141
  posthuman, 6, 242, 244
  racial, 5, 69–80, 84, 89, 118, 124; *see also* racial representation
  scientific, 2–3, 89, 101, 266, 271
  star, 5, 11, 43–4, 45, 185–99
  supernatural, 55–7, 61, 87, 108, 192, 239
  unruly, 42–53, 148, 149, 150, 152, 154, 155, 168, 198, 221
bodily turn, 2, 3
boundaries, 46, 47, 52, 57, 61, 64, 81, 82, 86, 87–8, 89, 91, 92–3, 106, 113, 123, 149, 152, 227, 228
Bourriaud, Nicholas, 174–84
Burke, Edmund, 106, 109–14
Burton, Tim
  artistic manifesto, 174–84
  CalArts, 16, 18, 19
  career, 2, 7, 16, 18, 18–19, 43–4
  unruly appearance, 43–5

cannibalism, 17, 135–47, 242
carnivalesque, 48–9, 53
Catwoman (character), 185–99

Charlie and the Chocolate Factory (2005), 135–47, 161–73, 235–59, 294
children's horror film, 94–104
companion animal, 83, 98, 100, 101, 102
companion species, 83
consumerism, 135, 136, 137–9, 147
corporeality *see* corporeal bodies
Corpse Bride (2005), 2, 27–41, 42–53, 54–66, 86, 148–60, 162, 172, 294
  as unruly bride, 46–9
  origins of, 36, 56
  transformation of, 39–40
costume, 32, 59, 126, 127, 148–60, 189–91, 193–6, 211, 246, 252, 262
  and posthumous embodiment, 148–60
  and seams, 148–60
  and somatic integrity, 148–60
  and stitching, 148–60
  fabric, 148–60
  gloves, 144, 167–70, 173, 216, 257
  goggles, 167–73
  in *Batman Returns* (1992), 148–60, 189–91, 193–6
  in *Corpse Bride*, 32, 59, 148–60
  in *Nightmare Before Christmas*, 148–60
  Victorian, 149, 151, 152, 153, 156, 157

Dark Shadows (2012), 8, 186, 294
death, 2–3, 4, 7, 46, 51, 53, 54–66, 81–93, 94–104, 135–47, 148–60, 193, 196, 197, 198, 203–4, 205, 206, 211, 213, 217, 220, 227, 235, 270, 271
Deetz family, 22, 23, 26, 204–8, 210
Depp, Johnny, 114, 141, 143, 145, 185, 249, 251
dialogic, 260, 261
Disney studios, 16, 19, 34, 44
dogs, 81–93, 94–104, 105, 260–72
Dumbo (1941), 118–32, 295
Dumbo (2019), 118–32, 295
Dyer, Richard, 5, 187, 188, 189, 199

Ed Wood (1994), 295
Edward Bloom, 219–232
Edward Scissorhands (character), 162, 164, 170, 189, 192, 193, 211, 214, 215, 245–59
Edward Scissorhands (1990), 16, 73, 164, 166, 167, 211–14, 217, 245–59, 260–72
elephants, 118–32
expressionism, 112, 174, 176; *see also* German Expressionism

eyes, 20, 23, 62, 65, 86, 100, 111, 126, 129, 130, 131, 145, 161–73, 175, 180, 193, 205, 208, 210, 234, 237, 241, 242, 264

facework, 165, 169, 172, 173
Faerie Tale Theatre: Aladdin and His Wonderful Lamp (1986), 2, 295
fairy tales, 15–26, 34, 56, 62, 76, 139, 196, 219, 225, 233, 239, 241, 243, 247, 261
fish, 219–32
Frankenstein (Shelley 1818), 154, 155, 211, 213, 217, 260–72
Frankenstein (Whale 1931), 89, 94, 103, 164, 184, 212, 216, 226, 262
Frankenweenie (1984), 81–93, 94–104
Frankenweenie (2012), 2, 81–93, 94–104
Freud, Sigmund, 57, 58, 63, 245–59, 270

genre hybridisation, 10, 54, 56, 65
German Expressionism, 7, 175, 219, 262
Gothic *see* bodies
grievable life, 100, 101, 102, 103, 104
grotesque *see* bodies

hands, 20, 24, 144, 145, 152, 161–73, 212, 214, 215, 250, 251, 252, 253, 254, 255, 258, 262
The Hollows, 233–44
horses, 105–17, 131
human/animal divide, 10, 120–1, 123–5

intertextuality, 101, 242–3, 260–72
The Island of Dr Agor (1971), 2, 295

Jack Skellington, 86, 95, 148–60, 162, 220

Karl the Giant, 219–32
The Killers' videos, 2, 210

Lacan, Jacques, 247, 252–3
Land of the Dead, 29, 35, 36, 57, 86, 152
Land of the Living, 29, 35, 36, 64, 86, 152, 153, 156, 157, 158
Luau (1982), 44, 295

Mantell, Emily, 27–41
Mars Attacks! (1996), 72, 82, 85, 87, 89, 119, 147, 295
masculinity, 5, 105–17, 188, 196, 197, 255

mask(s), 22, 23, 162, 164, 193, 195, 196, 197–8, 214, 239, 241
metaphor, 12, 80, 123, 136, 137, 140, 142, 161–73, 203, 227, 231, 253
Mattfield, Monica, 105–17
metonymy, 161–73
Miss Peregrine's Home for Peculiar Children (2016), 2, 9, 147, 203–18, 233–44, 295
modernity, 161, 162, 164, 165–7, 168, 170, 171, 173

non-verbal communication theory, 245, 246, 248–9, 251, 253, 255, 257, 258
normalcy, 181, 213, 214, 216, 220, 221, 222–6

outsider, 10, 12, 18, 19, 26, 36, 44, 73, 80, 120, 149, 160, 186, 205, 245, 260, 263, 267, 268, 269, 271

Pallant, Chris, 16, 18, 20, 21, 44
Pee-wee's Big Adventure (1985), 2, 43, 74, 296
the Penguin, 119, 151, 152, 164, 165, 185, 192, 195, 197, 198, 214–17, 231
petification, 103
pets, 81–93, 94–104, 115, 179, 265
Pfeiffer, Michelle, 185–99
phallic stage, 250, 252, 258
Planet of the Apes (Boulle 1963), 69, 75, 76
Planet of the Apes (Burton 2001), 75–80, 296
Planet of the Apes (Schaffner 1968), 70–2, 296
proto-feminism, 260–72
psychosexual development, 245–59

racial representation *see* bodies
  and ethnography, 70
  in Burton's films, 69–80
resurrection, 51, 101, 157, 192, 266, 267
Rowe, Kathleen, 42, 45, 46, 47, 48, 52–3

sadism, 249
Selina Kyle, 150, 155, 156, 159, 186, 188, 189, 195; *see also* Catwoman
sexuality, 3, 45, 153, 230, 245–59
Sleepy Hollow (1999), 105–17, 145, 176, 296

Snow White (Fleischer 1933), 20, 21, 23, 26, 296
Snow White (Hand 1937), 18, 20, 24 296
social anxiety, 245–59
social outcast, 203–18
Stainboy (2000), 2, 147, 296
star image, 11, 185, 186, 187, 188, 199; *see also* Richard Dyer
    problematic fit, 187, 189
sublime, 106, 109, 110, 111, 117; *see also* Edmund Burke
suburbia, 12, 73, 164, 203, 211, 212, 264, 269
supernatural *see* bodies
Sweeney Todd: The Demon Barber of Fleet Street (2007), 11, 15, 135–47, 161, 165, 166, 170–1, 296
synecdoche, 161–73

technology, 6, 119, 120, 128, 129, 131
Tim Burton's The Nightmare Before Christmas (1993), 33, 34, 36, 50, 73, 80, 86, 148–60, 296
transgression, 6, 10, 42, 44, 45, 47, 56, 82, 88, 93, 107, 177, 236

twins, 222, 224, 226, 229, 231, 234, 238, 239
    Identical Twins (1967), 225

the uncanny, 17, 18, 54–66, 233, 239, 240
    and doubling, 54–66, 91; *see also* twins
    and the Gothic, 12, 44, 54–66, 81–93, 95, 105, 107, 111, 117, 136, 148–60, 164, 167, 233, 234, 235, 242, 264; *see also* bodies
    and the supernatural, 55, 56, 57, 61, 87, 108–9, 192, 239; *see also* bodies

villains, 61–2
Vincent (1982), 15, 88, 95, 151, 296

Wells, Paul, 15, 17, 20, 34, 38, 118, 123, 129, 131
Willy Wonka, 135–47, 167–70, 245–59
Wood, Aylish, 52
wound culture, 6

zoos, 118, 120, 121–2, 123, 127, 129